Praying with Saint Mark's Gospel

Daily Reflections on the Gospel of Saint Mark

Edited by Father Peter John Cameron, O.P.

M<small>AGNIFICAT</small>®

Foreword

Father Peter John Cameron, O.P.

Two of the most mystifying verses in all of the New Testament are found in the Gospel of Mark: "Now a young man followed him [Jesus] wearing nothing but a linen cloth about his body. They seized him, but he left the cloth behind and ran off naked" (Mk 14: 51-52). Many have endeavored to "uncover" the mystery of this unclothed man's identity. But the only satisfying solution is one that answers a more nagging question: Why is this man's story part of the Gospel of Mark in the first place? If this episode has been included, it must be because there is something crucial in it for our life of faith. Explaining *who* the young man is means revealing *why* we need to know about him.

The rich young man?

As soon as we hear the expression "a young man," we probably think of the Gospel story of the Rich Young Man. In fact, in the Gospel of Matthew, this fellow is "young"; in the Gospel of Mark he is "rich"; and in the Gospel of Luke he is a "ruler." But we commonly blend these attributes to speak of the Rich Young Man. Mark's version of the encounter of the Rich Young Man with Jesus occurs in Mk 10: 17-22. The man "ran up, knelt down before [Jesus], and asked him, 'Good teacher, what must I do to inherit eternal life?'" When the Lord indicates the commandments, the man assures Jesus that he has observed them since his youth. Then we read this: "Jesus, looking at him, loved him and said to him, 'You are lacking in one thing. Go, sell what you have, and give to [the] poor and you will have treasure in heaven; then come, follow me.' At that statement his face fell, and he went away sad, for he had many possessions."

Venerable Thomas à Kempis in *The Imitation of Christ* sums up the dilemma of the Rich Young Man in all of us: "If you seek yourself, you will find yourself – to your own ruin. For the man who does not seek Jesus does himself much greater harm than the whole world and all his enemies could ever do."

So was this the end of the Rich Young Man?

The look that loves

As shocked and devastated as the Rich Young Man was at Christ's response, it is hard to believe that afterwards he simply returned to "business as usual." Could you? Even though he found the Lord's counsel outrageous, the way that Jesus looked at him prevented the Rich Young Man from dismissing his words: "Jesus, looking at him, loved him." When the Son of God turned his eyes on the man with such a loving gaze, he looked past all the man's self-importance, his preconceptions, his resistance, his materialism, his ambition, his "virtue." Christ's look of love pierces our fantasies, our self-sufficiency, our disordered priorities, our plans. It penetrates to our heart and lays bare our deepest, truest longings.

"Before temporal things are possessed," writes Saint Thomas Aquinas, "they are highly regarded and thought satisfying; but after they are possessed, they are found to be neither so great as thought nor sufficient to satisfy our desires, and so our desires are not satisfied but move on to something else." When Jesus looks at the Rich Young Man with love, the youth's desires move on to Something Else.

The repentant Rich Young Man

Some of the Fathers of the Church hold the opinion that the naked man in the Garden of Gethsemane is the repentant Rich Young Man. Repentance, after all, is one of the most prevailing themes in the Gospel of Mark. John the Baptist proclaims "a baptism of repentance" (Mk 1: 4). Christ begins his earthly ministry with the words, "This is the time of fulfillment. The kingdom of God is at hand. Repent, and believe in the gospel" (Mk 1: 15). Jesus proclaims: "I did not come to call the righteous but sinners" (Mk 2: 17). The newly commissioned apostles "went off and preached repentance" (Mk 6: 12).

But what moves us to repent? Repentance is not directed to some code of conduct. After all, as Pope Benedict XVI teaches, "Being Christian is not the result of an ethical choice… but the encounter with an event, a person, which gives life a new horizon and a decisive direction" (*Deus Caritas Est* 1). Repentance is always to a person… a person who looks at us with a love that awakens priceless truth and meaning we had neglected. Repentance is a change in what we set our heart on. Repentance is surrender to the personal transformation that God both desires for us and personally brings about in us.

Maybe the Lord's transfixing look of love changed the way that the Rich Young Man listened. Maybe it helped him remember what Jesus had said shortly before they met: "Amen, I say to you, whoever does not accept the kingdom of God like a child will not enter it" (Mk 10: 15). Maybe then he recognized how much childlike abandonment was the "one thing lacking" in him. Maybe the Rich Young Man continued to follow Christ at a distance and took it to heart when he heard the Lord declare, "The Son of Man… [came] to give his life as a ransom for many" (Mk 10: 45). Maybe the Rich Young Man was stunned at the way blind Bartimaeus "threw aside his cloak" – his sole possession in the world (see Ex 22: 25-26) – when Jesus Christ called him. Maybe, too, the sight of so many spreading their cloaks on the road before Jesus (Mk 11: 8) aroused a yearning to cultivate such detachment and munificence himself. Most of all, maybe observing the offering made by the poor widow in the temple was for him the clincher, since she gave "from her poverty,… all she had, her whole livelihood" (Mk 12: 44). Maybe the poor old widow inspired the Rich Young Man to sell all he had and give it to the poor, keeping only a linen cloth to wear for clothes.

The Gethsemane grace

In his newly acquired poverty, the Rich Young Man kept on following Jesus, even into the Garden of Gethsemane. The panic incited by the "crowd with swords and clubs" (Mk 14: 43) caused him to flee, leaving behind the last thing he owned.

But with that divesting came a great grace, for now the Rich Young Man was truly, totally poor... truly, totally free. Moments before the rabble arrived, perhaps he overheard the prayer of Jesus in his agony: "Abba, Father... Not what I will but what you will" (Mk 14: 36). That is, he heard Jesus himself accept the kingdom of God like a child. And that was all the Rich Young Man needed to be able to do the same.

When the women go to Christ's tomb very early on Easter, notice that it is not an angel they encounter (Mk 16: 1-8). There in the tomb, sitting on the right side, is "a young man," dressed in a white robe – dressed like the transfigured Christ (see Mk 9: 2-3) – who speaks to them: "You seek Jesus of Nazareth, the crucified. He has been raised." Because the repentant Rich Young Man has lived the whole of his life in Christ's look of love, he has become completely transformed and clothed with Christ... so much so that he is sent to evangelize others. "The beginning of the gospel of Jesus" (Mk 1: 1) for us is our obedience to that transfiguring look of love modeled by the most mysterious man in Mark.

Introduction
The Suffering and Glory of the Messiah

Mary Healy

They saw the man who had been possessed by the legion, sitting there clothed and in his right mind. And they were afraid... Jesus told him, "Go home to your family and announce to them all that the Lord in his mercy has done for you." So he went away and began to proclaim in the Decapolis what Jesus had done for him; and all were amazed.
(Mk 5: 15, 19-20; author's translation)

The whole of Mark's Gospel is encapsulated in this unlikely scene. Jesus has just delivered the Gerasene demoniac, a man whose pitiable condition Mark describes in graphic detail. The man lived among the tombs, captive to evil, alienated from human society and consumed by self-hatred and despair. It is an image of fallen humanity, wounded and disfigured by the consequences of sin. But this wretched man has been transfigured by his encounter with Jesus, who with a word expels the evil spirits that had held him in bondage. The man is now "clothed," his human dignity restored, and his guilt and shame taken away. He is "in his right mind," able to clearly perceive the truth about himself and about the Lord who delivers him. The people of the town, having witnessed this stunning transformation, are seized with fear – the typical biblical reaction to a theophany.

Living Witness

Having experienced Jesus' liberating power, this man is now qualified to be his witness. And Jesus' commission – "Go... and announce... all that the Lord... has done for you" – makes him, in effect, the first Christian evangelist! This seemingly unpromising missionary, previously known throughout the region for his degradation, has become a living witness to the Good News, visible to all as healed and full of joy. Indeed, the effectiveness of his testimony appears later from the new openness Jesus meets on his second visit to the area (compare 5: 17 and 7: 31–8: 9).

The liberated man is the first fruit of the Gentiles, a prelude to the Church's worldwide mission that will begin after Jesus rises from the dead.

This movement from encounter with Jesus, to deliverance from the power of sin, to fervent zeal in sharing the Good News with others is the underlying pattern of Mark's Gospel. Mark writes so as to lead his readers into the same movement that has transformed his own life and that of Jesus' first disciples. It is nearly impossible to read his work as a neutral bystander. At every turn the evangelist invites his readers to see ourselves reflected in the disciples, in the people who come to Jesus for healing, or even at times in those who disbelieve and resist Jesus' message. Like them we are confronted with the challenge of how to respond to the provocative words and astounding deeds of the carpenter from Nazareth.

Who Then Is This?

"Who then is this?" the disciples ask in awe after Jesus calms the storm at sea (4: 41). It is the question at the heart of Mark's Gospel. Jesus himself poses this question to his disciples: "But who do you say that I am?" (8: 29). Mark has already provided the answer at the beginning of his work (1: 1): Jesus is the Messiah, the long-awaited descendant of David who would fulfill the hopes of Israel and bring about the reign of God. Even more, he is the Son of God, the beloved Son with whom the Father is well pleased (1: 11). But it is not enough merely to understand the words; one must allow their full reality to come to light by spending time with him and listening to his word, as the disciples do.

The title Messiah (or Christ) reappears at a pivotal moment in the narrative. In the center of the Gospel is Peter's confession of faith, "You are the Messiah" (8: 29). Peter's statement was a penetrating insight that transcended the current political notions of what the Messiah would be. Yet it was only a partial revelation. To grasp *that* Jesus is the Messiah is not yet to understand what it means to be the Messiah. After Peter's confession, Jesus begins to unveil the mystery of his vocation to be a *suffering Messiah* who will lay down his life for his people – and the disciples' call to follow in his footsteps.

The mystery of suffering would have had special resonance for the first readers of Mark's Gospel. According to ancient tradition, Mark served as assistant to the apostle Peter, and wrote his Gospel based on Peter's preaching in Rome. He writes at a time when the Roman Christians are suffering social ostracism and brutal persecution under the emperor Nero. Some are martyred by crucifixion, others are set on fire or thrown to wild beasts in the arena. Many are tempted to abandon the faith. Mark's narrative of the events in Jesus' life is designed to encourage his readers, showing that God's purposes are not foiled by human failure or opposition. The violent hostility of Jesus' enemies, and even the weaknesses of his followers, only play into God's marvelous plan of salvation.

The Way of the Cross

After Peter's confession, Jesus begins a journey to Jerusalem that he knows will lead to the culminating events of his life. As the disciples follow him on the "way" to Jerusalem, they are learning about the "way" of Christian discipleship, and gradually discovering that it is the way of the cross. Along the way, Jesus foretells his Passion three times with increasing clarity and detail (8: 31; 9: 31; 10: 33-34). Each time, his disciples respond with utter incomprehension, which in turn becomes an occasion for Jesus to provide further teaching on discipleship.

After Jesus' third prediction that he will suffer and die, James and John exemplify the perennial temptation of his disciples – and of all human beings – to earthly ambition. "Teacher… grant that in your glory we may sit one at your right and the other at your left." There could hardly have been a more tactless moment for their request. Yet Jesus doesn't rebuke their aspiration to greatness, a desire God himself has placed in the human heart. Rather, he redirects it: "Can you drink the cup that I drink or be baptized with the baptism with which I am baptized?" Jesus' cup is the cup of suffering, willingly embraced out of love for the Father (cf. Mk 14: 36); likewise, his baptism is his atoning death (cf. Lk 12: 50). Only on Golgotha will the deep irony of the brothers' request become clear: those at the right and left hand of the Messiah-King are the two thieves crucified with him! Yet Jesus takes James and John's willingness seriously: they will indeed drink his cup, and be plunged into his baptism. From now on the privilege and joy of Jesus' disciples will be to share his glory by sharing in the act of love in which he gives his life for us.

On another level, "baptism" and "the cup" also allude to the two foundational sacraments of the new covenant, baptism and the Eucharist – the way that Jesus' disciples for all time will be joined to him and share in his very life. Jesus' question to the two brothers is an invitation to readers of the Gospel: Are we willing to receive the limitless grace poured out for us on the cross? Are we willing to let this divine life be released in its full power in our lives?

The Tearing of the Heavens

Mark's Gospel is framed by two events of cosmic significance. At the beginning, in an act of unfathomable humility, the Son of God submits to John's baptism of repentance for sins (1: 9). It is an act of obedience to the Father's will for his messianic mission, and a gesture of total solidarity with sinful humanity – a solidarity that will lead inexorably to the cross. Jesus' immersion in water is a symbolic anticipation of his Passion. In response to this act of self-abasement, the heavens are "torn" asunder (1: 10) – a decisive sign that the barrier between God and man is being removed. The same verb "tear" reappears at the climax of the Gospel, at Christ's death, when the curtain of the temple is torn from top to bottom (15: 38). The reconciliation of heaven and earth that began at his baptism is now complete. By his obedient death, Jesus has opened access to the Father.

But the cross is not the end of the story. The Gospel ends with the Easter proclamation, "He has been raised!" and the joyous promise of an encounter with the risen Lord (16: 6-7). Every reader is invited, along with the faithful women, to accept in faith the testimony to Jesus' resurrection, and having received his forgiveness and freedom, to "go into the whole world and proclaim the gospel to every creature" (16: 15).

An Invitation to Saint Mark's Gospel
Good News for the Young at Heart

Andrew Matt

My son Samuel's at that age where he gobbles up stories. At five and a half, he not only loves getting new books from the library, but also clamors for me to tell him new stories. Or, rather, new "Michael Moe Stories," as he calls them, after the main character he's created: a talking red excavator with a magic claw. "Tell me a Michael Moe story!" he blurts out at the breakfast table or in the car or at bedtime. And without fail, he'll then add, "And with a PROBLEM!" For the "problem" is key – to see how Michael Moe and his friends will solve the problem I concoct.

As I scramble to come up with an adventure and then launch into it, I notice how Samuel takes it all in. Very seriously. He gets quiet; his gaze becomes focused, his body inches forward, alert as a cat. Whenever the plot slows down a bit, he's right on top of me, "And then what? And then what happens?" I've got to stay on my toes. All of which makes me take it seriously too. As anyone who's told stories to kids knows, it's hard work. But because it's hard, serious work, it's also the most fun. Because it's all suddenly real.

And Michael Moe is real.

"Here comes his claw, right over our heads!" I exclaim, pointing.

Samuel looks up, and quickly ducks. "Whoa, that was close!" he says.

The story takes on a real presence that is so encompassing that we feel we're both inside it. It's embracing us from all sides, and we just can't wait to find out how Michael Moe will save the day this time: "And then? And then what happens after that?" Samuel demands with wide-eyed urgency.

Saint Mark's Magic: Childlike Immediacy

This sense of urgency and immediacy, this childlike sense of living fully in the moment permeates the Gospel of Mark. The Evangelist is so excited about the event of God walking straight into history that his exuberance becomes part of the very story he tells, pulling us into the action. We suddenly find ourselves reading the Gospel "not as a word of the past, but as the living Word, which is addressed to us today and involves us" (Pope Benedict XVI).

How does Saint Mark do it? We will focus only on two pivotal ways: a pair of key words and the vivid description of Jesus' emotional life.

"*And... immediately.*" One of Mark's favorite ways of conveying and sustaining immediacy occurs through the recurrent use of "And" (*kai*) and "immediately" (*euthys*), often used in combination. "And when he came up out of the water, immediately he saw... the Spirit" (1:10, RSV). "And immediately the Spirit drove him out into the desert" (1:12, author's translation). "And immediately [Peter and Andrew] left their nets and followed him" (1:18, RSV). And on and on it goes. Mark maintains this momentum by beginning an astonishing 410 of his 678 verses with "And," while peppering his narrative over forty times with "immediately." Like the persistent pounding of waves, this repetitive rhythm attunes us to Jesus' palpable presence on every page. As Saint Jerome aptly puts it: "When we are listening to the Word of God, Christ's flesh and blood are being poured into our ears."

Raw emotion. Saint Mark is like a film director who relishes shooting unscripted footage. Unlike Saints Matthew and Luke, who sometimes "edit out" Jesus' powerful emotions, Saint Mark does not hesitate to portray Christ in all his emotional complexity: compassion (1:41; 6:34; 8:2); love (10:21); sympathy (5:36); indignation (10:14; 14:48-49); amazement at disbelief (6:6); anger and exasperation (3:5; 7:18); distress and sorrow (14:33-34). Indeed, the force of Jesus' personality often triggers strong counter-reactions of bewilderment or disapproval, even by his own family. Only in Mark's Gospel, for example, do his relatives attempt to stage an intervention: "They set out to seize him, for they said, 'He is out of his mind'" (3:21). Saint Mark portrays a profoundly human Jesus: the Son of God who is truly the Son of *Man*.

Saint Mark's Unique Detail: Jesus the Child

While Saints Matthew and Luke famously present us with the story of the Christ Child at the outset of their Gospels, Saint Mark unveils the divine Child at the end. He alone records how Jesus in Gethsemane addresses the Father with an Aramaic term of endearment: "*Abba*" (14: 36). *Abba* is the intimate form of speech a child uses with his father, meaning Daddy. Thus, when Jesus utters this affectionate word as his agony begins – when in anguish he calls not upon the Father Almighty but rather upon his "Daddy" – then the beating heart of Mark's Gospel is suddenly laid bare before our eyes. Like the heavens "torn" asunder at his baptism by the voice of his Father (1: 10), Jesus "tears" his heart wide open in prayer, revealing heaven to us. In a split-second we are granted a mysterious glimpse of the eternal Child's trusting receptivity of his Father, who cradles his beloved Son in the eternal embrace of the Holy Spirit.

And immediately we recognize the life-giving source from which Saint Mark's own childlikeness springs: "And [Jesus] took a child… in his arms [and] said to [his disciples], 'Whoever receives one such child in my name receives me; and whoever receives me, receives not me but him who sent me'" (9: 36-37, RSV). Having gazed long upon this living parable of Christ's own filial relationship with his Father, Saint Mark has so identified himself as a child in the arms of Christ that in a flash of inspiration he sees what he must transmit to the Church. In one tiny word he gives flesh to the paradox of the Child who goes with wide-hearted love to the cross for all children – for us! – in obedience to his *Abba*. Mark's mission as Evangelist is thus an invitation to open our own hearts wide in filial immediacy to our Father who always hears us and awaits us with loving arms.

The Promise of God

Father Donald Haggerty

The beginning of the gospel of Jesus Christ [the Son of God].
As it is written in Isaiah the prophet:/ "Behold, I am sending my
messenger ahead of you;/ he will prepare your way. A voice of
one crying out in the desert:/ 'Prepare the way of the Lord,/
make straight his paths.'" (Mk 1: 1-3)

God's awareness of all history is a profound mystery. Everything past, present, and future is known to God all at once in a single eternal gaze. This may be an impossible thought for our minds to comprehend. But on occasion we do receive the grace to realize how precious time itself is in our lives. Every day of our lives is an unrepeatable gift, never again to be lived. I remember that in the last two years of my father's life before he died at ninety, he often used to say in one version or another: "I have lived many years and am very old now, but I can assure you life is much shorter than you may think."

For God every period of life anticipates and prepares for what follows. God always wants to bring to completion what he has planned. The importance of every present hour is in part this link to the next hour. The same is true of the central moment in human history when the Son of God took our flesh and lived an earthly existence. First God prepared the hearts of people for his coming in Jesus. John the Baptist announced from the desert that the day of great longing would soon be manifest. The exalted hour of God's revelation was about to take place. This reminds us even now to be alert to God's effort to prepare our hearts for an encounter with him.

Perhaps at times we experience some unease when our thoughts turn to the future. Is this not to forget God's entry into this world in Jesus Christ? Just as the coming of Jesus was prophesied, we too have a promise from God of his constant presence in our lives. The Eucharist itself is a continual experience of this. A life of beauty and happiness awaits us always when we trust in God's goodness and love. A promise from God is irreversible and always faithfully kept.

Father in heaven, all things are known in your eternal wisdom and love. I give you thanks and praise for all you have chosen, and most especially for your Son Jesus Christ.

The Desert

Father Donald Haggerty

John [the] Baptist appeared in the desert proclaiming
a baptism of repentance for the forgiveness of sins.
(Mk 1: 4)

The first evangelical impulse is ordinarily to go where the crowds are. In places where greater numbers are found, one can expect a wider reception and ultimately hope for more conversions. It is interesting, then, that John the Baptist is not inspired by God to establish residence in Jerusalem for his preaching. Instead God draws him into the harsh Judean desert for an unknown length of time in solitary preparation, and then keeps him there as John begins to proclaim his prophetic message. What is it about the desert that fits aptly this divine choice for John's life and preaching?

I remember a trip to Israel I made in 1981 and a visit to the still active fifth-century monastery of Saint Sabas, located in stark desert terrain about seven miles from Bethlehem. Journeying over desert hillsides on a makeshift road of rocks, and with the monastery now in sight in a valley, we climbed to the top of one larger hill and suddenly came upon a view that stretched mile upon mile into a distant desert horizon. It was an extraordinary landscape of rolling hills of sand. To this day I keep a small snapshot photo of that view in a frame.

With this in mind, it is easier to venture a thought about God's intention to set up his last prophet's pulpit in the desert. There is indeed a kind of spiritual encounter with limitless reality when the eyes gaze out upon on the desert's boundless expanses. The journey into the desert by those who sought out John opened them to this spiritual churning of soul. In the middle of a desert stretching far on all sides, perhaps many who came to John felt their souls moved profoundly in that location. The endless expanses of the desert may have provoked a graced realization of the profound depth and worth of their souls in God's eyes.

Almighty Father, help me to appreciate more deeply the value of my soul in your eyes, and to remember the sacredness of every human person.

The Prophet's Appeal

Father Donald Haggerty

*People of the whole Judean countryside and all the inhabitants
of Jerusalem were going out to [John] and were being baptized
by him in the Jordan River as they acknowledged their sins.*
(Mk 1: 5)

The movement of crowds can have a contagious quality. A kind of collective curiosity can sweep through people, especially when someone unusual is beginning to draw interest. No one wants to be left behind and miss seeing some person of public fascination. This observation may be valid when a politician, a sports star, a media figure walks the streets of a city. But is this an adequate explanation for the throngs of people journeying far on foot into the desert region near the Jordan River to see John the Baptist? What was the magnetic appeal in this case?

We can assume that both natural curiosity and a supernatural impetus of grace provoke the Jewish crowds who go out to John. From what we know historically, the Jewish expectation of the Messiah had been intensifying for some time under the Roman political domination. When John the Baptist makes his appearance, he surely arouses such thoughts. The combination of his ascetical features with the commanding fire of his words no doubt lead to speculation that he might be the promised Messiah. It is no surprise that everyone wants to see him.

But God also fills this man with a prophet's spirit to achieve a purpose of grace. Real conversions are the direct fruit of John's preaching. There is no suggestion that only a minority accepts his demand for immersion in the Jordan as a sign of their sincere sorrow for sin. It appears this is a general response by the multitudes that come.

Yet what happens later? Many of these same people who had returned from their encounter with John dramatically touched by grace nonetheless refuse to accept Jesus when he reveals himself in his divinity. It reminds us how precarious the work of grace is, and how humble we must be in our commitment to our Lord.

*Loving Father, keep me firmly rooted in my faith and in my choice
to follow your Son Jesus through all events of my life.*

Spiritual Radicality

Father Donald Haggerty

John was clothed in camel's hair, with a leather belt around his waist. He fed on locusts and wild honey.
(Mk 1: 6)

Christianity has always deeply respected the radical lifestyle as a sign of a greater commitment to God. During the first three centuries, such radicality was ever-present in the risk of bearing witness to the name of Jesus Christ. Under the Roman Empire, Christians had embraced a dangerous creed, and thousands suffered martyrdom in periodic waves of Roman hostility. In the fourth century, after the Roman persecutions ended, a new impulse replaced the possibility of dying for one's faith as a sign of ultimate commitment. Men and women began to venture into the burning deserts of Egypt and Syria to take up what today seem to be impossible hardships. In reading the lives of these desert monks we marvel at their physical endurance in surviving on little food or sleep under the rage of the desert sun. But perhaps we forget the interior passion that animated them to give all for God. These lives indeed became the model for monastic life in the Church, which, thankfully, does not demand today the extremes of ascetical deprivation that the desert monks practiced. Nonetheless monastic life has always been inspired by a notion of a prophetic witness to a soul's complete gift to God.

In a quite real sense, John the Baptist is a brother to all who receive this special call from God. Not simply because he clothes himself in the bristles of camel's hair or feeds on locusts, but because he finds the God of infinite being speaking to his own soul in the solitary quiet of the desert. We neglect a proper appreciation for John if we neglect his communion with God in prayer. The desert is his chapel before it becomes the site of his preaching. The passion of his soul for God is the source of his profound capacity to touch souls. This pattern must likewise become our own whatever our vocation is.

Father of all goodness, grant to me a greater attraction for prayer and for time alone with you; give me the courage to pray even when I find it difficult.

17

The Test of Humility

Father Donald Haggerty

And this is what [John] proclaimed: "One mightier than
I is coming after me. I am not worthy to stoop and loosen
the thongs of his sandals. I have baptized you with water;
he will baptize you with the holy Spirit." (Mk 1: 7-8)

A reliable sign of genuine holiness in a person is the sudden surprise he or she displays at the realization of being used by God in a special manner. Such a sign may show itself visibly when a holy person is praised or treated with some importance. I remember, for instance, Mother Teresa in a documentary film quickly deflecting a comment about her heroic actions for the poor with a reply that this is God's work and with a request to pray that she and her Sisters will not spoil his work. She refuses to entertain a thought of her fruits and contribution because she does not consider them her own. She has simply cooperated with God by surrendering to him.

John the Baptist gives similar evidence of this kind of spontaneous humility. John's proclamation of his unworthiness even to bend down and loosen the thongs of the Messiah's sandals is likely provoked by admiration and praise directed at his own person. While today we know him in his greatness as the last prophet and the forerunner of the Lord, John no doubt has a profound sense of his temporary role relative to the One who is to come. He expresses this awareness explicitly in John's Gospel after the baptism of Jesus when he affirms, "He must increase; I must decrease" (Jn 3: 30). His closeness to God may allow him to anticipate that he will disappear swiftly after his mission is completed with the coming of Jesus.

A powerful lesson in humility is offered to us here. There is nothing greater in a human life than to recognize God's will and fulfill his plan for us with a generous spirit. In most cases this may not involve dramatic accomplishments. But it will always entail a humble awareness, inspired by the Holy Spirit, that we belong ultimately to God.

Father, give me the grace of a humble heart and soul, and a
stronger realization that your Son's gift to me deserves the
complete surrender of my life to him.

The Favors of God

Father Donald Haggerty

*It happened in those days that Jesus came from Nazareth
of Galilee and was baptized in the Jordan by John.*
(Mk 1: 9)

When we recall that John is offering a "baptism of repentance for the forgiveness of sins" (Mk 1: 4), we may be puzzled why our Lord consents to undergo the ritual. Could this be a semblance of playacting? Why should Jesus make a gesture of symbolic repentance that contradicts his actual sinlessness as the Son of God? On the other hand, let us remember that while Jesus has no sin himself, he is willing to be considered a sinner on the cross. In this regard the baptism of Jesus at the Jordan is inseparable from the crucifixion. The immersion in the Jordan's waters becomes, three years later, the dreadful immolation of the cross.

There is a thought to consider in this regard. When an adult convert is baptized into the Catholic Church, we can expect that such a person has been moved at some point by the sight of a crucifix and the realization that the man nailed there is God in the flesh. In the prison facility where I offer Mass on Saturday nights, I have known a seventy-eight-year-old man, formerly Jewish, who was baptized after some months in the jail. His wife of fifty-four years had been suffering from terminal cancer. One night, using an old 1950s gun, he shot her to end her misery. He called 911 and, with the police operator on the phone, pulled the trigger four times to end his own life. But the gun malfunctioned each time. The operator interrupted, "Do you think maybe God is trying to tell you something?" In time this man had his own encounter with a crucifix, and perhaps in that hour he was given the full answer to the operator's question.

The favors of God are indeed unfathomable. Let us remember that his mercy is often prepared for us through some expression of the humility of God, as we see in Jesus accepting baptism from John.

Father, help me to see in your Son's humility at the Jordan River an invitation to deepen humility in my own life, acknowledging always my need for your mercy.

Divine Immersion

Father Donald Haggerty

On coming up out of the water [Jesus] saw the heavens being torn open and the Spirit, like a dove, descending upon him.
(Mk 1: 10)

The images are very striking in their symbolism. The Lord Jesus plunges into the waters of the Jordan. Then he emerges, and the heavens tear open. The descent of Jesus into these waters can signify the healing touch of God's hand upon his creation accomplished in the incarnation. Jesus as God sanctifies the waters by entering into them, just as he makes holy the flesh of humanity by uniting himself fully to our nature. Indeed at the Jordan all creation receives a sign of the restoration that occurs in Jesus Christ after the fall of Adam and Eve. Everything that exists is blessed by God as a consequence of the divine Son becoming man.

Then the heavens are visibly torn open to the eyes of Jesus. This is a sign of his own union with God. But it is also an anticipation of what is to occur. His suffering on the cross will unlock a door closed by sin and make accessible to us a companionship with God for all eternity. We are informed as well that the Spirit descends upon Jesus "like a dove." The description is again evocative. A dove is an image of innocence, purity, simplicity, qualities that we are less accustomed to apply to Jesus, yet certainly radiant in his human nature. But the dove recalls another event in Scripture. When in Genesis the flood waters began to recede after the deluge, Noah sent a dove to fly off in search of land. On its second flight it returned with an olive leaf, the sign that the earth would soon be habitable again. Jesus is himself this sign of ultimate hope, and the image of a dove descending upon him heralds the promise of abundant grace that is soon to be revealed in him.

Let us allow Jesus to immerse himself in our inner spirit, that we may find wide open to us a door to heaven within our soul.

Almighty Father, I ask you to send your Holy Spirit upon my own life, so that I may faithfully live the promises of my baptism to the end of my days.

The Father's Love

Father Donald Haggerty

And a voice came from the heavens,
"You are my beloved Son; with you I am well pleased."
(Mk 1: 11)

The Father does not wait long to testify to his love for his Son. After the hidden years in Nazareth, the baptism at the Jordan River is Jesus' initial entry into a public life. It is a largely quiet event, and even after it our Lord remains still unknown to the crowds, ordinary to any observer. Yet he is not unknown to the Father, and indeed Jesus is capable of moving his Father to an outburst of love. As Jesus emerges from the water, the skies tear open and the Father's voice is heard in a personal tribute to his Son. It is as though the heavens cannot be contained and must release already the secret that will await full disclosure over the next three years.

Notice that the words are addressed directly to Jesus: "You are my beloved Son." This testimony is a first revelation that ought to shape everything we read subsequently in the Gospel account. The statement suggests that the words are spoken for Jesus to hear in a private intimacy of recognition. The crowds do not hear them. But we can ponder now their infinite value. They are a divine sentiment that will deepen as Jesus gives pleasure to his Father by a complete submission to his will – even to his death on the cross. This love of the Father for Jesus is a love that God in turn wants to direct to us.

This past year, after my father's death, I spent some time rummaging through old family photos. One photo showed my father holding in his arms his first-born son as a baby. The joy of love in the face of this man is striking, and it moved me to gaze on it. But is this not an infinitesimal image of the love the Father bears for his Son Jesus? The Father knows that Jesus will give all for love of him, and he declares already in anticipation his great pleasure at this self-gift.

Heavenly Father, you love your Son with an infinite delight in him; help me to be a true child of your love, always faithful to you.

Satan's Temptation

Father Donald Haggerty

At once the Spirit drove [Jesus] out into the desert, and
he remained in the desert for forty days, tempted by Satan.
He was among wild beasts, and the angels ministered to him.
(Mk 1: 12-13)

Immediately after his baptism Jesus is compelled by the Spirit to seek the wild solitude of the Judean desert. Tradition has it that he climbs a rocky mountain in the desert not far from Jericho, where he has an expansive vista before his eyes in the daytime, and dwells at night in a cave carved into the side of that mountain. It is a time of testing, a time to confront Satan in a direct manner. Even the Son of God has to face temptation, and we may wonder at this.

The temptations of Jesus in the desert, described in detail in Matthew and Luke, are not ordinary. They suggest that Satan suspects the presence of divinity in Jesus without knowing certainly. In the desert our Lord does not evade Satan's questioning, nor flee the attempt to uncover his true identity. In each temptation he parries the devil's thrust aimed at distorting his self-awareness as the Son of God. In each case he conquers a temptation by humbly reciting a passage from Scripture. The humility of Jesus in these exchanges is more profound inasmuch as Satan in his arrogance assumes a power to grant him favors.

Satanic temptation in our lives may have its own sinister drama. Often it involves some presumption of an independence from God, as though our choices can be made without a consideration of God. The devil may not tempt us with the words, "If you are the Son of God" (Mt 4: 3). But he may well use the suggestive whisper, "If you would be great, if you would be rich, if you want to get ahead in life…" A young lawyer, for instance, in order to win an important case and advance his career, might prepare his defendant for a perjurious testimony. Or he can discern the devil's presence in this opportunity. How important it is to listen to the voice of God in our conscience.

Merciful Father, protect me always in the time of temptation, so that I may please you by relying on your help and grace in every danger.

Laying the Groundwork

Father Donald Haggerty

After John had been arrested, Jesus came to Galilee proclaiming the gospel of God: "This is the time of fulfillment. The kingdom of God is at hand. Repent, and believe in the gospel."

(Mk 1: 14-15)

When Jesus begins to preach in Galilee he does not proclaim his divine identity in its fullness. That will come later, after many healing miracles and more exposure to his mysterious attraction as a man. Only near the end of his life does he declare fully his oneness with the Father as an ultimate truth, and of course that revelation will cost him his life. But God is orderly in his ways, in creating and in the interventions of his grace. He takes a single step, as it were, then another, building upon his prior work. At the beginning of his public life, Jesus both echoes and deepens John's prophetic announcement that the time of fulfillment has come. Again, it is God's manner of acting and speaking – a gradual unveiling that will move always toward a deeper exposure of truth. The first preaching of Jesus also suggests an order and pattern in coming to know God. "Repent, and believe in the gospel." Humbling ourselves in sorrow for sin is a necessary act for belief in a Savior.

The story of Blessed Charles de Foucauld's conversion is a dramatic example of this pattern. He had abandoned his Catholic faith entirely in youth. One day he approached a priest asking to learn about the Catholic religion, since he had no faith now. The priest told him that he needed a pure heart to believe and commanded him first to kneel and make his confession, promising that God would then help him. After some protest, Charles did so and experienced in that confession the mysterious touch of God upon his soul. Ever after he identified this as his hour of salvation.

The initial proclamation of Jesus in Galilee to repent and then believe continues to bear fruit to this day in those who allow God to lift them from the misery of sin to a renewed awakening of faith.

Merciful Father, help me to deepen my faith by knowing more clearly my need for your mercy; forgive me for all the ways I have offended you.

Fishers of Men

Father Donald Haggerty

As [Jesus] passed by the Sea of Galilee, he saw Simon and his brother Andrew casting their nets into the sea; they were fishermen. Jesus said to them, "Come after me, and I will make you fishers of men." Then they left their nets and followed him.
(Mk 1: 16-18)

Surely Jesus knows the two brothers Andrew and Peter already. As John's Gospel describes it, Andrew and a companion (who must be John himself) first meet Jesus at the Jordan River after John the Baptist pointed to Jesus as the Lamb of God. Andrew then brings his brother Peter to Jesus. Yet afterward the brothers apparently go back to Galilee and their fishing. In that first meeting near the Jordan River, Jesus may have inquired about their work and heard that they were fishermen in Galilee. If so, he may not have been simply passing at random along the shore when he sees them casting their nets into the sea. He follows after them from the desert region with the purpose of inviting them to follow him. In Galilee he does not make a long persuasive speech. Indeed, how appealing is the simple proposal he makes to them: "I will make you fishers of men." Men who had labored for the fish of the sea are to fish for a much greater prize, the souls of men.

We sometimes remark on Jesus' choice of a rough, hardy set of first companions, workingmen familiar with daily sweat and toil. It is indeed an eloquent testimony to God's own humility that he prefers common men without status to be his apostles and take his Gospel throughout the world. But it is the heart of the fisherman in these first apostles that may have most attracted Jesus. I remember a fisherman on a boat telling me once that endurance is the test of his profession; each day does not always bring home a happy catch. And is it not true of every follower of Jesus Christ that we are called to pursue the catch of souls in a spirit of perseverance? Each day does not always provide the satisfaction of bringing a soul to the knowledge of Jesus Christ and his loving mercy. Yet for the joy of one such day, the reward of being a follower of Christ is boundless.

Father, you continue to call men and women to give their lives for the sake of souls; help me to hear that invitation also in my present circumstances of life.

Abandonment for Love

Father Donald Haggerty

[Jesus] walked along a little farther and saw James, the son of Zebedee, and his brother John. They too were in a boat mending their nets. Then he called them. So they left their father Zebedee in the boat along with the hired men and followed him.

(Mk 1: 19-20)

These fishermen, two pairs of brothers and fellow partners in business, drop everything to set off immediately with Jesus toward unknown destinies. In the case of James and John it can seem at first callous that they forsake their father so precipitately, with no explanation, leaving poor Zebedee to answer to their mother for their unexpected disappearance. But their quick departure reminds us that these men had already been affected by the divine presence of Jesus in a previous encounter at the Jordan. The first chapter of John's Gospel recounts the meeting of Andrew and Peter with Jesus, and presumably John as well. Back in Galilee after that initial encounter with Jesus they no doubt talked passionately about the man they had met through John the Baptist and the possibility that he was the One promised by God to Israel. When Jesus invites these same fishermen to abandon everything and follow him now as fishers of men, their souls are already full of a desire to discover more of him. All the same it is a profound risk they undertake. They show courage and a great trust to respond to this invitation.

We should ponder this example if God is calling us to a more total gift of our life. No vocation to the priesthood or religious life, no decision to marry, comes without a need to make an ultimate surrender to God. When I look back on my decision to become a priest, I wonder now why I hesitated for some years, avoiding the signs of God's call. Then one day with grace it became clear that it was not simply my choice, but God's invitation urging me to choose. Even spoken quietly in our soul, the words "Follow me" can become irresistible. It is our happiness that is being offered to us in this command. As I discovered for myself, we need only cross a threshold of trust to experience this happiness.

Loving Father, your attractions of grace lead us to your will in our lives; help me to respond more fully to your desires in all things in my life.

Words of Authority

Father Donald Haggerty

Then they came to Capernaum, and on the sabbath [Jesus] entered the synagogue and taught. The people were astonished at his teaching, for he taught them as one having authority and not as the scribes. (Mk 1: 21-22)

Jesus dons no scribal robes, fastens no tassel of honor when he enters the synagogue in Capernaum and begins to preach. On the contrary, he stands in front of the religious assembly as the working carpenter he is. But his words are different, unlike any previous speaker commenting on Scripture. In this man there is nothing of a need to impress the crowd, no impulse to perform or draw applause. He is not like others who compete and seem to have a rival preacher in mind. He proposes no interpretation to shock or sound original. Nonetheless he possesses what we would call today a presence about him, a charismatic quality that turns eyes on him and keeps the minds of his listeners captive as soon as his voice begins to flow. Something intangible in him moves people; the voice and the words he speaks, in their simplicity and strength, convey an aura of absolute truth.

At this early stage of the public life of Jesus, we witness the transition from his hidden life to what will become in time the full radiance of his divine revelation. Before any miracle has healed a broken body, Jesus already shines with the divinity that was one with his manhood. The man who until now has drawn little notice suddenly holds all eyes, even on the small scale of a synagogue in Capernaum. This is not surprising. The authority that permeates his being as the Son of God is released for open view as he enters his public life as Lord. There is a parallel for us in the life of the Church. The appearance of a priest or religious can of course be utterly drab and nondescript. But when priests are faithful to him, our Lord uses them to convey his own presence and even to speak again as he did in this life with the authority of his divine truth.

Almighty Father, grant me the grace of listening more carefully to your Son's words in the Gospel, that I may more faithfully follow him in everything.

Confrontation with Evil

Father Donald Haggerty

In their synagogue was a man with an unclean spirit; he cried out, "What have you to do with us, Jesus of Nazareth? Have you come to destroy us? I know who you are – the Holy One of God!" (Mk 1: 23-24)

As Jesus returns quietly to Galilee after his forty days in the desert, a great commotion is surely taking place elsewhere. The underworld of demonic spirits has been stirred like a nest of hornets in observing him repel the temptations of Satan. A fear of what is to come spreads rapidly among the demonic spirits. They are not oblivious to the threat Jesus poses. They know the prophecies of a promised Messiah. They are aware of John the Baptist's message and the profound anticipation he has aroused. In all this a contagious terror likely invades the dark Satanic underworld. They have no way of knowing what consequence to their own status as damned creatures might ensue with the coming of Jesus Christ. We hear this fear from the demon in Capernaum: "Have you come to destroy us?" In shouting these words, he includes with them a reluctant testimony of the truth. "I know who you are – the Holy One of God." It is a truth, however, that arouses no desire to draw closer, only a panic that with the coming of Jesus something dire is now inescapable.

This mention so early in the Gospel of the demonic recognition of Jesus reminds us that spiritual warfare constitutes an essential Christian challenge. Jesus vanquishes evil by his own suffering and death on the cross. Nonetheless we face in this life the destructive malice of the fallen angels. Their hatred for God is directed toward our own lives. As a priest I have seen that malice of the evil one on a few rare occasions. Once it seemed to occur immediately after a confession in a prison when a look of cold contempt and utter disdain was shot unexpectedly at me as I passed another inmate. A strange and foreboding stare was in that man's eyes. I was happy to walk away and soon found peace in praying a series of silent Hail Marys.

All-powerful Father, your Son conquered for ever the enemy of souls; grant me a strong confidence always to resist evil with Jesus at my side.

Divine Power at Work

Father Donald Haggerty

Jesus rebuked him and said, "Quiet! Come out of him!"
The unclean spirit convulsed him and with a loud cry
came out of him. (Mk 1: 25-26)

Exorcism is an ancient rite of the Church, a powerful weapon of select prayers used in rare cases of demonic possession. But it is not simply a recital of prayers that expels the demonic presence. The command of the priest exorcist plays a significant part in this act of spiritual healing. After using the ritual prayers, the exorcist orders the demon to leave by the authority of Jesus Christ. Often he must make this command repeatedly, sometimes in a number of sessions, before the departure of the demon. Jesus, we know, exorcises demons on numerous occasions in the Gospel. His word of command shows an invincible power over demonic spirits. This is a sign of his divinity that he can strike grave fear in the demons and send them immediately to flight when he pronounces his order to depart. It is apparently not so easy for exorcists.

I remember once an experienced exorcist recounting the stubborn obstinacy he had encountered often in exorcisms. He told me that there was one spiritual ploy, however, to be used in a difficult case of demonic possession. It is to inform the demon that unless it leaves without more delay, the priest will pray to our Lord to increase the punishment in hell of the recalcitrant demon once he does depart. And this, he said, seems to work with marvelous effectiveness.

Perhaps we witness something of this fear of further punishment in the demon when it departs so quickly at Jesus' rebuke. The convulsion it causes in the possessed man and the loud cry come like a last protest at the power of God over it. Is this a power to inflict a punishment of never disturbing another human person again until the end of time? We should believe that God does indeed exercise this power on our behalf. He is always ready to assist us in our struggles with the evil one.

Merciful Father, your strength is greater than my weakness; help me always to trust in your assistance in every struggle with temptation.

The First Poverty

Father Donald Haggerty

All were amazed and asked one another, "What is this? A new teaching with authority. [Jesus] commands even the unclean spirits and they obey him." His fame spread everywhere throughout the whole region of Galilee. (Mk 1: 27-28)

The startling impact of Jesus' exorcisms is quickly felt in Galilee. No one had ever expelled demons in this manner, with such lasting results. Until this time any sign of the demonic simply terrified people, and the possessed were customarily banished far from towns and villages. Yet here is a man fearless before demons. There is a singular power in his presence. At his mere word the spirits cower away into darkness, never to return. This is one of the first impressions Jesus makes as he begins his public life in Galilee. He comes as a liberator to estranged souls – truly the poorest of the poor in their spiritual suffering.

Sometimes the comment is made that these possessions are simply cases of mental illness. But that is surely false. On the contrary, it may be that demonic manifestations are intense in this period, with much spiritual disturbance and agitation. The coming of Jesus Christ into this world is akin to the outbreak of war in the supernatural realm. And yet Jesus' divine authority over demonic spirits is immediately evident. As we continue to read the Gospel, it may appear that Jesus shifts his attention away from this early work. In fact it is a work that continues to this day.

Once I attended a session of exorcism, stunned and shocked initially by a real personal presence of evil speaking in the dramatically altered voice of a poor possessed woman. At one point, there was a break in the session. Still unconvinced about what I was observing, I went across the room, poured some bottled water in a cup, and secretly blessed it. Offering it then to the woman, she drank and immediately sprayed the water out of her mouth, screaming at me that I had given her boiling water. By the end of that session the woman was quiet and subdued. The power of Jesus over evil remains to this day a power of liberation and healing.

Father, your Son Jesus turns always to the poor; help me to see in my encounters with every spiritual poverty a reason to pray and sacrifice for souls.

Bringing Jesus Home

Father Richard Veras

On leaving the synagogue [Jesus] entered the house of Simon and Andrew with James and John. Simon's mother-in-law lay sick with a fever. They immediately told him about her. He approached, grasped her hand, and helped her up. Then the fever left her and she waited on them. (Mk 1: 29-31)

A parishioner recently told me why she became a Eucharistic minister. Not long after she felt called to deepen her relationship with Christ and had begun to frequent the sacraments more, a parish priest asked her to bring communion to a woman dying of cancer. She protested that she didn't feel worthy to be the bearer of the Eucharist.

The priest told her with loving certainty, "But you're being called! I didn't ask if you were worthy, I asked if you were willing!" The parishioner said yes, and thus began a life-changing friendship between her, the woman to whom she bore the Eucharist, and Jesus himself. She now brings the Eucharist to two other homebound men in our parish, and her love for these men is truly moving; and she herself is clearly a woman whose life is moved by the love that Christ shows her by calling her and sending her.

This event in my parish has its origin in the event recounted in this short Gospel passage. Simon and Andrew are called by Jesus, and they attend the synagogue with him on the sabbath. On leaving the synagogue they bring Jesus home, to the sickbed of Simon's mother-in-law. The God who is worshiped in the synagogue has come to her very bedside. On being healed, Simon's mother-in-law serves Jesus out of gratitude, returning the love he first gave to her.

The service of Simon's mother-in-law is not a payment, but a joyous overflowing of the love of Christ. My friend in the parish does not bear Christ to others as a way of achieving worthiness, or paying him back for what he has done for her, but as a way of continuing the dynamic and loving relationship that Christ has begun with her. And this relationship overflows and embraces and invites the people that she serves into this same relationship that began two thousand years ago, and continues for ever.

Eternal Father, may you accompany me from the Eucharistic table into every aspect of my life, that your presence may heal my sin, and my presence may bear your mercy to those to whom you send me.

The Tenderness of Time

Father Richard Veras

When it was evening, after sunset, they brought to [Jesus]
all who were ill or possessed by demons. The whole town was
gathered at the door. He cured many who were sick with various
diseases, and he drove out many demons, not permitting them
to speak because they knew him. (Mk 1: 32-34)

I f the demons knew him, why wouldn't Jesus let them speak? Why not let them reveal the truth that he is the Son of God and Savior?

Let's imagine that you have fallen in love with a girl at college who happens to live near your family's house. When you get home from school for the summer you tell your family all about this girl who lives in the next town over. You are not exactly boyfriend and girlfriend – yet – but you are sure that this is the girl you are going to marry!

On Memorial Day, you invite this girl over to your family's barbecue along with some other friends from school. At a certain point, your devilish little brother comes over and grinningly interrupts the fascinating conversation you are having with your intended to ask, "Hey, is this the girl you said you were going to marry? Hello, future sister-in-law!"

At that point, you probably want to kill your brother, or at least place his face firmly upon the barbecue grill. "Why?" your brother might snidely protest, "I was only telling the truth!"

Yes, he told the truth. But time needs to pass between you and this girl so that love and trust can grow into a solid relationship such that she will one day rejoice in your proposal of marriage.

Jesus has become human, and as with any human relationship, his relationship with his disciples needs time to develop. If in those first days he said, "Hello! I'm the Son of God and I have come to save you," few would be ready to trust or follow.

Jesus knows that our faith and our following will never flourish if they are based only on words, even if those words be memorized and repeated. The foundation of our communion with Christ is life lived with him and time spent in the places and with the faces through whom he is most clearly alive and present.

Almighty Father, grant me your patience for my lack of faith, and grant me the patience I need to walk in my journey of faith with your Son Jesus Christ who accompanies me through his Mystical Body, the Church.

Rising to Real Prayer

Father Richard Veras

*Rising very early before dawn, [Jesus] left and
went off to a deserted place, where he prayed.*
(Mk 1: 35)

I once heard a wonderful little joke on a retreat, and I hope I can repeat it faithfully. There were two monks reciting their office together in the monastery chapel. As they were going along, loud peals of thunder and frightening flashes of lightning pierced the calm of the chapel. The wind made a branch scrape against a chapel window. At this point, one monk said to the other, "Hey, we'd better put our breviaries down and start praying!"

Weren't they supposedly praying already? It's so easy to reduce prayer to a task to do, or a debt to pay to God, rather than something that springs from our real need. Often our true need for God and our desire for the manifestation of his love and truth are far away from our minds during the times we set aside for prayer, whether that be Mass, a rosary, the daily office, or even silent prayer time.

For Jesus, prayer before his Father was a need, a necessity. His human life is inconceivable without it. He doesn't rise before dawn to please his Father, but to abandon himself to the eternal love of the Father in which he exists with the Holy Spirit. What is attractive and effective about Jesus is his communion with the Father and with the Spirit. Contrary to what many have imagined about him, he is not "Superstar" but "Son."

If I do not pray sincerely, from my need, then I might be able to know a lot of things about Jesus, and I might even be able to do a lot of things that look Christian, but I will not know Jesus himself. If Christianity is not an overflowing of the knowledge of the love of Christ that comes through prayer, then it will become a burden that is heavy and empty.

If we faithfully follow Jesus in prayer, we will joyfully follow him in his easy task and his light burden.

Loving Father, draw me to the love of your Son, that all my prayer may be an expression of my need and my gratitude for your Fatherhood.

32

Everyone Is Looking

Father Richard Veras

Simon and those who were with him pursued [Jesus]
and on finding him said, "Everyone is looking for you."
(Mk 1: 36-37)

Simon is truly a prophet when he tells Jesus, "Everyone is looking for you." For everyone truly is looking for Jesus. Anyone who seeks true love seeks Jesus, for God is Love. Anyone who seeks truth is seeking Jesus, for he is the way, the truth, and the life.

The audacious claim of the Church is that the depth of the heart of every person, Christian, Jew, Muslim, Buddhist, agnostic, or atheist, is beating longingly for Jesus. How could this be true?

When I have to book a flight to visit my parents in Florida at Thanksgiving, I want the least expensive flight I can find that leaves Wednesday evening and returns Saturday evening (I need to be home for Sunday Masses at the parish!). What I am looking for is the least expensive flight at the times convenient for me. I will ultimately come to discover that the flight I am looking for actually has a particular number and a particular name. There is a particular plane out there waiting to bring me to Florida in the most economic and convenient way.

Every human being longs for love and truth and meaning. Some might have ideas of what this will be, some are actively searching, some may have given up the search. However, none of us can stop the longing. At some point in time or outside of time, we are destined to discover that the love, truth, and meaning which our hearts have ever desired is a particular person, with a particular personality and a particular name. He is Jesus of Nazareth. He sits for ever at the right hand of the Father and he sits daily in countless particular spaces and places throughout the world. Everyone is looking for him. And he is truly waiting, lovingly and patiently and particularly, for everyone.

Loving Father, may I take my life seriously enough to go to the depths of the desires that you have placed within me to draw me to your Son, who will draw me to you through the grace of your Spirit.

You Are the Purpose

Father Richard Veras

[Jesus] told [Simon and those who were with him],
"Let us go on to the nearby villages that I may preach there also.
For this purpose have I come." So he went into their synagogues,
preaching and driving out demons throughout the whole
of Galilee. (Mk 1: 38-39)

I have always been impressed with the story of Blessed Teresa of Calcutta in which she was washing a poor dying man in the streets of a slum and he asked her, "Why are you doing this?" Her answer was simply, "Because I love you."

Imagine that man's awe at the fact that someone had come for him. He was her purpose. He was the reason she came.

This is why children in sports events or plays will look into the stands. They are looking for their parents, or their grandparents or aunts or uncles or siblings. Anyone in those stands is there for one reason and one reason only, out of love for that child. It's not like a family gathering where the whole family is the purpose for attendance. The presence of your grandpa at that event is for you.

"For this purpose have I come." What moving words of Jesus. He had in mind the people in the village synagogues. He was coming for them, and I think we can certainly say he was coming for each one of them, to embrace each one of them.

There are moments in the Gospels when Jesus speaks of us, he prays for us who will live in later times, believe in him because of the apostolic preaching, and encounter him in the apostolic Church.

You are the purpose for which he came. It is for you that he went to the synagogues, for you that he called Saint Paul to reach the Gentiles, Saint Thomas to reach the Indians, Saint Patrick to reach the Irish, Our Lady of Guadalupe and Saint Juan Diego to reach the Mexicans, and so on and so on and so on. He wants to reach us one by one with the gaze that a man on the streets of Calcutta saw in Blessed Teresa's eyes, and that Simon saw in the eyes of that mysterious carpenter.

Loving Father, through the face of your Son made present in the world through the action of the Holy Spirit, let me recognize and rejoice in your personal love for me, and never reduce you to a generic god.

Heart to Heart with Jesus

Father Richard Veras

A leper came to [Jesus] [and kneeling down] begged him and said, "If you wish, you can make me clean." Moved with pity, he stretched out his hand, touched him, and said to him, "I do will it. Be made clean." The leprosy left him immediately, and he was made clean. (Mk 1: 40-42)

I was about twelve years old and was coming out of the movies with my friend. In the lobby was a boy of about nine and his sister of about six. They were sitting on the floor by the phone booths, I assume waiting to be picked up by their parents. I was deeply moved by the sight of them. To this day when I recall this moment, significant only because I have inexplicably remembered it, I see the faces of me and my own little sister. There is a certain tenderness in my heart that belongs only to her (even at the ages of forty-five and forty-two!). I was moved at that moment because I know the love of brother and sister, the simple joy of being at a movie together. There is something deeply and mysteriously human that was moved in me and is moved even as I write about it.

How could Jesus be so moved by that leper? Because he had become human. He knew the trustful and faithful beseeching that came from that poor man when he said, "If you wish, you can make me clean." For Jesus must have stretched his own hands out to his foster-father and to his mother many times in his younger days. He knew that deeply human mystery that welled up in that request, in that humble and certain beckoning. Jesus' response, "I do will it. Be made clean," must have arisen from that deeply human place in his own self. Taking on human flesh means taking on a human heart and entering into the very depths of the mystery of our humanity.

Perhaps I am most truly myself in those moments when I can recognize my own face in the face of that leper. When the depth of my humanity cries out and is touched by the depth of Christ's humanity, and somehow divinity happens.

Heavenly Father, in your tenderness take pity upon me to my very depths, that my belonging to you through your Son Jesus Christ may deepen daily.

The Prescribed Ritual

Father Richard Veras

Then, warning [the man] sternly, [Jesus] dismissed him at once.
Then he said to him, "See that you tell no one anything, but go,
show yourself to the priest and offer for your cleansing what
Moses prescribed; that will be proof for them."
(Mk 1: 43-44)

Religious rituals can get a bad rap. It is true that ritual can easily turn into formalism, but we must not discount the value contained in the ritual itself. Jesus certainly did not scoff at ritual, for in this passage he clearly prescribes it to the healed leper.

I know many people who have become Catholic after years of "going through the ritual" of attending Mass with their Catholic spouse and children. I know many families whose children's enduring faith can trace itself back to a family rosary prayed with ritualistic regularity.

And I will never forget one night at the hospital. I had been called out by the daughter of a dying woman to pray at the bedside. I anointed the patient and then prayed a rosary with the family. In the silence after the rosary, I thought about the Apostolic Pardon that is in the ritual book for the sick and dying. It asks that the dying person be welcomed into paradise and released from all punishments. I knew the prayer was in the book, but I didn't know the page! I knew I would look slightly awkward thumbing through the book, but decided that this woman's salvation was more important than the impression I would leave on the family.

When I found the prayer and laid my hands on the patient and prayed the words, at the very moment I finished saying "Amen" the woman let out a deep sigh and passed away.

I knew I was not seeing things when the daughter, visibly moved, said to me as I was leaving, "Did you see that? She departed at the Amen!"

I try to recall this incident whenever I take for granted the rituals that Jesus prescribes to his priests and his faithful through his Church. These rituals are openings into the depths of reality. They are gifts that we would be foolish to ignore.

Our Father, who art in heaven, hallowed be thy name; thy kingdom come, thy will be done on earth as it is in heaven.

God's Hand in Shattered Plans
Father Richard Veras

*The man went away and began to publicize the whole matter.
He spread the report abroad so that it was impossible for Jesus
to enter a town openly. He remained outside in deserted places,
and people kept coming to him from everywhere. (Mk 1: 45)*

This passage reveals how Jesus lived his circumstances. Look back to Mk 1: 38-39 to see Jesus' original plan. He wanted to travel from village to village.

Well, the leper has "ruined" that plan. Now that the leper has directly disobeyed Jesus and told everyone what happened, Jesus cannot enter a town openly but must remain outside the town. The leper disobeyed and the original plan is dashed. But Jesus moves on without a complaint. For nothing, in the end, has been ruined. Jesus sees his Father behind everything. There is nothing that happens that can thwart the plan of the Father. There is no seeming setback that cannot be taken up by the Father to reveal even more splendidly his truth and majesty.

Notice that staying in deserted places did not stop people from coming to Jesus. And, in fact, the people who came were more ready to meet Jesus in those deserted places than they would have been in the town.

What does it take to walk to the center of the village to get a glimpse of the young rabbi people are talking about? In the populous places Jesus would probably attract lots of curiosity seekers, and the import of his presence could be reduced to the latest religious fad.

Those who take the trouble to travel outside the town to a deserted place must truly be looking for something. The effort of the journey would serve to purify them. And when they returned to town visibly changed and clearly moved, others who would have been mere curiosity seekers had he come to town may now go out with hearts that were open and ready for the encounter with Jesus.

"No one can come to me unless the Father who sent me draw him" (Jn 6: 44). No sin or disobedience can ruin the Father's plan, because the Father uses everything to open our hearts and draw us to his Son.

Merciful Father, help me to recognize and receive your tenderness toward me in the midst of what looks like turmoil, as your beloved Son did throughout his ministry and most especially on Calvary.

The Crowds around Jesus

Father Richard Veras

When Jesus returned to Capernaum after some days, it became known that he was at home. Many gathered together so that there was no longer room for them, not even around the door, and he preached the word to them.

(Mk 2: 1-2)

What kind of people were in that crowd? Were they all faithful Jews who worshiped regularly and sincerely? Were the better ones up front? Among those who could not even get close to the door, were there devout people who might have deserved a closer spot? Might there have been undeserving types situated in some of the prime spots?

Jesus does not distinguish. He preaches the word to all of them. He offers himself to any who will listen, and leaves the response to their freedom. He is sowing the seed, and the condition of the soil will make itself known. Some listeners may come to believe quickly, some may deepen the belief that they already had, and some might walk away today and come back after a time.

It is easy for us to get a bit annoyed on days like Ash Wednesday, Palm Sunday, Christmas, and Easter when many people come to the church that we don't normally see at other times. I deeply regret, for instance, losing patience with a gentleman one Ash Wednesday who wanted to get his ashes and go. It had been a long day and I didn't give the time to listen to his story.

What drew him to seek ashes? Did he have a worthy reason? God knows… not me. I do know that Jesus can reach him through whatever reason brought that man to the church that day.

Let us recognize these crowds as evidence of the presence of Christ among us. Whatever the reasons that bring them, they are there. And Jesus is there. And I don't doubt that somehow he will preach the word to them. He will cast the seed, and the condition of the soil will make itself known in God's time. We tend to be impatient. But God has a fatherly patience which is directed toward our salvation.

Merciful Father, may I realize the patience you have always had with me, and grow in my desire to reflect that patience to all who are in need of it.

The Moment of Truth

Father Richard Veras

They came bringing to [Jesus] a paralytic carried by four men.
Unable to get near Jesus because of the crowd, they opened up
the roof above him. After they had broken through, they let
down the mat on which the paralytic was lying.
(Mk 2: 3-4)

It must have been a frightening moment for that paralytic. Not just the experience of being hoisted over a roof and lowered down in the midst of a large crowd, but the experience of leaving his paralysis behind. Exciting, to be sure, but perhaps somewhat frightening.

Recall that Saint Augustine once prayed to be given chastity, "but not yet." A whole way of life, and a certain role and place in the lives of others, was on the brink of extinction. He must have known as his friends were getting him closer to Jesus that he was likely facing a point of no return. This is not a dream any more. There are no more "what ifs" or "wouldn't it be greats," for there is a moment of truth that is fast approaching. There is a possibility of a change that will change everything. This is not a game, this is extremely serious.

I recall the excitement of asking admittance to the seminary, but it was also a bit scary. This was not a game. I was not embarking on a role in a play, a job for a time; I was putting my life before Christ. It was the same at ordination; as I am sure it is the same at the moment of engagement and the moment of the wedding.

There can be the same scariness before confession, or before any serious encounter in which I open myself to correction and intervention. I can ask for healing in prayer, I can tell those closest to me that I want a change in my life, that I want to let go of this habit or that sin. But what do I really want? Do I want Jesus? Do I desire him more than whatever lesser thing I am holding closer to myself? Will I risk the fear of letting go of my old way of life and freeing myself to open my arms to Christ?

Almighty Father, let me not turn back or hesitate before the conversions that will lead me to the happiness of communion with you.

The Real Problem

Father Richard Veras

When Jesus saw their faith, he said to the paralytic, "Child, your sins are forgiven." Now some of the scribes were sitting there asking themselves, "Why does this man speak that way? He is blaspheming. Who but God alone can forgive sins?"
(Mk 2: 5-7)

What must the bearers of the paralyzed man be thinking? Didn't their struggle to get him through the roof so clearly express that they were looking for a healing? What is their initial thought when Jesus looks at the paralyzed man and simply says, "Your sins are forgiven." If it were I, I would probably think, "Is that all? All he's going to get is the forgiveness of his sins?!" This shows me how radically God's ways are not my ways.

To help the students in my parish understand Jesus' thinking in this instance, I ask them to imagine being wounded to the point of bleeding. When you get to the emergency room, an alarmed looking doctor comes over to you and says, "My goodness, look at all that blood!" and then he takes your shirt off and runs with it to the laundry. You are left there bleeding and helpless. There is clearly something wrong with the doctor's priorities. The shirt is not the real problem; the problem is you!

For Jesus, the real and ultimately the only problem is union with God the Father and, therefore, for the paralyzed man and for all of us the priority is the forgiveness of our sins. Many people have full use of their limbs and are unhappy. Many suffer from chronic disabilities and are at peace. Jesus goes to the root of the problem which is the paralyzed man's heart, the core and source of his life which Jesus has come to save. Forgiveness and reconciliation are the priority. The paralysis, i.e., the difficult circumstance of his life, is not the priority because it cannot prevent his communion with Christ. Saint Paul reminds us that no circumstance, no matter how difficult, can separate us from the love of Christ.

So let us follow Jesus who says, "Seek first the kingdom [of God] and his righteousness, and all these things will be given you besides" (Mt 6: 33).

Father, let me let go of complaints in the midst of difficulty, let me trust that your Son always holds my salvation as his highest priority, let me grow in the knowledge that my happiness is union with you.

When You Love Someone

Father Richard Veras

Jesus immediately knew in his mind what [the scribes] were thinking to themselves, so he said, "Why are you thinking such things in your hearts? Which is easier, to say to the paralytic, 'Your sins are forgiven,' or to say, 'Rise, pick up your mat and walk'?" (Mk 2: 8-9)

When you love someone, you become familiar with that person's reactions. You come to know how he or she thinks. Without a word being uttered, you can understand the one you love.

With the exchange of a glance, my parents can communicate a lot, and if I see the glance exchanged, I can pretty well know what they are both thinking.

One of my best friends has a wonderful way of knowing what I am thinking. He is a true friend, and so he takes the liberty to correct me if he sees that I am misunderstanding something, or taking something the wrong way, or just "checking out," or allowing my prejudices to keep me from being open.

There are people who know you so well that you cannot put one over on them. You cannot lie to them and you cannot pretend that something is not bothering you when they know very well that it is. This can seem inconvenient at times, but it is the fruit of having someone love you.

Perhaps it is not his divinity that allows Jesus to know what the scribes are thinking to themselves. Perhaps it is his humanity. He knows their way of thinking and reacting. He knows that they are not there because of an openness toward him but because of a prejudice against him. He is very well aware of what they are thinking about him and about what he says and does.

And why is this possible? Because he loves them. He loves them with all of his humanity. He is moved by their predicament and will risk whatever he must to free their hearts to receive his love. Whether they realize it or not, he is the best friend they have ever had. Jesus' pity is not just for the paralyzed man, his pity is for these scribes who are ignorant to the depth of their own poverty.

Loving Father, help me to look into the depths of my darkness through the truthful and merciful gaze of your Son, Jesus Christ.

Merciful Authority

Father Richard Veras

"But that you may know that the Son of Man has authority to forgive sins on earth" – [Jesus] said to the paralytic, "I say to you, rise, pick up your mat, and go home."
(Mk 2: 10-11)

The first thing people noticed about Jesus was that he spoke with authority and not like the scribes (see Mk 1: 22).

The scribes know many facts about the things God has done and the law he gave, but Jesus knows God as Father. Jesus doesn't repeat facts, he bears witness to his experience. Every fiber of his being communicates the fatherly love of God.

It must have been indescribable to be in the presence of Jesus and this substantially different authority that had never been seen before his coming into the world. Perhaps it seemed to some doubters to be too good to be true. Surely the scribes and Pharisees were working hard to give that impression to people. The old way of thinking about God and the fear of the law must have been deeply engrained, and the enemies of Jesus wanted to encourage these doubts and this resistance.

The healing of the paralyzed man was an act of mercy not just to him, but to all those who were gathered around that house that day. All the Jews would know that only God can forgive sins. By claiming this authority Jesus was claiming to be God. And to verify that claim he heals the paralytic. Jesus explicitly states that the reason he is healing the man is to offer evidence that he indeed does have the power to forgive sins, that he indeed is the face of God present in their midst.

To those who were tottering toward faith, Jesus extends a merciful and authoritative hand. This mercy is extended to all who are gathered there, whether they be able-bodied or paralyzed, friends or enemies. All are accompanied by Jesus on their path toward faith, no matter where on that path they may be.

Heavenly Father, help me to be open to the deepening of my faith which you continually offer through daily signs and verifications.

The Chosen

Father Richard Veras

[The man] rose, picked up his mat at once, and went away in the sight of everyone. They were all astounded and glorified God, saying, "We have never seen anything like this."
(Mk 2: 12)

My first assignment as a priest was in a parish in the Little Italy section of the Bronx. My Italian left a lot to be desired. I could stumble through a conversation and, with a lot of help and practice, I could preach in Italian. If I strayed too far from my written text, I would usually use wrong conjugations or tenses. I was blessed with an Italian professor from a nearby university who would critique me after my homilies.

One Sunday, I became very passionate about the subject of my preaching, and I hardly looked down at my paper. In the midst of it I remember being amazed because the words were flowing out and I was pretty sure they were grammatically correct.

After Mass, my professor friend came up to give her weekly critique and said to me, "That was the Holy Spirit! Because your Italian is not that good!"

I was not the least disappointed by her blunt assessment of my poor Italian skills, because I was completely moved by the fact that the Holy Spirit had worked with me and through me. No amount of compliments regarding my skills could awaken my heart as much as being chosen by God to be a sign of his Spirit working among us.

My friend was not kidding about my skills, and she was not kidding about the Holy Spirit. She was glorifying God!

As I think of that healed paralytic walking away in the sight of everyone, I am sure whatever joy his walking abilities gave to him was as nothing compared to the joy of knowing he had been loved and chosen, and that his paralysis and his healing were exalted to be for ever a sign of God's presence among us.

There is no deeper joy than knowing that you are a witness to God's love, not because of your ability, but because you have received his mercy.

Heavenly Father, may your love be known on earth; and your children in this world be continual witnesses of your love that comes from beyond this world.

An Unexpected Call

Father Richard Veras

*Once again [Jesus] went out along the sea. All the crowd came
to him and he taught them. As he passed by, he saw Levi, son
of Alphaeus, sitting at the customs post. He said to him,
"Follow me." And he got up and followed him.*
(Mk 2: 13-14)

I t was after a swimming practice when I was in the seventh grade. We were all gathered at the side of the pool and the coach was on the deck giving us a pep talk. I wasn't paying a whole lot of attention because I was not a star swimmer and didn't consider that the pep talk was much meant for swimmers like me. Then it happened! The coach said my name! He said, "Look at Richie Veras, he comes through for us, we can always rely on him for points." I was a part of the team! The coach noticed me. I, and my consistent third place showings, were valued.

Think of Levi at the customs post. He is just sitting there. He doesn't seem much interested in the fact that Jesus is passing by even though there is a whole crowd following and listening to his teaching. Was he looking up, was he listening at all? Perhaps, since his job as a tax collector has alienated him from his people, he figures that this man Jesus and his teachings don't have much to do with people like him.

He may have been pretending not to notice Jesus, but Jesus noticed him. Can you imagine what it must have been like when he saw Jesus looking straight at him? Perhaps he was expecting a rebuke, as he must have already received from so many. Perhaps he was too taken by the whole thing to know what to expect. And then the words, "Follow me." Jesus didn't rebuke him; he actually wants Levi to be with him!

And here is where my swimming analogy limps. I, at least, had scored some points for the team. Levi had, as far as the Jews were concerned, betrayed his people. Nothing made him worthy of the preferential attention Jesus gave to him. And so how much sweeter, how much more life-changing, must the loving gaze of Jesus have been!

*Merciful Father, increase my awareness of your ever loving gaze
upon me, which not even my inattention, not even my sin, can
turn away.*

That First Supper

Father Richard Veras

While [Jesus] was at table in his house, many tax collectors and sinners sat with Jesus and his disciples; for there were many who followed him. (Mk 2: 15)

How horrifying it must have been for the fishermen when Jesus called Levi. Everything was going so nicely, why invite this tax collector along? Perhaps they were even hoping that Jesus would rebuke him when he saw him at the customs post.

Even more difficult was that dinner. These were respectable fishermen; why was Jesus bringing them to the house of a tax collector to eat with even more tax collectors and sinners?

I think the supper at Levi's may be second in importance to the Last Supper. At the same table you had resentful enemies. Fishermen who had felt themselves cheated by tax collectors, and tax collectors who had been looked upon mercilessly by "upstanding" men like these fishermen.

How was unity possible? Through Jesus. Jesus must have been so happy to see that the joy of Levi spilled over into the invitations he gave to his friends. He must have been so amazed at what his Father was doing. The desire and openness of these known sinners were witnesses to Jesus of the generous workings of his Father's mercy.

When someone you love is joyful, that person's joy becomes infectious. When my young nephews and nieces would see their parents and grandparents and uncles and aunts laughing, they would laugh along even if they didn't understand the subject of the laughter; the joy of the adults had given rise to joy in them. This must have happened to the fishermen and the tax collectors. They were so caught up in the joy of Jesus, their humanity was so exalted by his human joy, that they met each other within his new gaze. His gaze is a gaze of joy and truth. After that moment there would be no going back. Their mutual resentments were simply lies that covered the truth of the unity they shared in their common love for their one Lord and Savior.

Almighty Father, may the joyful presence of Christ in the Church heal whatever wounds of sin and division exist among us. May the unity of Christians become a beacon to those who suffer alienation in their own lives.

A Pivotal Decision

Father Richard Veras

Some scribes who were Pharisees saw that [Jesus] was eating with sinners and tax collectors and said to his disciples, "Why does he eat with tax collectors and sinners?" Jesus heard this and said to them [that], "Those who are well do not need a physician, but the sick do. I did not come to call the righteous but sinners." (Mk 2: 16-17)

It is one thing to join Jesus for dinner with tax collectors and sinners, but once they are seen by the Pharisees, the fishermen are called to a greater risk, a deeper belonging to Jesus, because now their belonging will be public. The Pharisees are sure to tell the townspeople that these fishermen have defiled themselves with sinners. Perhaps they will encourage people to buy fish from other boats. It is not the fishermen's religious or devotional life that is on the line, but their whole lives and livelihood. For Jesus calls all of me to himself.

It is one thing to go on a date with a girl, but it is quite a different thing to introduce her to your friends, then to your family, then to your parents. And quite another to marry, and thus publicly acknowledge your belonging by sharing one name and one life.

The disciples are called to follow Jesus publicly, to link their lives inextricably to his. They probably cannot explain why Jesus is eating with sinners, but the experience they have had at that dinner and in these first days and weeks while following him have convinced them that being with this man is the truest thing they have ever done.

They can get up from that table and salvage their reputations and go back to life as it was. But they stay, for they have found someone whose love has dispelled their fear of the Pharisees. In their fearless decision to stay, they not only share Jesus' joy, but they have begun to share in his authority.

Jesus, affirming his unity with his disciples, answers the question for them; and his answer is not a rebuke of the Pharisees, but an invitation. For all the Pharisees have to do is admit their own need and immediately they will be welcomed to the same table, the same joy, the same life. And they will finally learn what real authority is.

Almighty Father, let me never be ashamed of my belonging to the Father, the Son, and the Holy Spirit through your one, holy, catholic, and apostolic Church.

Jesus in Reality

Father Richard Veras

The disciples of John and of the Pharisees were accustomed to fast. People came to [Jesus] and objected, "Why do the disciples of John and the disciples of the Pharisees fast, but your disciples do not fast?" (Mk 2: 18)

Jesus' way of being with his disciples is bothering some people. They object because he doesn't act like they expect a holy man should act. Don't holy men fast? Isn't that part of the package? The problem is that Jesus is not part of anyone's preconceived package. He is a real person that we don't create with our imaginations. One of the ways we know that he is a real person is that he tends to bother us on a rather regular basis.

Remember the story of *The Stepford Wives*? Men want their wives to stop bothering them with their personhood. They prefer instead to have robots who will fit their preconception of what a wife should be and how a wife should act. Real life and real love are exchanged for death and emptiness.

If a long time goes by without Jesus bothering me, I begin to get suspicious. Am I following the real Jesus in the Church or am I following a "Stepford Jesus" I have conjured in my head. Am I being led toward life or am I drowning in my own emptiness?

The Jesus in my head might be the nicest person I can imagine. The problem is that he is a figment of my imagination. This imaginary figure might always agree with me and coddle me.

Or perhaps the Jesus in my head is a strict and tough supervisor who hates me if I falter or fail in regard to whatever expectations he has.

The real Jesus, through the community of the Church, and its Scripture, tradition, and teaching, will correct me in love and truth. In confession, the real Jesus might give me mercy that I have difficulty accepting.

If he calls me to continual conversion, he must be Jesus. If I am never bothered and never have any questions and have everything figured out, then I must surely be lost in my imagination.

Loving Father, grant me the grace to follow Christ in truth and to welcome the corrections, the contrition, and the offers of mercy which are essential to my Christian path.

To Recognize the Bridegroom

Father Richard Veras

Jesus answered [the people], "Can the wedding guests fast while the bridegroom is with them? As long as they have the bridegroom with them they cannot fast." (Mk 2: 19)

The spring before going from the minor seminary to the major seminary, my classmates and I were invited for a dinner to meet the new rector. There we were in the dining hall talking among ourselves and waiting for the evening officially to begin when a priest came and shook my hand and asked me who I was. I told him my name and then I asked him, "And who are you?" When he told me he was the rector I felt like a complete idiot. I was so distracted by whatever conversation I was having that I didn't notice the rector had entered the room. In that moment I was so oblivious to the reason we were there that I didn't put two and two together and figure out who this priest must be who is going around and shaking hands.

The people asking Jesus about fasting are distracted and oblivious. What is the point of fasting? It is to recognize my need for God and my dependence upon him, so that I may always be waiting for his gracious presence in my life. At this moment God is standing right in front of them in the flesh, having said and done many things to verify the truth of his presence, and they are asking theological questions, oblivious to the fact that the Purpose and Answer to every question is right there before them! They are asking about a practice which is supposed to make me ready to recognize and welcome God into my life. Clearly whatever fasting they have already done has not done them much good. For they may have become good at keeping penitential practices, but their hearts are not hungry. Their human need is so buried that it does not recognize and rejoice in Jesus the Bridegroom.

Those whose hearts are truly hungry are those who cannot help but rejoice when the Bridegroom makes himself present.

Almighty Father, help my heart always to be ready to welcome your presence when you make yourself known through your Son by the power of the Holy Spirit. May I rejoice in you for ever.

Do You Miss Him?

Father Richard Veras

"But the days will come when the bridegroom is taken away from them, and then they will fast on that day."
(Mk 2: 20)

When I moved out of my parents' house into my first apartment, I remember feeling such a longing for my family, for that daily presence that I had so taken for granted. When I have been asked to move on to new priestly assignments, suddenly all that is good and beautiful about my current assignment is so much more evident to me. I am sure this happens with all kinds of separations and farewells in life. You wish you could turn back time and be more attentive, more aware of the gift that has been given to you.

Jesus knew that this reality would be extremely acute for his disciples, who had experienced a relationship of love, truth, and beauty beyond anything anyone had experienced to that point. For this reason, he promised that he would rise from the dead and give them the Holy Spirit. The Holy Spirit continues to make Christ present in the Church so that we can have the same experience as the disciples.

So if the Bridegroom is still present, why is fasting still part of our tradition? Because we can take the presence of Christ for granted. We can reduce Jesus Christ to an abstract and sentimental construction. We can reduce Christianity to rules and traditions (even really good rules and really nice traditions!).

When we fast in the penitential liturgical seasons, or embark on a personal fast, it is to bring us back to that acute longing of the apostles.

If I can avoid it, I don't want a deathbed conversion. I don't want to look back on all the ways that Christ has revealed his presence to me, and all the good that he has given to me and realize that I let it slip by.

Fasting is not meant to take away my joy, but to reawaken me to my need for Christ and lead me to true joy, that joy which rejoices in his presence.

Loving Father, you have created my heart to be restless until it rests in you. Heal my heart of its hardness and awaken in me the need to beg for and rejoice in the abundance of your love.

Faithfulness to His Newness

Father Richard Veras

"No one sews a piece of unshrunken cloth on an old cloak. If he does, its fullness pulls away, the new from the old, and the tear gets worse. Likewise, no one pours new wine into old wineskins. Otherwise, the wine will burst the skins, and both the wine and the skins are ruined. Rather, new wine is poured into fresh wineskins." (Mk 2: 21-22)

One summer I had returned to the parish with a busload of high school students and some other priests and teachers. We had just come back from a five-day retreat. At this retreat it was made clear to all of the adults that we were not chaperones, but that we were retreatants as well. We were not to see ourselves as "experts" but rather to recognize that we were in need of a renewed encounter with Christ just as much as the students.

The retreat was full of miracles, and the movement of Christ among us was palpable. The joy and energy that lasted throughout those days was the living grace of God.

As we got off the bus, one mother said to me, "Father, you made it through! You must be so relieved to see these kids driving away with their parents!" I smiled and said, "Yes," because it seemed like the polite and expected response. That's how a chaperone is supposed to react at the end of such a long trip.

I have often remembered that moment and that response as a kind of betrayal. Something new had happened on that retreat, and I did not bear witness to it. Instead, I responded as if it had been the same old thing – taking credit as if I had done something generous when it was Jesus who was generous to me.

Christ bursts through our old way of thinking and interpreting things. I pray to have the loyalty and courage to bear witness to that newness and not to fall back on the same old way of looking at life. The first one I need to bear witness to is myself. I am the first one to let the newness of Christ go to "ruin" when I fail to remain in wonder at the unimaginably new things he is doing in his Church today, when so many have reduced him to something old-fashioned.

Eternal Father, eternally young, and eternal source of all life and joy, may our hearts flourish in the newness and light of your love, and may our lives bear witness as you continue to make all things new.

Minding Your Business

Father Richard G. Smith

As [Jesus] was passing through a field of grain on the sabbath, his disciples began to make a path while picking the heads of grain. At this the Pharisees said to him, "Look, why are they doing what is unlawful on the sabbath?" (Mk 2: 23-24)

There's a scene at the end of Saint John's Gospel that, sadly, isn't included in the three-year cycle of Sunday Mass readings – it certainly deserves a wider audience than it receives as part of the weekday Mass cycle. You may remember: after Peter has made his threefold declaration of love for Jesus, Peter turns and sees the Beloved Disciple following behind. Peter asks Jesus, "Lord, what about him?" Jesus replies, "What if I want him to remain until I come? What concern is it of yours? You follow me." That's Jesus' way of saying, "Peter, mind your own business!"

The Pharisees in this passage from Saint Mark's Gospel would do well to heed Jesus' advice to Peter. The Pharisees had no official status or authority in Jewish society – instead, whatever influence they had on the people came from their knowledge of the law and their own personal holiness. Here, though, they seem to imagine themselves as a secret police force, spying on Jesus and his disciples. As soon as they see the slightest (perceived) transgression of the law, they pounce: "Look, why are they doing what is unlawful on the sabbath?" As the story progresses it becomes clear these men are spending so much time minding Jesus' and his disciples' business that they've lost sight of their own vocation to holiness.

There's something harsh in the saying "Mind your own business!" But it's also wise advice. When we mind other people's business, chances are we're missing what's going on in our own lives. Sometimes we're like the Pharisees, watching for someone to slip up, taking satisfaction in someone else's misfortune. Other times, we're jealous of the blessings and talents someone else receives in life. Either way, we're missing our own call to holiness and the ways God acts in our lives. In dealing with us, God is overwhelmingly generous and loving. It's a good thing to mind our business!

Kind and generous Father, open my eyes to see the good things you do in my life and in the lives of my brothers and sisters. Empty my heart of any pettiness and jealousy so I may always give you thanks and praise, and more faithfully follow Jesus.

The Prism of Love

Father Richard G. Smith

[Jesus] said to [the Pharisees], "Have you never read what David did when he was in need and he and his companions were hungry? How he went into the house of God when Abiathar was high priest and ate the bread of offering that only the priests could lawfully eat, and shared it with his companions?" (Mk 2: 25-26)

In one of his more technical works, *On Christian Doctrine*, Saint Augustine explains how Sacred Scripture ought to be interpreted. He explains the proper interpretation of any part of Scripture always involves a building up of Jesus' twofold command to love God and neighbor. Love is the prism through which we read God's word.

The Pharisees prided themselves on their knowledge of the Scriptures. But, at times, they forgot the purpose of the Scriptures and failed to read it through the prism of love. As Jesus tries to open their hearts and minds to the authentic meaning of the Sabbath, he invites them to consider an incident related in Scripture. The scene to which Jesus alludes occurs in the second Book of Samuel. David understands that laws surrounding temple worship, important as they are, are not as important as the hunger and real need of his companions. In order to meet the needs of his friends, David gives them the showbread only the priests were permitted to eat. While David violates the letter of the law, he does not forget the heart of the law. David understands God's word, God's command, through the prism of love. Jesus asks the Pharisees to understand the laws concerning sabbath rest, as important as they are, through that same prism.

Jesus teaches us that he comes not to abolish the law, but to fulfill it. He shows us that the law is always to be viewed through the prism of love. For us who follow Jesus, the commands of the Lord are never a cold arbitrary set of rules given so we can prove ourselves. The law is only ever a means to an end – a guide in our coming to know the Lord ever more deeply. God's commands make sense in the context of a living friendship with the Lord.

Loving Father, in Jesus, your Son, you reveal the full extent of your great love for us. Help me always to understand your will for me with Jesus as my guide. May I never lose sight of the love at the heart of your Word to me.

Resting in the Lord

Father Richard G. Smith

Then [Jesus] said to [the Pharisees], "The sabbath was made for man, not man for the sabbath. That is why the Son of Man is lord even of the sabbath." (Mk 2: 27-28)

"The sabbath was made for man" – of course, Jesus here is responding to the legalism of the Pharisees. In their rigidity concerning the law, they've lost all sight of the purpose of God's law. In our own time, at least in the area of Sunday rest, we're rarely tempted to such legalism. Instead, we frequently find ourselves at the other extreme – completely disregarding God's command to keep holy the sabbath.

For the people of Israel, keeping the sabbath rest was a great *gift* from the Lord. It allowed the people of Israel to *rest* in the Lord, to be more deeply attentive to the presence of the Lord in their daily lives and actually to *imitate* the Lord who himself rested on the seventh day of creation. In fact, the concept of a day of rest was unique to Israel in the ancient world. The keeping of the sabbath rest became one of the primary ways the people of Israel defined themselves.

At the end of his *Confessions*, Saint Augustine looks forward to the fulfillment of the sabbath in eternal life. In the created order, every sabbath has a sunrise and sunset. But the eternal Sabbath will have no sunset. On *that* Sabbath, Augustine boldly hopes, we will rest in God and *God will rest in us*. We are meant to taste something of that peace and joy each week on the Lord's Day, the Christian Sabbath. The summit of the Christian Sabbath is the celebration of the Eucharist where Jesus comes to us in word and sacrament. He rests in us and we in him. It's important, though, that our Sabbath doesn't end where it's supposed to begin. For us Christians, Sunday is a day of rest, a day of vacation, when we can simply relax in God's love and become more aware of his presence in our daily lives.

Eternal Father, you are the center of my life; I ask for the gift of simply resting in your love for me. In the midst of my busy daily schedule let me be more and more aware of your constant and gentle presence.

Setting Agendas

Father Richard G. Smith

Again [Jesus] entered the synagogue. There was a man there who had a withered hand. [The Pharisees] watched him closely to see if he would cure him on the sabbath so that they might accuse him. (Mk 3: 1-2)

It's never good to come to Jesus with an agenda. Almost without fail in the Gospels, and especially in Mark's Gospel, anyone who comes to Jesus with an agenda walks away disappointed, frustrated, or even enraged, as we will see a few verses later in this scene. For the Pharisees, the man with a withered hand is simply a test case for their understanding of the law. This is the moment for which the suffering man has been waiting perhaps his whole life. The One who could fill his every need stands right before him in a moment of pure grace. Instead of seeing a real human person in real (perhaps desperate) need, instead of seeing the great joy of the moment, the Pharisees only see an opportunity to trip Jesus.

What's remarkable here is that they "watched [Jesus] closely," but they fail to *see* Jesus at all. The hearts of these men have become so entangled in bitter argument and controversy over the finest points in God's law that they've lost all sight of the purpose of that law in the first place. Instead of being a means to an end – a gentle guide toward deeper intimacy with the living God – the law has become an end in itself for them. Because of what Mark will later call their "hardness of heart," they can only come to Jesus with their own agendas, wanting to pull Jesus into their own drama.

There's always the temptation to do the same in our relationship with Jesus. At times, prayer can be reduced to our telling Jesus what the problem is, how it ought to be fixed, and when he ought to fix it. It's far better to come before Jesus with open hearts ready truly to *watch him closely*, allowing *him* to set the agenda. Jesus' plan is always far more joyful and life-giving than anything we can imagine.

Most merciful Father, cleanse my heart and make it a less complicated place where I can meet the living Jesus and discern his plan for my life.

54

Full-Throated Praise

Father Richard G. Smith

[Jesus] said to the man with the withered hand, "Come up here before us." Then he said to [the Pharisees], "Is it lawful to do good on the sabbath rather than to do evil, to save life rather than to destroy it?" But they remained silent. (Mk 3: 3-4)

Over and again in his magnificent homilies on the Psalms, Saint Augustine teaches us that the human person is created to praise. Every human person praises someone or something – that, for Augustine, is a given. The question always is who or what are we praising?

In the Gospels, an authentic response to Jesus' preaching and actions always involves joy and praise. When people understand his words or when they discern the hand of God acting when Jesus heals or works a miracle, they can barely contain themselves for joy. They praise God.

When Jesus invites the man with the withered hand to come up before him and the Pharisees, he asks a loaded question: "Is it lawful to do good on the sabbath rather than to do evil, to save life rather than to destroy it?" Clearly, what Jesus would like to do in this suffering man's life is entirely good and entirely life-giving. But his words here (and his action in a few more moments) fall flat on the Pharisee's hearts. There is no joy, and certainly no praise of God in them. Instead, as Mark writes, "they remained silent." You can almost hear Mark's sigh behind those words. It is not too harsh to say the law has become their god and the object of their praise. In the presence of Jesus, as he speaks a word of life and restores the life of a broken man, the only response these Pharisees can muster is silence.

We're never meant to point at someone in Scripture and shake our heads at him or her. Scripture is a sort of mirror that can allow us to see ourselves more clearly. There are very many things that can become a god for us, very many things we can choose to praise with our words and actions. The living God alone is worthy of our undivided hearts and our full-throated praise in life.

Almighty and eternal Father, I give you thanks and praise for the wonders you work in my life and in the lives of my brothers and sisters. May I never be silent in the face of your Word, through whom and in whom all good things come.

The Finger of God

Father Richard G. Smith

Looking around at [the Pharisees] with anger and grieved at their hardness of heart, [Jesus] said to the man, "Stretch out your hand." He stretched it out and his hand was restored.

(Mk 3: 5)

Jesus commands, "Stretch out your hand!" The magnificent fresco of the creation of Adam by Michelangelo in the Sistine Chapel comes right to mind. The strong, life-giving hand of the Father reaches out to the limp hand of Adam, just barely outstretched toward the Father, as he receives the gift of life. It's a stroke of genius on Michelangelo's part to depict Adam's creation in this way. Genesis relates God's *breathing* the "spirit of life" into Adam's nostrils, and so Michelangelo might have chosen a more literal representation of the scene. But it's awkward, if not impossible, to portray convincingly the act of breathing in paint. And so, Michelangelo uses another scriptural image of God's Spirit and creative power – the finger of God – to great dramatic effect. The touch of the Father in the Sistine fresco *is* the sharing of the "spirit of life" and the moment of Adam's creation.

We can imagine the dramatic scene of the man with the withered hand stretching out his own limp hand to Jesus, through whom and in whom everything was created! The man gets much more than physical healing from Jesus; he gets a new life from him. The touch of Jesus is the moment of this man's renewed creation. From this point on, the man will be able to earn a living and lead a full life instead of being at the mercy of others for his basic needs. He will shed the social and religious stigma surrounding physical deformity, and take his place in the community. We are very much like the man in Mark's Gospel at each Eucharist in which we share. We too need healing and forgiveness – we need salvation. The same Jesus who came to him comes to us and, through the awesome gift of the Eucharist, he touches us. That touch *is* the sharing of healing and new life.

Eternal Father, you alone are the source of all life and of all that is good. I ask you once again to stretch out your hand and touch me with the gifts of your life and love.

Surprised by God

Father Richard G. Smith

*The Pharisees went out and immediately took counsel
with the Herodians against [Jesus] to put him to death.
Jesus withdrew toward the sea with his disciples.*
(Mk 3: 6-7a)

A few years ago, on a return trip from Rome, my mother sat next to a woman who was coming back from her first visit there. As my mother related the beautiful churches and museums she had visited, the great meals she shared, and the warm people she met, the other woman listened quietly. The woman then shared that her experience of Rome was entirely different, and that it seemed a miserable place to her. She explained she did not speak Italian and was terrified to take public transportation from the airport to the city – so she decided to spend her vacation locked safely away in an inexpensive hotel close to the airport, far from the beauty and warmth of Rome. How different her experience would have been had she taken a risk and allowed herself to be surprised by the new place in which she found herself.

The Pharisees we so often hear about in the Gospels are not bad people. In fact, they are deeply religious people, focused on God's word and the importance of acknowledging the presence and action of God in every part of daily human life. The great fault of at least some of the Pharisees, though, is imagining they have God all figured out. They are so certain of what God will and will not do, even what God *can* and *cannot* do, that they are no longer able to be surprised by God. And so, the Pharisees in Mark's Gospel scene miss the entirely beautiful and *new* thing God does in the ministry of Jesus; their response to Jesus is completely thrown off as a result. Instead of being awed by Jesus healing this man's withered hand, they are enraged to the point of wanting to murder Jesus. How different their lives would be if they only took a risk on God and allowed him to surprise them.

Heavenly Father, you are always far greater than my own thoughts and words about you. May I never allow a sense of familiarity with you to obscure the new and surprising ways you choose to work in my life and in the world.

Leave Everything to Follow Jesus
Douglas Bushman

A large number of people [followed] from Galilee and from Judea. Hearing what [Jesus] was doing, a large number of people came to him also from Jerusalem, from Idumea, from beyond the Jordan, and from the neighborhood of Tyre and Sidon.
(Mk 3: 7b-8)

Bees need no command to seek nectar. They simply comply with the laws of their nature to accomplish God's will. Similarly, great crowds follow Jesus with a conspicuous spontaneity, no external command, nothing forced. Learning that Jesus is near suffices to trigger an act of free will, a decision to seek him. What a great grace so readily to hearken to the inner voice upon learning that Jesus is near!

That morning everyone awakes with expectations for the day: meals, work, chores, prayer, a gathering or celebration. Following Jesus is not scheduled. When news of him arrives, suddenly the mundane, daily activities dwindle in importance. If for only a short while, they leave everything behind to follow him (see Mk 10: 28-29).

Jesus puts everything in perspective. In him God is near, and with God comes the fullness of meaning and purpose to every moment and activity of life. His presence unexpectedly drives home what is so easily crowded out of consciousness: "the world in its present form is passing away" (1 Cor 7: 31). We are made for another world, for heaven; this is why we are drawn to prophets, saints, and miracles. They confirm that our hearts are not deceived in saying that life is more than "the world in its present form."

Every day, if only for a short time, we should leave all things behind to seek Jesus in prayer and sacrament. Like the crowds returning to the daily routine enriched by meeting him, our daily encounter with Jesus makes us aware that God's kingdom is coming and his will is "done on earth as it is in heaven." We become more at home with him than in "the world in its present form," which indeed is passing away. Jesus makes it possible to live in the world yet not be of the world, for though he meets us on earth he abides in heaven, where we are most at home.

Heavenly Father, I thank you for sending Jesus to transform the world with your love. Grant me the grace to leave all things behind every day to seek him in prayer.

Jesus Always Has More to Give
Douglas Bushman

[Jesus] told his disciples to have a boat ready for him because of the crowd, so that they would not crush him. He had cured many and, as a result, those who had diseases were pressing upon him to touch him. (Mk 3: 9-10)

In Jesus, God comes close to the sick and infirm. His love heals, and this provokes a predictable rush upon him of all for whom God is their only hope. How long has their hope remained buried, aware that their needs are beyond the skill of physicians? Jesus brings a resurrection of hope. The crowds draw close to the God who, in Jesus, has already drawn close to them.

Perplexingly, Jesus seems to withdraw. He is still present, but he creates a buffer: the crowds on land, he in a boat. In reality, he creates a space for reflection on what it all means. Jesus wants them to be open to another way for him to love – by teaching. He does not heal all, but he does teach all.

Jesus wants us to know why he heals, by what power, and how this relates to the coming of God's kingdom. The pause in healing is only apparent, for in teaching he heals at a deeper level. He cures our ignorance about God's love. He wants to heal all souls with saving truth. He desires that we be one with him in this truth.

Doubtless, at first the inability to touch him to be cured of disease gravely disappoints. Had he not aroused this hope? Indeed, he did, but more profound hopes remain buried in the human heart: hopes for God's kingdom of forgiveness and reconciliation, for justice and peace in families and among nations. These, too, need be resurrected. Jesus raises our aspirations beyond the physical and material, awakening such hopes because he desires to fulfill them. He wants our desires to be his own. He withdraws from healing the consequences of sin to cure sin itself.

Jesus always has more to give! It is great wisdom to look beyond his first gifts, to see in them a pledge of even greater gifts, and to receive from him the highest gifts of his love.

Most loving Father, I praise you for resurrecting my hopes today, in Jesus. With confidence in the power and love revealed in him, I pray: Heal me of my sins.

Deliver Us from the Evil One

Douglas Bushman

And whenever unclean spirits saw [Jesus] they would
fall down before him and shout, "You are the Son of God."
He warned them sternly not to make him known.
(Mk 3: 11-12)

Jesus interacts with demons quite differently than with men. With demons his mode is command: "Quiet! Come out of him!" (Mk 1: 25). Eternally set against God, the demons' choice is irrevocable and conversion is impossible. Though aware that Jesus is the Son of God, they cannot align their wills to the truth. They cannot receive his love; their relation to him is reduced to power.

With men, who can receive his love, Jesus always works to bring about conversion. He can be demanding. He can call us to be perfect, to love our enemies, and to pick up our daily cross. He can reprimand the apostles. But every word is a word of love. It may be more apparent in the words of forgiveness spoken to the penitent woman and the woman caught in adultery, but even his chastisement of the scribes and Pharisees is love. Every word and every action is love, because he is God, and God is love.

At the very center of the drama of Jesus' mission is his appeal to our freedom that is God's first gift to us. His constant refrain is: "Will you let me love you?" Love cannot be forced upon another, nor can it be gained by effort. It can only be received. Jesus' every word and gesture is a plea to open our hearts to receive his love. The depths of God call to the depths of man.

Only by sin is God's love rejected. Only by conversion is his love received anew. This is the central truth about Jesus and his mission. Both demons and men have sinned, but only men can receive this love anew. This is why Jesus commands demons not to speak about him, for they cannot witness to his love, while he directs his disciples to proclaim the Good News of his love by the witness of their lives, and thereby to bring hope to the entire world.

Father of infinite love, let not Jesus' words of love fall on deaf ears.
Here I am; send me to proclaim the Good News of your merciful
love to those I meet today.

One with Jesus in Mission

Douglas Bushman

[Jesus] went up the mountain and summoned those whom he wanted and they came to him. He appointed twelve [whom he also named apostles] that they might be with him and he might send them forth to preach and to have authority to drive out demons. (Mk 3: 13-15)

Jesus is not alone on the mountain. Far removed from daily activity, the mountain is the place of encounter with God. Jesus is at home there. There he is with his Father. Jesus is never alone, even when he descends to take up his mission: "The one who sent me is with me. He has not left me alone, because I always do what is pleasing to him" (Jn 8: 29). The Father's will is that he save the world and establish the Church. For Jesus, being with the Father and doing his will are one and the same thing. He is sent *by* the Father, but he is not sent *away from* the Father.

Jesus does not cling to this "being with" the Father and "being sent" by him as a privilege for himself alone. Rather, he extends it to the apostles, and to all of his disciples, by calling them to be with him and to be sent by him as associates in his mission. We must first be with him, even as he is with the Father. From this "being with" comes mission, as Jesus was sent by the Father. Jesus invites us to enter into the dynamism of "being with" and "being sent" that defines his own way of relating to the Father.

"Being sent" flows from "being with"; communion is the condition for bearing fruit in mission: "I am the vine, you are the branches. Whoever remains in me and I in him will bear much fruit" (Jn 15: 5). Mary is the model. The grace of the Immaculate Conception established her without sin, in perfect communion of "being with" God. This prepared her for the mission to be the Mother of God. Mary teaches us that mission, "being sent," is not a leaving behind. It is communion or "being with" in action. In this way God is present in all the activities by which we accomplish the mission he entrusts to us.

Almighty Father, through the intercession of Saint Mark and Mary, let me always desire to be with Jesus and to fulfill the mission – the vocation – he has entrusted to me.

Jesus Works with the Apostles

Douglas Bushman

*[(Jesus) appointed the twelve:] Simon, whom he named Peter;
James, son of Zebedee, and John the brother of James, whom
he named Boanerges, that is, sons of thunder; Andrew, Philip,
Bartholomew, Matthew, Thomas, James the son of Alphaeus;
Thaddeus, Simon the Cananean, and Judas Iscariot
who betrayed him.* (Mk 3: 16-19)

Jesus chooses twelve apostles and prepares them for his final words: "Go into the whole world and proclaim the gospel to every creature." They were not left alone to do this: "And they went forth and preached everywhere, while the Lord worked with them" (Mk 16: 15, 20).

Jesus works with the apostles. When he sends them to preach, to heal, to exorcise, and to baptize in his name it is his divine authority that they exercise. In reality, he exercises his authority through them. Jesus is present and active, working with the apostolic Church. Therefore faith in Jesus is also faith in the apostolic Church. Once he promises to work with the apostles, the two cannot be separated. To believe in the apostolic Church means to believe that Jesus keeps his promise.

This continues a pattern established by God with Moses. After witnessing what God did through Moses – ten plagues, the parting of the sea – Israel "believed in him and in his servant Moses" (Ex 14: 31). Faith in God means believing that God works through his chosen servants. At the times of Moses, to seek God and his blessings means to be in a right relationship with Moses. Similarly, to seek Jesus and his blessings after his ascension means to be in a right relationship with the apostolic Church.

Jesus' pledge to work with the apostles extends to their successors, the popes and bishops, because his promise surpasses the apostles' lifetime: "The gates of the netherworld shall not prevail" (Mt 16: 18); "I am with you always" (Mt 28: 20). Faith perceives that Jesus teaches, heals, and sanctifies through the apostles and their successors, the bishops. As God is present in the human nature of Jesus, so Jesus is present in the human dimension of the Church. Catholic faith leads all who seek Jesus and his blessings to establish a right relationship with his apostolic Church.

Most wise Father, yesterday I prayed, "Let me always desire to be with Jesus." Today I pray, "Let me always desire to be with Jesus in his apostolic Church."

Hoping against Hope

Douglas Bushman

[Jesus] came home. Again [the] crowd gathered, making it impossible for them even to eat. When his relatives heard of this they set out to seize him, for they said, "He is out of his mind."
(Mk 3: 20-21)

Again the crowds seek Jesus. His teaching and miracles enliven their hope that God's promises are being fulfilled. They live in the expectation of this hope, like Simeon, the righteous man, "awaiting the consolation of Israel" (Lk 2: 25). Jesus' miracles indicate that he is fulfilling this hope. The waiting is almost over.

Through the generations, beginning with Abraham, this hope is received and passed on. Abraham's desire to have a son seemed destined to remain unfulfilled. His spirituality is "hoping against hope" (Rom 4: 18). Against a merely human hope, which is no hope at all, he trusts in the Lord, for whom nothing is impossible. The lowly virgin who became the Mother of God also lives this hope. "How can this be?" she asks. And the answer: "Nothing will be impossible for God" (Lk 1: 34, 37). Hope is purest when we cannot see how God's promises will be fulfilled, because then it rests entirely in God.

In a startling way, God fulfills the hopes of his people by first dashing them, leading us to the precipice of despair. The disciples from Emmaus thought that the death of Jesus was the final chapter of his life: "We *were hoping* that he would be the one to redeem Israel" (Lk 24: 21). Their hope had to die with Jesus in order to rise with him. Resurrected hope is the purest hope.

The crowds gathering around Jesus have no idea how their hope would have to be transformed. Like Jesus himself, it will have to die and then be raised to a new life. Our hope, then, approaches its perfection precisely at those moments when all that remains is to hope against hope. At such times a cloud of witnesses – Abraham, Mary, the disciples from Emmaus, all the saints – rise up to proclaim: "Study the generations long past and understand;/ has anyone hoped in the Lord and been disappointed?" (Sir 2: 10).

Father of all goodness, I hope in your promises, and I trust in your power to fulfill them. Grant me the grace to persevere in hope, especially when all seems hopeless.

Discerning the Signs of the Times
Douglas Bushman

The scribes who had come from Jerusalem said, "[Jesus] is possessed by Beelzebul," and "By the prince of demons he drives out demons." (Mk 3: 22)

"Whoever is not with me is against me" (Lk 11: 23). There is no middle ground when it comes to Jesus. Everyone must decide whether to be with or against him. Everyone must answer the question: "Who do you say that I am?" (Mk 8: 29). Jesus' claim to be the Son of God dictates the terms of the answer. He either is or is not who he claims to be. The decision to be with or against Jesus is based on the judgment whether Jesus is with or against God.

Jesus gives us all the signs required to decide, the same signs he gave to John the Baptist so that he could judge who Jesus is (Lk 7: 16-23). "Are you the one?" John asked. This is the one question that unlocks the meaning of the signs. They are only meaningful for those who search for God in the truth. They point to Jesus as the unimagined answer to the ultimate questions that we must ask about the purpose of our existence and thus about the goodness and wisdom of God.

John the Baptist was sent to prepare the way of the Lord. His mission is necessary in our day. It is necessary to keep alive the question about who Jesus is, and whether he is the one. Without these questions, the signs cannot lead us to Jesus. Other questions, banal in comparison, seem to command attention: health, career, financial security. Preoccupation with these renders us blind to the signs that Jesus gives.

It is not I.Q. and advanced degrees that train us to see the signs. It is what takes place in our hearts that matters, the humble search for truth. The blind man whom Jesus healed saw very clearly: "It is unheard of that anyone ever opened the eyes of a person born blind. If this man were not from God, he would not be able to do anything" (Jn 9: 32-33).

Father of all wisdom, give me a heart to seek the truth in all things, so that I may discern the signs of your love, revealed in the teaching and actions of Jesus, today.

Jesus Reveals Us to Ourselves

Douglas Bushman

Summoning [the scribes], [Jesus] began to speak to them in parables, "How can Satan drive out Satan? If a kingdom is divided against itself, that kingdom cannot stand. And if a house is divided against itself, that house will not be able to stand. And if Satan has risen up against himself and is divided, he cannot stand; that is the end of him." (Mk 3: 23-26)

More occurs in today's reading than Jesus refuting the charge that he expels demons by the power of Beelzebul. By confronting the scribes with an internal inconsistency in their argument, Jesus reveals them to themselves. He does this out of deep love for them, and a profound regard for their God-given freedom. Knowing that the human mind is fashioned by God for truth and consistency, Jesus' purpose is to place the scribes in a state of profound interior tension.

If their accusation (yesterday's reading) is rooted in an honest search for truth, then they are simply mistaken, and they will correct themselves. If his words cause them to realize that their accusation is rooted in prejudice against him, then they can still correct themselves. These are the two ways of conversion. The first, primarily intellectual, presupposes a good will and a desire to follow the truth wherever it leads. The second is moral in nature. It entails coming to a judgment that one has not honestly sought the truth, and it requires a realignment of the heart – taking sides with truth against oneself.

Jesus desires to create moments of truth in our hearts because he desires the most profound unity with us, and this is unity in truth. This is why his entire life stands before us as one great trial. In Jesus, God places himself on trial, so to speak, and makes us the jury. Will we accuse him of blasphemy, as being a pretender, as a partner of the devil? Or will we acknowledge, in faith, the truth that he is the Son of God and that in him the love of God is revealed definitively?

In the great trial of Jesus, man himself is also on trial. Will we weigh the evidence truthfully, justly? The decision that each one of us makes about Jesus is in reality a verdict on ourselves. "For as you judge, so will you be judged" (Mt 7: 2).

Father of truth, thank you for creating me with the dignity of being made for truth. Whenever Jesus stands to be judged in my conscience, may my judgment be truthful.

Blasphemy against the Holy Spirit
Douglas Bushman

"But no one can enter a strong man's house to plunder his property unless he first ties up the strong man. Then he can plunder his house. Amen, I say to you, all sins and all blasphemies that people utter will be forgiven them. But whoever blasphemes against the holy Spirit will never have forgiveness, but is guilty of an everlasting sin." For [the scribes] had said, "He has an unclean spirit." (Mk 3: 27-30)

Like bookends to his Gospel, Saint Mark shows Jesus accused of blasphemy: at the outset of his ministry (Mk 2: 7), and at the end (Mk 14: 64). The Gospel is the unfolding of the drama of this charge of blasphemy. Everyone must decide: Is Jesus a blasphemer?

What occasions this accusation? Jesus identifies himself with God by forgiving sins. For his detractors, by pardoning sinners Jesus blasphemes, showing contempt for God and his prerogative to forgive sins. The irony is that, as the eternal Word of God, only Jesus can reveal the full truth about sin and God's love. Those who accuse Jesus of blaspheming are the real blasphemers.

By enduring death as the penalty for blasphemy, Jesus offers a sacrifice for sin. His heavenly Father accepts it and sends the Holy Spirit into the world. He, the Spirit of truth, is the ultimate criterion of all blasphemy. He is, in Jesus' mind, the bottom line when it comes to truth and blasphemy, love and sin. Why? Because the Spirit bears witness in our hearts that Jesus is the Son of God and that by his sacrifice sins are forgiven. His mission is to "convict the world in regard to sin" (Jn 16: 8). He enlightens consciences about sin, but never without simultaneously witnessing to Jesus' death as the sacrifice that gains forgiveness. The Spirit gives us all the evidence we need to decide: Is Jesus guilty of blasphemy? Or is he the Son of God and Lamb of God who takes away the sins of the world?

It is clear in Saint Paul. Before his conversion, he judged Jesus as a blasphemer. After his conversion he accused himself of blasphemy (1 Tm 1: 13) and saw his persecution of Christians as an effort to force them to blaspheme (Acts 26: 11) by renouncing their faith in Jesus. By the gift of the Holy Spirit's witness to sin and to his mercy, Jesus forgives blasphemies against him.

Father of the eternal Word of truth, this day may I be faithful to the witness of the Holy Spirit and proclaim in thought, word, and deed that Jesus is Lord.

The Family of Jesus
Douglas Bushman

[Jesus'] mother and his brothers arrived. Standing outside they sent word to him and called him. A crowd seated around him told him, "Your mother and your brothers [and your sisters] are outside asking for you." (Mk 3: 31-32)

Responding to those for whom this passage shows that Mary had children besides Jesus, apologists point out that the language used here refers to the extended family of cousins. The Church has never seen a contradiction between this verse and Catholic faith in Mary's perpetual virginity. Jesus was her only child. What Saint Mark's account points to is the contrast between the positions of these relatives of Jesus, including his mother, and those in the crowd, who remain nameless. The crowd is close to him, around him, while twice Saint Mark describes Mary and his relatives as being "outside." It is intended to underscore the universal nature of Jesus' mission.

Jesus knows himself as the object of the eternal love of his Father. He knows himself as the focus of Mary's most perfect maternal affection. From these he derives an unparalleled personal security and assurance of his own goodness, and this makes him free to give himself to others. In language of our day, Jesus is the most perfectly affirmed of human beings. He makes himself available to others in the power of this affirmation of love. The divine perfection of the Father's love and the human perfection of his mother's love fill him to overflowing with goodness and make him a man for others. The gift he makes of himself reveals the perfection of the gift of love he has received.

Countless souls in need of love and affirmation populate our world. Their hope lies in the generous self-giving of those who have been filled with love from God and their parents, who represent God to their children. The crowning glory of God's love and of parents' love is children who grow to Christ-like maturity in love, who are capable of giving themselves to others by embracing vocations to the priesthood, religious life, and marriage. Every vocation simply specifies the vocation to love.

Most loving and faithful Father, you call me to love as Jesus loves. Fill me with your love, the Holy Spirit, so that I may bring love to those who need love.

The Church Is God's Family

Douglas Bushman

*But [Jesus] said to [the crowd] in reply, "Who are my mother
and [my] brothers?" And looking around at those seated in
the circle he said, "Here are my mother and my brothers.
[For] whoever does the will of God is my brother and sister
and mother." (Mk 3: 33-35)*

What a compliment it is to Joseph and Mary that Jesus should draw on his experiences of love and unity with them in order to convey the bond of communion with all those who do his Father's will. Putting God first in all things was the unifying power of the Holy Family. This unity of wills in loving obedience to the will of God the Father is the DNA of the family of God.

Obedience to his Father's will is the essence of Jesus' mission: "I came down from heaven not to do my own will but the will of the one who sent me" (Jn 6: 38). Doing the Father's will is the nourishment that sustains his life: "My food is to do the will of the one who sent me and to finish his work" (Jn 4: 34). This sheds light on the meaning of the Eucharist, which is the spiritual nourishment of the family of God, received from the supper table at which we come together. Jesus' sacrifice of loving obedience definitively fulfills the Father's will. In the Eucharist his food of obeying and fulfilling the Father's will becomes our food. In the Eucharist the whole family of God is united in loving obedience to the Father's will.

Our entire lives are meant to be a living out of this Eucharistic obedience. Doing God's will means to fulfill all the duties that come with one's vocation, and to accept all that happens as a mysterious manifestation of the Father's love. Mary is Mother of the Church, of God's family, and our model of this obedience: "I am the handmaid of the Lord. May it be done to me according to your word" (Lk 1: 38). Her entire attention is fixed on the Lord, ready to do his will at every moment, like a servant with eyes fixed on the master's hands in order to discern the very first indications of his will (Ps 123: 2).

Our Father, who art in heaven, hallowed by thy name. Thy kingdom come, thy will be done on earth as it is in heaven. Give us this day our daily bread.

By the Sea

José Enrique Aguilar Chiu

On another occasion [Jesus] began to teach by the sea. A very large crowd gathered around him so that he got into a boat on the sea and sat down. And the whole crowd was beside the sea on land. (Mk 4: 1)

Anyone who has visited the Holy Land readily grasps why Jesus liked to preach on the shore of the Sea of Galilee. This magnificent body of water lies amidst a breathtaking landscape, inviting us to broaden our horizons and to gaze far and wide at the hills on the other shore and at the sky that silhouettes them in such beauty. It is here that Jesus calls his first disciples as he walks along the shore (Mk 1: 16), and the crowd follows after him to listen to his words (Mk 2: 13).

The shore is something unique. It allows us to remain on firm ground, but at the same time sets before us a limit; we are unable to leave the earth and go walking on the water. We gain a deeper feel for things as we walk along the seaside: we become aware of our limits and our limitations. And we also become aware that there is something more than all our everyday backing-and-forthing on earth would have us believe. Being on the seashore helps us to expand our horizons. This attitude grounds us, giving us the humility and openness we need if we are to listen well to Jesus.

Jesus gets into a boat, the Evangelist tells us, and seats himself in order to teach. This gesture signals his authority. The crowd comes to hear the Master's word, which carries authority. Then Jesus heals countless sick people (Mk 1: 32-34) and forgives sins (Mk 2: 5). The words of authority that he uses to teach the crowds are the very same words that heal and forgive sins.

Jesus communicates his teaching while seated in the little boat. From the first centuries, the Fathers of the Church have seen this boat as a symbol of the Church, which traverses the waters of the world with its hardships and perils. Jesus continues today to send us his word, from the bark of the Church.

Heavenly Father, help us to dispose ourselves adequately to hear your Son's mighty, merciful word that he speaks through the Church, inviting us to widen our horizons.

Hear This!

José Enrique Aguilar Chiu

And [Jesus] taught [the crowd] at length in parables, and in the course of his instruction he said to them, "Hear this! A sower went out to sow. And as he sowed, some seed fell on the path, and the birds came and ate it up." (Mk 4: 2-4)

Why does Jesus teach in parables? It is a question that many continue to ask. Perhaps the reason for this form of teaching stems from the very nature of what Jesus is teaching: the mystery of God's kingdom (Mk 1: 15; 4: 11). In order to understand this mystery, one must have recourse to the simple, yet powerful, language of images. Some realities can only be understood through images. Saint Paul is aware of this when he writes to the Corinthians: "And we speak… describing spiritual realities in spiritual terms" (1 Cor 2: 13).

The parable reveals itself to the person who listens to it with attention, and who seeks to understand it. Its message is concealed, however, from the person who makes no attempt to understand it. In order to hear Jesus' word, one must desire to hear it and understand it. This is the key point of the parable, which is Jesus' first teaching in Saint Mark's Gospel.

In the Book of Deuteronomy, God addressed the people through the mouth of Moses, inviting them to open their ears: "Hear, O Israel" (Dt 6: 4). Jesus makes the same exhortation (Mk 4: 3). This appeal is well exemplified in the parable, since, in order for the seed to bear fruit, it must first strike root. A seed that falls without entering into the soil produces no fruit, and is devoured by the birds.

This opening parable in Mark's Gospel constitutes, in itself, the general doctrine of all of the Gospels, for it invites us to listen. In this regard, Mary points the way for us: she listens and reflects in her heart on all that she has heard (Lk 2: 19). And Mary not only listens but she also seeks to understand the word of God so as to put it into practice. She asks, "How can this be?" (Lk 1: 34).

Loving Father, you sent your Son to sow the seed of the Gospel in us. Grant us the grace to listen with the attentiveness of Mary to what you say to us, that we might bear abundant fruit.

Spiritual Foundations

José Enrique Aguilar Chiu

"Other seed fell on rocky ground where it had little soil. It sprang up at once because the soil was not deep. And when the sun rose, it was scorched and it withered for lack of roots."

(Mk 4: 5-6)

Walking along the streets of Manhattan in New York, you sometimes find yourself gazing around awestruck at the height of the buildings everywhere. But what you see towering overhead is not everything. A great part of the city lies hidden beneath the surface: the subway and train lines, underground shopping malls, water and gas mains, electrical grids, the massive pillars supporting the skyscrapers. Without this subterranean root system, so to speak, the Big Apple could not survive.

The same thing applies to our spiritual life. To achieve the tasks God gives us, we need strong spiritual "pillars." Otherwise, our lives will mirror what happens in the parable: the seed will fall "where it had little soil," and it will bear no fruit.

Readers have always been surprised by the fact that the Gospels almost never tell us anything about the first thirty years of the life of Jesus. Saint Mark in particular completely omits these early years of Jesus' life. Nevertheless, this silence is important: these hidden years make up the vast majority of the Lord's time on earth. Thus they constitute the unseen yet indispensable pillars that were crucial for his mission.

Some writers of the second century gave themselves to the task of writing "apocryphal gospels," which depict the child Jesus performing stupendous miracles, even as a child. But this is not what the canonical Gospels teach us. There is always the temptation to sprinkle on some artificial fertilizer so as to speed up the plant's growth. But if the seed sprouts too soon, it may be a sign that "the soil was not deep" enough.

Likewise in our lives, we must cultivate those moments that no one sees, but that are so necessary for the Gospel to bear fruit: times of prayer and attentive listening to the word of God (Mt 6: 6).

Gracious Father, give us the humility we need to sink our roots deep in prayer so that your Son's word may grow strong in us, and bear an abundant harvest in our lives.

The Sower Sows Everywhere

José Enrique Aguilar Chiu

*"Some seed fell among thorns, and the thorns grew up
and choked it and it produced no grain."*
(Mk 4: 7)

One might surely wonder about the aptitude of the sower described in the parable. What could have made this person sow on such unfavorable ground as a highway, rocky soil, or land full of thorns? If the seed produces no fruit, is this not perhaps the fault of the sower? Saint John Chrysostom posed himself this question long ago, and gave us his answer. The parable shows that the Lord sows the seed of the Gospel in all persons, regardless of their attitude or availability, their social status, race or gender, hoping in each case that they may somehow receive it and produce fruit.

Such an attitude on our Lord's part ought to inspire our own lives as well, leading us to deal with everybody equally, without distinction of persons. As the Gospel warns, "If you love those who love you, what recompense will you have?" Jesus preaches to everyone – fishermen, sick people, women, soldiers, scribes, and priests. In a world in which these groups tended to be excluded, Jesus preached to all without distinction, inviting them to be his brothers and sisters (Mk 3: 35). Jesus is not a "poor sower," but rather a generous sower, brimming with mercy.

On the other hand, the success or failure of the Gospel does not depend so much on external causes. It depends on our own attitude. If in our lives we afford the word of God no opportunity to take root, then we can be sure that a thousand distractions will quickly consume us, devouring what has been sown: the seed will be plucked up by birds (Mk 4: 4), scorched by the sun (Mk 4: 6), or choked by thorns (Mk 4: 7).

If the Gospel does not yield fruit in us, we cannot point the finger at our neighbor, or work, or what's happening at home. If we lack sufficiently fertile soil for the Gospel to take root, any pretext will do for extinguishing its message in us.

Merciful Father, may your word take root in our hearts, that we may sow it in our lives among everyone we meet, without distinction or preference, for we are all siblings in your Son.

Becoming Holy Fruit

José Enrique Aguilar Chiu

*"And some seed fell on rich soil and produced fruit. It came up
and grew and yielded thirty, sixty, and a hundredfold." [Jesus]
added, "Whoever has ears to hear ought to hear."*
(Mk 4: 8-9)

The lives of the saints offer us examples to imitate in our
own lives. They are very different from one another, and
there is always the possibility that one of those lives will
resemble our own situation more than another. But reading the
lives of those who faithfully followed the Gospel can also entail
a difficulty as well: it can seem as if the saints are very different
from ourselves. Why? Because every saint has performed at least
one miracle. In view of our poor condition as sinners, we might
become discouraged; instead of trying to imitate the lives of the
saints, we might lose heart and give up.

But the message of this parable affords us consolation and encouragement. It is not required that we perform miraculous acts
in our lives in order to be able to share in the kingdom of God. In
fact, Jesus tells us that the seed sown here yields crops of "thirty,
sixty, and a hundredfold." And guess what? These various yields do
not depend on the quality of the soil, which is described as "rich"
in each of these cases. Saint Paul himself writes to the Corinthians
that not all persons have the same function in the Church. "Are all
apostles? Are all prophets? Are all teachers?" (1 Cor 12: 29). What
is important in each case is that there be love (1 Cor 13: 1-3).

True, the Lord invites us all to be "perfect, just as your heavenly
Father is perfect" (Mt 5: 48). But if for any reason we cannot arrive at that perfection, the Lord still considers us "rich soil." For
the Lord, who is the good farmer, it is never too late to hope for
the seed to yield fruit. On the cross, he announces that the violent
robber next to him "will be with me in Paradise" (Lk 23: 43) as this
man yields his little fruit by means of his repentance.

*Heavenly Father, you summon us to be perfect in love. Grant us
the grace to embrace this holy call by imitating your Son, without
being discouraged by our faults, for you are rich in mercy.*

Seeking Jesus Alone

José Enrique Aguilar Chiu

*And when [Jesus] was alone, those present along with
the Twelve questioned him about the parables.*
(Mk 4: 10)

We have all had the experience of desiring to talk to someone in particular about an important matter, and of seeking to do so when he or she is alone, free from possible distractions or interruptions. In the same way, Jesus' disciples approach him to question him when he is "alone."

This attitude on the part of the disciples ought to encourage us to consider our own attitude. Do we seek to approach Jesus when he is "alone"? Or, better yet, do we seek to be "alone" with him? In order to hear his word and to penetrate it, it is necessary to be "alone" with the Lord. Otherwise, other people, places, and activities may distract us. Granted, it is very difficult, not to say impossible, to be alone with an important persona such as the Pope, the President, or any well-known public figure. What wouldn't we give to get fifteen minutes alone with someone like this in order to present this person with our desires or problems!

And yet, do we appreciate the privilege afforded us by our heavenly Father of being able to approach Jesus whenever we desire, and to converse with him all "alone"? Absolutely nothing stands in the way of our spending time "alone" with him, except ourselves.

Here is another detail that merits our attention: the evangelists Matthew and Luke tell us that it is "the disciples" alone who approach Jesus. Mark, on the other hand, informs us that this group also includes "those present along with the Twelve." In this detail we see how Mark, in writing his Gospel, clearly has his readers in mind. This little twist should encourage us to seek out some solitary time with Jesus every day, if only for a few minutes each time, and ask him about the most important questions in our life.

*Ever-loving Father, inspire us to seek and find moments of solitude
with your Son, so that our lives may share ever more deeply in his
loving communion with you.*

Granting the Mystery of the Kingdom

José Enrique Aguilar Chiu

*[Jesus] answered [those present along with the Twelve],
"The mystery of the kingdom of God has been granted to you.
But to those outside everything comes in parables, so that/ 'they
may look and see but not perceive,/ and hear and listen but
not understand,/ in order that they may not be converted
and be forgiven.'" (Mk 4: 11-12)*

Of all of the verses in Saint Mark's Gospel, these may be the most difficult to appreciate. How is it possible that Jesus would preach and at the same time try not to be understood? This paradox can be explained in part by the words of the prophet Isaiah: "They may look and see but not perceive" (see Is 6: 9-10).

Isaiah was called by God to preach to the people (Is 6: 8-13) even though God knew that they would not believe his message (Is 29: 10-11). What's worse, the prophet's preaching would cause the people to harden their hearts all the more. Finally, the people would reach the point of deliberately refusing to understand, out of fear of being converted to the Lord! A similar example of hard-heartedness was the "closing up" of King Ahaz, who decided not to ask for a sign from God that would help him believe in the word of Isaiah (Is 7: 12).

Jesus himself feels that these words of the prophet Isaiah were being fulfilled all over again in his own experience, seeing that the multitude is so unwilling to believe. One might ask, then: Would it be better not to preach to these unbelieving people? Not at all. The people will finally understand, when they receive the Spirit of the God who will open their minds and their hearts. In preparation for that moment, however, it is necessary above all that the word of God be preached (Rom 10: 14). And the moment when God grants his Spirit to the people will occur when Jesus fulfills his mission – on the cross. It is then that the centurion is able to recognize Jesus' divinity (Mk 15: 39).

To those who are truly disposed to become disciples, Jesus offers access to the mystery of the kingdom, which is none other than his very own Person. And this is the teaching we continue to receive through the Church.

God our Father, we give you thanks for granting us knowledge of the mystery of your kingdom, which is none other than your Son, Jesus Christ, who died and rose to make us heirs of your kingdom in the Spirit.

Hearing and Understanding

José Enrique Aguilar Chiu

Jesus said to [those present along with the Twelve], "Do you not understand this parable? Then how will you understand any of the parables?" (Mk 4: 13)

Saint Mark alone records this rebuke of the disciples by Jesus. Indeed, in his Gospel he repeatedly calls attention to how sluggish the disciples seem to be when it comes to understanding the actions and words of Jesus (Mk 6: 52). But the Evangelist levels the same indictment at Jesus' followers in Rome, and in all parts of the world. "Do you not understand?" No believer can be completely safe from the danger of spiritual blindness. It is not simply a matter of "hearing." It is also a matter of "understanding."

In the Bible, "understanding" something does not mean merely putting words or ideas into one's mind. Above all, it means putting them into practice. So, for example, when the Virgin Mary asks the angel, "How will this be?" (Lk 1: 34), she does so with the whole-hearted intention of accomplishing what has been announced (Lk 1: 38).

Saint Anthony of the Desert, founder of monasticism, and Saint Francis of Assisi, founder of the Franciscans, both read the following Gospel verse: "If you wish to be perfect, go, sell what you have and give to [the] poor, and you will have treasure in heaven. Then come, follow me" (Mt 19: 21). After reading these words, neither went on to read the next. No, they immediately put into practice what they had read. Many of us, on the other hand, are often distracted – interested in knowing what the Gospel says on the next page, or what it said on the previous one. And we forget what we have just read. But Jesus says, "Hear and understand" (Mt 15: 10; Mk 7: 14).

If we have not understood, it is because we have not truly listened to what has been said (Jn 8: 43). And the first step in the quest to understand the Gospel is to begin to put it into practice, as did Saint Anthony and Saint Francis.

My Father, you sent your Son to preach to the multitudes who yearned to hear his Voice. Give us ears to hear and understand your teaching, putting it into concrete practice in our lives, so that we may truly be your disciples.

How to Soften Hard Soil

José Enrique Aguilar Chiu

"The sower sows the word. These are the ones on the path where the word is sown. As soon as they hear, Satan comes at once and takes away the word sown in them."
(Mk 4: 14-15)

Jesus explains this parable by comparing the diverse qualities of the soil to those who hear the word of the Gospel. A first group consists of those in whom the Gospel does not succeed in striking root, due to the hardness of their hearts. These are compared to the soil "on the path." The worst thing here is that this soil allows the birds of the air (that is, the Evil One) to swoop down and make off with the word that has been scattered.

To become hardened means to become closed in on oneself. This condition can have many causes: some people experience personal problems or tragedies, some have their dignity trampled upon, while others become utterly disillusioned as a result of countless disappointments. Whatever the case may be, such soil needs to be softened and loosened up, so that the seed of the Gospel may have a chance of bearing fruit. This type of soil cries out for rain to moisten it and make it soft.

In the Old Testament, we read of the prophet Elijah's prayer to God to send rain upon his homeland, which has been made barren and desolate by a great drought. Although the prophet's prayers have no effect at first, he patiently persists until at last it pours down rain (1 Kgs 18: 41-45). Saint James speaks of this incident and exhorts Christians to follow Elijah's example to pray with perseverance (Jas 5: 17-18).

We, too, can ask God for a "rain" to soak and soften hardened hearts, that they may be open to the Gospel. Saint Monica, the mother of Saint Augustine, gives us a fruitful example. Decades of prayer, offered with many tears, finally won over for Monica the conversion of her stubbornly prodigal son. The Lord is the one who sows the seed, but he also wants us to help irrigate the hard soil, praying that it become receptive to the seed of Life.

Father of all fruitfulness, you sow your word of love in all hearts. Give us the perseverance we need to pray without ceasing for those whose hearts are most in need of healing, hope, and mercy.

77

Pretending and Being

José Enrique Aguilar Chiu

"And these are the ones sown on rocky ground who, when they hear the word, receive it at once with joy. But they have no root; they last only for a time. Then when tribulation or persecution comes because of the word, they quickly fall away."
(Mk 4: 16-17)

Unlike the preceding case "on the path" where the Evil One gobbles up what has been sown, here "on rocky ground" the word of the Gospel manages to bear fruit, but only for a moment. In either case, the outcome is the same: there is no fruit to be reaped. In this passage, the "rocky ground" refers to those who seem to receive the Gospel, but they do not genuinely allow it to penetrate into their hearts. Faced with an obstacle, what they had initially received with joy is promptly forgotten.

Our modern consumer society, which inclines us more to "pretend" and to "have" than to "be," can be compared to the rocky terrain in the parable. We have grown accustomed to having things delivered to our doorstep, instantly. The same goes for our faith – what we ask for in prayer we want right now and without a catch. The result, however, is that we end up with a "pretend faith," one that looks like faith on the outside to others, and even to ourselves. But the Gospel cannot abide pretense. The Gospel deals with "being," with what's real. It wants to reach beneath the surface to the heart, and really strike root there. Indeed, Jesus says, "Pray to your Father in secret. And your Father who sees in secret will repay you" (Mt 6: 6).

The wisdom writers of the Old Testament knew that the trials and tribulations of life ultimately yield a positive effect – they put the human heart to the test, to see whether one really loves God. Thus we read, for example, "The crucible for silver, and the furnace for gold,/ but the tester of hearts is the Lord" (Prv 17: 3). It takes more letters to spell the word "pretend" than the word "be," but pretending yields only ephemeral fruits, while being yields imperishable ones.

Father of our hearts, help us to receive your word with sincerity and simplicity, so as to bear true fruits of peace and love, even in the midst of adversity and affliction.

Essential Priorities

José Enrique Aguilar Chiu

"Those sown among thorns are another sort. They are the people who hear the word, but worldly anxiety, the lure of riches, and the craving for other things intrude and choke the word, and it bears no fruit." (Mk 4: 18-19)

Sometimes there can be too much of a good thing. For example, a friend of mine once went into a new supermarket looking for toothpaste, and it turned out to be the most difficult purchase of his life. He stood there virtually paralyzed by the dozens of brands staring back at him. The same thing can happen in our spiritual life: we can cram so many things in our heart that we risk losing touch with what is most important.

This parable warns us against crowding Christ out of our heart. Our lives can actually become so busy that we no longer know what we are living for. And not because the things or events that occupy us are necessarily evil, but because we don't stop to distinguish between what is essential and what is not. The problem arises when we lose the correct hierarchy of values.

The story of Martha and Mary is a good case in point. The words Jesus addresses to Martha remind us of what's essential: "Martha, Martha, you are anxious and worried about many things. There is need of only one thing" (Lk 10: 41-42). This is why Saint Paul exhorts the Thessalonians not to let the voice of the Spirit be extinguished within them (1 Thes 5: 19). The Desert Fathers were intimately acquainted with the paradoxical benefits of desolation and privation; how a desert wasteland could be an excellent means of centering one's life around what is most necessary. There they could better hear the word of God with few distractions and no clutter. But we don't need to travel to a literal desert in order to set our priorities straight and purify our life. Carving out a few minutes of desert silence in our busy daily routine becomes second nature when our relationship with Christ becomes our first priority.

Almighty Father, you have entrusted all creation into our human hands. Help us never to lose sight of the source of all beauty and goodness, for only in your word can we find peace and happiness.

Amazing Fertility

José Enrique Aguilar Chiu

"But those sown on rich soil are the ones who hear the word and accept it and bear fruit thirty and sixty and a hundredfold."
(Mk 4: 20)

The conclusion of this parable inspires us to reflect upon the wondrous fertility of the word of God. We have the example in Abraham, to whom God promises, "I will make of you a great nation,/ and I will bless you" (Gn 12: 2). When Abraham begins to doubt, God reaffirms, "Look up at the sky and count the stars… Just so… shall your descendants be" (Gn 15: 5). While well aware that he and his wife were of advanced age, Abraham nonetheless believes in God's word, and Isaac is born. In the fullness of time, God fulfills this promise in an unheard of and definitive way in the resurrection of Christ (cf. Acts 3: 25-26). Jesus is the true descendant of Abraham (Gal 3: 16), to whom every believer is united (Gal 3: 28-29), and through whom offspring as numerous as the stars of heaven are born.

We have another example in David, to whom God proclaims: "I will raise up your heir… and I will make his royal throne firm forever" (2 Sm 7: 12-13). David's son Solomon believes that this promise is fulfilled in himself (1 Kgs 8: 20), once he builds the temple and confirms his authority in the kingdom. But God intends to fulfill his promise in a manner immeasurably more grand. As the apostles later declare, God keeps his word in a marvelous fashion in the resurrection of Christ, Son of David, to whom God grants a seat at his right hand for ever (Acts 2: 34-35).

The parable of the mustard seed (Mk 4: 31) presents us with a similar teaching. The fruit that God will reap is immense. Yet the only thing God asks is that "good soil" be receptive to his word. No saint has ever imagined what would become of his or her life after saying yes to God. We, too, shall never fathom what God has prepared for those who love him (cf. 1 Cor 2: 9).

Loving Father, you fulfill your promises in ways beyond our imagining. Inspired by Mary's "yes," help us to open our hearts wide to your word each day, for the glory of your name and the good of your Church.

Lighting the Way to Joy

Father Richard G. Smith

[Jesus] said to [those present along with the Twelve], "Is a lamp brought in to be placed under a bushel basket or under a bed, and not to be placed on a lampstand? For there is nothing hidden except to be made visible; nothing is secret except to come to light. Anyone who has ears to hear ought to hear."
(Mk 4: 21-23)

On the south-westernmost coast of Ireland stands a decommissioned lighthouse called Mizen Head. It is located in one of the most beautiful and remote places of the country – the nearest small village is miles away, itself in the middle of nowhere. In years past, the lighthouse served a vital role in protecting boaters approaching the coast, warning them of the location of a particularly shallow and treacherous area. Until relatively recently a team of men served at the lighthouse in shifts lasting months at a time to ensure its proper functioning. Visiting the complex around the lighthouse today, it is easy to imagine how lonely and isolated the men must have felt during their weeks of service. The sacrifice of being away from family and friends for such long stretches must have been great. It was a sacrifice made for the well-being of others.

When Jesus asks us, "Is a lamp brought in to be placed under a bushel basket or under a bed, and not to be placed on a lampstand?" he's inviting us to do something very bold. The Gospel we have received as Christians and the joy of the friendship we share with Jesus should not be hidden away. We are meant to be heralds of that Gospel and joy. Put another way, we are meant to be bright beacons reflecting the true Light of the world, leading the way to Jesus. Often, in our interactions with people at work or at school or even among friends, it is much easier and more comfortable to keep quiet about our faith. We fear what others might say or think about us if we give clear witness to Jesus. Yet, the world *needs* our witness and light, because the world desperately *needs* Jesus! Like those men at Mizen Head whose sacrifice provided light for others, Jesus asks us to sacrifice our own comfort and security to be his light right now.

Almighty Father, thank you for the gift of faith shared with me through Jesus, your Son. May I have the grace to witness boldly to that faith as a light of hope for my brothers and sisters.

Empty, Opened Hands
Father Richard G. Smith

[Jesus] also told [those present along with the Twelve], "Take care what you hear. The measure with which you measure will be measured out to you, and still more will be given to you. To the one who has, more will be given; from the one who has not, even what he has will be taken away." (Mk 4: 24-25)

The Carmelite Monastery in Lisieux, France, makes available reproductions of photographs of their best-loved Sister, Saint Thérèse of the Child Jesus. For years, a popular photograph has been a close-up of Saint Thérèse's hands, folded across her lap, cropped from a larger community photo. At first glance, it's a strange image – who wants a picture of someone's hands? Yet, such a focused photograph invites focused attention. By nature, Thérèse was a strong-willed woman who was not afraid to take control of a situation. By God's grace, Thérèse was also a woman who emptied herself entirely and came before God with empty, opened hands, confident in God's awesome love for her. There is something of that openness in the photograph of her hands. From someone so strong-willed, we might expect tight, clenched fists. Instead, her hands are entirely relaxed – no doubt made so by her continually coming before the Lord with empty, opened hands.

Jesus says to us, "The measure with which you measure will be measured out to you, *and still more will be given to you.*" Jesus isn't proposing a quid pro quo in which we'll get his gifts so long as we're good or generous enough with others. Instead, he states a reality. Jesus wants to give us nothing less than himself. Nothing surpasses the joy of knowing Jesus as our friend, the One who loves us without any conditions at all, the One who saves us and brings us Life. But if we are selfish in our dealings with others or stingy in actively loving our brothers and sisters, the person we are becoming might not be able to receive the gift Jesus offers. Saint Thérèse teaches us that we don't need to earn God's love, which is a free gift. Instead, we ask to be prepared for that love by being love in the heart of the Church, and then coming before the Lord with empty, opened hands.

Good and generous Father, you are all that I could ever need or want in life. I come to you with empty, opened hands trusting that your love and your grace are sufficient.

Growth in the Kingdom of God

Father Richard G. Smith

[Jesus] said, "This is how it is with the kingdom of God; it is as if a man were to scatter seed on the land and would sleep and rise night and day and the seed would sprout and grow, he knows not how. Of its own accord the land yields fruit, first the blade, then the ear, then the full grain in the ear. And when the grain is ripe, he wields the sickle at once, for the harvest has come."
(Mk 4: 26-29)

In the Dominican Church of San Clemente in Rome, there is a beautiful twelfth-century mosaic of the crucifixion in the apse above the high altar. At the base of the cross is a large acanthus plant out of which vines grow until they cover the entire surface of the apse. It is easy to get lost in the small details of the mosaic. In the branches of the vines the artists have placed all sorts of birds, animals, and flowers in bloom. There are scenes of everyday contemporary human life – monks at work and at prayer, aristocrats conversing with their stewards, shepherds caring for their flocks, even a woman feeding birds. No part of God's creation falls outside the embrace of the vines growing from the cross.

The scene of the crucified Jesus triumphant on the cross, which has become the Tree of Life, is very clearly inspired by the theology of John's Gospel, in which Jesus says, "I am the vine and you are the branches." It also illustrates the idea of *growth* stressed by Jesus here in Mark's Gospel. Jesus proclaims and makes present the kingdom of God promised in the Old Testament. His words and actions in the Gospels are like so many small seeds, scattered on the soil of the hearts of those who encounter him. Jesus' preaching and healing ministry culminates on the cross where the logic of love is revealed as far stronger than the logic of fear and violence. From these apparently small beginnings, the kingdom grows into every time and place until it comes to perfection on the Last Day – the harvesting of the grain.

The San Clemente mosaic shows us we are part of the sprouting and growing of God's kingdom begun in Christ Jesus. No part of our lives and no part of God's creation falls outside the embrace of the new life of God's kingdom offered in and through Jesus.

Loving Father, in all my words and actions today may I be part of the growth of your kingdom into every time and place as it moves toward the perfection of your great harvest.

Nothing Is Casual or Small
Father Richard G. Smith

[Jesus] said, "To what shall we compare the kingdom of God, or what parable can we use for it? It is like a mustard seed that, when it is sown in the ground, is the smallest of all the seeds on the earth. But once it is sown, it springs up and becomes the largest of plants and puts forth large branches, so that the birds of the sky can dwell in its shade." (Mk 4: 30-32)

The Sisters of Life are a religious community of nuns founded by the late John Cardinal O'Connor in the Archdiocese of New York a few decades ago. The nuns have a special apostolate to protect and enhance the sacredness of all human life. Part of their religious habit is a medal of our Lady with the inscription "Nothing again would be casual or small" on the reverse. It is meant to be a reminder that all human life, no matter however seemingly small or insignificant in the eyes of others, is important. The great beauty of the human person, created in the image of God, begins with the joining of just two small cells.

Jesus likens the kingdom of God to the smallest mustard seed that grows into a large bush teeming with life when properly nurtured. There is something wonderful, even miraculous, in the way something as small and seemingly lifeless as a seed can grow into a flower or plant or tree. Over and again in the creation and in God's word, we discover God likes to start with very small things in order to do something great and awesome. He doesn't need much at all from us to make wonderful, even miraculous, things happen in our lives and in our world. We may imagine that what we have to contribute is so small as to be completely insignificant. With God, though, nothing is casual or small. Just like the small infant in a mother's womb, or the tiny seed planted in the earth, or the small community of Christian disciples who set their world on fire, God acts in surprising, unexpected ways. A seemingly small and insignificant kind word or gesture or sign of Christian witness on our part can take root and become something awesome and life-giving in the kingdom of God.

Loving Father, nothing in my life is casual or small. I give all that I am and do and say to your purpose and will, trusting that I may serve you in all my thoughts, words, and actions today.

Jesus' Gentle Accommodation

Father Richard G. Smith

With many such parables [Jesus] spoke the word to [the people] as they were able to understand it. Without parables he did not speak to them, but to his own disciples he explained everything in private. (Mk 4: 33-34)

Jesus consistently and gently makes accommodations for the human hearts of his followers. Mark tells us that Jesus "spoke the word" to people in the crowds "as they were able to understand it." Those closer disciples of the Lord receive a deeper explanation of everything "in private." Jesus recognizes the differences among those who come to hear and see him – some come out of curiosity, others seek answers to their real questions, still others follow with a heart more committed to Jesus. He speaks to all of them, as their hearts are able to accept his words.

We can imagine that somehow the first disciples of the Lord were far more fortunate than we later disciples in that they were able to live with Jesus, see him, touch him, and hear him daily. We might imagine that they had some special insight into Jesus because of a unique physical proximity to him that we can never have. It's clear throughout the Gospels, though, that even Jesus' closest disciples didn't always understand Jesus' words and actions, and that their full meaning and significance only gradually unfolded for them after Jesus' resurrection from the dead. Jesus planted seeds in their hearts that would only gradually bear fruit in understanding.

After the ascension, Jesus' ministry of teaching and healing continues in the sacraments. Jesus still speaks his word to us daily through the Scriptures, through his teaching and praying Church, through the silence of our private prayer, and through our brothers and sisters in need. Above all else, Jesus is present among his disciples in the Eucharist. We too can say we live with Jesus, see him, touch him, and hear him daily. And the same gentle and accommodating Jesus we discover in the Gospels comes to us now, speaking the word as we are able to understand, planting seeds in our hearts that gradually bear fruit in understanding.

Father in heaven, may I always come before your Word with a simple, open, accepting heart. I ask for the grace of insight and understanding as I pray with your Word.

Jesus, the Still Center

Father Richard G. Smith

On that day, as evening drew on, [Jesus] said to [his disciples], "Let us cross to the other side." Leaving the crowd, they took him with them in the boat just as he was. And other boats were with him. A violent squall came up and waves were breaking over the boat, so that it was already filling up. Jesus was in the stern, asleep on a cushion. (Mk 4: 35-38a)

The nineteenth-century French Romantic painter Eugène Delacroix is not known as a great religious painter. However, he seems to have had a fascination with the calming of the storm by Jesus, and he depicted it on canvas after canvas. One of these paintings, *Christ Asleep during the Tempest*, hangs in the Metropolitan Museum of Art in Manhattan. It's a small canvas of deep, heavy greens, grays, and blues – Mark's "violent squall" is about to overwhelm the small Galilean fishing boat. Crammed into the boat are ten men reacting to the threat of death in various ways – one thrusts his hands to heaven, crying out in despair; another takes control of the situation by grasping the rudder; another reaches for an oar floating just out of reach; still another embraces the stern, paralyzed by the fear of his imminent death. The sole source of light in the painting is the halo above Jesus, asleep and seemingly unaware of the unfolding tragedy. Delacroix adds a detail not contained in the Gospel: a disciple, himself asleep, rests on Jesus' heart.

In every human life, storms arise that threaten to overwhelm and destroy us. Christian discipleship is not an exemption from the very real storms that form around our health and the health of those we love; the storms of misunderstanding in our marriages, families, and friendships; the storms of war, violence, and terrorism in the world. There are any number of ways we can respond to these inevitable storms. Like the disciples in Delacroix's painting, we can despair, or work against the storm as though everything depended on us alone, or we can become paralyzed by fear. Or we can follow the lead of that one disciple who does not see Jesus' silence as a sign of apathy or absence, but as an invitation to rest in his love, confident that he will bring life where there seems to be only death.

Loving Father, in the face of the difficulties I face in life, help me to find rest in Jesus, your Son, and to be confident in your love, which is far stronger than my fears.

Storms of the Heart

Father Richard G. Smith

[His disciples] woke [Jesus] and said to him, "Teacher, do you not care that we are perishing?" He woke up, rebuked the wind, and said to the sea, "Quiet! Be still!" The wind ceased and there was great calm. (Mk 4: 38b-39)

A Latin poem called *Carmen de Jona et Ninive*, for centuries (incorrectly) attributed to the early Church theologian Tertullian, is an extended meditation on the Book of Jonah. The poet fills between the lines of Scripture, expressing the inner thoughts and motives of the biblical characters. In Scripture, Jonah flees from God's calling to be a prophet to the people of Nineveh, and leaves on a ship bound for Tarshish. A wild storm, not unlike the one in Mark's Gospel scene, threatens to destroy the boat and all in it. It is not until Jonah is thrown overboard and swallowed by a great fish that the storm is calmed. In the midst of that storm in the Latin poem, Jonah cries out, "I am the storm! I am all the world's insanity!" In both the poem and Scripture, the great storm is really an outward expression of the inward reality of Jonah's heart.

Some of the greatest storms we face in life originate in our hearts. What originates in the heart can quickly spread to more obvious aspects of our lives. When we are not centered on Jesus, when we turn away from the Lord in sin, when we allow fear to take hold of us, everything in life is thrown off as a result, and we can feel ourselves adrift at the mercy of the storm. When we do not have inner peace, we cannot expect outward peace and order in life. Jesus commands the sea, "Quiet! Be still!" and because he has authority over all of creation and because his word is effective, the sea is calmed. Before anything can begin to happen in our friendship with Jesus, we need to hear Jesus speaking those same authoritative words to our hearts: "Quiet! Be still!" In the calm and stillness Jesus brings to our lives, we can begin to discern his presence and voice more clearly.

Loving Father, I ask you to come into my heart in a deeper way today. Calm the storms that can rage there at times, and help me to see and hear Jesus more clearly.

Awe then Fear

Father Richard G. Smith

Then [Jesus] asked [his disciples], "Why are you terrified?
Do you not yet have faith?" They were filled with great awe
and said to one another, "Who then is this whom even wind
and sea obey?" (Mk 4: 40-41)

The disciples are "filled with great awe" by the immensity of Jesus and what he has done. And yet, as Jesus so pointedly reminds them, they are still terrified, still lacking confidence, trust, and faith in him. Despite all they have seen and heard from Jesus, they still don't "get it."

Most of us can see ourselves in these disciples. We see signs of Jesus' love and presence around us all the time – and looking back on the trajectory of our lives, we can often discern the gentle but firm hand of Jesus guiding our course. Each of us can be thankful for the fact that our loving God has cared for us and brought us to this point in our lives. Like those disciples, there are many times in our relationship with Jesus when we experience ourselves as "filled with great awe."

But then, suddenly, we find ourselves living in a state of anxiety and turmoil. Our fears are often all too real – we all have our personal lists of the things that threaten to overwhelm and even destroy us. Instead of trusting that the same God who has cared for us so far will *continue* to love and care for us, we fall into fear. We hear Jesus ask those questions of us, "Why are you terrified? Do you not yet have faith?"

The most frequently repeated command in the whole of Scripture is "Do not be afraid." It's repeated so frequently, no doubt, because we need so much to hear it! With Jesus, *all is grace*. In this present moment, we are not alone. In fact, we have *never* been alone and *will* never be alone. Jesus is always with us, loving us, providing for us, making all things work together for good. If we are confident of his love, there is nothing we need fear.

Loving Father, nothing is more important than your love. May I always stand confident in that love, trusting in your mercy and providence.

Exiled

Father John Dominic Corbett, o.p.

[Jesus and his disciples] came to the other side of the sea, to the territory of the Gerasenes. When [Jesus] got out of the boat, at once a man from the tombs who had an unclean spirit met him. The man had been dwelling among the tombs, and no one could restrain him any longer, even with a chain. (Mk 5: 1-3)

The gifts of the spirit work in a holy variety of ways. Evil, on the other hand, is monotonous and repetitious in its journey to nowhere. In the following reflections on the story of the Gerasene demoniac, we will trace out some of the features of evil that are repeated again and again.

One of the marks of evil is that it is always alienating. It always separates a man from his own home and his own self.

Jesus told a story about this. A young man grew up to be very spoiled and very used to having his own way. He loved his comforts and privileges and eventually very little else. This cut him off from his father and his brother first spiritually and then physically. He left his home and spent his inheritance in a land where he knew no one and no one knew him. He lost it all, of course, and eventually came to envy the local pigs.

But the man in question here was in deeper trouble than the Prodigal Son. The Prodigal Son may have lived among pagans and may have been cut off from his family, but he still lived among human beings. The terrible thing is that it is possible to cut off even this contact and live in a spiritual isolation and loneliness so profound that the only way truly to describe it is to say that it is living in the graveyard. There are those so cut off as to be fairly described as living among the dead. This loneliness makes a man the special prey of the devil.

Jesus comes to us in our inaccessible places, in those terrible solitudes in which our grip on reality and our grip on ourselves are most radically challenged. He provides us with the most basic and humanizing help. By his very presence, he assures us that we are not, after all, alone.

Father, stay with us and help us stay close to you. Be with us in our solitude. When we begin to lose contact with you, your Son, and our neighbors, call us back to life.

Enslaved

Father John Dominic Corbett, O.P.

In fact, [the man] had frequently been bound with shackles and chains, but the chains had been pulled apart by him and the shackles smashed, and no one was strong enough to subdue him. Night and day among the tombs and on the hillsides he was always crying out and bruising himself with stones. (Mk 5: 4-5)

Some people think that we are basically alone. Of course, these people know that we all have fathers and mothers, and that the lucky among us have friends, and the luckiest fall in love and have happy families. But they still think that there is a basic aloneness to the human condition that is incurable. If that were true then aloneness would be natural and community would be something artificial. Community would be a construct, and even the most basic rules of the community would be something that we basically make up. Even the most basic moral convictions would be like the rules of monopoly or poker. They would be useful but they would also be disposable; first of all in the case of a moral emergency, but finally also in the case of a whim.

What governs us then? We are left in the hands of our own freedom. The only thing that can control us is something that we forge. Our moral laws would be experienced as self-forged chains.

In the end the chains fail. We find ways of getting around the restrictions that we place on ourselves. Like computer-savvy kids, we know how to undo the parental controls that we have devised. "No one was strong enough to subdue him."

Left to himself in his terrible solitude, he is left with a tyrant of demonic power. This tyrant, precisely because he acknowledges no law which governs or guides his freedom, never really attains what is truly good, and never finds rest. Instead he is always "crying out and bruising himself."

Motorcycle kids, Goth kids, desperate housewives, madmen, admen, how many bruise themselves and cry out because of their own terrible strength, which breaks every chain except the ones their own empty freedoms forge. Jesus comes not to take away our freedom but to take away our self-forged chains, and to give our selves back to us, back with our right mind.

Father, help us to understand the precious gift of freedom that we have from you. Help us to see that we can only be free in service to the truth that your Word speaks.

Paranoid

Father John Dominic Corbett, O.P.

Catching sight of Jesus from a distance, [the man] ran up and prostrated himself before him, crying out in a loud voice, "What have you to do with me, Jesus, Son of the Most High God? I adjure you by God, do not torment me!" (He had been saying to him, "Unclean spirit, come out of the man!")
(Mk 5: 6-8)

There is something profoundly unsettling about a free choice to do wrong. It involves judgment to go against a judgment. This is not just about how things ought to be but also about how things are. When we do wrong we go against ourselves and we place ourselves in opposition to reality itself. And we somehow know that somehow somewhere we will answer for it and pay a penalty. There is no free lunch in the spiritual world and a choice to sin involves at some deep level a choice to go to war with reality. This choice brings a justified fear of retribution and punishment. It also brings with it a loss of perspective as though the whole world must now be viewed through the lens of guilt and subsequent fear. These are distorting lenses, and they can make the world appear as a madhouse – a place in which there is scarcely a place to hide from the unbridled fury of retribution.

Now this is the world the demons inhabit. They are locked in their evil choice, and their choice cannot change. This means that they are also locked in dread and fear, and at the approach of Jesus would be convulsed in terror at the thought of being despoiled of their prey and being left with – nothing.

It is important to remember that the Savior came to save us from our sins, not to change the nature of sin. Sin always was and always will be terror-inducing. But Jesus has the power to cast our sin away, and to take away the nightmare of guilt and hiding which it brings. If sin brings fear and ultimately insanity into our lives, Jesus' power is ordered to saving us from that in order to live, not in terror, but in confidence in the Father's changeless love.

Father, we are your children and you are the Lord. Help us to see that in you we need not fear the shadowy terror of sin. Help us to know your love and forgiveness.

Divided

Father John Dominic Corbett, O.P.

[Jesus] asked him, "What is your name?" He replied, "Legion is my name. There are many of us." And he pleaded earnestly with him not to drive them away from that territory. (Mk 5: 9-10)

D r. Robert Lifton's medical practice was in psychiatry. His scholarly interest was in that twilight zone where the human mind and feelings encounter evil. He listened to victims of trauma in war. He also listened to perpetrators of trauma. His book *The Nazi Doctors* showed how the men who experimented on human beings during the day could go home to play with their children and look at sunsets and listen to classical music and believe themselves to be, after all, decent civilized men who, during the daytime hours, were simply doing their admittedly unpleasant duty. They were able to regard themselves as fine doctors and exemplary human beings. How is this possible?

It is possible through the phenomena called doubling. The person cannot live with what he has become, and so he becomes in essence two or more persons. There is a sealed off and idealized section of his being where what he does and what he is cannot be acknowledged. He is one person at work and another quite different person at home. The Bible knows about this and calls the wicked man a person of double heart.

Jesus asks the demon his name. Asking for a name in the Bible is asking for more than a label. It is asking for the inmost essence of a person. The demon answers Jesus, "Legion," which means that the inmost essence of that spirit in its condemned state is "many" or "divided" or "at perpetual civil war" or "never at peace."

By way of contrast, Jesus is "at one" with the Father. He is "at one" with the Holy One. This undivided state is what the Bible means by purity of heart. Those who follow him are likewise at one with the Father and at peace with themselves. Blessed are they who have no need to hide from themselves. As their will is increasingly to do the will of the Father they find themselves "one person" in Christ.

Father, grant us purity of heart. Grant us freedom from inward division and grant us integrity as we strive to serve you.

Grudge Match

Father John Dominic Corbett, O.P.

Now a large herd of swine was feeding there on the hillside. And [the unclean spirits] pleaded with [Jesus], "Send us into the swine. Let us enter them." (Mk 5: 11-12)

The demons plead to be allowed to enter a place. Why? It isn't obvious that a spirit who has no body would need a place.

This business of "needing" has always been their problem. The angels were created to be with God, but first they had to undergo a test. The test was about autonomy. They were made so high in rank that they could be their own world. Men are so obviously dependent on a million things like air, water, food, and friends. Only the most insane would insist on an absolute independence. However, the angels were created with dazzling minds and with proportionately powerful wills. Having no bodies that could tire, sicken, and ultimately die, they had no kind of dependence on anything created. They did depend upon God, of course, but on nothing else. So they could turn their attention to God the giver of their being, and adore and obey him, or they could refuse to do that, and instead only focus on and adore themselves. This was their suicidal choice.

They made this choice with reference to the Lord Jesus. The Father showed the angels the incarnation. He showed them that the second person of the Trinity would become man. This outraged the pride of the angels who would never consent to adore one who took on, of all things, a body. Jesus would have a body that would need food, sleep, a place to be, air, and in this body, now glorified, he would reign as Lord over heaven and over all times, places, and persons on earth as well.

So the unclean spirits have a need. They need to rage against Christ in his human and glorified body. They also need to attack and degrade his image: man. Expelled from his image, they are defeated in their pride. They claimed to need nothing. They found they needed pigs.

Humility before God and special love for man, God's creature and image, mark our Lord, his Mother, and all those who follow him.

Father, by sending your Son into the world as its Savior, you showed special honor to man made in your image. May we honor that image in everyone we meet.

Degraded

Father John Dominic Corbett, O.P.

And [Jesus] let them, and the unclean spirits came out and entered the swine. The herd of about two thousand rushed down a steep bank into the sea, where they were drowned. The swineherds ran away and reported the incident in the town and throughout the countryside. (Mk 5: 13-14a)

Jesus "let them" go into the swine Why? How can Jesus and the demons possibly come to agreement on anything? Perhaps he lets them go into the pigs to signify their degradation. The demons that tormented the man are demoted by being sent into something less than man. Perhaps also Jesus lets them go into the swine because granting this request is a reception of their surrender to his authority.

In any case, the demons plunge the swine in the waters of the sea. The water is the traditional abode of demons. It is a realm in which there is no form. It recalls the world before the world had taken its form and shape from God's almighty and creative hand. The demons want to undo the work of God, and so they want to dissolve creation. Hence they find satisfaction in destroying even as humble a part of creation as a herd of swine by plunging them into a watery grave.

But that is not the whole of the story. The swine and the demons may have had common purpose. The pigs flee down the hill because they cannot abide the presence of the unholy ones, and they instinctively know that death itself is preferable to their company.

Is there any lesson for us in the pigs' desperate plunge into the water? We must remember that the waters were hallowed by the spirit of God brooding over them on the first day of creation. The waters of the Red Sea were used to drown Pharaoh's armies. Christ was baptized in the waters of the Jordan River. The waters of baptism effect death to sin and a new creation in Christ. Perhaps we do not sufficiently realize that our own flight from evil will plunge us into a fatal cleansing begun with our baptism, to be sure, but only completed by our death in Christ.

Father, your Son paid a terrible price for our redemption and freedom. Give us a love strong enough to want "to complete what is lacking in the suffering of Christ."

Sanity and the Fear of God

Father John Dominic Corbett, O.P.

And people came out to see what had happened. As they approached Jesus, they caught sight of the man who had been possessed by Legion, sitting there clothed and in his right mind. And they were seized with fear. (Mk 5: 14b-15)

Why are these people seized with fear? You would think that at long last they have good reason not to be afraid. A man who was strong enough to break chains and was strange enough to live in graveyards and who was under the control of entities who were themselves enslaved to murderous hatred of God had lived in dangerous proximity to them. This was a man to be greatly feared. This man is healed by Jesus, and the destructive horde which had tormented them all is gone. The people come out to see what has happened, and they find a man clothed and in his right mind and no longer a threat to anyone. And yet it is only then that the people begin to be truly afraid.

Perhaps the key that unlocks this mystery is found in that phrase "in his right mind." What does it mean to be in one's right mind? Presumably, it means to be normal. But the word "normal" has a couple of distinctive meanings. It can be understood as "normative." It also can be understood as "statistically regular."

If this man is restored to his right mind in the sense that he is more or less like all of his neighbors, then the people wouldn't be afraid. They would be reassured. He would share their quirks, idiosyncrasies, and prejudices. He would be strong where they are strong and weak where they are weak. The quality of his mind would be simply a reflection of theirs.

If, on the other hand, the man is restored to his right mind in the sense that he now is in possession of the truth about God and about himself and about his neighbors, then he might be very disturbing indeed. Actually, if we were ever to see what is normal and normative in God's eyes we would realize how much we need to change, and we would be afraid too.

Father, we are often deaf to your call because we do not understand how much we need to change. Give us the love that will make us willing to listen.

Collaborators

Father John Dominic Corbett, o.p.

*Those who witnessed the incident explained to [the people]
what had happened to the possessed man and to the swine.
Then they began to beg [Jesus] to leave their district.*
(Mk 5: 16-17)

They are told about what has happened to the possessed man and the swine. Apparently, they are just as interested in what happened to the swine as they are in what has happened to the man. The man in his new state is frighteningly normal. The pigs are gone. So is the livelihood of the swineherds. What has Jesus done? He has brought healing to a man and healing to a community (for they have all been terrified of the man). Nevertheless, Jesus has brought disruption as well.

We are of two minds about healing. On the one hand, we truly need it and desire it. Illness can destroy our lives and the suffering that it brings can make them seem not worth living. The relief and restoration that healing brings is always desired.

On the other hand, we can get used to illness. We can grow accustomed to the routines that our illnesses require and to the exemptions that our illnesses afford us. A sense of entitlement can grow. A sense of accountability can begin to wither.

In the same way, we can become accustomed to others' illnesses. We work around them and can derive some sort of residual benefit from them. People who have alcoholic members of their families get used to caring for them and to being needed in all sorts of ways. One becomes a hero. One can tell tales that magnify one's virtue. Above all, one can derive an identity around caretaking for those in need.

Up to a point, this is all right. However, it can be carried to an extreme if one would rather continue with the illness than chance the form of new life that would come were healing permitted to do its work.

They beg Jesus to leave their neighborhood. No wonder. If he were to stay, he would heal even more people and disrupt who knows how many more settled and sick routines.

Father, we derive benefits from our sins. Help us to see them as they are. Help us to know that we are harmed by our collusion with evil. Give us desire for what you promise.

Commissioned

Father John Dominic Corbett, O.P.

As [Jesus] was getting into the boat, the man who had been possessed pleaded to remain with him. But he would not permit him but told him instead, "Go home to your family and announce to them all that the Lord in his pity has done for you."
(Mk 5: 18-19)

The townspeople have seen marvels. They have literally seen pigs fly and they don't know whether to compose an epic poem or praise their pagan gods or file a lawsuit claiming damages from Jesus. But they have seen amazing things that day.

It's no wonder that they practically forget about the formerly possessed man himself. What about him? What is he supposed to do now that he is free of the nightmare that had turned all his days into one unending night? What is he supposed to do with his days now?

He is in such unfamiliar territory and it is no wonder that he desires to cling to the one man who knows what to make of it all. He pleads to be able to remain with Jesus.

But Jesus has completed his cure. One of the effects of evil as well as one of its causes is alienation. Think again of the Prodigal Son. He rejected his relationship with his father and brother. He left his native land. He lost even the use of his own language. Everyone in sin is in this situation of lost bearings, family, and friends. Being liberated from the grasp of evil involves the recovery of these important relationships.

That is why when Jesus casts out the demons his work is not yet done. The cure is not complete until the man is restored to his family. This is why Jesus tells him to "go home" and be restored to his rightful world. He tells him to go home and reclaim his humanity. He tells him to go home and reclaim all that made his life worthwhile.

And Jesus tells him to tell his family that this restoration is the work of the Lord's special compassion for those wanderers who even today are lost in the night.

Father, we lose so much when we sin. Help us to know that your desire is that we should recover what has been lost. Help us in our recovery.

Life in the Big Cities

Father John Dominic Corbett, O.P.

Then the man went off and began to proclaim in the Decapolis what Jesus had done for him; and all were amazed.
(Mk 5: 20)

We should notice that our text does not say that the man returns home and does exactly what Jesus has said. Instead, the Gospel tells us that he "went off and began to proclaim in the Decapolis what Jesus had done for him." The Decapolis is an area of ten cities in pagan territory. You see what has happened? He has taken and expanded Jesus' charge to him. He has shared what Jesus has done for him not only with his family but with perfect strangers.

There are three things to remember here. The first is that our man is a Gentile. He knows nothing of God except what glimmers of truth pagan legend might afford. Indeed, the very term Gentile means "one who is ignorant of God."

The second is that he is beginning to know God in the same way that the chosen people began to know him. They began to know him as he came to act on their behalf. In Egypt, the Hebrews had forgotten the very name of their God. They relearned it as the Lord intervened on their behalf and rescued them from the slavery of Pharaoh. "I AM," the Divine Name, can be rendered as a promise of rescue. So in receiving the intervention that God has made on his behalf, the man has also learned who God essentially is.

The third is that the man begins to "proclaim" and the crowds are amazed. To "proclaim" is to announce the deeds of God and to be "amazed" is to perceive that these events are truly acts of God. To be amazed is to be astounded at a divine act. The crowds are amazed, which means they have received revelation too and begin to see God as he is. They begin to see him as the one who truly loves man and saves him from the powers of darkness still prowling the world seeking the ruin of souls.

Father, you revealed yourself to one who did not know you, and you used him to reveal yourself to a people who had not known you. Please send such preachers again into our world.

The Fall That Saves

Monsignor Gregory E. S. Malovetz

When Jesus had crossed again [in the boat] to the other side,
a large crowd gathered around him, and he stayed close to the
sea. One of the synagogue officials, named Jairus, came forward.
Seeing him he fell at his feet. (Mk 5: 21-22)

I t had been a beautiful day out on the boat: friends, lunch, conversation, and two golden retrievers. Upon returning home, we docked the boat and spent time cleaning and securing it. Moondoggie, one of the retrievers, sat on the dock watching the activity. He had been swimming most of the day, and now seemed content to wait for us to finish. Inexplicably, he leaned to one side, and then fell into the water. As he was an accomplished swimmer, we were shocked and then panicked when he didn't immediately resurface. When he did, we struggled to get his hundred pounds back on the dock, almost falling in ourselves. Moondoggie shook himself dry, gave us a grateful look, and then walked down the dock to the car.

When Jairus fell at the feet of Jesus, I imagine it was more like collapsing. He was an accomplished synagogue official, a man to whom others looked for guidance and support. Coming upon this moment, those who witnessed Jairus fall before Jesus might have been shocked to see him drowning in despair and desperation. Jairus approaches Jesus in the hope that this man can lift the terrible weight and prevent him from drowning in life's disappointments.

Through the waters of baptism, Jesus gives us a promise. He will enter the struggles of life with us. He does not stand on the dock watching us secure our boats, or watch bewildered when we fall. Jesus enters our lives – he dives into our disappointment and despair – so that we can be restored to life.

Every day someone falls on the journey of life. Sometimes it is from the stress of work or family life; other times it is from addiction, illness, or broken relationships. We may be tempted to think we will be saved by good intentions or a stroke of good fortune. But it is in the falling before Jesus that we find our way home.

Gracious Father, I place before you those who have fallen because
of loss or pain. May I stand with them, and in doing so reveal the
saving presence of Jesus.

Remember the Grip

Monsignor Gregory E. S. Malovetz

*And [Jairus] pleaded earnestly with [Jesus], saying,
"My daughter is at the point of death. Please, come lay your
hands on her that she may get well and live." He went off with
him, and a large crowd followed him and pressed upon him.*
(Mk 5: 23-24)

His smile was huge; his face young and handsome. And he looked nervous. As a group of people entered the elevator, we joined a young father holding tightly to the car seat containing a sleeping baby. He kept looking down, as if to check that the sleeping baby was still there, tightening his grip each time. His smiling face became an invitation for us to discover he was a new dad. It was his first child, the mom was at the pool, and he was in charge. The lights of the elevator landed on his floor, and he exited holding firmly onto his child. Another man on the elevator had a far-off look in his face when he said to everyone and to no one, "I remember that smile, and I remember that grip."

How many smiles was Jairus remembering when he pleaded with Jesus? What moments of joy did he recall as he now choked back tears in his request? As a father, Jairus must have often held the hand of his daughter, believing he could guide and protect her on the road of life. Now he was losing grip, as he realized he could not save his daughter. In losing his grip, he was losing himself. It was only the hand of Jesus that could save them both.

As disciples, we find our true selves in Jesus. The meaning of our lives is found not in what we possess, but in placing our lives in the hand of Jesus. Along the road of life, we lose our way. Distracted by many things, our hands slip from the hand of Jesus and we find them filled with anxiety, worry, or anger. It is the hand of Jesus that will heal. The healing can only come when we grip tighter to the hand that will save us.

*Loving Father, I place my life in the hands of your Son. May the
challenges of this life never cause me to let go of his love.*

Someone to Listen

Monsignor Gregory E. S. Malovetz

There was a woman afflicted with hemorrhages for twelve years. She had suffered greatly at the hands of many doctors and had spent all that she had. Yet she was not helped but only grew worse. (Mk 5: 25-26)

I was filled with worry and some fear the minute a computer-generated voice prompted me to press number one. Within seconds I was entangled in what companies erroneously advertize as the "customer help line." As the command over the phone told me to speak or press the appropriate number, I found my spirit sinking. Overcome by the sense of falling deeper into chaos, I was moving farther away from an answer to my problem. After fifteen maddening minutes, I finally continued to press zero in frustration. A live human voice came on and said, "My name is Robert, how may I help you?" I responded, "I'm not mad or angry, but I just want someone to listen."

I am not sure what health care looked like during the time of Jesus. There is something poignant though about the afflicted woman going from doctor to doctor in search of an answer. In seeking help, she exhausted not only her savings, but her energy, her dignity, and her hope as well.

The afflictions many of us carry require something more than a brilliant physician or adequate health care plan. We may carry resentments from childhood, a sorrow that broke our heart, or a hurt that no bandage can repair. So we run from one thing to another, thinking if I just had more money, or a different job, or a nicer family, or another drink, I would be fine. The truth is that what we need is the grace to know that God is near. It is God who will hear us, and it is God who will heal.

Someone today is looking for help. They have exhausted their energy, their dignity, and their hope. In their search for healing they will encounter you along the way. "I have no answers," you may insist when they come to you. But you are a follower of Christ. The answer is to be the someone who will listen.

Father of peace, I know you hear my voice. Give me the grace to be a disciple with a listening heart.

Recognizing the One Who Serves

Monsignor Gregory E. S. Malovetz

[The woman] had heard about Jesus and came up behind him in the crowd and touched his cloak. She said, "If I but touch his clothes, I shall be cured." Immediately her flow of blood dried up. She felt in her body that she was healed of her affliction.
(Mk 5: 27-29)

One evening a friend and I went to a local restaurant for dinner. As we were led to our table, we immediately recognized our waiter. He had waited on us several times previously, but not here. He had been our waiter at not one but two other restaurants within a few months' time. He recognized my friend and me, and laughed when I asked if he was stalking us. We learned that he was attending college, and as a hard-working young man he was taking shifts at several restaurants to earn money. Each of the restaurants required him to wear a different kind of slacks and shirt. Despite wearing different clothing in each place, he was the same gracious, helpful, and friendly server each time. Before we left the restaurant he leaned in and asked what restaurant we would be eating in next so he could apply for a job there.

Given the culture and times in which he lived, we can assume that Jesus did not have many changes of clothing. People knew Jesus not from what he wore or the color of his tunic. They knew him from the experience they had when encountering him. Even in a crowd, Jesus touched people with compassion, with understanding, and with grace. The woman in need of healing wanted to touch not the garment of Jesus, but the gracious and life-giving presence people experienced in him.

We encounter the gracious and loving presence of Jesus in the Eucharist and in the Word. It is there that we touch the One we know can cure us of the things that keep us hidden in the crowd. Jesus is also found in the great crowd we call the community of believers. He is touched when we are the gracious servers who recognize those who need to be cured, and clear the path to Jesus.

Loving Father, your loving presence guides my journey. May I become the kind of servant who finds you in the lives of others I meet along the way.

The Power That Is Always Here

Monsignor Gregory E. S. Malovetz

Jesus, aware at once that power had gone out from him, turned around in the crowd and asked, "Who has touched my clothes?"
(Mk 5:30)

The storm had been raging for hours, with brutal winds and driving rain. The radio reported that power outages were widespread. As I drove home, the route became one long detour, with fallen trees creating an obstacle course. I noticed the dark houses along each street, and expected to find my home in complete darkness as I turned the corner. To my great surprise, the houses on my street were all still lit on this stormy night. The power had not gone out.

And then it happened. I no sooner got into the house than the lights flickered and then went out. I stood frozen in the darkness, my eyes not yet adjusted, trying to remember where the flashlight, candles, and matches were. As I started to make my way, the lights came back on. The paralyzing feeling of the darkness was lifted by the return of the power.

We all have had the experience of the power going off and then coming back on in our homes. In this Gospel passage we are told that Jesus felt the power *had gone out from him.* What was the sensation Jesus experienced that made him aware power had gone out from him and into the life of another person? I would like to think it was the experience he had each time someone came to him, whether looking him in the eyes or hiding in a crowd. Jesus saw the light returning to the darkness of someone's life, a darkness that was caused by sin, depression, discouragement, or fear. The depth of his love rekindled in others a meaning to their lives that had gone dark.

Darkness can enter our lives like an unexpected power outage. A loved one dies, the doctor says the news is bad, or a job is lost. In a crowded world we feel alone. But when we adjust our eyes to the dark, we see Jesus and his power are there.

Father of Light, may I always know the power of your love, even in the darkest hours of my life.

The People We Choose to See

Monsignor Gregory E. S. Malovetz

But his disciples said to [Jesus], "You see how the crowd is pressing upon you, and yet you ask, 'Who touched me?'" And he looked around to see who had done it.
(Mk 5: 31-32)

The sun was already high in the sky and the heat intense as we entered the field. Some friends had bought a share at one of the cooperative farms in central New Jersey. Right before going on vacation, they suggested that another friend and I could have their share of the crops for that week. We would just have to go and pick the vegetables and herbs.

Despite being urbanites, my friend and I were excited at the opportunity to be farmers for a few hours. Armed with bags and the list of what the co-op indicated we could pick, we began. This was no mere walk down the produce aisle of the supermarket. Picking blackberries required that we look carefully through the bushes for those that were ripe. Picking okra meant looking close to the ground for those that were ready to be cut. As we walked through the vast fields I soon realized the true work of harvesting the vegetables involved looking carefully. As we got back in the car, my friend said, "I'll never look at shopping for vegetables the same way again. There was a real intentionality about doing this."

When Jesus looked around to see who had touched him, the disciples insisted it was impossible to identify the person. But there was nothing impossible about it for Jesus. Throughout his ministry, Jesus intentionally looks at people. He sees the wounded souls, the ones in need of healing, and the person who believes her life does not matter. He does not rush mindlessly through the aisles of life. Jesus takes his time so that when he looks, he really sees.

Along the road of life, there are people we do not see. We are too busy to notice, or we look the other way. Yet they press upon us, demanding that we who are the disciples intentionally choose to see them.

Gentle God, in this crowded life, you see me. Give me the vision to see the hurting hearts of those the world chooses not to see.

The Truth That Brings Life

Monsignor Gregory E. S. Malovetz

The woman, realizing what had happened to her, approached in fear and trembling. She fell down before Jesus and told him the whole truth. (Mk 5: 33)

When I recently realized it was time to renew my passport, it was a pleasant surprise to learn that the renewal forms could be found online. This was a welcome change in the ten years since I had last renewed this document. Since it was a busy week for me, my administrative assistant downloaded the forms and started to fill them out. She then left them on my desk to review and make the necessary changes. I went down each line, making sure the personal information was accurate. And then I came to the line for hair color. She had typed in gray. While I am not a vain person, it was really stunning for the truth to be spelled out in front of me. The ten years that had passed since the last renewal had seen my brown hair disappear. This part of the renewal process was not a welcome change.

Like Jairus, the trembling and fearful woman falls before Jesus. In that moment she tells him the whole truth. Her truth-telling is more than an admission that she has touched the garment. It is a moment to admit the truth of her life: she needs to know that God has not abandoned her. Through the many years, what never changed was her desire to be healed and know that in her suffering she had not been forgotten by God. As she places that truth before Jesus, all the tears of disappointment dry up. The affliction of hopelessness was healed by Jesus' renewing love.

As we look in the mirror, we may see more than a few changes indicating the passage of time. Our lives may be marked by disappointments that give us more than gray hair. They cause us to lose hope. Jesus knows our struggles. It is in telling ourselves the whole truth that we find our way to him.

Loving Father, give me the grace to see my life as you see it. As years go by, may I never stop believing that the truth of my life is a blessing to you.

The Promise of Peace

Monsignor Gregory E. S. Malovetz

[Jesus] said to her, "Daughter, your faith has saved you.
Go in peace and be cured of your affliction."
(Mk 5: 34)

The promises kept coming faster and with greater urgency. "I swear I am going to stop smoking and eating unhealthy food; I am going to start to exercise." The voice came from behind a curtain in a hospital emergency room. Years ago, I had been taken to the hospital for a minor medical emergency. I was left alone in an area of the emergency room where patient cubicles were separated by a series of curtains. From what I heard, it seems that the woman in the next cubicle had been brought in because of breathing problems. She had erupted into a series of promises to change her life if the doctor returned with good news. While I don't remember the entire diagnosis, I know the doctor returned saying basically all was well and that she needed to take better care of her health. A great cheer went up by the woman and her friend, and soon they were gone. As they left I wanted to stick my head out of the curtain and ask, "But what about all those promises?"

What jubilation the woman cured of her affliction must have felt as Jesus sent her away. But she was sent away with a reminder and a task. The reminder is that only God can give our lives meaning and help us find the way. That is how faith saves us. She is also given a task: those who have been healed and cured must live as people of peace.

I often wonder what happened to that woman who encountered Jesus, and what happened to countless others like her. Did she return to her life a more grateful person, ready to live an authentic human life? Was she better prepared to breathe peace into the world because of this encounter? What happened to her?

And then I realize, we are that woman when, having been healed and forgiven, we live as people of peace.

Loving Father, I stand grateful for the healing love you have given to me. Help me always to remember that I have been sent to be a bearer of peace.

Message on the Road

Monsignor Gregory E. S. Malovetz

While [Jesus] was still speaking, people from the synagogue official's house arrived and said, "Your daughter has died; why trouble the teacher any longer?" Disregarding the message that was reported, Jesus said to the synagogue official, "Do not be afraid; just have faith." (Mk 5: 35-36)

Even at the end of the rush hour, the congestion was still huge on 125th Street. I was driving to a wake being held for the mother of a friend in the Bronx. I inched my way toward the bridge, and saw up ahead a woman standing in the middle of the street. She was a woman of a certain age, with a face beaming a bright smile. She was selling bottled water from her place in the midst of the traffic. A friend driving with me urged that I roll down the window. The woman was selling the water for considerably less than what it would cost in a convenience store. My friend handed me twice the amount she was asking for, and we bought two bottles. She continued the bright smile as we thanked her. Her message was as wide and uplifting as her smile: "You have a good day, baby!"

Every day we receive messages. We check our email, the mailbox at our door, and instant messages on our cell phone. In the time of Jesus there was one way of communication: by word of mouth. In this terrible moment, the crowd stands in the street. You can almost imagine their arms crossed, faces contorted with grief and anger. "Why bother?" is their message. That message continues down the centuries by countless people. "Why bother" when structures oppress, when the powerful are unjust, when life gets complicated, or when death comes and sorrow breaks our hearts?

The message of Jesus is not one of naïve optimism. It proclaims the saving presence of God's grace on every road of life. The message says grace is even there when the road is dark and we lose our way. The disciple of Jesus is willing to stand in the middle of the road and speak a message of hope that is as refreshing as water on a hot summer day.

Merciful Father, let me never embrace the messages that deny your love or the possibility of new life for me.

Companions on the Journey

Monsignor Gregory E. S. Malovetz

[Jesus] did not allow anyone to accompany him inside except Peter, James, and John, the brother of James. (Mk 5: 37)

We heard the noises and the sound of cheers. On the last night of my vacation, I emerged from the house I was renting to a night sky that was filled with fireworks. The house sits directly on the Long Island Sound, with a dozen or so other houses on either side. Most in the neighborhood were renters; this was the last night before packing up and turning in the keys.

I looked up and down the beach. People were emerging from their houses, having heard the noise and seen the light. Some folks, in the midst of dinner, came out with cocktails in hand. Children tumbled out of the doors and stood on the beach, mesmerized by the brilliant colors. And when this impromptu end of the season celebration concluded, a large cheer and applause erupted from all those who had been watching. For one brief moment, the light had united us.

The disciples of Jesus accompanied him to many places. They went with Jesus to more than towns and villages. They would enter people's lives. They would stand with people in moments of celebration and in moments of despair. They would stand with them in ordinary daily life. In those encounters they discover there are no strangers. We are all the children of God to whom the light is given. The disciples learn that they were not a select few individuals given the privilege of accompanying Jesus. Those who were in the company of Jesus were to expand the circle, and bring others into the light.

As we make the journey of our life, we enter into one another's lives. Sometimes those who accompany us are people we will know our entire life. Others may be individuals we meet for just a moment. We must never forget to be grateful for those who stand with us in his light.

Loving Father, I breathe a prayer of gratitude for friends and strangers who in my life have brought me into your light.

You Take the Sting

Monsignor Gregory E. S. Malovetz

When [Jesus, Peter, James, and John] arrived at the house of the
synagogue official, [Jesus] caught sight of a commotion, people
weeping and wailing loudly. So he went in and said to them,
"Why this commotion and weeping? The child is not dead but
asleep." And they ridiculed him. Then he put them all out.
(Mk 5: 38-40a)

The beautiful day made the outdoors perfect for the pictures. Before she left for the church, the bride posed by herself, and with various members of the wedding party. As the pictures were taken, the photographer's assistant stood with a diffusion panel that was circular and large enough to prevent unwanted shadows in the picture. As the bride was being photographed alone, a bee circled around the assistant. The assistant saw it and made several discreet attempts to keep the bee away from the bride. At one point the bee moved too close to the assistant who, in his panic, jerked his body in such a way that he hit the bride in the head with the panel. She was uninjured but the photographer was mortified. The embarrassed assistant whispered, "What was I supposed to do, it was coming at me." In a voice loud enough for all to hear, the photographer responded, "You take the sting."

Peter, James, and John may have been nervous when they encountered the commotion, weeping, and loud wailing at the house. The stinging ridicule directed at Jesus may have made them, in panic, want to run. But Jesus stands there. He takes the comments, but is not distracted or deterred by them. Jesus was no stranger to words that hurt, and understood why people spoke them. As in so many other moments, Jesus listens but does not stop. He moves forward to be a living word of hope when all seems lost.

In our lives, we are often distracted or deterred by what others say. It can be mean comments, unfair judgment, or criticism that hurts deeply. Those words can paralyze and cause us to believe we cannot move ahead. We give power to words that do nothing more than cause commotion and tears. The disciple of Jesus is called to trust in the word of the One who is willing to take the sting.

Father, when words bring pain, let me hear only your Word of
Love. Let the words of my mouth always bring peace.

Taking a Chance

Monsignor Gregory E. S. Malovetz

[Jesus] took along the child's father and mother and those who were with him and entered the room where the child was. He took the child by the hand and said to her, "Talitha koum," which means, "Little girl, I say to you, arise!" (Mk 5: 40b-41)

She was skeptical at first. And a little worried. Every summer I take two of my nieces for a day in Manhattan. One year we went to a play and planned for dinner at a restaurant. As we emerged from the theatre, I suggested the easiest way to get to the restaurant was taking the subway. One of my nieces was enthusiastic; the other, not so much.

My less enthusiastic niece skeptically followed me on that hot summer afternoon down the steps to an even hotter subway platform. She looked a little worried as we got on the crowded subway. After dinner we took another subway to the parking garage.

We did not talk much about the subway experience after that. But riding the subway, even begrudgingly, must have given her a new kind of confidence. That fall, my niece spent time in London and Paris. It was interesting to hear how enthusiastically and successfully she negotiated the London Underground and the Paris Métro.

Gathered around a bed, Jesus stands with parents and disciples who are more than a little skeptical. In grasping the young girl's hand, he is doing more than bringing her back to life. He is giving her, and those in that room, a new way of looking at their lives. They will be given a power greater than themselves – the Spirit of God – to help them find their way. Wherever the journey of life takes them, they will live as people who believe a new beginning is always possible. But it would be possible only if they were willing to take a chance and get on the journey of discipleship.

Discipleship is like finding yourself on a subway platform. We might be hot, worried, skeptical, or unsure. It is the choice of holding back or getting on which indicates whether we have understood the meaning of Risen Life.

Loving Father, give me your Spirit that I may arise each day, believing a new beginning is always possible.

Listening to the Stories

Monsignor Gregory E. S. Malovetz

The girl, a child of twelve, arose immediately and walked around. [At that] [the child's father and mother and those who were with Jesus] were utterly astounded. [Jesus] gave strict orders that no one should know this and said that she should be given something to eat. (Mk 5: 42-43)

Beverages, crackers, cheese, a cutting board, and a candle. For most travelers, none of those are standard items to be packed for a trip. But they were for my friend Trish. It happened when she was traveling to Rome, to a wedding in Arizona, or down to the New Jersey shore. Even in the most unusual circumstances, Trish could always be counted on to have a delicious treat or refreshing beverage among the things in her suitcase. She would pay special attention to who would be on the trip, making sure favorite items were included. Among her friends, she became known as the Queen of the Packed Snack.

Her motivation was not hunger. It was a way of gathering the group, discussing the day's events. It was her opportunity to hear their stories. She not only had the snacks, but a listening heart too.

There are many stories in the Gospel in which we find Jesus feeding people. As he fed them, he gave them a vision of what it means to be his disciples. Those who were fed by Jesus were then sent to feed others. Most were not sent to far-off places to be missionaries. They were sent back to their daily lives with the mission to feed others with the same listening heart Jesus had given them.

When Jesus directs the parents to feed their daughter, he is doing more than providing a meal. He was restoring her to the routine of family life. It is in our daily lives with family and friends that we live our discipleship. The moments that challenge us are not always ones of great crisis or trouble. It is the willingness to take the time, over a cup of coffee, to listen to someone's story.

Trish went home to the Lord one summer morning. Each time I share a drink or snack with friends I remember her. And I remember what discipleship really is.

Father, I am fed by the love of your Son. Let me never be so busy that I miss the opportunity to find him in the stories of those I meet on the journey of life.

It's Just Astonishing!

Father Jacob Restrick, O.P.

[Jesus] departed from there and came to his native place, accompanied by his disciples. When the sabbath came he began to teach in the synagogue, and many who heard him were astonished. (Mk 6: 1-2a)

"Many who heard him were astonished." Imagine that! We can imagine that because it's still going on: many are still astonished by what Jesus teaches. This can be taken in different ways. Some may be stupefied or overwhelmed with joy by what Jesus teaches, for example: the kingdom of God is within you; you are more precious and valuable to God than all the birds and lilies of the field. It's astonishing to learn that God loves me – always has, always will. Or they can find it all too incredible.

I heard a middle-aged woman, who had come through a battle with alcoholism and prescription drug addiction, say that she didn't pray because she didn't think God wanted anything to do with her. She thought that he had more cosmic problems to deal with. She was astonished to learn that God loved her and made her. She was unique in all the world. She was astonished when she came to realize that God was with her through the struggle of recovery, and loves her with an infinite love. She was astonished to learn that prayer is more than asking; it's more like listening. She was astonished when she began to read the Gospels as a disciple, and not an outsider.

One could also be astonished or even scandalized by what Jesus teaches. He teaches that whatever we do to the least of his brothers or sisters, we do to him. He teaches that the tax collectors and prostitutes and sinners are entering the kingdom of heaven. He teaches that he and the Father are one. Astonishing!

By extension, many people are astonished by the Church's teachings. The Church teaches the truths about life and death; marriage and family; the Eucharist and sacramental reconciliation; heaven and hell; and the sacredness of all human life. It's just astonishing!

Loving and glorious Father, do not stop astonishing us with the words of Jesus, your incarnate Word. Teach us to listen and to heed his words today, for he is Lord for ever and ever.

From Astonishment to Offense

Father Jacob Restrick, O.P.

[Many] said, "Where did this man get all this? What kind of wisdom has been given him? What mighty deeds are wrought by his hands! Is he not the carpenter, the son of Mary, and the brother of James and Joses and Judas and Simon? And are not his sisters here with us?" And they took offense at him.
(Mk 6: 2b-3)

Perhaps they took offense at him because he was too human. He was too much like them, and they wanted to keep God and the kingdom of God separate from their ordinary life. They wrestled with it all in their heads and hearts: how can Jesus be God? He is flesh and blood, as we are. He walks and talks and breathes the same air we do! His relatives are our friends and neighbors; we're very familiar with them. Is God familiar with us?

The human nature of Jesus is still a stumbling block for people. That Jesus is God in the flesh is too much to believe. For many today, it's downright offensive because it's too exclusive. They want Jesus to be just one among other religious and spiritual men: Buddha, Confucius, Zoroaster, Mohammed. After all, if Jesus is just another "holy man" we can relate to that, but God in human flesh – unbelievable!

One friend told me that he wants to keep Jesus as a holy man, teacher, a "spirit-friend" but nothing more, because then his teachings are just his opinion, as good as they may be for his time and people, but nothing more. And opinions one can take or leave; it's a matter of personal preference and subjective taste.

How precious is the gift of faith! To be fascinated by his every word, and actually to know him and relate to him; to belong to his family! It's all still quite astonishing. The Lord, of course, is not separate from his Church. Nor is the Church just one religious institution among many others, each with its own opinions and world views. We hold it is astonishing and wonderful, and not offensive, that the Church teaches with divine authority and is preserved from error in matters of faith and morals.

Loving Father, when you gave us your Son, you gave us a holy communion in him. You gave us a Church. May we be astonished at all you do in him, for ever and ever.

Home: Exception to the Rule

Father Jacob Restrick, O.P.

Jesus said to them, "A prophet is not without honor except in his native place and among his own kin and in his own house."
(Mk 6: 4)

Every preacher, every priest and religious, indeed, every devout Christian knows what Jesus is speaking about. It is "easier" to speak words of wisdom and to counsel others when they're not your family.

I know a number of home-schooling mothers. Most are raising large families, teaching, cooking, and making their home a "seat" of Catholic culture! Family celebrations give the Church's feast days a whole new impetus. And beneath all that, hopefully, one can discover so many virtues and holiness of life being taught simply by example and practice. Large families today all undergo many sacrifices, but they live life to the full. And sometimes it's the extended family members who are most discouraging, critical, or unsupportive. If that be the case, the devout parents of the large family may not be able to share with their extended families the wonderful fruits and joy and challenges of living the faith. I've come to realize that anyone practicing his faith in a serious and joyful way may not always find support or sympathy from within the "hometown" community of believers. Charity begins at home; that isn't a new exception to the rule, but charity makes itself known in each home in unique ways. Acceptance and gratitude really help!

I felt terrible once when criticizing some parishioners who habitually come to Sunday Mass late, and one of the mothers kindly explained that she had six kids to get up, washed, and dressed, and into the car peacefully... and I understood. I hadn't realized the family routine is not like my own. I felt like the hometown mayor who missed the extraordinary good of his own local citizens. But take courage! The Lord knows exactly what it is like to be criticized and even rejected by one's own. It didn't move him off course for a second!

Loving and gracious Father, may I be faithful to the graces you give each day; courageous in times of opposition, and compassionate when misunderstood. We ask this in the name of Jesus, who is Lord, for ever and ever.

Divine Amazement

Father Jacob Restrick, O.P.

So [Jesus] was not able to perform any mighty deed there, apart from curing a few sick people by laying his hands on them. He was amazed at their lack of faith. (Mk 6: 5-6)

Just four verses before reading that Jesus is amazed at their lack of faith, we read that all who heard his teaching were astonished. (Except in his hometown.)

We may also be amazed at peoples' lack of faith when we read the Gospels. These people saw stupendous miracles: the dead brought back to life; blindness, deafness, and leprosy healed in an instant. Maybe we're sometimes amazed at peoples' lack of faith today, especially if they know there are "miracles" in our midst.

Take Billy W., for example, alcoholic and recovering drug addict. By all human calculation he should be dead. Not only was he physically and emotionally wiped out by drinking and drugging, he was spiritually bankrupt. He had a "soul-sickness" which brought him to the brink of despair and suicide. Crash! He hit bottom, which also included a telephone pole, a neighbor's dog, and a DWI. He was riddled with guilt and fear, and didn't want to stop drinking because it took away the pain, and because he couldn't stop.

The court system sent him to rehab, and rehab introduced him to Alcoholics Anonymous, and A.A. introduced him to a Power greater than himself who took away the desire and compulsion to drink or take pills. When he celebrated a year of being sober and clean from all mood-changing drugs, he told a room full of other alcoholics and addicts: "I'm a miracle!" He told them that he came to believe that God saved him from destroying himself, and even more, that God's love and care are infinite.

Faith can move mountains that we can't imagine. But if we're attuned to his grace each day, and praying to do his will, we will discover little miracles in our own lives. Open the eyes of faith, and be amazed.

Merciful Father, how tremendous your care. Look not at our sins, but at the faith of your Church, and work miracles in our lives today.

The Walking Sticks

Father Jacob Restrick, O.P.

[Jesus] went around to the villages in the vicinity teaching. He summoned the Twelve and began to send them out two by two and gave them authority over unclean spirits. He instructed them to take nothing for the journey but a walking stick – no food, no sack, no money in their belts. They were, however, to wear sandals but not a second tunic. (Mk 6: 6b; 7-9)

The Lord's instructions to his apostles, sent out two by two to preach and to cast out unclean spirits, causes most of us "modern day apostles" to smile because we schlep our bags through airport security with everything *except* a walking stick, unless one is sporting a cane.

I was driving my car into Canada where I was going to preach a retreat to a community of Dominican Sisters. It was during the year following 9/11, and the border security was very scrupulous about checking every vehicle in and out of the country. I had to empty the trunk of the car, which had everything the Lord tells us *not* to take, in triplicate, plus three portfolios of poster-size icon reproductions. My retreat uses these images in each conference. They depicted the mysteries of the faith, like we meditate on in the rosary, as well as images of our Lady and the saints.

I was frustrated and impatient, but understood the precautions, as we all did. The hidden blessing was the opportunity to explain to the border control officer the meaning of icons, and what a retreat was. I don't think I cast out any unclean spirits, but made of it an opportunity to speak about the Lord and our Lady. He was almost childlike in his eagerness to learn.

The Lord gives us all opportunities on the journey of life to speak about him, maybe even in dark places or where the mind has set up "borders" that keep out the Holy Spirit and his gifts of faith, hope, and love. Let these be our *walking sticks*, along with the companionship of a friend, a brother, a sister in the faith. When we cross the "Final Border," may his image be found in our trunk – or better still, in the driver's seat!

Loving Father, we bear the image of your Son since our baptism. Renew the life of faith, hope, and love in us that his image may be our most intimate companion.

Please Pass the Dust-Shaker

Father Jacob Restrick, O.P.

[Jesus] said to [the Twelve], "Wherever you enter a house, stay there until you leave from there. Whatever place does not welcome you or listen to you, leave there and shake the dust off your feet in testimony against them." (Mk 6: 10-11)

Shaking the dust from one's feet would be as common a practice in ancient Middle Eastern culture as wiping our shoes on a doormat before entering a house is for us.

People in the Lord's time also walked a lot more than we do. The roads were not nicely asphalted streets and litter-free highways. One's footwear was usually open-toed sandals. And so upon arrival an act of gracious hospitality and welcome was warm (or cool) water poured over one's dusty feet. How often during walking would one stop and shake the dust and pebbles from one's feet! Our closest identity to this dust-shaking action might be shaking the sand from our feet after being on the beach. And even then, sand usually gets all over the place and clings between one's toes and takes up residence in one's socks. The "sand-shaker" doesn't always work!

It's not easy to shake off bad *habits* either. These may be sandy little sins, like venial sins, which we've carried around for years, maybe even a lifetime. They may be irritating at times, but we get used to them and may even forget all about them, taking up space in our socks! But when we discover the sand in our shoe, it's time to become "dust-shakers." I find this is a grace of growing older, and we look back at our lives with a different perspective.

If there are people, places, and things that become occasions of sin for us, that do not "welcome" holiness, grace, peace, forgiveness, faith, and love in the house – shake that dust from your feet and move on. I think of that every time I see someone trying to dance the Macarena. Human dust-shakers!

The confessional, of course, is a great "feet-shaking" place, and you leave with a lighter step; no irritation; no dirty socks.

Heavenly Father, hallowed be thy name. May my heart be a place of true hospitality for all who walk the dusty roads and sandy paths to cross over my threshold. May I welcome you in them.

117

After the Fall Previews – Sacraments!

Father Jacob Restrick, O.P.

So [the Twelve] went off and preached repentance.
They drove out many demons, and they anointed
with oil many who were sick and cured them.
(Mk 6: 12-13)

Today's verse from Mark certainly indicates a preview of the sacrament of the anointing of the sick. It clearly shows this sacramental gesture (or "rite") as instituted by Christ to give grace – the grace of physical and spiritual healing, forgiveness, and repentance. It's a wonderful sacrament for all who are seriously ill, undergoing a serious surgery, or burdened with a chronic illness.

After more than forty years since Vatican II, most people do not refer to the sacrament as the anointing of the sick, but as the "last rites." This, of course, is incorrect, as the sacrament is for all those who are seriously sick, who may or may not be dying. When someone is dying, it's the most wonderful sacrament to prepare their soul and strengthen them in the face of suffering. Even fewer people refer to it as "extreme unction," a name denoting the sacramental use of oil. While four of the seven sacraments include an anointing with oil (baptism, confirmation, holy orders, being the other three), the anointing of the sick requires oil as the necessary matter for the sacrament. There is a specific oil blessed by the bishop or a priest called the oil of the sick.

The anointing may very well be the last touch of God's love (rite) given by and through his Church to prepare a soul for that awesome moment of being born into eternal life. "By this holy anointing, may the Lord help you by the grace of the Holy Spirit. May the Lord who forgives your sins, save you and raise you up." It's a beautiful and powerful prayer.

Do not be afraid to be anointed or to have a loved one who is sick anointed. It is Christ touching, strengthening, consoling, healing, and loving. It is all his grace. It is the gift of the Holy Spirit. No more previews – it's the real thing.

Father of all consolation, Lord of mercy, you have given us the comfort and strength of your Holy Spirit in this beautiful sacrament – like being anointed with your love. Thank you.

Wake Me Up, Lord Jesus

Father Basil Cole, O.P.

King Herod heard about it, for [Jesus'] fame had become widespread, and people were saying, "John the Baptist has been raised from the dead; that is why mighty powers are at work in him." (Mk 6: 14)

Someone's fame is another person's envy, which is precisely what brings Jesus to the cross. The Pharisees and scribes want him out of the picture because he threatens their self-image and their alleged fame with the people. But the people's high regard for Jesus is based also upon false expectations, which he repeatedly tries to dispel. Over and over again he asserts that he is not in the work of making direct political or economic changes in their lives by freeing them from Roman domination. He comes for much deeper and higher purposes. However, they will not listen to his total message because their feelings get the best of their minds, as they do with all of us from time to time. Our minds become clouded by negative feelings, and objectivity thus becomes difficult for us in trying to understand how Jesus works, which is ever so silently.

Often our prayer lives are based upon certain illusions we may have of Christ, just like the people who foolishly imagine he is John the Baptist risen from the dead. We think we can manipulate him to do our will because we feel he is mercy without justice. Likewise, our prayers may be infrequent because we are terrified of his justice without believing in his loving mercy, or we feel he is just so distant. Why does he not intervene more often when we cry out in the face of impossible situations we find ourselves in? I can think of all the prayers for twenty years begging God to remove the depressions from my mother, seemingly to no avail. Our impatience gets in the way of truly perceiving how much he loves us. Our esteem of him diminishes because we have false expectations of him. But our ignorance does not diminish his love for us. Jesus keeps trying to help our wounded personalities to accept him as he really is, even when we feel frustrated.

Loving Father, help me accept your Son on his terms.

Prophets Are Truth-Sayers

Father Basil Cole, O.P.

Others were saying, "[Jesus] is Elijah"; still others,
"He is a prophet like any of the prophets."
(Mk 6: 15)

Well, not really, he is not like any of the prophets because Jesus is true God and true man. We are stamped with an indelible mark at baptism and confirmation which gives us a share in the prophetic office of Jesus. We exercise that office when we teach and defend this beautiful treasure called "the faith" or sometimes called "the deposit of the faith." Those of us who are theologians attempt to develop a deeper understanding of the faith with prayer, study, and penance. Even those who write hymns, poems, or paint and sculpt do something quite similar. We live a more hidden life behind books, and our cross is often our desk. This does not mean that theologians do not experience the joy of publishing or the delight of being illuminated by the gifts of the Holy Spirit. Like prayer itself, it has many dry hours. Sometimes we fail miserably by not defending the faith, evading it, or teaching contrary to it because we are fallible and weak, but think otherwise.

Before I ever went to kindergarten, my mother had already taught me many prayers, as my father belonged to no religion at that time of his life. The Church reminds us in her many documents that parents are the first proclaimers of the Gospel to their children. They hand on not merely ideas but divine knowledge about realities beyond reason and the senses. This divine knowledge is more certain than anything scientists can come up with. Parents' prophetic office is aided by the two sacraments of initiation and the grace which comes from holy matrimony. And this office lasts until the child leaves the nest, and continues throughout one's daily encounters.

The faith is in need of simple people reminding others that there is another world besides this one. We are not made for this life ultimately but for a better one that will eventually include even a new earth.

Father, give me clarity and conviction when I have to explain your revelation in Jesus Christ either to our loved ones, to the indifferent, or to our enemies.

We Want to Believe What We Desire

Father Basil Cole, O.P.

*But when Herod learned of it, he said, "It is John
whom I beheaded. He has been raised up."*
(Mk 6: 16)

Did Herod say this because he was mouthing the opinions of his people about Jesus? Perhaps he wanted to be "with it," or as was often said in the 1940s and 50s, "hip." When we are spiritually blind, we want to follow what "they say," perhaps the Gospel of what we hear on ABC, CBS, or NBC. No, John was not raised up physically. But Herod knew he would have to change. It is very important to remember that the very first words John proclaims are "Repent, for the kingdom of heaven is at hand!" (Mt 3: 2). But if Herod was not willing to do this with John, how could he be willing to listen to and believe in Jesus?

Yet, Jesus came to redeem and save even Herod. Redemption is not an idea. We were not redeemed by ideas, even if they came from God. We are saved by that divine person who became incarnate, that is, took a human nature unto himself and poured himself out in blood. He left us himself as our life in the Eucharist, as a model to imitate, and taught us many things beyond the scope of our weak intellects. Nevertheless, it was his Passion, death, and resurrection that formed the nature of our redemption.

Like Herod who killed John, Pontius Pilate also physically killed Jesus, together with the soldiers, the chief priests, and the Pharisees. But strangely, popular opinions got it wrong again, and were convinced he was dead! Today, many still think that he was crushed out of existence, and those of us who believe in the triumph of Christ are living in illusion. But to serve our King, Creator, and Redeemer is to reign with him. Washing dishes, cooking, or working at a firm which makes computers may not seem to be serving our King, but when done with love in our hearts and a sense of a personal vocation from him, yes we are!

Heavenly Father, teach me to revere and seek intimacy with your Son Jesus Christ as my Redeemer, and to be his servant and disciple.

To Hold a Grudge Is to Be Held Captive by It

Father Basil Cole, O.P.

Herod was the one who had John arrested and bound in prison on account of Herodias, the wife of his brother Philip, whom he had married. John had said to Herod, "It is not lawful for you to have your brother's wife." Herodias harbored a grudge against him and wanted to kill him but was unable to do so. (Mk 6: 17-19)

Grudges are the cause of a lot of families not getting along together. They are caused by real or seemingly unjust acts or speech on the part of another. When the situation is not remedied either by forgiveness or discussing misunderstandings, then bitterness sets in and this closes off all communication. This is the work of the grudge.

In the case of Herodias, she was both Herod's niece and his sister-in-law. Herod had married her, which was forbidden by divine law and even natural law. It is a form of an incestuous relationship. When John the Baptist then criticized Herod, both he and his wife harbored ill feelings toward John because he not only embarrassed them publicly, but also stirred up guilt feelings as well. As a result of this bitterness, Herodias had a strong desire to kill John. In some ways, grudges can not only be against the love of neighbor, but can also be anti-life. Only prayer and repentance can solve this problem.

I have met many people who were angry because their parents left them out of their will even though they stayed home to care for them. Sometimes they did not marry while the other siblings did very little to help them or their parents, yet received financial remuneration. Worse, the siblings refused to share the bounty with the ones who took care of their parents. This can lead to much bitterness unless the hurt person prays and prays and forgives.

In the case of Herod and Herodias, what they did was wrong, and instead of changing their lives, they refused. They are like those who hear the harder truths of the Gospel message but then close in on themselves and fight against the teachings of the Church, as if the pope or bishops or the local priest were the enemies of their lives. Sometimes we do not want to hear the truth of our lives because it challenges our own false image.

Father, let me not be ruled by resentment and bitterness when people turn against me or when someone corrects my shortcomings.

Do You Enjoy Homilies?

Father Basil Cole, O.P.

Herod feared John, knowing him to be a righteous and holy man, and kept him in custody. When he heard him speak he was very much perplexed, yet he liked to listen to him.

(Mk 6: 20)

"Oh, Father, that was a great sermon you gave yesterday. I liked it very much. We need to hear about that subject so much from the pulpit." How often I have heard such praise, but when I probed a little deeper, it made no real impact because some people love to hear homilies for the style of the preacher, the use of images, the voice, and even the content when it is well presented. A great homily is a work of beauty like the other arts. But for some reason, the homily stops there. The preacher's words cause delight but there are obstacles that his words cannot break through. This was Herod's problem.

John the Baptist presented a great image of strength and character, which appeals to most people since the inclinations or seeds of virtue are in all of us. But then, we have to make decisions about ourselves and try to take strategies of change in our lifestyle to conform ever more to what is truly right and virtuous. This Herod would not do because his moral problems were massive, though not definitive, as in the bad angels. We human beings, no matter what we do that is wrong, can change with the help of God's grace. We can re-make ourselves and return to the true image of God within us by turning to God in obedience.

Why did Herod fear John? And why do we sometimes fear good preachers? John had already exposed Herod's immorality and stirred his conscience. He probably feared John because, unlike most preachers, John spoke directly to his whole being, not just to his mind. In other words, he feared him because he could sense that John might know other areas in Herod's life that would need changing, which Herod was unwilling to give up. He didn't want any more guilt feelings because they were threats to his comfort zone.

Father, do not let me fear your Word when he exposes my selfishness and lack of love, and help me to do something about making a change.

Foolish Promises

Father Basil Cole, O.P.

[Herodias] had an opportunity one day when Herod, on his birthday, gave a banquet for his courtiers, his military officers, and the leading men of Galilee. Herodias's own daughter came in and performed a dance that delighted Herod and his guests. The king said to the girl, "Ask of me whatever you wish and I will grant it to you." He even swore [many things] to her, "I will grant you whatever you ask of me, even to half of my kingdom." (Mk 6: 21-23)

I once attended a troupe of Spanish flamenco dancers giving a concert in San Francisco. It was very beautiful, but I didn't want to give away anything to the dancers! It was just pure joy. Poor Herod must have had a great ego to exalt this child of his brother. He also wanted to show off his power to the guests attending the party by being able to give away some of his kingdom as well. What a fool!

Parents sometimes exaggerate the talents of their children, using them to reach goals they themselves could not achieve because of their own lack of talent or resources. Perhaps Herod was a frustrated dancer himself! Teachers today complain that when they give a low grade to their students or discipline them for disrupting class, parents no longer back them up but defend their children as if they were angels or geniuses or both.

The Gospel says Herod swore many things to the girl, traditionally called Salome. In this context, swearing does not mean using bad language but making unreasonable promises and even professing an oath or two. Herod certainly went overboard in this regard. Promising too much to children leads to grave disappointments, even if fulfilled in adolescence, because it raises high expectations for the unknown future. On the other hand, our Lord indubitably promised the joys of heaven beyond our ability to understand now, but we have to work to receive divine things now to get there at our end.

We have a tendency to promise many things to ourselves, family, and the world at large, which we are unable to fulfill. The original sin that we have inherited, and, if baptized, that has been wiped away, has its remaining residue of rebellion in our mind, will, and emotion. It takes a lifetime to forge great virtue. Character is the effect of hard work, but that work is a road to the bliss of heaven.

Heavenly Father, keep us from self-delusion and help us face ourselves as we really are so that we can be apostles of truth to others.

Blind and Really Dumb

Father Basil Cole, O.P.

[Herodias' daughter] went out and said to her mother, "What shall I ask for?" She replied, "The head of John the Baptist."
(Mk 6: 24)

Intellectual, athletic, or artistic abilities – such as being able to dance very well – are wonderful gifts from God. However, they do not necessarily mean someone has wisdom or holiness. Salome typifies those teenagers whom we could classify as utterly dense. She is so dependent on "Mommy," she cannot think or decide for herself. Perhaps Herodias made her excessively dependent on her every wish and whim as a mother. We see Salome does not even protest when her mother asks for the head of John. She is definitely not pro-life because she will be cooperating in the death of an innocent and holy human being. Like mother, like daughter.

Is Salome unaware of the horribly immoral request? Does she not know the fifth commandment? Maybe they are just words to her with no personal meaning. Perhaps when she learned them, they did not get to the inner recesses of her soul. One can kill people directly with a gun or indirectly by failing to do one's duty to protect life, and this girl together with her mother used a false promise to get John killed. Herodias must have convinced her daughter that John was a real enemy of the family. But was he?

Behind every negative divine command stands a positive aspect. In the case of the prohibition against killing innocent people, it is the great call to respect and reverence the image of God in everyone. While we cannot harm God in himself, we can injure gravely the mystical Christ united in many different ways to Jesus. In a private revelation, Saint Paul was told he was harming Jesus by killing early Christians. In a private revelation to Saint Margaret Mary Alacoque, Jesus wanted to be consoled by people praying before the Blessed Sacrament. Strictly taken, no one can console the risen Lord in himself, but we can bring consolation to his members by prayer.

Dear Father, help us to respect human life, even when it means we have to deal with the burdens of others and sacrifice ourselves for them.

Cruelty at Its Worst

Father Basil Cole, O.P.

*[Herodias' daughter] hurried back to the king's presence
and made her request, "I want you to give me at once on
a platter the head of John the Baptist."*
(Mk 6: 25)

It is interesting that Salome used the words "I want." She was in collusion with her mother on this issue. Complicity in evil is a terrible thing in contrast to collaboration in works of love and mercy. But why the emphasis on a platter? Platters are normally used to carry and serve food. As if the killing of John were not bad enough, now humiliating his person is worse, as if he were merely fodder or foodstuffs. Such public cruelty must have come from Satan's influence on Herodias and her daughter. And why did she not ask for more than the head of John? All we can do is speculate because the Scriptures do not give us an answer. But we can understand something of the meaning of cruelty. It is a desire to punish beyond what is reasonable. It goes so far as to take immense delight when inflicting punishment because the latter becomes an end in itself. Torture is like that as well. This is why our Lord was called "meek and gentle" of heart because he does not delight that people throw themselves into the torture of hell.

The daughter is also forcing the hand of Herod who bragged so much to her in the face of all his guests. She and her mother want Herod to share the evil of killing John, which he will do but, unlike themselves, with some reluctance. Reluctance however is not enough to change an immoral action to a moral one. It takes humility and gentleness to control one's judgments leading to harm. A king or anyone in charge of the common good of a country is supposed to be a protector of life, not its destroyer. So Herod lacked that self-possession which made him fear what his friends would say if he did not give in to Salome's requests. He was a people-pleaser rather than a God-pleaser.

*Wonderful Father, give us the grace to keep us gentle and humble
of heart lest we live rashly and so harm others.*

Unreasonable Promises, Evil Results

Father Basil Cole, O.P.

The king was deeply distressed, but because of his oaths and the guests he did not wish to break his word to [Herodias' daughter]. So he promptly dispatched an executioner with orders to bring back [John's] head. (Mk 6: 26-27a)

What kind of distress was Herod under? It was old-fashioned fear of displeasing others. We call that attitude giving in to "human respect." It is a false respect. Fear is a good emotion when it alerts us to dangers, bodily and spiritual. We try to escape from them. With bodily ills, we go to doctors and hospitals to get cured from minor or major illnesses. One of the gifts of the Holy Spirit is called fear of the Lord, which in this context means we love him so much that we fear our capacity to lose his friendship by our sins.

Then there is a wrongful fear based upon false loves and desires. We may love material things so much that we fear their slightest loss as a blow to our very being. In the case of Herod, as a braggart he feared the opinion of his guests in large part because he wanted affirmation from them. Braggarts love to exaggerate their talents and accomplishments. Ultimately this flows from a lack of self-worth and wanting others to affirm us excessively. This in turn comes from a lack of humility which leads to being unable to see and accept one's limitations calmly. From this inner mess, and contrary to the very nature of his being, Herod contradicted an obvious law of nature. He had John killed because he feared what people would say if he were not true to his promise to give Salome anything she wanted.

Often we are afraid of what others might think or say if we defend the teachings of the Church or of natural law. We know something is not right, but we keep it to ourselves rather than speaking out against it. This can happen with children or on the job when it is necessary to take a stand, but fear eats us up.

Dear Father in heaven, I want to remain always in your love and promise to keep to the way of meekness, as Jesus taught us, in my life.

Complicity in Action

Father Basil Cole, O.P.

[The executioner] went off and beheaded [John] in the prison.
He brought in the head on a platter and gave it to the girl.
The girl in turn gave it to her mother. (Mk 6: 27b-28)

Can you imagine how any teenager would feel seeing a person's head, still bleeding fresh from being executed, and holding the platter in her hands? It feels gruesome. What kind of a young girl is this? Why give it to her mother except to fulfill her cravings for revenge at the outspoken words of the holy preacher of God.

Let us look at the decapitated head in our meditation. John chose to speak the truth of life rather than obscure it to save Herod and Herodias both from themselves. In sticking to the plan of God, John allowed death to take him brutally rather than sacrifice truth. Obviously this defiance of John took great courage in contrast to the executioner, Herod, Herodias, and Salome. The martyr for truth loves life and hates death, but loves the truth that comes from God even more. He must have experienced great loneliness in his jail cell and was undoubtedly surprised that he would be killed so quickly without so much as a trial or the ability to defend himself. Why did not Herod at least go and speak with him and convince him that he needs to keep quiet about Herod's sin? Why not offer to bribe John and make promises as he did to Salome? He knew by a certain instinct that John was implacable. It would take more than that to change his mind.

It takes uncommon conviction to grasp what truly fulfills a person and what does not. Leadership in the family means there is no compromising on fundamental moral principles. Likewise, it is equally true in guiding a business properly so that a good product emerges and there is honesty about its quality. Above all, those who help make the product are to be treated with dignity and true justice. Day in and day out, one must adhere to what is right with the help of God.

My Father, may I live in your grace and do what you do from your very being and overcome all cowardice to do the right thing always.

Work of Mercy

Father Basil Cole, O.P.

When [John's] disciples heard about it, they came
and took his body and laid it in a tomb.
(Mk 6: 29)

Traditionally, one corporal work of mercy is burying the dead, usually in a sacred tomb. Why would this be so important? Because it shows a sign of reverence to the person created in the image of God, who was a bodily being informed by a spiritual principle called the soul. We also bury in order to honor the good works that the deceased did. That redounds to our benefit because it reminds us of the importance of doing good works for others and the glory of God. Finally, when a loved one dies, we need consolation, and this is afforded through the ritual of the Catholic Church, and such would have been similar for the disciples of John. We need reminding that the deceased's life is not completely over. Jesus has conquered death and given us hope that, at the end of time, we will also return back to life.

The Dominicans of the West have a wonderful custom of burying all of their dead in their beautiful cemetery of Benicia, California. When I am on vacation in the West, I visit that cemetery to pay my respects to my parents who are also buried there. Then I make the rounds of the Dominicans I knew, and pray for them. Old memories of my formative years come back to me. Even if a professor I did not care for is there, I pray for him too because I know he too tried his best to help me along.

Finally, funerals remind us of the fragility of life. God has a plan for all of us that can bring good out of the physical evil of death. We are not made ultimately for this world in its present condition. Yet, while we are definitively made for a life of eternal friendship and bliss with God, it will include a new earth and new heavens as well.

Heavenly Father, help us keep in mind that at some point our lives will end so that we may be aided in keeping you as our final destiny, and not the attractive things of this world.

Rest a While

Father Andrew Hofer, O.P.

The apostles gathered together with Jesus and reported all they had done and taught. He said to them, "Come away by yourselves to a deserted place and rest a while." People were coming and going in great numbers, and they had no opportunity even to eat. So they went off in the boat by themselves to a deserted place. (Mk 6: 30-32)

The most important thing in life is not hard work. But, for many of us, we too frequently measure others and ourselves simply by work. How much are *you* getting done today? The hours of our day come and go largely around a cycle of jobs to do; the same holds true for the days of the week, the weeks of the month, and the months of the year. Resting can seem like only a "necessary evil" – a temporary suspension of labor due to our own inadequacy to be able to work all the time.

Within his fast-paced account, Mark reports how the apostles go back to Jesus after they had been sent out with authority over unclean spirits. They preached repentance, drove out demons, and healed the sick. Jesus now invites the apostles to "rest a while." Mark suggests that this time of rest would allow the apostles to eat, since they were too busy even to take some food. But even more than eating, the Evangelist stresses that the rest is to be in a deserted place, a place to be alone together. It's a beautiful image. The apostles can have Jesus all to themselves.

Jesus invites us to share in that rest. Our commitment to prayer is not some distraction from the real work we ought to do. It's resting together with Jesus. As for me, I love to be able to rest in the presence of the Blessed Sacrament. The practice springs from my childhood. When I was a kid growing up on a Kansas farm, my mother would stop her work on Saturdays to take me to town so that I could get library books and we could make a brief visit in the church. Thinking back on that rest, I have learned a lesson. The most important thing in life is not hard work. It is to be together with Jesus.

Almighty Father, I give you thanks that your Son calls me to rest a while. Pour forth your Holy Spirit upon me so that my heart may always treasure that rest of being together with Christ.

Wait for the Lord

Father Andrew Hofer, O.P.

*People saw [Jesus and the apostles] leaving and
many came to know about it. They hastened there on foot
from all the towns and arrived at the place before them.*
(Mk 6: 33)

The people want what the apostles have: Jesus! Can you blame them? When they see the apostles sail off with Jesus, they run to the place where they know the boat will land. And so what must they do upon reaching that side of the sea? They wait.

There's a saying: "Hurry up and wait." It drives some people crazy. Why should you hurry just to wait around? But we know that people will hurry and wait when something important will occur and people need to be ready for that occurrence. For example, think of all those who hurry and wait for a sports event or a musical performance; they want to have their places ready before the athletes or musicians come out to begin playing.

We can imitate the people in the Gospel and hurry up and wait in the spiritual life for something very important. How so? Jesus will come. How do you think Jesus will come in your future? Where would you expect to find him? How will you be ready? If we give up on the coming of Christ, then there's no point to hurry for him, no point to wait for him. But Jesus will come, and he wants us to hurry and wait for him. That's also what happens at the end of Mark's Gospel. We find that the disciples are supposed to go to Galilee in order to see the risen Lord. In our lives, it may not necessarily be a physical movement, but a spiritual movement that is needed for us to experience the coming of the Lord. We can go to a place in our heart which is deserted, free from the entanglements of the world, where we expect Jesus will come, and wait for him there. We follow the Psalmist's own words: "Wait for the Lord, take courage;/ be stouthearted, wait for the Lord!" (Ps 27: 14).

Loving and merciful Father, let your Holy Spirit guide me so that I can hurry to a deserted place, free from sin, where Jesus will come. I will wait for him there.

Moved with Pity

Father Andrew Hofer, O.P.

When [Jesus] disembarked and saw the vast crowd, his heart was moved with pity for them, for they were like sheep without a shepherd; and he began to teach them many things.

(Mk 6: 34)

To attract the attention of many important people we must earn it. We want to outshine others in all sorts of ways, such as in job performance, financial assets, social skills, humor, intelligence, athletic ability, or various other talents. We have to be the best in order to have just the right someone take notice of us. Perhaps that would give us the edge we need to succeed in life.

When thinking of our spiritual lives, we may be tempted to apply that worldly model of earning attention to our relationship with the Lord. We may even think, "God will more likely look upon me with his favor if he sees how wonderful I am." But today's Gospel passage, like so many other depictions of Christ's action in the Gospel, gives a very different picture. Christ does not teach the people many things because they have proven themselves extremely bright and capable students with tremendous aptitude for future brilliance. No. He teaches them because they are like dumb sheep without anyone to care for them. They are pitiable and in need of his mercy.

It is this approach that we take for our prayer before the Lord, and especially when we come together in the Mass. The penitential rite at Mass allows us to place ourselves in the posture where the Lord will take notice of us, not because we're great, but because he is. At the beginning of the Holy Sacrifice, we don't recount for the Lord our past accomplishments. Rather, we attract him by asking for his mercy upon us who need it. At Mass, we are the vast crowd in great need for Christ to teach us many things. We come to know him not as the one who is simply our Judge, but our merciful Savior. His heart is moved with pity for us.

Heavenly Father, I give you praise that you have sent your Son to be my Savior. Fill me with his Holy Spirit so that I may know more deeply that his heart is moved with pity for me.

A Solution Half-Right

Father Andrew Hofer, O.P.

By now it was already late and [Jesus'] disciples approached him and said, "This is a deserted place and it is already very late. Dismiss them so that they can go to the surrounding farms and villages and buy themselves something to eat."
(Mk 6: 35-36)

D o you ever tell Jesus the solution for a problem you see? I do. I try to be very helpful to the Lord for lots of problems in the world. I inform him about what is wrong, and then I tell him what he should do and why he should take that course of action. I have a precedent for this kind of prayer. It's what the disciples do in this day's reading from Saint Mark's Gospel.

Jesus must have preached at great length that day, and perhaps behind the disciples' words lies even some implicit criticism against the Lord for preaching without being sensitive to the needs of the people: "Shouldn't he know that it's late and the people are hungry? Why does he keep talking to them? He should stop and tell them to go find something to eat for themselves." On the one hand, what the disciples do seems to make sense. They seem to be caring for the people, and they give a quite reasonable response to the need. On the other hand, the disciples have failed to understand the one who is teaching the people. As Saint Mark will soon tell us, Jesus already has a plan, a plan that shows how the disciples are wrong.

But could their solution be called half-right? The disciples go to the right person. They go to the Lord. He will take it from there in the Gospel, and he will take it from there in our lives. We can learn to make Christ's own prayer our own, leaving all things up to the divine control even after we have made our human intention: "Abba, Father, all things are possible to you. Take this cup away from me, but not what I will but what you will" (Mk 14: 36). It may seem already very late, but know that it's not too late for the Lord to act for what is best.

Most merciful Father, for some problems in the world it is already very late. Send your Holy Spirit upon me so that I may turn with confidence to Jesus, your beloved Son. He will not fail.

Do It Yourself

Father Andrew Hofer, O.P.

[Jesus] said to [his disciples] in reply, "Give them some food yourselves." But they said to him, "Are we to buy two hundred days' wages worth of food and give it to them to eat?"
(Mk 6: 37)

Jesus turns right back to the disciples after they tell him what to do. They want the people to be dismissed so the people can travel some distance and buy their own food. Jesus gives the disciples an order that seems absurd to them. The disciples seem to be thinking, "Huh? We can't give them food. We don't have that kind of money. That's an impossible task!" What we will find out is that the disciples will, in fact, give the entire crowd more than enough food. But they can't do it on their own. After they recognize their own insufficiency, they will be able to feed the great multitude. They will be the Lord's ministers, his servants, to the people he loves.

The lesson that the disciples learn is the lesson that I learn and re-learn. I'm called to serve God's people hungry for the Word of God. Jesus wants me to feed them, but I can't feed them on my own. I don't have the resources needed to satisfy hearts that yearn for the One who made them. God help me if I ever think that I can preach to people by myself! I can't do it. Yet, the Lord wants me as his preacher, and he will provide for his people.

All of us who are Christ's disciples are called to tasks that exceed our nature. We cannot do them on our own, and yet God wants us to do them. And so in his great compassion, God the Father sends the graces of the Holy Spirit upon us disciples not only to heal and elevate our own souls, but also to be of service within the Church. All disciples become servants at the disposal of God's almighty power that works not only for us, but through us. He works these mighty deeds through us this very day.

Heavenly Father, you have told me to do something that would be impossible without you. Send your Holy Spirit upon me that I may do it in the service of Christ.

Go and See

Father Andrew Hofer, O.P.

[Jesus] asked [his disciples], "How many loaves do you have?
Go and see." And when they had found out they said,
"Five loaves and two fish." (Mk 6: 38)

"Go and see." Jesus wants his disciples to go and see how much bread they have on hand for the crowd of five thousand men. They find only five loaves, and so perhaps because they find so little bread they also report what else they could scrounge up: two fish. When we hear, "Five loaves and two fish," we immediately think of Christ's miraculous feeding. But put yourself in the position of those disciples who are reporting back. Five loaves and two fish must have appeared pathetic to them. I can imagine the courage it took from the disciples to present so little to Jesus for such a great need. I can also imagine Jesus surprising the disciples by being pleased at such an offering given to him. The offering, pathetic in itself, will turn into a bountiful feast. This miracle will not only change the loaves and fish, it will also change the disciples, from being dejected at offering something so pathetic to being joyfully amazed at what Jesus does.

Now think of something in your life where there's a tremendous need. Jesus wants you to "go and see" just what you have. When I think of the need in my life and what I really have, I become dejected. What little I have is really pathetic. "Go and see" becomes an examination of conscience for me, and I find myself wanting. At times I lack the courage to present to the Lord what little I have. What use is it? But Jesus can work with whatever we bring to him. For example, if he's asking us to go and see what we have for love, we may find that we don't have much love – but we'll bring to him what little love we have, and we'll throw in a little faith, too. He will work miracles.

Mighty and wonderful Father, fill me with your Spirit's gift of courage so that I may bring to the Lord Jesus what little I have in my life.

Satisfied

Father Andrew Hofer, O.P.

So [Jesus] gave orders to have them sit down in groups on the green grass. The people took their places in rows by hundreds and by fifties. Then, taking the five loaves and the two fish and looking up to heaven, he said the blessing, broke the loaves, and gave them to [his] disciples to set before the people; he also divided the two fish among them all. They all ate and were satisfied. (Mk 6: 39-42)

Why does the Lord Jesus work this miracle? The most basic reason should not be forgotten: people are hungry. There's a real need. If people didn't need food, Christ wouldn't have performed this miracle. Could he have blessed the people so that they would not be hungry? Yes, he could have, but something would be missing in their participation, their experience of God's wondrous works. In his loving compassion, Christ uses the littleness of what the disciples have, only five loaves and two fish, to show the greatness of grace. He also uses the disciples to set the miraculous meal before the people. He graces the ordinary to be extraordinary. After the blessing, breaking, and distributing there is enough to satisfy all. The people cannot mistake their eating for some sort of hallucination. A full belly testifies to the Lord's generosity, and gives cause for them to praise.

This miracle shows us the beauty of the Holy Eucharist. Christ gives us himself because we are hungry. We have a real need. If we didn't need Christ, he would not have given himself to us. We need him. Could he just enter our souls without the sacramental use of bread and wine? Yes. But he wants to use the littleness of creation to show the greatness of his grace. Ritual actions make present the actions of the Last Supper, foreshadowed by this Gospel account of the multiplication. Christ wants to show in the Eucharist's blessing, breaking, and distributing that there is enough for all, enough for the multitudes of "every nation, race, people, and tongue" (Rv 7: 9). When my soul is hungry, I know that the Lord continues to work a miracle of love for me in the Holy Eucharist. He alone satisfies my inmost being, and I pray that my soul may be so full as to proclaim the greatness of the Lord.

Loving Lord God, let your Holy Spirit inspire me today to tell the world that Jesus is the joy of my heart.

Wasting Nothing

Father Andrew Hofer, O.P.

*And [the disciples] picked up twelve wicker baskets full
of fragments and what was left of the fish. Those who ate
[of the loaves] were five thousand men. (Mk 6: 43-44)*

I hate to have anything go to waste. I abhor, in particular, throwing good food in the garbage after a meal. Food is always a sign of God's generosity, even if you do the work of growing it, cooking it, and serving it. In the prayer before meals, we ask for God's blessing upon both us *and* our food. Food becomes an occasion of grace. Excess food thus not only reminds us of the grace of God at the meal, it will be available to feed the hungry later!

After the multiplication of loaves and fish, the disciples pick up the extra bread and fish. These leftovers from the feeding of five thousand men far exceeded the original amount of five loaves and two fish, and they testify to God's sustaining power. The disciples who ate the bread and fish after that miracle would have surely recalled what had happened, and their subsequent hunger would again be satisfied.

This can help us understand about wasting not only food but God's action in our lives. When God acts in our lives, there's always a remainder. Something continues after the event. We could throw that away by forgetting about it, or we could be in contact with that to remind us of God's action in the past. It would also sustain us again when our spiritual hunger is aroused. For example, when we pray the Mass, God feeds us in ways that exceed our capacity at that time. After the Mass, we could just forget about what we heard and experienced at that Mass – or we could keep what remains in our memory. Deep inside of us is a spiritual tabernacle where we remember what Christ did for us at the Mass. No one can remember all the details of a Mass, but think back on what fragments remain with you. Keep them in your spiritual tabernacle. They will be available to feed the hungry later.

Almighty Father, I thank you for the spiritual bounty that you give. Pour down your Spirit upon me so that I may save the fragments of your action in my life. I ask this in the name of Jesus.

The Loneliness of Prayer

Father Anthony Giambrone, O.P.

Then [Jesus] made his disciples get into the boat and precede him to the other side toward Bethsaida, while he dismissed the crowd. And when he had taken leave of them, he went off to the mountain to pray. (Mk 6: 45-46)

A s Mark informs us, Jesus chooses the Twelve precisely "to be with him" (Mk 3: 14); yet there is evidently a line of intimacy that their apprenticeship does not cross. The Lord reserves his *prayer* as a profoundly private mystery: a mode of his incarnation with no pass of privileged access. It is the Son's secret spot of commerce with the Father.

Jesus' habit of solitary prayer has a special place in Mark's description. It appears as the programmatic conclusion to Jesus' famous first day in Capernaum (Mk 1: 35). The Lord retires for a moment from his ministry to be alone in a desert place and pray. With this bent for prayer in seclusion, it is no accident that this Gospel never records the Our Father or Christ addressing his High Priestly Prayer. In the Markan revelation, Gethsemane is the only glimpse of Jesus' interior prayer – and what a glimpse! We, who might imagine his contemplation as pure consolation, must behold the terrible truth of a Son who could collapse under the stern face of the Father, who could knock and *not* have the door opened.

Whether or not Christ agonized here on the mountain is impossible to say. The beheading of John was just recounted (Mk 6: 14-29), and the prospect of a similar fate must have pressed on Jesus' spirit. Regardless, the lesson Mark's Christ teaches here concerns content more than company. Prayer is solitude with God; it is *a retreat from the demands of living and an acknowledgment of the humanly incommunicable.* Even when the Lord invites Peter, James, and John to "be with him" in the garden, he finds himself more alone than ever. In this sense, profound loneliness surrounds the experience of prayer. If our prayer is thus made on the master's model, we will know and even court this grim solitude; we will seek the Father in that unutterable place where no one understands us.

Father in heaven, we do not know how to pray as we ought. Teach me to seek you in silence and groan in the Spirit. May I find you in my loneliness and so sanctify my solitude.

Rowing against the Wind

Father Anthony Giambrone, O.P.

When it was evening, the boat was far out on the sea and [Jesus] was alone on shore. Then he saw that [his disciples] were tossed about while rowing, for the wind was against them. About the fourth watch of the night, he came toward them walking on the sea. He meant to pass by them. (Mk 6: 47-48)

If Jesus' buoyant behavior appears to be a rescue mission to save his sea-tossed friends, the final short sentence puts an end to such illusions. The Lord means to walk right past them. This is a curious fact when we consider the disciples' evident distress and the *compassion* Jesus just showed for the crowds. What, then, is the meaning of this miracle on the water? Is Jesus intent only on efficient transportation?

The revelation of his desire to slip past the disciples (a detail found only in Mark) allows us to glimpse a private sphere of Christ's experience. It seems to be almost *an accident* (were that possible) that he is caught in this marvelous maneuver, and we are certainly meant to wonder what else he is hiding. "Who is this man?" As at the theophany of Tabor, the curtain is momentarily pulled back on the subtlety of Jesus' glorified form, and we perceive that this human body – by day content to plod along in clumsy wooden boats – is, in fact, veiling some vast secret. Christ's epiphany over the waters, therefore, is not classed as a mere "mighty deed" fitted to the narrow dimensions of human need; it is a free and radiant burst of divine splendor.

It is not uncommon in our experience to find ourselves rowing against the wind. In such moments, faced with some stern and stubborn opposition, we can often perceive the Lord almost blithely ignoring us, as though he were content coldly to leave us to our own meager forces. When our desperate prayers hit an iron heaven, however, and we labor fruitlessly against the wind, we are graced to behold God's sovereign freedom, serenely unperturbed by the gusts and gales we fear. Our salvation then is to recall his proven compassion, take comfort he has seen our plight, and worship this wondrous Lord, who hides a might far greater than our perilous, rocking boat.

Father in heaven, help me worship your marvelous glory and see beyond my problems. When I am oppressed and failing, let me remember your compassion and bow before your wisdom.

The Holy Ghost

Father Anthony Giambrone, O.P.

But when [the disciples] saw [Jesus] walking on the sea, they thought it was a ghost and cried out. They had all seen him and were terrified. But at once he spoke with them, "Take courage, it is I, do not be afraid!" (Mk 6: 49-50)

It is quite possible to mistake Jesus for a ghost: a half-real threat from stories we've heard about which we've not made up our minds. Does a crucified and resurrected Lord really exist? Have we ever actually seen him? Or have we just been taken in by a lot of campfire tales at Sunday school – spooked by fear of the fire of hell?

The image of God as a great boogeyman is common enough. In his little book *The Pilgrim's Regress*, C.S. Lewis records the (auto-biographical) story of a boy in "Puritania" fed on ghastly tales of an unseen "Landlord" who enforced his countless rules with the awful threat of the "Black Hole." With such an unsavory picture of God, it is understandable that folks might be unwilling to grant his existence.

The truth, of course, is that we've made the monster; and the Lord's words here help shatter the illusion. "Take courage, it is I, do not be afraid!" The Lord dispels fear. His identity puts it to flight. Ghosts and landlords have no interest in losing their edge of fear; they have no hope of winning our love. The sign of the true God, in contrast, is that *he weans us from our fears; for he is confident that to know him is to love him.* This indeed is the mark of coming to see God as he is: when our servile fear gives way to holy awe.

There is, it is true, a kind of terror that sin and judgment should inspire; but hearing the Lord pronounce "Take courage" should reveal his true intention. "God did not send his Son into the world to condemn the world, but that the world might be saved through him" (Jn 3: 17). May we remember this truth whenever we fear to follow the way of Christ. He is not a shade leading down to Sheol, but the risen Lord who shows us the path to life.

Father in heaven, save me from servile fear and cast out every false image of your being. Help me to see you as you are, and so know you as to love you.

Breaking Through to Hard Hearts

Father Anthony Giambrone, O.P.

[Jesus] got into the boat with [his disciples] and the wind died down. They were [completely] astounded. They had not understood the incident of the loaves. On the contrary, their hearts were hardened. (Mk 6: 51-52)

Hardheartedness is a harsh way to describe a lack of understanding. It is striking, however, that there is no word of reaction following the miracle of the loaves. The wake of enthusiasm that typically trails behind Jesus on this occasion, incredibly, leaves no record. It will be worse after the repeat performance (Mk 8: 1-10), when Jesus himself will complain: "Do you not yet understand or comprehend? Are your hearts hardened? Do you have eyes and not see, ears and not hear?" (Mk 8: 17-18). If impatience with the disciples' blindness is a theme in Mark's Gospel, it raises a basic question. Why did the disciples fail to profit from such miracles and perceive Jesus' true identity? There is a mystery of human dullness here, as much as a mystery of divine epiphany.

The disciples themselves were, of course, highly engaged in "the incident of the loaves." It was they who noted the crowd's need to eat, they who supplied Jesus with the bread and fish, they who distributed the food to the people, and they who gathered up the fragments. It would be wrong simply to psychologize the disciples' hard hearts – an inscrutable divine action is at work here. Still, we might imagine that the disciples' very instrumentality somehow clouded their eyes. Mighty deeds in which we play no part somehow strike us as more mighty. This explains why the gratuitous apparition on the water produced such sudden astonishment. There was no deceptive mixture of things human and divine.

Jesus' words, "Give them some food yourselves" (Mk 6: 37), give a humble cover to his miraculous intervention. We must wonder how often the Lord so mutes his omnipotence under our agency. Can our spiritual eyes discern his compassion intertwined with a series of natural causes? Or are our hearts so hard that we must see the Lord walking on water before we are ready to believe him?

Father in heaven, replace our hearts of stone and give us the hearts of flesh you have promised. Open my eyes to see the wonder of your goodness in every hidden act of your compassion.

Holy Shamelessness

Father Anthony Giambrone, O.P.

*After making the crossing, [Jesus and his disciples] came to land
at Gennesaret and tied up there. As they were leaving the boat,
people immediately recognized him. They scurried about the
surrounding country and began to bring in the sick on mats
to wherever they heard he was. (Mk 6: 53-55)*

Jesus moves about in a cloud of commotion. He is a center of
activity, yet there is nothing of the celestial rose in his circle.
The human halo that surrounds the incarnate Son is a scut-
tling mass of busybodies and invalids.

That the King Christ should travel in such an entourage is in-
dicative. It reveals the precise crowd of courtiers he chose: a band
of shameless beggars. We might prefer more semblance of deco-
rum, an honor guard less ill-mannered, contagious, and pushy.
The Lord's dignity suffers no slight, however, from the needy company he keeps. After all, the truth is that in the presence of this
man, all the world is a hanger-on and a beggar. He who made himself a little while lower than the angels has by right the ceaseless
worship of the seraphim, the praise of all nine choirs. For such a
Lord to walk in this world of mortal clay is to clothe himself with
rags. What would it do to clamor here after the paltry trappings of
human glory?

To see Jesus wearing this humble corona should stir our hearts
and show us the unimaginable favor God holds for the human
race. The Letter to the Hebrews says we ought confidently to draw
near to the throne of grace to receive help in time of need (Heb 4:
16). How undeterred we should be by protocol! It is not that we
should bear no sense for the divine majesty. As Teresa of Ávila
(and others) said, we should give the Lord at least the respect due
any human potentate. All the same, we must not let that swell our
own sense of importance. No, we should take an example from the
humble people in this passage: *recognize* Jesus as our hope and salvation, then hound and harry him with importunate supplication,
lugging our maladies on mats and piling into his presence every
ugly thing that infects us.

*Father, give me a holy shamelessness. Let me never dress up my
sicknesses or posture in false dignity. Reproduce in me your Son's
humble neglect of self-importance, so that I may abide in his
company.*

Touching His Tassels

Father Anthony Giambrone, O.P.

*Whatever villages or towns or countryside [Jesus] entered,
[the people] laid the sick in the marketplaces and begged him
that they might touch only the tassel on his cloak; and as many
as touched it were healed. (Mk 6: 56)*

A poverty of our time is to live in a disenchanted age. Christian affectivity is a major casualty, and one cannot help but lament other side-effects of living in a demythologized world like ours. Yet how worthy of an Arthurian romance is this tassel of Christ's cloak! It is like Longinus' Bleeding Spear, a mysterious relic radiating power, well worthy of having a history all its own. It is fit to be the garment made to heal the Fisher King.

Obviously, indulging such fantasy is embarrassingly foreign, and folks might whisper about feeble-minded *poesis*. It is the product of a thoroughly Catholic sensibility, however; and the health of our devotion might be helpfully measured by our comfort with a charged world of healing mantles. Perhaps we are too reserved and self-conscious to imagine reaching out for the Lord's tassels. Perhaps our divinity is more "spiritual," asking only movements of the heart. We might take our temperature thus: Do sacramentals have a real dignity in our estimation, or is it pious and kitschy claptrap for those void of taste? Make no mistake: sacraments are not spells, and superstition is a sin; but a little dose of magic fires the imagination and amplifies our grasp of the incarnation. The eternal Son has assumed matter as his instrument. There is henceforth a depth and destiny to this messy world of things that is never exhausted by knowing its chemical compounds.

The tactile impulse has been grievously blunted in the West. Our digitized world has sublimated everything from money to music into disembodied vapors, shades of the concrete *realia*. Yet the Word became man to come *touch* us. He used stuff like mud and spittle to make us feel how close he really is. In devotionals, his tassels still dangle around us. May we never be too proud to clamber and cling even to the humblest vestige of this God come in the flesh.

*Heavenly Father, confirm my faith in the scandal of the incarnation.
Help me grasp for you in the nearness of your presence. Give me the
grace to reach out, to grab you and be healed.*

Unwashed Hands

Anthony Esolen

Now when the Pharisees with some scribes who had come from Jerusalem gathered around [Jesus], they observed that some of his disciples ate their meals with unclean, that is, unwashed, hands. (Mk 7: 1-2)

I have never quite known on what side of the plate the fork and spoon go, and at a restaurant I can hardly remember to spread the napkin out on my lap. I am, you might say, challenged by etiquette, and many a social convention leaves me simply confused.

The scribes and Pharisees here come from Jerusalem, that great city, the center of Jewish worship. What do they find but a ragtag band of disciples from the backcountry, who apparently do not know any better than to begin eating with unwashed hands. We can't tell for certain why they are doing so. Perhaps they were hungry, and there was no water nearby.

Whatever the reason, their hands are not clean, and in the minds of the Pharisees, that uncleanness seems to suggest irreverence toward God. But there is another way to look at it. Before we approach the sanctuary to receive the Holy Eucharist, we acknowledge, in effect, that our hands are not clean. We repeat the words of the centurion, saying, "Lord, I am not worthy that you should enter under my roof." We place ourselves in the position of the tax collector in Jesus' parable, who stood at the back of the temple with his unclean life, pleading, "Lord, have mercy on me, a sinner." Or with the thief who was crucified at Jesus' side, who acknowledged his guilt, and begged the Lord to receive him into his kingdom.

It is not that Jesus is content that we remain unclean. Indeed he commands us to be holy, even as the Father is holy. But he comes to meet us in our weakness. He lays upon us none of the burdens of trying to appear what we are not. Rather, he seeks to reveal to us our own hearts, beneath all appearances. In this lies our great hope. For whose hands are clean before the Lord?

Father, give us the confidence to approach you as we are, for only you can cleanse us of our sins, through Jesus Christ, in whose blood we are made clean.

Not by Tradition

Anthony Esolen

(For the Pharisees and, in fact, all Jews, do not eat without carefully washing their hands, keeping the tradition of the elders. And on coming from the marketplace they do not eat without purifying themselves. And there are many other things that they have traditionally observed, the purification of cups and jugs and kettles [and beds].) (Mk 7: 3-4)

The Pharisees, Saint Mark tells us, kept "the tradition of the elders," washing their hands, purifying themselves when they came from the marketplace, and cleansing "cups and jugs and kettles." And I am afraid I have some sympathy for the Pharisees. That is not because they practiced a cleanliness that must have protected them against disease. Nor because, in their rites of purification, they paid respect – or perhaps were supposed to pay respect – to the holiness and purity of God.

No, I must confess that I am a traditionalist at heart. I believe that in the preserving of tradition, one gives grateful honor to one's forebears, and partakes in a culture that both spans and transcends the generations. It's what Chesterton called "the democracy of the dead," whereby we give a vote, so to speak, to people who are no longer with us. And it would be far too simplistic to see in Jesus a rebel against tradition. He celebrated the Jewish feasts with solemnity and gratitude. He knew the Jewish scriptures through and through – and when he was but twelve years old, he delivered his learned opinions about them to the rabbis in the temple.

What is the trouble, then? I think there is a subtle danger to being a traditionalist, one that in a strange way approaches the danger of rebellion. It is that we will come to esteem ourselves for our dutiful habits, and will thus replace gratitude with pride. This pride is all the more poisonous as it is masked by religious devotion. "We at Saint Joseph's celebrate benediction on the feast of Corpus Christi" – nothing wrong with that; everything *right* with it, until it is tainted and spoiled by the sense of personal superiority. Instead of submitting ourselves to tradition, we subordinate tradition to ourselves, using it to parade our own righteousness and wisdom.

Father in heaven, give us always the wisdom to accept in humility what your Church has handed on to us, that we may be faithful stewards, small in our own sight, through Jesus Christ, our Lord.

The Light of the Holy

Anthony Esolen

So the Pharisees and scribes questioned [Jesus], "Why do your disciples not follow the tradition of the elders but instead eat a meal with unclean hands?" (Mk 7: 5)

The Pharisees approach Jesus, Saint Mark says, to ask him why his disciples do not "follow the tradition of the elders but instead eat a meal with unclean hands." Their question might well stand as the most irrelevant in the history of the world. For let us consider the situation. They have before them the Anointed One, the long awaited Messiah of God. He has been traveling the length of Palestine, making the blind to see and the deaf to hear, healing the lame and the crippled, and preaching the kingdom of God to a people in captivity. He is the image of the Father, from whose will he never swerves. He is, whether people nowadays care to admit it or not, the man who has come to change history for ever. And what do the Pharisees ask? Why his disciples do not wash their hands before eating.

How strange is our blindness to the holy! We think that the holy should present us with an experience of overwhelming light and goodness, unmistakable and irresistible; but we forget the darkness of our hearts, and our desire to duck and skulk and hide. We want only so much light as will comfort us, without shedding its terrible glare upon our sins. We want only so much goodness as will not challenge us to abandon our old ways and give ourselves up to God. The saints are the most beautiful witnesses to the truth of the Christian faith; and for that very reason they are slandered, as Father Damien of Moloka'i was, and as Mother Teresa, of all people, has recently been; or they are cast out of polite society, or put to death. If that is true of the saints, how much more so Christ, the ultimate sign of contradiction? The Pharisees have the light of the world before them, and they blink.

Father, shed your light upon us and grant us the grace that we may seek that light always, proceeding from light into light, through Jesus Christ our Lord and Savior.

Where Are Our Hearts?

Anthony Esolen

[Jesus] responded, "Well did Isaiah prophesy about you hypocrites, as it is written:/ 'This people honors me with their lips,/ but their hearts are far from me;/ In vain do they worship me,/ teaching as doctrines human precepts.'/ You disregard God's commandment but cling to human tradition." (Mk 7: 6-8)

"This people honors me with their lips," Jesus says, quoting the prophet Isaiah, "but their hearts are far from me." That is something that warrants close examination. It is one thing to be the kind of hypocrite who does not believe what he says, but who dons the robe of righteousness to please or to fool his neighbors. But I wonder whether that is the hypocrisy Jesus is accusing the Pharisees of here. For the "heart" of a human being is mysterious to us; it is his core, the central essence of who he is. We cannot even depend upon knowing our own hearts. We talk much, but talk is cheap. We pray, but allow our prayers to settle into a comfortable feeling of devotion, of being all right with God, with nothing crying out for change. We assume that if we were alive in the days of the Roman martyrs, we too would have gone to the arena to face the wild animals, or to be burnt alive; yet when Jesus calls upon us to give up our least comfort – to go beyond our habits, say, and to approach the beggar in the shantytown by the railroad tracks – we blanch.

God is closer to us than we are to ourselves. We know our lips; we hear from them all the time. We do not know our hearts, but God does. That means that we run the risk of being no better than the Pharisees. We can reduce devotion to God to the practice of certain human habits – perfectly reasonable and upstanding habits, but human no less. We must instead stop ourselves, even amid our prayers, and ask, "Where is my heart?" That might mean that we cease to move our lips for a while, so that we can hear the promptings of God once again.

Father, grant us a teachable spirit, so that we may never mistake human precepts for your commands, and so that our hearts will rest in your will alone, through Jesus Christ our Lord and our Teacher.

Honor Thy Father and Thy Mother

Anthony Esolen

[Jesus] went on to say, "How well you have set aside the commandment of God in order to uphold your tradition! For Moses said, 'Honor your father and your mother,' and 'Whoever curses father or mother shall die.' Yet you say, 'If a person says to father or mother, "Any support you might have had from me is qorban"'" (meaning, dedicated to God), you allow him to do nothing more for his father or mother." (Mk 7: 9-12)

Jesus looks with disdain upon a practice of his time: a son would wriggle out from under his responsibility to support his aging parents, by declaring that anything they might receive from him was *qorban,* or dedicated to God. And the leaders of the synagogue would look aside.

Now that would violate the commandment of God, delivered to the Hebrew people by Moses: "Honor your father and your mother." But the sin is more complicated than we might at first suppose. When we look at the ten commandments, we see that the commandment to honor our parents stands between the commandments that reveal our duty to God, and the commandments that forbid wickedness against our neighbor. That is fitting, since our parents are a kind of bridge between God and neighbor. From our parents we first learn to pray; many a saint's heart has been formed by the piety of father and mother, kneeling before the holy cross. From our parents too we first learn to render justice and kindness to those around us; we learn the value of honest labor; we learn what it means to live in community. So it is that the commandment faces in two directions. If we are hardhearted to our parents, how likely is it that we will welcome the poor and the sinful into our midst? And if we do not recognize our parents as givers of law, how likely is it that we will respect the law of God?

So the people of Jesus' time who sought to protect their assets were not just sinning against their parents. They were sinning against the very authority of God, whence derives the authority of father and mother. It is as absurd as if one were to curse one's father in the name of the Father. All of which may explain the severity of Jesus' rebuke.

Father, soften our hearts toward those who brought us into the world, and who reflected your goodness by their love for us and their labors on our behalf, that we and they may give you glory together, through Jesus, the Son in whom you are well pleased.

The Purity That Counts

Anthony Esolen

[Jesus] summoned the crowd again and said to them, "Hear me, all of you, and understand. Nothing that enters one from outside can defile that person; but the things that come out from within are what defile." (Mk 7: 14-15)

"Nothing that enters one from outside," says Jesus to the crowds overhearing his confrontation with the Pharisees, "can defile that person." Rather it is the things that come out from within us that defile. What does he mean?

When I was a boy I took a veritable pride in how black my ankles and elbows got, from playing ball on a dusty sandlot, or clambering over hills of coal and shale in my Pennsylvania town. "You have to eat a peck of dirt before you die," my father used to say, and I did my best to bear out that wisdom. No shame in that. All of God's creation is good, from the skies vaulting above our heads to the black earth beneath our feet. Many were the ways in which the pious Jew following the law of Moses could incur ritual impurity; touching a corpse was a sign that one had brushed against the mystery of death, over which God alone had supreme authority. But Jesus is concerned not with the sign but with the reality. He does not care about the blackness of ankles and elbows. He wants more than the signs of purity. He wants the real thing.

It's a lesson we don't find easy to learn. For we extend the category of "unclean" to include not only objects but people too. The saddest examples are the so-called untouchables of India. They suffer under the caste system of Hinduism, but there is something of that disdain for the "unclean" in the Pharisees also. Behind their condemnation of Jesus' disciples lies a condemnation of Jesus, as if he were defined by merely touching and eating with such sinners. It does not occur to them that they too are sinners. They too come to the table with smudged souls. And Jesus will break bread with them too, if they would but welcome him.

Father, in whose presence nothing impure can stand, cleanse us of our impurities, that we may enter the wedding feast well-dressed, and celebrate the banquet of your Son the Lamb, through the same Jesus Christ our Lord.

The Friends of Jesus

Anthony Esolen

When [Jesus] got home away from the crowd his disciples
questioned him about the parable. He said to them,
"Are even you likewise without understanding?"
(Mk 7: 17-18a)

When the disciples ask Jesus what he means, that nothing that enters a man from without can defile him, the Lord turns to them with real disappointment. How can they have spent so much time with him, and yet still be so slow to understand?

Jesus is a man on fire. His entire being is filled with the urgency of his message, the news that the kingdom of God is at hand. He comes not to abolish Moses and the prophets, but to fulfill them, by instilling in the hearts of his followers the law of love. And his own love was so profound that he would suffer death for his enemies, even death upon a cross. Yet what did he encounter, in his three years of traveling and preaching in Galilee and Judea? Throngs of people brought him their sick, that he might cure them; but we are never told how many sought him out, that his words might heal their souls.

In his humanity Jesus turned to others for friendship, but he seems never to have known the pleasure of standing beside someone who would catch his meaning, whose thoughts would be his. Peter tries to persuade him not to go up to Jerusalem. James and John jockey for positions of honor in the kingdom. Philip asks him to show them the Father. The disciples rebuke the women who try to present him with their children, to be blessed. Before the descent of the Holy Spirit at Pentecost, there seems to be not the slightest hint that the apostles themselves really understood the Lord with whom they had walked for so long, and spoken, and broken bread. I am not sure if there is a patron saint for the lonely. If not, there is Jesus, all the lonelier in that he is consumed with love for us, who understand him but a little, and often turn away.

Father, send forth your Spirit upon us, to kindle in our hearts a conflagration of love for your Son, that we may overcome the solitude of sin, through the same Christ, our Lord.

Food for the Heart

Anthony Esolen

"Do you not realize that everything that goes into a person from outside cannot defile, since it enters not the heart but the stomach and passes out into the latrine?" (Thus [Jesus] declared all foods clean.) (Mk 7: 18b-19)

What woman would consider herself flattered by a man who said, "I love you with all my intellect," or "My stomach and my appetites are wholly yours"? Rather what she wants to hear – or not, as the case may be! – is, "I love you with all my heart."

When we say so, we do not mean, "I love you with that part of my body that pumps blood to all my organs." We mean instead to call upon everything we are, at the profoundest core of our beings. The heart refers not simply to what we think, or even to what we desire, but to what makes us ourselves. In giving our hearts, we give our all. It is a complete surrender in love.

So when Jesus says that when we eat, the food enters our stomachs but not our heart, he is distinguishing between the superficial and the central. For the food, whatever it may be, enters us but does not enter *us*. It does not touch us at the core. Therefore it cannot render us unclean. And thus, in one magnificent gesture, showing forth his authority as Lord and teacher, Jesus, says Saint Mark, "declared all foods clean," much to the chagrin of the Pharisees, who wished to prove their own cleanness, and the uncleanness of others, by their hewing to the dietary laws of Moses.

But perhaps I have spoken too quickly. There is one food that is meant to enter our hearts. Jesus himself provides, and is, that food: it is the bread of the angels, the Eucharist. Under the old law a man might render himself unclean by eating the wrong thing – meat mingled with blood, for instance. But the Eucharist is that food which purifies the sinner who consumes it reverently, praying that it will indeed enter under his roof, and heal his soul.

Father, create in us a clean heart, and renew a right spirit within us, that we may give our hearts entirely to you, loving you with all that we are, through Christ our Lord.

Dust upon the Heart

Anthony Esolen

"But what comes out of a person, that is what defiles. From within people, from their hearts, come evil thoughts, unchastity, theft, murder, adultery, greed, malice, deceit, licentiousness, envy, blasphemy, arrogance, folly. All these evils come from within and they defile." (Mk 7: 20-23)

What a catalogue of evils Jesus enumerates here! Nor does he simply name evil deeds, such as theft and adultery and murder. As always, Jesus searches the heart. He reminds us of the breach between our outward actions and our inward dispositions. For from the heart come not only deeds but the principal motives of our deeds: such dispositions as greed, malice, envy, and arrogance.

All these are the evils that defile us, says Jesus. And this warrants a closer look. If I am a reaper harvesting the grain, I may be covered with dust and straw and grimy sweat after a day's labor in the fields. Then I can wash, and make myself clean. But if I steal a sack of my neighbor's grain, what can I do? Even if I restore it twice over, I still may not be able to repair the broken trust between us. And I have stood as an example for others, that they might go and steal in turn. If I commit adultery, breaking my vow to keep myself only for my wife, even if I promise never to commit the sin again, and even if she accepts the promise, the shadow of the deed will come between us.

What is true of deeds is truer still of dispositions. If I have allowed greed to harbor in my heart, what single thing can I do to make things right again? If I have given myself up to blasphemy, what words can I utter to cleanse myself of the defilement? If I am arrogant, will one hour upon my knees heal me? It would take a renewal of my heart – a conversion, a turning to the Lord with my whole being. Jesus is calling the people to just such a turning. That, while they are worrying about dusty hands.

Father, search my heart and all my soul, and heal every unsound spot within me, that your Spirit may have a pure temple wherein to dwell, through Jesus Christ, our Lord.

The Desire for Solitude

Father Basil Cole, O.P.

From that place [Jesus] went off to the district of Tyre.
He entered a house and wanted no one to know about it,
but he could not escape notice. (Mk 7: 24)

Today's iPods, cell phones, e-mail, and the internet makes being alone difficult. They are the new noise of our times. Yet being alone from time to time is essential for growing in the spiritual life. Too much talking, chatting, texting, viewing pictures, makes intense thinking and praying very difficult because these activities require silence. This is not to say that modern means of communication are evil, but excessive use of them is not helpful either for the spiritual life. To be able to think through to a solution of a problem cannot be done with noise. Solitude is a great help for this kind of activity, but it too is not the be-all and end-all of the spiritual life either. It is rather an important means for growing in meditation and contemplation. It makes for great preachers and teachers.

Jesus wanted to be alone. But he was now in Phoenicia, Gentile territory. Nevertheless, needy people found him. He did not simply disappear but gave them his time and talent to help them grow into the life of virtue. Even priests and religious, if not parents themselves, often have to leave aside their sweet times of prayer and study to minister to the needs of others, or they betray their vocation to love their neighbors or children as well.

Often what we want to do must yield to merciful love for others. And Jesus did this more often than not without giving up solitude altogether. He knew how to balance these realities perfectly. Without meditation and contemplation in one's life, the desire to grow in greater service of God will not take place. To prepare ourselves for future trials requiring new bursts of virtue will not take place either. However, while it is true that we discover Jesus in prayer before the Blessed Sacrament or reading the Bible, he is also found in the faces of people, especially those who may need us.

Heavenly Father, never let me be so taken up with communication that I neglect being alone with you, or so taken up with being alone with you that I abandon people in their needs when they call upon me.

Prayer as Begging

Father Basil Cole, O.P.

*Soon a woman whose daughter had an unclean spirit heard
about [Jesus]. She came and fell at his feet. The woman was
a Greek, a Syrophoenician by birth, and she begged him
to drive the demon out of her daughter. (Mk 7: 25-26)*

Prayer first of all means "to ask" in most languages. It is the sign of depending upon God and also an expression of divine hope. It can be both a petition for oneself or for another. In this case, it is for the removal of a daughter's demon who seems to possess her. When we ask for favors not owed to us in justice, we are appealing to God's infinite mercy. But it may be that what we ask for is against his plans for us and ultimately harmful to our eternal destiny. Yet we are unable to fathom that. It requires faith and confidence in God. In the case of the daughter, being possessed by a demon is not intrinsically evil. Being possessed by mortal sin is terribly evil and far worse than diabolical possession because it excludes one from heaven and many helps of divine grace as well. Some sins are mortal because they kill the life of grace in the soul, expel the indwelling of the Trinity, and the theological virtue of charity disappears while faith and hope are weakened. Diabolic possession does none of this, yet it can lead – but not with necessity – to mortal sin. It is similar to a physical and psychological ailment.

Notice how humble the Greek woman is. She falls at the feet of Jesus. This is a good beginning for growing in prayer because humility removes obstacles from a relationship with God. She knows she can do nothing to cure her daughter of this terrible reality. Notice she "begs." This is another good sign because one who prays has no rights in justice to stand on when it comes to interceding for others. While Jesus as God already knows the situation of her daughter, he wants to cure her because her mother is begging, not demanding. Many of our prayers for others and for ourselves often lack these two qualities.

*Merciful Father, teach me how to ask from you through your Son
so that my communication with you may always bear fruit even
if you say no to my requests.*

The Seeming Cruelty of God

Father Basil Cole, O.P.

[Jesus] said to [the woman], "Let the children be fed first. For it is not right to take the food of the children and throw it to the dogs." (Mk 7: 27)

I s our Lord being insensitive here? Calling the Greeks dogs and throwing food to them seems like a cruel answer. To the Jew of the time it was a term of contempt for the Gentiles. Jesus seems to be calling the woman herself a dog. But the Greek word our Lord used is more like a pet dog, a small lap dog looked upon with affection rather than a wild dog from the streets. Notice, however, he does not say "no" absolutely, but only says that children are fed "first," which does not exclude that Gentiles or the woman be "fed" second, in this case with a favor, the healing of her daughter from the devil's grip.

When we pray for an important favor for others and even for ourselves, often the Lord does not answer immediately. Sometimes the situation gets worse. The more I prayed for my own mother who was filled with depression, the worse she seemed to become and she never was cured except at death. In retrospect, it seemed cruel at the time, but it forced me to help Mom anyway and keep on praying for her and surrender to God's mysterious designs, which I did not understand. My mother's unmet burdens became the occasions of purifying my trust in God and continuing love for my mother.

God never leaves prayers unanswered, but not in ways we will appreciate in this life. Behind a "no" is a "yes" that requires faith and trust, sometimes in the face of a sea of darkness. Sometimes, when we lose a son or daughter to an early death after praying to our Lord, our Blessed Mother, and the saints, we have to give these persons back to God. Ultimately, they are his, not ours, and his plan for them is none of our business, but we always have to believe it is a loving plan since he is infinite love.

Wonderful Father, help me accept you as you are and not try to put limits on you when my prayers seem to be rejected.

The Humility of Prayer

Father Basil Cole, O.P.

[The woman] replied and said to [Jesus], "Lord, even the dogs under the table eat the children's scraps." (Mk 7: 28)

I do believe that our Lord must have been smiling when he heard the reply of the Phoenician woman. It was a great repartee on her part, showing respect to Jesus and at the same time using his words to her advantage. She seems to understand that he came for the Jews first and the Gentiles second, and is willing to accept that position.

Most people want to aim for and achieve excellence in some way. We have been designed with many talents and gifts that are still in potentiality even if we are aged. But we all have a problem: we do not easily accept our limitations. We only look at what we can do but refuse to see what we cannot do or what needs improvement. Humility keeps us from exaggerating what we can do or have done. It also keeps us from thinking that we can save ourselves by ourselves, or that we can do great things without the help of God.

Humble prayer opens up the heart of God, as it were. The humble person does not attempt to bribe God with promises that probably won't be kept, as if he can do everything on his own to please God. Humility recognizes that it is God who must first give the grace of prayer to be able to receive efficaciously a favorable answer.

Our Lord promised to exalt the humble and humble the proud. Sometimes, we need to be humbled by dry prayer that perseveres when all seems lost, or worse, a waste of time. This is a prayer that purifies us and prepares us to receive many graces. Then there are times when prayer is delightful and seems to intensify our desires to work even harder for the glory of God and the salvation of others. Then we know we've been exalted.

Father, teach me to understand that it is your will and kingdom I need to want, not my own will and kingdom.

Qualities of Prayer

Father Basil Cole, O.P.

Then [Jesus] said to [the woman], "For saying this, you may go. The demon has gone out of your daughter." When the woman went home, she found the child lying in bed and the demon gone. (Mk 7: 29-30)

Was it because she tricked him with words that Jesus gave her such a favor? Can we create beautiful speeches to God, which will force him to give us what we want? This was the problem of the Pharisee who spoke eloquently to God about what he did not do, whereas the publican simply begged for mercy. It was not the speech of the woman that brought about the favor but the heart attitude behind her words.

Saint Thomas Aquinas in his *Summa Theologiae* teaches that the prayer of petition first must ultimately be directed to achieving eternal happiness, not simply a favor for its own sake for self and for others. Second, the request for something should fall under what someone hopes is necessary for salvation. Third, one has to ask piously or humbly. Fourth, one should ask with perseverance because sometimes God wants us to grow in desire for him through the prayer of petition.

Prayer is not simply asking for favors from God, but is a loving communication with him as the Syrophoenician woman had to a great degree. She asked with loving affection toward him. Eventually, prayer goes on to become loving converse with the Lord, not only prayers of petition but of love, adoration, praise, and thanksgiving.

Finally, since prayer is a loving conversation with God, it needs to include a spirit of listening. Often we Catholics are good at speaking to the Triune God and not with God. Often he speaks to us through reading. I discovered my vocation to the Dominicans through books. But God can often speak to us through people we think are beneath us, even a child. Perhaps when a child receives First Holy Communion, he or she may be able to prompt a parent to get to confession and receive also. What a grace!

Loving Father, I am not a saint but I fall down before you and ask your help to keep me always seeking to know you, love you, and serve you now and for ever.

Gentile Territory: Do Not Enter

Father Jacob Restrick, O.P.

Again [Jesus] left the district of Tyre and went by way of Sidon to the Sea of Galilee, into the district of the Decapolis. And people brought to him a deaf man who had a speech impediment and begged him to lay his hand on him.
(Mk 7: 31-32)

Saint Mark is doing more than giving geographical stage directions, like a Scriptural GPS! He's underlining that the Lord has entered into Gentile territory. The deaf man represents all of us who can't hear the word of God; who can't, therefore, speak clearly or pray clearly, with trust and confidence. Our prayer can be impeded by an inability to hear what the Lord may be saying.

I discovered the "Decapolis" (Gentile cities) within me. I can be slow to believe and hard of hearing, not just when the Lord tells me to repent, but when he talks to me about his love. Father Anonymous, a young and energetic priest, told me he doesn't always believe that God loves him. "It's so difficult to pray at times, and trust that God hears my prayer and really cares." It's especially difficult if one expects to feel God's love or see tangible fruits of it in one's life.

It's a temptation my young priest friend battles against, especially when he gets overwhelmed with the unbelief rampant in our culture. And then he met a poor woman who lived on the streets and frequently came into the church to sleep, to pilfer from the candle-money box, and hopefully to pray. "She prayed a lot," Father A. told me, "and seemed to be listening with a tilted head toward the tabernacle." He stopped her one morning leaving the church and asked what she was praying for. She told him she begs the Lord to lay his hands on her children whom she hasn't seen in years, and an older brother who has abandoned his faith. "Just making an intervention, Padre." Father A. realized then that the communion of saints was always there too, making "interventions" for all of us who are just a little bit – or a whole lot – deaf. And sometimes, it's not just the communion of saints in heaven.

Gracious and loving Father, may your healing touch take away my deafness that I may hear your voice in the Scriptures, in the teachings of the Church, and in the liturgy and prayers of your holy Church.

Closed for Business

Father Jacob Restrick, O.P.

[Jesus] took [the deaf man] off by himself away from the crowd. He put his finger into the man's ears and, spitting, touched his tongue; then he looked up to heaven and groaned, and said to him, "Ephphatha!" (that is, "Be opened!") (Mk 7: 33-34)

Jesus is the Sacrament of God's presence among us. He is the God who touches us by his incarnation – his words, his healing, his real presence, his sending forth his Holy Spirit.

Jesus is *the* Sacrament touching us, however, in seven ways or in seven *signs*. And Mark shows us how physical that may be. Jesus, of course, doesn't have to put his fingers in the man's ear, use his own spittle, or speak any dramatic words, like *Ephphatha*. Jesus heals by the mere intent of his will. But he often will say a word or words for our sake, and he will often touch to "out-form" the interior movement of his grace. It's all signs of his divine love.

The Lord continues to touch us this way in the sacraments, which are material signs and words and gestures, which give the actions their spiritual form, through which the Holy Spirit really comes to us. Jesus doesn't have to use outward signs and rituals to touch us with his grace, but he has chosen to do so this way. The sacraments are like nuptial gifts the Bridegroom gives to his bride, the Church.

When Jesus speaks, the words literally *do* what they say. To the deaf man in the Gospel, his ears are instantly opened at the word *Ephphatha*. This is true with all the sacramental words of the Lord: "I baptize you…" "This is my body…" "I absolve you of your sins…" "May the grace of the Holy Spirit help you."

One of my favorite reverts (former Catholics who leave and then return) calls himself a "sacramental Catholic." "It's the sacraments, especially the real presence in the Eucharist, that brought me back," he says when talking about his reversion. "I was closed to so much, but now my ears have been opened." If you're closed, when will you be open again?

Father Almighty, open our hearts each day to hear your word and to experience your saving touch in the sacraments of your Church.

Show and Don't Tell

Father Jacob Restrick, O.P.

And [immediately] the man's ears were opened, his speech impediment was removed, and he spoke plainly. [Jesus] ordered [the people] not to tell anyone. But the more he ordered them not to, the more they proclaimed it. (Mk 7: 35-36)

Friday mornings were my favorite days at Seventh Avenue Elementary School, at least in first and second grade. They were "Show and Tell" mornings. We'd get to bring in something really neat from home, show it to the class, and tell them all about it. It was a lesson in "preaching the good news" about something that made us happy.

The Lord was not suppressing "Show and Tell" when he ordered the gathered crowd *not* to tell anyone about this miracle, even though Mark mentions that the cured man now spoke plainly. It is early on in the public ministry of the Lord. Only gradually does he reveal who he is. By his miracles of restoring hearing to the deaf and sight to the blind, he fulfills the words of the prophets concerning the Messiah. His miracles are like the Father's "Show and Tell." Jesus shows the Father's love and mercy, and tells us not to be afraid to ask for it.

The day would come when he literally sends his apostles out to tell the whole world, but for now they are to keep it a secret. Some would say the Lord is being humble; others that he is being prudent. He knew if the word got out that he would be proclaimed king, the anointed one who would overthrow the oppressive pagan rulers. But his kingdom is not of this world. He is showing them an interior kingdom, and preparing them for the indwelling of the Holy Spirit, and then they will show the "kingdom, the power, and the glory" of God, and tell the whole world.

They didn't listen and proclaimed this miracle to all who would hear. Sometimes we just can't keep it all to ourselves, and need the grace *to show and tell* humbly and prudently because it's all about him, not about me!

Father in heaven, thy holy will be done. Show me this day the miracles of my life, and grant me the courage to obey you and to tell others by my gratitude and peace.

Astonishment Runneth Over

Father Jacob Restrick, O.P.

*[The people] were exceedingly astonished and they said,
"[Jesus] has done all things well. He makes the deaf hear
and [the] mute speak." (Mk 7: 37)*

Everyone on pilgrimage to Lourdes was excited to be making the trip to one of the most popular and powerful Marian shrines in the world. We were exceedingly expectant and very fervent in our prayers. There were several reluctant pilgrims, however, who were skeptical about "it all" and hardly prayed at all. One such was the father of a seven-year-old daughter dying from a terminal illness; it was just a matter of time. Daddy sat squished against the plane window, staring out at the darkness of night.

On the flight home he was talkative, exuberant, and prayerful. Why? Because he had been *exceedingly astonished* by the faith and hope of the pilgrims who had come to Lourdes; he had walked and prayed in the processions, pushing his sick child in a special wheelchair. She was not physically healed, but her spirit was touched with peace and joy. Accepting and embracing the crosses the Lord permits in our lives out of love and with him, through him, and for him is exceedingly astonishing!

Daddy experienced a miracle of love and faith at the shrine where the Lord draws us to himself through his holy Mother. Countless pilgrims are spiritually deaf and blind, but out of hope and love they make their way to Jesus through Mary. And they find faith, peace, and even joy.

When the time came during that next year for Daddy's little girl to make her pilgrimage into eternal life, he was exceedingly astonished again to let her go in peace because the Mother of God promised him that she would be there at the hour of death. "Lourdes came to us in her hospital room; we knew our Lady was there!" He goes back to Lourdes every year now, to push other children in their wheelchairs and to pray with their moms and dads.

Loving Father, dare us to ask to be exceedingly astonished by your presence in our lives and to be eternally grateful for all you do for us.

161

Jesus Shows Compassion

Father Romanus Cessario, O.P.

In those days when there again was a great crowd without anything to eat, [Jesus] summoned the disciples and said, "My heart is moved with pity for the crowd, because they have been with me now for three days and have nothing to eat. If I send them away hungry to their homes, they will collapse on the way, and some of them have come a great distance." (Mk 8: 1-3)

What a comforting thought! The God who created heaven and earth also concerns himself with provisions for hungry pilgrims. While we often think of God as governing the big moments in life, Jesus shows us that the divine compassion reaches down to meet our everyday needs. Many features of our technologically advanced culture subtly persuade us that we can control the usual happenings of our lives. Rapid communications and easy-to-make contacts leave us with the impression that we can manage daily events. When we allow this illusion to take hold, our attention to the loving providence of the heavenly Father recedes. And so we forget that what transpires in the world falls within the divine providence that governs everything.

When Jesus takes pity on the crowd, he confirms that the providence of his Father includes compassion. He assures us that divine providence does not intrude into our lives like a menacing source of external control. God cares lovingly for us, and we should pay attention to the patterns of this loving providence. To develop this disposition requires that Christians recognize in the little things that happen one by one the infallible signs of God's goodness. Only personal sin provides an exception to this rule. Divine providence allows but never causes sin. Otherwise, everything that happens displays the divine compassion. Of course, sometimes things arrive that we do not welcome; still the Christian views them as signs of divine providence. Given the sad sentence of death that the children of Adam and Eve stand under, even the hour of death follows the providence of God. We can prepare for this moment by living day to day in the compassionate love of God, Father, Son, and Holy Spirit. Anxiety finds no home in the person who delights in the providence of God.

Heavenly Father, grant me the grace to welcome your providence. Make everything that I say and do a reflection of the love that governs heaven and earth. Then I will rejoice in whatever comes my way.

Spiritual Discernment

Father Romanus Cessario, O.P.

His disciples answered [Jesus], "Where can anyone get enough bread to satisfy them here in this deserted place?"
(Mk 8: 4)

Confidence in divine providence relieves a weight that many persons, even of good will, carry on their shoulders. Many imagine that they must find a solution to each problematic event that comes along. Of course, certain circumstances require that someone know how to deal with problems. Teachers must know how to instruct the ignorant. Doctors must know how to cure disease. Parents must know how to raise their children. In short, what our professional responsibilities require us to know, we should know. All kinds of things happen, however, that fall outside our professional abilities, and sometimes things arise that baffle even the professionals. No teacher knows everything. The cure for some diseases escapes medical science. Parents often encounter limitations in rearing children. Additionally, many things occur in life for which no professional competence exists. When they gazed on the four thousand, the disciples of Jesus found themselves faced with such an occasion. So they wondered out loud: "Where can anyone get enough bread to satisfy them in this deserted place?" From a human viewpoint, their predicament appears all too genuine.

What Jesus' disciples learn from the multiplication of the loaves gives them a new perspective on problem-solving. They discover that God's compassionate providence provides solutions to problems that transcend whatever the human imagination can conceive. Who would have dreamt that Jesus would multiply the loaves? Although we cannot expect miraculous solutions to all life's difficulties, we should develop the practice of expecting help from resources other than our own. To receive special interventions of divine help, we should pray for them, and then we should learn to recognize these divine helps when they arrive. This spiritual sensibility – a proper kind of discernment that enables the spiritual person to treat spiritual things spiritually – brings us great consolation. And God relieves our burdens.

Loving Father, your provision for my needs surpasses all human expectations. Give me the grace to accept how you provide for my needs. Then I will rejoice in the company of your saints.

Miracles Do Happen

Father Romanus Cessario, O.P.

Still [Jesus] asked [his disciples], "How many loaves do you have?" "Seven," they replied. He ordered the crowd to sit down on the ground. Then, taking the seven loaves he gave thanks, broke them, and gave them to his disciples to distribute, and they distributed them to the crowd. (Mk 8: 5-6)

The saints often remark on the spiritual significance of the number seven. They interpret the number of loaves available to the disciples as pointing to Christ's compassion. The seven loaves of bread provide sufficient food to sustain four thousand people. Clearly the Evangelist wants us to recognize that Jesus works no stingy miracle, and that God amply provides for the material needs of those who remain close to him. He also provides abundantly for the spiritual wants that all human beings experience.

The number seven further points to the seven sacraments. Obviously, the multiplication of the loaves suggests to Catholics the multiplication of the Eucharistic bread that happens at each Mass. Recall the words that the priest speaks: "For on the night he was betrayed he himself took bread, and, giving you thanks, he said the blessing, broke the bread and gave it to his disciples." The remaining six sacraments each meets some spiritual hunger that devout Christians experience throughout their lifetimes. Before receiving the Eucharist, baptism bestows new life in Christ, and supplies the soul with a way to escape the limitations that our natural lives impose. Penance brings forgiveness from Christ, and provides the penitent with a remedy for the harm that sin introduces into our lives. Confirmation strengthens our life in Christ, and supplies what adult believers need to face the challenges that public witness to Christ requires. Holy orders and matrimony endow the Church with priests and married couples, and effect special sacramental consecrations to meet the responsibilities that each vocation in the Church imposes. Lastly, holy anointing prepares us for a holy death, and readies us to stand before God's throne of judgment. When we ponder the seven sacraments, we should come to appreciate the divine largesse that the feeding of the four thousand only foreshadows.

Almighty Father, renew in me love for the sacraments of Christ's Church. Conform my life to the rhythm that the sacraments establish in those who receive them worthily. Then I shall praise you for ever.

Seven Baskets Left Over

Father Romanus Cessario, O.P.

[His disciples] also had a few fish. [Jesus] said the blessing over them and ordered them distributed also. They ate and were satisfied. They picked up the fragments left over – seven baskets. There were about four thousand people.
He dismissed them. (Mk 8: 7-9)

While the multiplication of the loaves and fishes reveals the superabundance of the divine compassion, it also confirms the true identity of Jesus Christ. Taking pity on hungry people belongs to Christ's humanity, whereas the miracle that he worked to feed the hungry crowd confirms his divinity. A man feels pity. Only God multiplies foodstuffs. In one divine Person, two natures, God's and ours, are united. Jesus is the God-man.

The number seven reappears in the account of the leftovers. Seven baskets left over! Some authorities consider these baskets symbols of the seven gifts of the Holy Spirit: wisdom, understanding, counsel, fortitude, knowledge, piety, and fear of the Lord. The gifts belong to each baptized person. When the time comes to receive the sacrament of confirmation, young and other Catholics are told that this sacrament enkindles in them the sevenfold gift of the Holy Spirit. These seven gifts charge our human powers with divine energy, and so they affect directly the manner in which we conduct our lives. The gifts specifically shape the moral life of the Catholic believer. Wisdom enlightens us about divine truth. Understanding and knowledge assist the virtue of faith so that we grasp with insight what we believe. Counsel sharpens our moral judgment. Fortitude heightens our sense of those situations that require courage. Piety renders us supple to the requirements of justice. Fear of the Lord transforms a debilitating fear of punishment into an expression of childlike reverence for the heavenly Father.

When we consider the picture of the Christian life that these gifts present, we find ourselves pondering the face of the God-man. The gifts make us Christlike as only the munificence of God can accomplish. When we think of the leftovers from this miracle, we should rejoice that God gives so much to us.

Heavenly Father, make me seek heaven above all other pursuits. Give me the grace to long for the heavenly homeland more than the best consolations earth can provide. Then I will love here below as you love.

Signs, Signs, Signs

Father Romanus Cessario, O.P.

*And [Jesus] got into the boat with his disciples
and came to the region of Dalmanutha.
The Pharisees came forward and began to argue with him,
seeking from him a sign from heaven to test him.* (Mk 8: 10-11)

"Dear God, manifest yourself to me in a way that leaves no room for me to doubt your presence." This plaintive cry comes frequently to the minds if not the lips of people who hear the Christian Gospel. Because the Pharisees require a sign that pleases them instead of what the Lord provides, Jesus does not respond to their demand for "a sign from heaven." Were Jesus to succumb to this challenge for a sign of men's own choosing, the Pharisees would consider themselves exempt from the rule of living by faith. When the Pharisees demand "a sign from heaven," they also discount the very signs that Jesus did manifest on earth. They suppose that the feeding of the four thousand results from some magic trick, something even that a charlatan could perform. So these onlookers wait for the sun to stand still or stars to fall from the heavens. By demanding something that would transpire spectacularly in the starry sky, they seek to depreciate the miraculous multiplication of loaves and fishes.

What desperate foolishness from these onlookers who seek to test Jesus. Their demand for a sign urges us to recall instead the many benefits that God has bestowed upon us, and then to resolve not to put Jesus to the test. Tell Jesus rather that you believe in him, even though you expect no miraculous sign to confirm your reliance on his power. And cultivate the practice of living daily in the unseen presence of God through acts of faith, hope, and charity. The thought that seeing surpasses believing seduces many persons. While the seduction appeals to our common way of understanding, it destroys Christian living. For divine faith concerns things that remain unseen. The only signs Christians can expect today from God appear in the seven sacraments.

Eternal Father, give me confidence in your presence. Grant me the grace to live each day according to the love Christ shows me. Then I will meet our blessed Lady and the saints where you reign for ever.

Carnal Delights

Father Romanus Cessario, O.P.

[Jesus] sighed from the depth of his spirit and said, "Why does this generation seek a sign? Amen, I say to you, no sign will be given to this generation." Then he left [the Pharisees], got into the boat again, and went off to the other shore. (Mk 8: 12-13)

The Evangelist observes the intensity of the reaction that Jesus gives to the Pharisees' incredulity. These religious leaders represent those who do not recognize Jesus as the One sent by God to save the world from its sins. So Jesus sighs "from the depth of his spirit." Why does Christ react in this way? He knows that reliance on sensible manifestations demonstrates a reluctance to live by faith. His expression of sorrow also warns us that attachment to our senses can lead us awry. Appropriate bodily pleasures of course find their place in Christian living. For example, the pleasure that accompanies the love that husband and wife share in procreating children forms part of the sanctification of married life. The pleasures of the palate assist nutrition, while the pleasures of the eye satisfy our aesthetic sense. Christian life reprobates neither the body nor the pleasures that accompany bodily operations.

The Gospel message, however, does forbid the inordinate pursuit of felt pleasure. Christianity never abets hedonism. Why? Those who find themselves overly attached to pleasure of whatever kind discover that they grow dullish in their appreciation of supernatural goods. To appreciate spiritual realities requires at least a moderation in our enjoyment of carnal pleasures. Mortification supplies an ascetic gauge to ensure that the pursuit of felt consolation does not obscure the hidden presence of the Blessed Trinity. No wonder Jesus sighed deeply when he recognized that some persons wager everything according to what satisfies their senses. Overindulgence in carnal delights always works against Christian believing. Those who live by faith should remain vigilant lest their movements toward carnal delight obscure their capacity to welcome the spiritual realities that heaven contains. This warning does not create saddish and dour personalities. Jesus causes more joy in us than any carnal pleasure can produce.

Most merciful Father, forgive my sins. Grant what I need to remain steadfast in the faith of your Son's Church. Then I will find spiritual pleasure for ever in your presence.

Attitudes to Avoid

Father Romanus Cessario, O.P.

[The disciples] had forgotten to bring bread, and they had only one loaf with them in the boat. [Jesus] enjoined them, "Watch out, guard against the leaven of the Pharisees and the leaven of Herod." They concluded among themselves that it was because they had no bread. (Mk 8: 14-16)

The disciples frequently miss the point of what Jesus says. They show themselves to be slow learners. So when Jesus talks about leaven, the disciples assume that he is commenting on the varieties of bread available in first-century Palestine. This awkward conjecture helps us to identify with the disciples. We ourselves often move slowly when it comes to penetrating the full significance of spiritual realities. Truth to tell, Jesus mentions the leaven of the Pharisees and of Herod as a warning to his disciples of things to avoid. Some ancient authorities identify the leaven of the Pharisees as making the decrees of the divine law inferior to the traditions of men; preaching the law in word, while attacking it in deed; tempting the Lord, while at the same time disbelieving his doctrine and his works. The leaven of Herod, on the other hand, suggests adultery, murder, rash swearing, a pretense of religion, and showing hatred to Christ and to his forerunner, Saint John the Baptist. When Jesus mentions this leaven, how in the world could the disciples have been thinking about an insufficient supply of bread? In any case, we should flee the state of incomprehension that Jesus' disciples display while they were with him "in the boat."

To avoid missing the point of what Jesus teaches requires that we rely on the graces that he sends us. This grace makes us lovers of divine truth, not strategists for evil. The warning that Jesus gives to his disciples today alerts us to the danger of cynicism and self-satisfaction. We rather should rejoice in the divine goodness that envelops us. The more we embrace this divine goodness, the more we will find ourselves liberated from those things that destroy the human spirit, and joined to the One who perfects us in every good blessing.

Loving Father, conform my whole being to your law of love. Grant me the grace to flee all occasions of sin. Then I will discover the superabundance of your love that conquers all deceit.

What Makes Us Understand

Father Romanus Cessario, O.P.

When [Jesus] became aware of this he said to [his disciples],
"Why do you conclude that it is because you have no bread?
Do you not yet understand or comprehend? Are your hearts
hardened? Do you have eyes and not see, ears and not hear?"
(Mk 8: 17-18a)

When Jesus speaks about an ingredient in bread – leaven – his disciples assume that he frets over their depleted supply of foodstuffs. The reproving words Jesus addresses to his disciples are meant to console them. He wants his disciples to rise up and recognize divine truths, and not remain at the level of ordinary and everyday understandings. So in order to instruct them about the true nature of Christian wisdom, Jesus scolds his disciples. Then he instructs them about the danger of putting the worship of God at the service of exclusively human purposes and goals.

His warnings against the culturally dominant Pharisees and the politically minded Herod retain their force today. It can happen that human authorities of one or another kind attempt to place religious practices after sociological or political concerns. Jesus proclaims the politics of heaven. The Christian Gospel delivers a message about eternity. Eternal truth does not come only through reading books or following study-courses. To understand the things of heaven requires a gift from heaven. This Gift comes to us in the Person of the Holy Spirit. We say that the Holy Spirit dwells in the souls of those who remain in Christ's love. The language of indwelling emphasizes the proximity that we enjoy with this divine Person. The work of the indwelling Spirit remedies the defect that Jesus signals in the disciples. The Holy Spirit softens our hearts. He readies our eyes to see spiritual realities, and our ears to receive spiritual instruction. We invoke the Holy Spirit as Comforter the best. While many persons regard religion as an obstacle to human well being, those who welcome the Holy Spirit realize that the possession of divine truth completes the human person in a way that only God can provide. With this Truth, the soul rejoices.

Lord of heaven and earth, make me supple to the inspirations of your Holy Spirit. Let me abide always in his indwelling presence. Then I will find myself ready to enter the joy that lasts for ever.

Lots Left Over

Father Romanus Cessario, o.p.

"And do you not remember, when I broke the five loaves for the five thousand, how many wicker baskets full of fragments you picked up?" [Jesus' disciples] answered him, "Twelve." "When I broke the seven loaves for the four thousand, how many full baskets of fragments did you pick up?" They answered [him], "Seven." He said to them, "Do you still not understand?"
(Mk 8: 18b-21)

The two instances of miraculous feedings that Saint Mark records in his Gospel tell of Christ's power. The surplus fragments of bread that the disciples gather are meant to introduce them to the dimensions of Christ's authority over nature. When we ponder the feeding of the five thousand (see Mk 6: 34-44) and the feeding of the four thousand, we should find ourselves overwhelmed by the grandeur of divine providence. Christ's power over nature awakens in us the realization that God orders everything in the world of angels and men. Bread and fish represent the gifts that nature supplies for the sustenance of human beings. When the Lord multiplies these foodstuffs, he makes something out of nothing. Only God creates out of nothing. These miracles witness against the temptation to restrict religion to an imaginary world of the invisible. God's dominion over our lives includes his care for soul and body. Not only the biospheres but also uninhabitable places belong to God.

When we profess each Sunday at Mass that God is the "maker of heaven and earth, of all things visible and invisible," we come to regard created things differently. Those who acknowledge God as the maker of heaven and earth resist the naïve cosmological myths that people without reliance on divine revelation conjure up to explain the everyday working of the universe. Christian believers eschew all superstition, no matter how sophisticated. At the same time, the Christian believer acknowledges the limits that scientific investigation imposes on itself. No laboratory experiments can prove definitively the existence of the God who creates out of nothing. So Jesus prepares his disciples and us for this great truth by doing what only God can do. He makes something out of nothing. Our response must include gratitude for receiving this lavish divine consideration.

Gracious Father, create in me a spirit of piety. Make me cherish all that exists as your very own possessions. Then I will develop the right kind of respect for the world and those who dwell within it.

The Evacuation Route

Father Jacob Restrick, O.P.

When [Jesus and his disciples] arrived at Bethsaida, they brought to [Jesus] a blind man and begged him to touch him. He took the blind man by the hand and led him outside the village.
(Mk 8: 22-23a)

Jesus "took the blind man by the hand and led him outside the village." Only Mark tells this story and relates the special care the Lord shows for this man. We can only speculate as to why the Lord "led him outside the village." Sometimes the Lord leads us away from the business of the world, from our frenetic activities which occupy our minds and energy, and leads us into a kind of desolation. The "village" is full of noise and distraction, and we find we live there!

The Lord seems very kind and gentle when healing this man. The first things he would see would not be a noisy, exceedingly astonished crowd yelling and cheering. He would see the calm face of the Lord, full of peace. The Lord would heal him gradually to let him come to experience vision without fear or being overwhelmed by it all.

I wonder what blinds us today from seeing the truths which the Lord wants to reveal? What prevents us from seeing him in others? Are we too busy? Are we all involved in the sound and fury of the "village" and lose sight of our true end in life? When that happens to me, I have to let the Lord take me by the hand and lead me out of my own chaotic village. This may be in the form of a spiritual retreat, a time and place away from the norm, to devote to prayer and meditation, spiritual reading, and quiet reflection. It does us all a world of good to get out of the village from time to time. But if that's not possible, the interior cell, our soul, is a wonderful refuge from the worldly village in which we live. And prayer becomes the Lord taking us by the hand... or our hand grabbing hold of his!

Father of peacefulness and interior joy, lead me out of the noise and storms of my life to that place where I may rest in you. Thy kingdom come.

Well, Spit in My Eye!

Father Jacob Restrick, O.P.

Putting spittle on [the blind man's] eyes [Jesus] laid his hands on him and asked, "Do you see anything?" Looking up he replied, "I see people looking like trees and walking." (Mk 8: 23b-24)

The Lord, of course, did not spit in the blind man's eye, but took his own spittle, probably on his thumb, and pressed it onto the man's eyes. Another Gospel tells us that the Lord made a kind of mud from his spittle and the dirt. In ancient days it was commonly assumed that one's spittle contained great healing properties. Almost instinctively when we cut our finger, for example, we lick it. Animals by nature "lick their wounds," and so perhaps there is something "healing" in saliva.

We know the Lord could have simply willed it, and the man would see instantly. Or the Lord could have just touched his arm or his cheek and sight would have come. But sometimes the Lord uses matter and human touch to accomplish his miracles, as his Church would do in the centuries to follow. The rite of baptism of infants includes the priest or deacon touching his own thumb to his mouth and then touching the infant's ears and mouth. The Church prays that our ears and mouths be opened to hear and praise God for everything.

Seeing with the eyes of faith means to re-focus everything within our range of vision... everything in our lives. There may be wounds in need of healing, and amends to make to others. In the beginning it may seem that people look like walking trees. But do not be afraid – healing has begun, and it may sting or hurt for awhile. Maybe it draws us to pray a little more. A recent convert told me all she wanted to do was pray. It was a new way to see everything, and her "walking trees" came into real focus, and thus she came to believe in God's healing power. Are there any walking trees in your life?

Loving and compassionate Father, may I always be grateful for all the graces you have given to me and, when I am not seeing things too clearly, touch my eyes again, Lord, that I may see.

Return by a Different Route

Father Jacob Restrick, O.P.

Then [Jesus] laid hands on [the blind man's] eyes a second time and he saw clearly; his sight was restored and he could see everything distinctly. Then he sent him home and said, "Do not even go into the village." (Mk 8: 25-26)

The confessional, whether the box or face to face in a reconciliation room, is a place of healing. The Lord's mercy is literally poured out in abundance. The blind see and the deaf hear and those lame with sin walk away whole again... forgiven, healed, and hopefully with a firm purpose of amendment. It's not uncommon to listen to someone weeping in the confessional, sometimes out of contrition, and sometimes out of joy. It can be such a relief to let go of the guilt and burden of sin we carried into the sacrament.

A "weeping penitent" had returned to the grace of God in this sacrament after many years absence. His tears, he told me, were tears of gratitude because he now saw everything distinctly. His sin had blinded him. He needed to be absolved, and he was. And he understood my little admonition: "Go in peace, and avoid the near occasions of sin." If the penitent was familiar with Mark's Gospel, I could have said: "Go in peace, and do not even go into the village." When the Prodigal Son returned to his home and to his father, he never went back to visit the "village" where he became the penitent son. May none of us return to the people, places, and things that lead us into sin, or back to our spiritual blindness.

Staying close to others who walk the spiritual path is a big help. My penitent friend became a daily communicant, and it all began in that ominous wooden box in the back of church.

The confessional is a place of hope and where new life begins, strong in purpose of amendment, firmly resolving by the help of God's grace to avoid the occasions of sin and to amend our lives. May we return to the Lord and our family, by a different route!

Father in heaven, may it be so. Renew in me a contrite spirit that I may serve you more lovingly each day.

He Asked His Disciples

Father Andrew Hofer, O.P.

Now Jesus and his disciples set out for the villages of Caesarea Philippi. Along the way he asked his disciples, "Who do people say that I am?" They said in reply, "John the Baptist, others Elijah, still others one of the prophets." (Mk 8: 27-28)

N arrating the healing of a paralytic, Mark the Evangelist describes how some of the scribes were criticizing Jesus for saying that the paralytic was forgiven. Mark writes, "Jesus immediately knew in his mind what they were thinking to themselves, so he said, 'Why are you thinking such things in your hearts?'" (Mk 2: 8). He who searches the mind knows the scribes' thoughts – and yet he asks a question. That is the first question the Lord asks in Mark's Gospel. It is characteristic of God not only to forgive sins, but to ask questions. For example, the Lord God calls out to Adam after Adam's sin, "Where are you?" (Gn 3: 9). It's not that the Lord is ignorant, but he asks questions because he wants us to think rightly – such as to think where we are when we sin.

Now in Mark, chapter 8, we read the first of two questions that Jesus asks along the way to Caesarea Philippi: "Who do people say that I am?" Is he ignorant of what people think of him? No. But he wants his disciples to think of what others say about him. He will follow up with the more important question, "But who do you say that I am?" He wants them to think about who he is. They will then be able to see the contrast between mere opinion and real faith in him.

Jesus continues to ask questions. What question is he asking you to think about? One question he asks me is the same one we heard: "Who do people say that I am?" Some think that he is just a great teacher, prophet, or healer; some think he's a lunatic or merely a myth. When I am aware of the diversity of opinion about Jesus, I can appreciate even more my faith to think rightly about who Jesus truly is.

All-powerful and ever-living God, send your Holy Spirit to me so that I may hear the questions your Son asks me and answer them according to your will.

You Are the Messiah

Father Andrew Hofer, O.P.

And [Jesus] asked [his disciples], "But who do you say that I am?" Peter said to him in reply, "You are the Messiah." Then he warned them not to tell anyone about him. (Mk 8: 29-30)

Jesus doesn't want his disciples to think just about what others say of him. He wants them to think about who he is: "But who do you say that I am?" Peter gives his answer, an answer that he cannot fully understand: "You are the Messiah."

We, too, are called to give answers. We are not to mimic what the crowds say. Rather, the answers we give come from another source – not from ourselves, but from God through us. Ultimately, we will answer the question of Jesus' identity with our lives. The Christian life lived in God-given holiness, picking up the cross and following Jesus in obedience until death, is the most eloquent answer to the question of who Jesus is. It is also the most unique. Each of our lives is different from any other. As for our words, we can tell Jesus from our hearts in our own personal way what we think of him upon this earth. He doesn't want us simply to repeat what others say. He's waiting to hear from our hearts today.

O Jesus, many speak your name.
But who do you say that I am?
I know for some you win acclaim.
But who do you say that I am?
For others faith is just a game.
But who do you say that I am?
I have some friends who always pray.
But who do you say that I am?
Ask them, they know, is that okay?
But who do you say that I am?
At last in faith, "My Christ," I say!

Heavenly Father, let your Holy Spirit guide me so that I may be prompt to tell your Son in love what I think of him.

The Rejection of Jesus

Father Andrew Hofer, O.P.

[Jesus] began to teach [his disciples] that the Son of Man must suffer greatly and be rejected by the elders, the chief priests, and the scribes, and be killed, and rise after three days. He spoke this openly. (Mk 8: 31-32a)

When the Son of God came, he did not appear as a mighty warrior to slay his enemies, nor did he appear as one unmistakably loveable to all his friends. He came as the Son of Man. Jesus explains in the Gospel that the Son will be unloved, unwanted, and put to death. Explicitly, he says that he will be rejected by Israel's leaders; implicitly, this will mean that people will think that God rejected him. How could the elders, chief priests, and scribes not be following God's will? Moreover, Jesus himself on the cross will pray Psalm 22: "My God, my God, why have you forsaken me?" (Mk 15: 34b). The rejection of Jesus is a much bigger problem than mere human opinion; it looks like divine judgment.

We know that Jesus continues to be rejected today. He is rejected in those who are unloved and unwanted. He is rejected in those who are despised when they proclaim the mystery of the cross of Christ. When people see the rejection of Jesus occur even by those who are our social, religious, and intellectual leaders, they may be tempted to think this is what God really wants. For how else could heaven allow what we see to happen upon this earth?

But within the Gospel's first, formal prediction by Jesus of his suffering, we have that little phrase: "and rise after three days." The rejection of Jesus is not the end of the Gospel, and it's not the end of our world. Jesus tells those who reject him: "You will see the Son of Man seated at the right hand of the Power and coming with the clouds of heaven" (Mk 14: 62). By undergoing rejection with Jesus, we also experience the baptismal revelation of God's full, unqualified acceptance: "You are my beloved Son; with you I am well pleased" (Mk 1: 11b).

My God, my God, thank you for accepting your Son's offering of his own life in what seemed to be total rejection. Send his Spirit upon me so that I may bear witness today to him.

Thinking as God Does

Father Andrew Hofer, O.P.

Then Peter took [Jesus] aside and began to rebuke him. At this he turned around and, looking at his disciples, rebuked Peter and said, "Get behind me, Satan. You are thinking not as God does, but as human beings do." (Mk 8: 32b-33).

Do we know God's mind? Some people consider the claim to know what God knows to be the height of intellectual snobbery. They want a more modest stance, a stance that would not upset anyone by a claim to divine authority and its demands. If someone goes beyond what is socially acceptable, then it's that person who will bear the brunt of criticism. This happens on all sorts of levels when matters of Christ's identity, social justice, sexual morality, and a host of other controversial subjects come up in conversation. But the Christian faith is a response to revelation. We believe because God has shared his mind with us. If we who are called disciples rely on thinking merely as human beings do, we will find ourselves objecting to what God, in fact, is revealing. He reveals much more than what we could ever imagine.

Peter learns this lesson the hard way. He had just made this confession of faith: "You are the Messiah." After he hears how the Son of Man must suffer, Peter wants to correct Jesus. In polite fashion so that the other disciples do not hear it, Peter pulls Jesus aside. Mark the Evangelist uses the strong word "rebuke." It's also the word Mark uses to describe how Jesus reacts to Peter, but Jesus does so while "looking at his disciples." Jesus teaches Peter and all of us a lesson through this rebuke. It's not enough to think as human beings do. To think only as a human being, when the revelation of God is offered, is to be Satan. When we are tempted to think merely as human beings think, we can remember that, in faith, "we have the mind of Christ" (1 Cor 2: 16b). It is then that we really get behind Jesus as his followers.

All-knowing God, fill me with your Holy Spirit so that I may never object to the ways of your Son in my life.

Taking up the Cross

Father Andrew Hofer, o.p.

[Jesus] summoned the crowd with his disciples and said to them, "Whoever wishes to come after me must deny himself, take up his cross, and follow me. For whoever wishes to save his life will lose it, but whoever loses his life for my sake and that of the gospel will save it." (Mk 8: 34-35)

It's no accident that Jesus tells his disciples about their cross and new life only after he announces to them his own suffering, death, and resurrection. His title of Messiah in Mark's Gospel can be understood only through the cross. His identity, in a sense, becomes our identity. To be Christian means to find a new life only in the cross given to us. The cross is not meant to be just some inconvenience in life. It's meant to kill. For us who are sinners, the cross puts to death that which prevents us from attaining God. At times, we can become acutely aware of the pain. The cross hurts. But what makes the pain bearable? Life with Christ!

We don't take up our cross alone. We do it through him, with him, and in him. Jesus leads us in bearing the cross. He would not want us to undergo some suffering that he himself did not first undergo. At times, our suffering can seem so isolating, so peculiar to our individual circumstances. But the Lord Jesus is always with us. He will not allow anything of us to die without giving a far better life with him. Do you believe that? Life with Christ is much happier than what this world has to offer.

This motivates me to think not so much about how I can make the most of this day in my life by earthly standards, but how I can lose my life for the sake of Christ and his good news. I am called to lose my life, the time of this day, in the prayer and work that God has given me. Today is to be a waste, wasting my life for love of Jesus. It is only then that I can find my life's salvation.

Loving Father, grant me your Holy Spirit's anointing so that I may be more and more conformed to Jesus, the Messiah who died for love of me.

Not Ashamed

Father Andrew Hofer, O.P.

"What profit is there for one to gain the whole world and forfeit his life? What could one give in exchange for his life? Whoever is ashamed of me and of my words in this faithless and sinful generation, the Son of Man will be ashamed of when he comes in his Father's glory with the holy angels." (Mk 8: 36-38)

Saint Paul says, "I am not ashamed of the gospel" (Rom 1: 16a). That is the most succinct response to what our Lord says in our Gospel passage. We know all too well some alternatives to not being ashamed in the New Testament. Saint Mark records that after the crowd with swords and clubs came to Jesus in the garden on the night before he died, Jesus points out that he had taught openly in the temple area day after day. In short, he was not ashamed of what he said. And what is the response of the disciples who were with him on that night? They were ashamed of him. The Gospel records: "And they all left him and fled" (Mk 14: 50). On that long, cold night, Peter even denied him three times before a maid and various bystanders. When the cock crowed a second time, Peter remembered that Jesus himself had predicted this three-fold denial. Peter then became ashamed of himself. The Gospel says, "He broke down and wept" (Mk 14: 72).

We should be ashamed of our sins. But instead, we know there are all sorts of temptations to be ashamed of Jesus and his words in our generation. What are the temptations in your life to being ashamed of Christ and his teaching? By the grace of God, some manage to proclaim the Gospel by word and deed through the little things of each day. They don't give in to the temptations to deny Jesus when social pressure mounts, such as in the workplace. They know that Judgment Day is more important than payday. As a preacher, I realize that temptations lurk to modify what Jesus says so as to fit the Gospel for the world, and not fit the world for the Gospel. I need grace to give the witness of Saint Paul: "I am not ashamed of the Gospel."

Gracious and loving Father, let the grace of your Spirit fill my whole life so that I may always believe in my heart and confess with my lips that Jesus is Lord.

The Kingdom of God

Father Andrew Hofer, O.P.

[Jesus] also said to [his disciples and the people], "Amen, I say to you, there are some standing here who will not taste death until they see that the kingdom of God has come in power."
(Mk 9: 1)

Saint Mark records various parables about the kingdom of God. Several of these parables show how little or insignificant that kingdom seems at the beginning. It's like seed: the seed that is sown on all sorts of ground; the seed that sprouts and grows while the farmer knows not how; the mustard seed, which is the smallest of all seeds. When the kingdom of God is as small as a seed, it seems so powerless. You could even be ashamed of it. When the seed is fully grown, you could say that the "the kingdom of God has come in power." You could not be ashamed of it. Rather, it could put you to shame.

When does the kingdom of God come in power? Many answers could be given, but I think it is when we see who Jesus really is. He is the Messiah, the Son of God, the one crucified and risen for our salvation with authority in his Father's glory to judge us and to save us from judgment. On the last day, all will see who Jesus really is. He will judge the living and the dead. But even now, when our faith is unwaveringly firm, then the kingdom of God has come in power.

How much power does the kingdom of God have for us today? In the Gospel, we repeatedly find the disciples lacking faith. Jesus calls them to great faith. He says, "Amen, I say to you, whoever says to this mountain, 'Be lifted up and thrown into the sea,' and does not doubt in his heart but believes that what he says will happen, it shall be done for him" (Mk 11: 23). That is the kingdom of God come in power! Do you want that kind of faith? I do! Our faith is not in mountains, but in Jesus. May he show his kingdom's power today through our faith.

Almighty Father, fill your Church with the Holy Spirit so that all who bear the name Christian may see the kingdom of God come in power through faith.

The High Mountain and Love

Father Harry Cronin, C.S.C.

*After six days Jesus took Peter, James, and John
and led them up a high mountain apart by themselves.*
(Mk 9: 2)

L ove grows. It is never complete, never finished. There are stages and phases of love. That is why the best and most satisfying is the love that lasts a lifetime. The journey up the mountain is one moment in a growing love between Jesus and the disciples. Climbing a mountain is a perfect symbol for love. We don't fall in love. We mount to love.

They have known Jesus. They have called him by name. As they perform this simple act of climbing, their love grows.

And so – the mountain. Of course. The mountain.

Love does not embody ideas or thoughts. It embodies feelings: profoundly transforming feelings. It is what the two people in love have been holding in their hearts, what they have been wanting to say, what their hearts have cried out to hear. When it is finally said, there is a peace and joy. Words have been found. No more vague, inchoate, imperfect feelings.

When Jesus takes his disciples up a high mountain, that experience has already happened. They have finally called Jesus by name. They have finally entered into the wonderful mystery of who this man really is. They have recognized him and, of course, been recognized themselves. That experience is part of their journey.

They have been able to say "I love you" to Jesus. They have said, openly and clearly, that he is the Messiah, the Son of God. But the reality is that they have said "I love you" in a special and important way. And then – they go up to a high mountain.

It must have been freeing finally to find the words for a deep and wondrous feeling. They said that he was the Son of God – finally said it. But the thought, the idea, the notion, the wish, the prayer – all of that had been inside them. It had grown in them like a tiny seed and had finally burst out.

Father, may we know your Son.

A New Way to See

Father Harry Cronin, c.s.c.

*And [Jesus] was transfigured before [Peter, James, and John],
and his clothes became dazzling white, such as no fuller on
earth could bleach them. Then Elijah appeared to them along
with Moses, and they were conversing with Jesus. (Mk 9: 2b-4)*

We see people in different ways. This is especially true of people we love. We lay expectations and hopes on them. It is, if you like, a downside of love: wanting the one we love to be whatever we want them to be. It's a downside, because these expectations are hardly ever met. Parents want their children to grow up and be happy. Sometimes their expectations are more specific. Sometimes they want their children to grow up and be doctors or lawyers.

The same was true of Jesus' disciples. They had expectations. They had clear ideas what they wanted Jesus to be – or what they hoped he would be. That's why the moment of transfiguration was so important: because they saw him in a different way. Jesus had not changed. He was the same. He was the same friend, the same companion, the same leader, the same towering inspiration. He was the one they followed with a particular and acute love. He had not changed. What happened was that the disciples saw him in a different way.

What Jesus' disciples saw was the glory of Jesus: a new and changing view of who Jesus was and what he was doing. He was the eternal Word of God who had become flesh. As that Word, the Son of God, he had been conceived in the Trinity's light. It was that eternal brightness which framed him now. They saw him in the light of his own unique glory, and the vision astounded them. They saw him in the light of a joyful creation. They saw him in the light of his Father's radiance. He was Jesus, the Son of Mary. But he was also the eternal Word, the Son of God. Saint Paul would later assert boldly that Jesus was the model and template of all creation, that everything was made through him.

Their wonder grew and would continue to grow.

Father, give us the gift of wonder.

A Bad Idea

Father Harry Cronin, C.S.C.

Then Peter said to Jesus in reply, "Rabbi, it is good that we are here! Let us make three tents: one for you, one for Moses, and one for Elijah." He hardly knew what to say, they were so terrified. (Mk 9: 5-6)

I t doesn't take us long to grasp the fact that our minds and intellect are limited. In a complex and confusing world, we soon realize – sometimes tragically – that we simply can't grasp it all, can't understand it all, can't comprehend, can't take it all in.

A tent for Jesus. A tent for Moses. A tent for Elijah. How perfectly ridiculous. And yet – how completely understandable. The disciples were being slowly and relentlessly overwhelmed by a splendid and amazing vision and, of course, they didn't want to lose it. There was even an air of desperation. They knew that the vision they saw contained inklings of another world, a world beyond both them and time, a world marked by eternity. But they also realized that, no matter how stunning it all was, they still lived in time. When a lover receives a bouquet of flowers, the immediate first reaction is to put the flowers in a vase of water. Try to preserve the gift. Try to keep the precious moment. The disciples wanted to hold on to what they were seeing and feeling. So they said: if I put a tent around it, then I can hold on to it; then I can capture it. And then, even more confusing and more mysterious comes the final thought, the longer and more complex hope: maybe, just maybe I might even be able to understand it.

The three – Jesus and the two prophets from their people's past – were there before them, glowing, existing in a view, in a life that was both living and present. Jesus was one with the prophets. He was in their company. The past and the present were fusing in wonderful and amazing ways. Perhaps they had the strong conviction that no one had ever seen this before; that perhaps they were the first humans ever to witness such a light. So put a tent over it. Cover it. Hide it.

Father, keep us open and always aware of your beauty.

The Joy of What We Hear

Father Harry Cronin, C.S.C.

Then a cloud came, casting a shadow over [Peter, James, and John]; then from the cloud came a voice, "This is my beloved Son. Listen to him." (Mk 9: 7)

Listen to him. Parents say this to their children all the time. You listen to me! The words are usually followed by a strong warning or a dire threat: if I have to come in there... If I ever catch you again... wait until your father gets home.

But the words of the Father in this amazing moment of vision and splendor are neither warning nor threat. They are short, concise, and exact words: simple in what they declare and lucid and clear as water. Listen to this man because of who he is. The words fit the reality they express and fit exactly. What the words declare is simple as well.

There is before you a mighty and wonderful love. It is a love that matters to you because it is a love that matters to the whole world. It is everything that matters.

The Father speaks words that come from the deep, the origin, the soul. They are words that come from the heart that beats at the very center of the world. The words announce a fact: This is my Son. From the fact flows a command. Listen to him.

The words are neither warning nor threat. Don't listen to him because of what might happen if you don't. Listen to him because of the joy that will transpire if you do.

Listen. Just listen. Listen to him because the words he speaks are golden and they are words about life. And only about life. This is true because his words are life bringing, life bearing, and life giving. Everything this man says is life. His breath is life. His body is life. So listen. Just listen. No one has ever spoken like him. For there has never been one like him. He is sole and unique. He is the one and only. Be deaf to him and you will be deaf to life. And that will be sad. So listen. Just listen.

Father, let us listen. That's all. Just let us listen.

No One But Jesus

Father Harry Cronin, C.S.C.

Suddenly, looking around, [Peter, James, and John]
no longer saw anyone but Jesus alone with them.
(Mk 9: 8)

They saw only Jesus. The vision of the two prophets – that was gone. They were not there any more. The dazzling light had faded to the ordinary. The moment of vision, the instant of wonder, the quick glimpse of another reality – all of that had vanished. They were seeing only Jesus. They sensed, probably in a dim and inchoate way, that somehow Jesus was the purpose of the vision. It had all been about Jesus. The Father had wanted the disciples to know who Jesus was. More than that, the Father wanted them to know who he was precisely and exactly. He wanted the disciples to know not only Jesus, but to know his mission, his beginnings, and his destiny.

And so now, the vision dimmed, they saw only Jesus. The person of Jesus. His flesh, his face, his body.

Somehow that was enough and it was good. Very good.

It was like the comforting conclusion of a story. "They lived happily ever after."

They certainly didn't realize it, but they had discovered what the whole world would eventually know: that Jesus, their friend and companion, was indeed the sum total and final conclusion of everything that is. It all comes down to Jesus; or – perhaps more accurately – it all rises to Jesus.

Look at it this way. Waves crash on the seashore. They are relentless and indiscriminate. Wave after wave, hour after hour. The waves rush in, break into foam, and vanish. Another wave follows.

It is permanent. Jesus is permanent as well. He is like the waves of the sea: always there, but not always in our awareness.

Express it as you wish because every expression is inadequate. Jesus is the sun that makes the shadow. But don't look at the shadow or mind it or let it frighten you. The light creates the shadow. It is the light that is wonderful.

Father, bathe us in your Son's light.

185

A Question about Rising

Father Harry Cronin, c.s.c.

*As they were coming down from the mountain, [Jesus] charged
[Peter, James, and John] not to relate what they had seen to
anyone, except when the Son of Man had risen from the dead.
So they kept the matter to themselves, questioning what rising
from the dead meant. (Mk 9: 9-10)*

Good question. What does it mean to rise from the dead?
It is not a topic for discussion that regularly occurs in
day-to-day conversation. It is not a usual item of ordinary vocabulary. We don't discuss "rising from the dead" the way
we might chat about what the neighbors are doing or whether it
might rain today.

The disciples had heard these words spoken in the midst of a
vision. It was an astounding event which shattered their senses
and was, in every sense of the word, beyond belief. The problem
was, however, that they had actually seen it, and so the question of
believing or not believing had become irrelevant. And the words
about rising from the dead were beyond belief as well. The vision
is gone. They are left with the bare words and they are forced back
into the clumsy realm of meaning. What do the words mean?
What does it mean "to rise from the dead"? The question is both
compelling and urgent. Because it is the consequence of an even
more wrenching question: what does it mean to die?

Everyone dies. Everyone. It is an event both universal and feared.
What does it mean to die? We know the bare facts, of course. Everyone dies. But does death have any meaning?

For the murderer, of course, death has a meaning. It is punishment and retribution for crime. But for most of us, death is a random and meaningless running into darkness.

But at this point we descend into a blank confusion. What does
it mean to rise from the dead? What does it mean to die? And
then, the final clap of thunder: what does it mean to live?

The question goes deep, to the very core. But the answer is there.
Jesus. He is what it means to live.

Father, give us Jesus, the hope of our life.

When Elijah Comes

Father Harry Cronin, C.S.C.

Then [Peter, James, and John] asked [Jesus], "Why do the scribes say that Elijah must come first?" He told them, "Elijah will indeed come first and restore all things." (Mk 9: 11-12a)

The return of Elijah was revered by the Jewish people as both a hope and a promise. The return of Elijah was the "See? I told you so" of God's promise. The return of Elijah was one more guarantee of a trustworthy and faithful God.

It will all be restored.

That is an absolute certainty.

Everything will be brought back, assembled, collected, saved.

The reason for this universal rescue is vitally important. It is because absolutely everything, all of it, is of immense value. This is true even if we don't see the value of it. All of it is important, even if we are too dim to comprehend it.

That is why it will all be restored.

That is why nothing will be lost.

What Jesus means in particular is that, in our union and company with him, we have the glowing and priceless opportunity to see the past and the future in a changed way. Past and future are continuous wonder. Past and future are matched and joined, linked together in a precious scheme and purpose, planned scrupulously and carefully by God, a cunning strategy etched by the creator himself on the blank screen of time.

We see the past as we stand on the platform of the present. And the future? Well, we wonder about it. All the time. Sometimes we wonder in fear, knowing that things don't always work out, that there are horrors that occur without warning. And the two – future and past – are joined together in the ambiguous instant we call the present. Our only tool for viewing the past is our memory. Our only tool for surmising the future is our imagination. And we stand here, in the present, and view the past and muse about the future. We view them inadequately. But God sees them both from the better platform that is called eternity.

Father, give us the joy of honoring our time.

Pain and Glory

Father Harry Cronin, C.S.C.

"Yet how is it written regarding the Son of Man that he must suffer greatly and be treated with contempt? But I tell you that Elijah has come and they did to him whatever they pleased, as it is written of him." (Mk 9: 12b-13)

Suffer greatly and be treated with contempt. He calls himself "the Son of Man." That is the destiny he picked for himself. He chose that destiny from an infinite list of possible destinies. He chose to be "the Son of Man." And with that choice of destiny, he became nothing but vulnerable. To be a "Son of Man" was to be liable to every conceivable indignity. As "Son of Man" he would be totally and completely without protection. None at all. The only way he could protect himself would be to marshal immense force and power. He could have done that, but he did not. He did not choose the way of force and power, and as a consequence he died naked and bleeding, fastened with nails to a wooden cross. The "Son of Man" became an outlaw, a criminal, buried finally in a tomb that belonged to someone else. The destiny he chose became a bloody, agonizing destiny. He chose – actually chose – to "suffer greatly and be treated with contempt." You and I want to be loved and admired. Jesus wanted to be treated with contempt. Is it possible on any level to comprehend this? How can we understand that? How can we understand the outrageous truth that glory is only forged in the cauldron of loss?

Yes. We can comprehend this if we understand the reason why. We want to be loved and admired, but at the same time we know that we are powerless to bring that about. To be loved and admired is a chimera we pursue and when it happens it is rare indeed. What happens most frequently is that, like Jesus, we suffer greatly and are treated with contempt. Jesus chose to be "Son of Man" so he could stand next to us and receive our indignities. Yes. It is true. Glory is forged only in the cauldron of loss.

Father, help us understand the mystery of pain.

Thoughts about Arguing

Father Harry Cronin, c.s.c.

When [Jesus, Peter, James, and John] came to the disciples, they saw a large crowd around them and scribes arguing with them. Immediately on seeing [Jesus], the whole crowd was utterly amazed. They ran up to him and greeted him. He asked them, "What are you arguing about with [the disciples]?" (Mk 9: 14-16)

Arguments and disputes have always been an integral part of Jewish religion. Debate among rabbis and teachers of the law had always been considered a way of arriving at truth. It has always been an important part of the process of obtaining religious knowledge. The fact that an argument was happening was hardly unusual or suspicious.

Arguments are about what is true and what is false. Arguments relentlessly center around facts: the seemingly endless dispute among human beings about what is right and wrong, true and false, real or not real. There is a time and a place for arguments. But, for the disciples who had seen this extraordinary vision, that time had passed. They were beyond the realm of simple argument. They had no idea of the realm they had entered. One fact, however, was immensely clear: there was no point in discussing or arguing.

The vision which the disciples had seen brought them to a place where facts, even the simplest facts, had become irrelevant. And it had altered – for them, at least – their simple perceptions. Time was no longer a measure of life passing. It was instead the measure of life growing, of love increasing, of taking part in a procession led by the spirit of God.

The usual anchors of thought had disappeared. True and false, right and wrong, seen and unseen, real and not real – all of these had vanished. The disciples had seen pure light. They had seen Jesus in the midst of joy. Suddenly, there was simply nothing more to argue about. There was no dispute. Because the light they had seen had embraced them and light was love and love was light and the light and love was Jesus. And all had changed, all had become distant and indistinct, and in this new and brilliant light they wanted to shout in ecstasy. And not argue.

Father, give us the beauty of your light.

Healing and Doubt

Father Harry Cronin, C.S.C.

Someone from the crowd answered [Jesus], "Teacher, I have brought to you my son possessed by a mute spirit. Wherever it seizes him, it throws him down; he foams at the mouth, grinds his teeth, and becomes rigid. I asked your disciples to drive it out, but they were unable to do so." (Mk 9: 17-18)

They bring the pathetic to Jesus. They bring him the wounded, the tormented, the tortured, and the lost. In this incident, they bring him a miserable young boy. He is unable to speak, unable to engage in the most elemental form of communication. He cannot say what his needs are, how he thinks, why he fears, what he wonders about. He cannot express love. And most important, he cannot declare faith. He is so lacking that one might wonder if the word "human" could be appropriately applied to him. He lives in a world bounded by torture and frustration. Whatever he wishes to say must remain a wish only. And if his grief is human, he certainly can't say this or even ask the question. And above all this unhappiness, he is the object of fear and scorn.

Those who bring the boy to Jesus simply want him to be human. Nothing more than that. Just make him human. Just let him speak. They bring the helpless to Jesus and his disciples when all else has failed and all others have failed. They know from Jesus' past that he has healed. But these healings have always been disturbing because the healings were never the end. They were always the springboard for Jesus to make other disturbing statements about gratitude and faith. Because the duty to believe and the duty to be grateful can be as burdensome and limiting as not being able to speak. They approach him with both fear and doubt. "There is something about him." Is it an air? An attitude? A readiness? No. It is a spirit. It speaks in the slightest, most subtle expression in his face. He is a friend of grief and has a unique understanding of those who suffer. There is healing here for the grossest and most pointless evil. There is healing.

Father, let us approach your Son even when we are not sure.

How Faithful? How Loving?

Father Harry Cronin, C.S.C.

[Jesus] said to [the crowd] in reply, "O faithless generation, how long will I be with you? How long will I endure you? Bring him to me." (Mk 9: 19)

Jesus doesn't want an answer to his question. He doesn't want someone to tell him how patient and long-suffering he will be. He is not expecting someone to shout out: "How about a month?" "How about a year?" "Two years?" He already knows. The question is rhetorical at best.

"I will put up with you for ever," says Jesus. "I will endure you until time has run out. I will willingly and eagerly tolerate the dirt and the grit and the lies. I will always say, at the bottom of my frustration, bring him here to me. Just bring him here. Let him be present to the sound of my voice. Bring him here so I can breathe on him. Bring him to me so I can speak a single, blunt, and gentle word of love. Bring him to me so I can touch him. I will not be repelled by the touch. I will not wince or shy away no matter how whining or self-pitying he might seem. Just bring him here. Let him see my smile. Let him touch it if he is blind. Just bring him here. My love is not like yours. My love for you will not be compromised by a fear of loss. I will never lose you. If you back away from my love, I will run after you. I have resources you will never know or comprehend. At the beginning, when the project of humanity was first designed by God's mind, I purposely devised the genius of human cleverness. I designed it in a way in which I would always be ready to overcome. I can surpass your cleverness because I made you that way. It's all part of a plan. I can be more clever still. I can overcome human avoiding, human fear, human derision, and human hate. So I know that my love will not run out."

Father, let my confidence in you be without end.

The First Terrorist

Father Harry Cronin, C.S.C.

They brought the boy to [Jesus]. And when he saw him,
the spirit immediately threw the boy into convulsions.
As he fell to the ground, he began to roll around and foam
at the mouth. Then he questioned his father, "How long has
this been happening to him?" He replied, "Since childhood.
It has often thrown him into fire and into water to kill him."
(Mk 9: 20-22a)

The boy's body is both target and host to a mighty and deadly force. Worse than that, the force is both wily and intelligent. It is a force that has been witnessing the human tragedy since the tragedy first began and since it first became tragic. It is a force both slow and relentless: not bent on destroying the boy, but on using the boy as a means to bring fear. It is a force that is motivated. It is a force that, in a brutal and sinister way, truly wants something.

The evil ensnares the boy, but the object is not the boy. The object is all those who must watch the boy's decline. It is a fearful show of force put on for the benefit of all those who love the boy and all those whom the boy loves. It is a display of terror. Its object is not only to frighten, but also to paralyze.

It is a force profoundly evil and entirely personal. Its first target is that part of us that is most vulnerable: the field of what we imagine. Its path of destruction is first to ensnare the human imagination, and then immobilize it.

It is bent on bringing those who must witness this ugly dance to the brink of desperation. It is bent on destruction. It is an evil deep inside: a virus, a cancer.

But this particular evil inside this boy has much grander ambitions. This spirit wants to sow deep discomfort and anxiety in the hearts of everyone who witnesses the convulsions. "Don't ever get comfortable," the spirit says. "Don't ever be at peace or try to capture serenity. Imagine the worst that will happen and then be sure, be absolutely certain that what will eventually happen will be more damaging than anything you can imagine."

No, Jesus says. No.

Father, take from us every fear.

Don't Say "If"

Father Harry Cronin, C.S.C.

"But if you can do anything, have compassion on us and help us." Jesus said to [the boy's father], "'If you can!' Everything is possible to one who has faith." (Mk 9: 22b-23)

Wait. Wait. Say that again. Everything? That's not possible. You're saying that everything is possible, and you seem intelligent and fluent and well-schooled, but the most ignorant dunce in the street knows the precise opposite, knows that possibilities are by their nature limited. What is possible, what can actually happen is a narrow, usually painful lane between what I dread and what I desire, and joy is occasional and rare. So don't tell me everything is possible. When you believe that you just get your hopes up and sometimes that's good, but most of the time it is not good at all. When you get your hopes up, you are disappointed, and so it is infinitely safer to live in despair, to live in a world with no hope. Despairing is painful, but not as painful as disappointment. It is better to have no hope at all than to have hopes dashed. So, please. Don't say that everything is possible.

But you say it is. You say it simply and with passion. That impresses me.

All right. All right. Answer me this. If everything is possible to one who has faith, please tell me how and why. The faith that you recommend has a consequence. It means that I enter into a new possibility – and even a new world. And I don't make this entrance by some kind of magic gift. I decide to enter. I say the words: "I believe."

What if I hedge? What if I say "if" to God? What if I say something like this: "If I promise to be good." "If my child does not die." "If I only get what I want." But that doesn't work, does it? The answer is: don't ever, ever say "if." God is God. His goodness has no conditions. He is pure love and pure light, pure forgiveness and pure grace. Whatever you do, don't say "if."

Father, let my prayer be as your love. Let it be without conditions.

When Faith Needs Help

Father Harry Cronin, C.S.C.

Then the boy's father cried out,
"I do believe, help my unbelief!"
(Mk 9: 24)

Try crying that out. Go outside, find a distant, quiet place where no one can hear you and then scream, shout at the top of your voice, "I do believe, help my unbelief!" You can't shout those words in a way that's fast and sharp. You have to shout that phrase slowly and it has to be peppered generously with tears.

When the boy's father shouted these words, he fell into the abyss. His whole being gave itself over to a deadly and dangerous free-fall. His eyes were fixed on Jesus, their eyes are locked and, for a rare and magnificent moment, he refuses to look at the brutal harshness we innocently call "the real world." He puts on new clothes, he enters a freshly furnished, just painted dwelling. The smell is new but the look and the feel, the whole experience, is frankly terrifying. There is nothing familiar, absolutely nothing that is within the realm of his experience. Besides that, there is nothing to negotiate: no wagers, no chances. And for this reason, the statement he makes is naked and vulnerable: I do believe. Help my unbelief. I do. I do believe. But my belief is wavering and inconstant. My belief is like dripping water. My belief is like a dying flower. My belief is like dust carried by a strong wind. So my belief needs help.

There is a dark place in my heart that laughs hysterically at the barest notion of believing. There is a dark place in my heart that keeps repeating, over and over, "faith is for fools, faith is for fools." It is the same dark place in my heart where I carefully store my fears. Help me there, Jesus. In that dark frightening place inside me. Help me there, Jesus. And Jesus does.

Father, help me when my belief is not strong enough.

New Life for Old

Father Harry Cronin, C.S.C.

Jesus, on seeing a crowd rapidly gathering, rebuked the unclean spirit and said to it, "Mute and deaf spirit, I command you: come out of him and never enter him again!" Shouting and throwing the boy into convulsions, it came out. He became like a corpse, which caused many to say, "He is dead!" But Jesus took him by the hand, raised him, and he stood up.

(Mk 9: 25-27)

An audience was assembling. The crowds of people sensed that something was about to happen. They didn't know exactly what was going to happen, but whatever it was, it would be worth watching. The tortured young man was the center of attention. Yes, they thought. This is going to be exciting. But what was really happening could not be seen. What was happening was not a spectacle. What was happening was an important and solemn lesson about life itself.

Life: it's what we live by. We can live by our wits or live by our gut or live by our intelligence. The problem is that each of these in turn will fail us. In the story for today, the boy is driven by pure embodied evil. It's as if he lives by that evil. In some mysterious way, the evil seems to own him. For that reason, when Jesus orders the spirit to come out of the boy – he seems dead!

The fact that Jesus came to us to destroy evil becomes very important when we see how desperately powerful evil can be. Evil has been overcome. But evil still strives to get up and keep fighting. It will be a losing battle, but it will be a battle. The outcome is never in doubt as long as we fight by the rules. The rules are simple: depend on God. Depend on his strength and power. Never rely on yourself. And when the invader leaves, when the false life fails us, well, yes – then we seem dead.

But Jesus is the provider of new life. The new life is free and ready for us to have. Turn in the old life and get a new one in return. Turn in the unclean spirit and be filled with the spirit of God's only Son who is nothing but love.

Father, open our hearts completely to your new life.

A Way to God

Father Harry Cronin, C.S.C.

*When [Jesus] entered the house, his disciples asked him in
private, "Why could we not drive it out?" He said to them,
"This kind can only come out through prayer."*
(Mk 9: 28-29)

Prayer opens a way to God. It is like a bridge, a channel, or a tunnel. Prayer links the mind of God to our mind and the heart of God to our heart. When we pray, we take advantage of an access to God which is, in every sense, deeply personal. For this reason we do not – and should not – tell God in prayer what we think God wants to hear. We should say to God only what we deeply want to say. We should say to God what is in our heart.

On a conscious level, when we pray we usually have something in mind, something that we want and something we can't get or bring about with our own power. So we pray. On the conscious level, when we pray we usually pray "for"… for health, for escape, for money, for love. For something. For whatever. We ask God. Sometimes these prayers are answered and sometimes not. But no matter the outcome, we may not be aware of the fact that the channel has been opened. We have made a connection with God, whether we realize it or not. This is the unconscious dimension of prayer.

When we come to God with our need, we have laid ourselves open to him, we have exposed our vulnerability. In the act of praying, in the process of opening this channel, something else has happened. What we need to realize is that our access to God gives us access as well to God's power. We don't pray to God the way a beggar in the street asks for money. We pray to God because we are his children. Our access to God is a special access.

The disciples were unsuccessful in their attempts to get rid of demons because they didn't avail themselves of prayer. The bridge, the link, the tunnel had not been opened.

*Father, prayer is our food, our life, and our breath. May we use
it always.*

"Be not afraid"

Sister Mary Timothea Elliott, R.S.M.

[Jesus and his disciples] left from there and began a journey through Galilee, but he did not wish anyone to know about it. He was teaching his disciples and telling them, "The Son of Man is to be handed over to men and they will kill him, and three days after his death he will rise." But they did not understand the saying, and they were afraid to question him. (Mk 9: 30-32)

During the homily at the Mass that formally opened his pontificate, Blessed John Paul II cried out, "Be not afraid! Be not afraid to open the doors to Christ!" Whenever this pope encountered young Catholics at a World Youth Day, he repeated the same message: "Be not afraid to open the doors of your hearts to Christ!"

Jesus is traveling with his disciples through Galilee, on the way to Jerusalem. At this time he wishes to instruct them and prepare them for what lies ahead. He does not want them to be frightened and scandalized by the cross. It is an intimate time for Jesus with his disciples alone. As they journey together, Jesus opens his heart and tells them, "The Son of Man is to be handed over to men and they will kill him, and three days after his death he will rise." The disciples are startled. Peter, James, and John recall their vision of Jesus' glory on Mount Tabor and wonder what this could mean.

"But they did not understand the saying, and they were afraid to question him." Why are the disciples afraid? Why do they refrain from questioning Jesus? Here he is among them and there are no jostling crowds begging for attention. Jesus attempts to gather them, to share with them his anticipation of betrayal, suffering, death, and resurrection. But they withdraw into silence, as if they do not hear what he is saying.

Each disciple knows himself to be loved by Jesus. Each knows that he was called by name to be "with Jesus," to preach the good news of the kingdom, to heal and cast out demons, to follow closely and be formed by the teaching of the Master. However, this message of betrayal, suffering, death, and resurrection just does not fit with their aspirations. They are afraid to open wide the doors of their hearts, to welcome a new depth of understanding and relationship with Jesus.

Heavenly Father, help us to so trust in your love that we may dare to ask the questions that will lead to new depths of relationship with you.

Dreams of Power and Glory

Sister Mary Timothea Elliott, R.S.M.

[Jesus and his disciples] came to Capernaum and, once inside the house, [Jesus] began to ask them, "What were you arguing about on the way?" But they remained silent. They had been discussing among themselves on the way who was the greatest.
(Mk 9: 33-34)

J esus and the disciples come to Capernaum in their journey through Galilee. Once inside the house, Jesus asks them, "What were you arguing about on the way?" The manner in which Jesus phrases his question suggests to us that the disciples lagged behind him on the way and spoke heatedly among themselves. Obviously they did not talk about Jesus' prediction of his Passion! A second time their response to Jesus is silence. This time it is not a silence of fear, but of embarrassment. "They had been discussing among themselves on the way who was the greatest."

How alone Jesus must feel among his chosen band who have rejected and forgotten the word of his approaching Passion and death. Their personal dreams of power and glory motivate them to follow Jesus at a distance and to argue and squabble over precedence in the group. Looking into the questioning eyes of the Master and realizing that he knows them in all their obtuseness and personal ambition, yet continues to love them, they could only be deeply embarrassed.

Saint Thérèse of Lisieux preferred to pray on the passages of Scripture where Jesus was alone, and she sought to keep him company in his solitude. Perhaps this is a passage that appealed to her. While Jesus was surrounded by the Twelve, nevertheless he was quite alone. The disciples repeatedly rejected Jesus' message of his approaching Passion and death – they rejected the cross. And, in fact, they rejected him as he attempted to reveal his true nature and mission. Their personal dreams of power and glory at the side of the Messiah interfered with the depth of relationship that he offered them.

Is it possible that I follow Jesus at a distance because my personal aspirations and goals conflict with the mission he has planned for me to accomplish in union with him?

Patient Father, we often prefer the human honors and glory that so easily pass away to the true glory of being your children by baptism. Help us to keep our eyes on the glory that never ends.

Paradox

Sister Mary Timothea Elliott, R.S.M.

Then [Jesus] sat down, called the Twelve, and said to them, "If anyone wishes to be first, he shall be the last of all and the servant of all." (Mk 9: 35)

In the accounts of the three predictions of the Passion in Mark's Gospel, a repeated pattern emerges. Jesus speaks of his approaching betrayal and being handed over to men, his suffering, death, and resurrection. The apostles respond with a rejection of the message in some form, and then as a consequence, Jesus instructs them on the true nature of discipleship.

In this second prediction, the apostles' rejection takes the form of silence and fear, and leads to an argument about who is the greatest among them. First Jesus sits down, in the posture of a rabbi about to teach. He then begins a serious lesson in discipleship: "If anyone wishes to be first, he shall be the last of all and the servant of all."

The saying involves a paradox that reverses all the conventional notions about greatness. Society says the great are first; they have the power; they have many possessions and servants who do their bidding; they have front-row seats, and everyone listens when they speak. Jesus says that greatness in the kingdom involves the exact opposite. The great among his disciples will take the last place; they will not enjoy prominence or prestige; indeed, they are to be the servants of all. With this teaching Jesus elevates and dignifies service.

After the third prediction of the Passion (Mk 10: 32-34), James and John respond with a striking example of ambition. Jesus repeats his message of service. "You know that those who are recognized as rulers over the Gentiles lord it over them, and their great ones make their authority over them felt. But it shall not be so among you. Rather, whoever wishes to be great among you will be your servant; whoever wishes to be first among you will be the slave of all. For the Son of Man did not come to be served but to serve and to give his life as a ransom for many" (Mk 10: 42b-45). Jesus models the perfection of service for his disciples.

Loving Father, you sent your Son Jesus as the servant of all, especially to the poor and the suffering. Greatest of all was his service of suffering and dying on the cross to free us from sin and eternal death.

Disciples and Children

Sister Mary Timothea Elliott, R.S.M.

Taking a child [Jesus] placed it in their midst, and putting his arms around it he said to them, "Whoever receives one child such as this in my name, receives me; and whoever receives me, receives not me but the One who sent me." (Mk 9: 36-37)

Jesus continues his lesson on discipleship. To do so, he takes a child, stands him up in the midst of the Twelve, and embraces him. It would not be correct to impose upon this scene our contemporary idealization of children, equating them with happy innocence, humility, and simple faith. The Jews at the time of Jesus regarded children as unworthy of consideration. If anything, they were the objects of total disregard and scorn. The Aramaic term for "child" is *talya*, a word which signifies both "child" and "servant." This word underscores Jesus' lesson about discipleship and service, and connects it to the previous verse.

When Matthew considers this incident, he has Jesus admonishing the disciples to become as children. "Amen, I say to you, unless you turn and become like children, you will not enter the kingdom of heaven. Whoever humbles himself like this child is the greatest in the kingdom of heaven" (Mt 18: 3-4). In Mark, Jesus' message is not a call to imitate the child, but to receive and care for the unimportant in society, like the child. He calls his disciples to loving service of the weaker members of the community; those on the margins; those who stand in the greatest need of service; those who are dependent and have no claim to greatness. Jesus identifies the child with himself by embracing it, and says, "Whoever receives one child such as this in my name receives me." A Christian is one baptized into the name of Jesus (Mt 28: 19) and who belongs to him. In receiving another because of his connection with Jesus, the disciple receives (serves) Jesus himself and in so doing welcomes the Father: "and whoever receives me, receives not me but the One who sent me."

Such is the dignity of the disciple's service. Jesus so identifies with those called by his name in baptism, that in receiving one of these little ones we serve Jesus himself. Moreover, we receive the Father who has sent him. The real competition among the disciples now becomes a competition to welcome and serve others.

Compassionate Father, I place myself in your embrace, grateful that you have claimed me as your child by my baptism. Enlighten my eyes so that I may see Jesus and serve him in the most needy people I meet.

Division or Union

Sister Mary Timothea Elliott, R.S.M.

John said to [Jesus], "Teacher, we saw someone driving out demons in your name, and we tried to prevent him because he does not follow us." Jesus replied, "Do not prevent him. There is no one who performs a mighty deed in my name who can at the same time speak ill of me." (Mk 9: 38-39)

As a child growing up in a neighborhood where Protestants outnumbered Catholic residents, and at the same time attending a Catholic elementary school, I was acutely aware of what it meant to "belong" to the Catholic Church. Those who did not belong to the Catholic Church I thought of as outsiders, living in darkness, and deprived of the true faith, the Mass, and sacraments. There was an aura of feeling "special," particularly loved by God, of having a direct line to Truth.

The Second Vatican Council and the ensuing years introduced a corrective to these attitudes that underscored separation and, instead, accented the expressions of our common Christian beliefs. We were encouraged to engage in dialogue, to explore the aspects of faith and practice that unite us as Christians, to recognize our common baptism and reverence for the Sacred Scriptures.

John speaks for the other apostles who have received from Jesus the authority to act in his name, to heal, and to cast out demons. He refers to "we" and "us." Jesus, on the other hand, recognizes in the one driving out demons in his name a genuine faith in his power. This is a person on the way to becoming a follower of Jesus, a disciple. Such a person should not be prevented in his approach by any false sense of exclusivity or defensiveness. He should be regarded as one on a journey toward unity. This one will not speak ill of Jesus.

It is important to recognize the action of the Holy Spirit in the hearts of those who act "in the name of Jesus" or adhere strongly to some of his teaching, and to welcome them in a dialogue which may lead to a full incorporation into the intimate circle of Jesus' disciples who make up the Body which is his Church.

Loving Father, you desire that all be saved and come to you through Jesus your Son. Give us welcoming hearts toward all those who share in the dialogue of salvation and seek the Truth of your kingdom.

For and Against Christ

Sister Mary Timothea Elliott, R.S.M.

"For whoever is not against us is for us. Anyone who gives you a cup of water to drink because you belong to Christ, amen, I say to you, will surely not lose his reward." (Mk 9: 40-41)

This passage is closely connected to the one that immediately precedes it. There, John uses the word "us" (v. 38) to signify the band of disciples united with Jesus. Here, Jesus uses the word "us" (v. 40) in the same way. He has so united himself with his disciples that they form one Body with him. As he claims that no one who performs a mighty deed in his name can at the same time speak ill of him, so also, one who recognizes the power of Jesus' name is already positively disposed toward him.

In this passage anyone who performs even a small act of kindness, like giving a drink of water because "you belong to Christ," receives a reward. "Belonging to Christ" is a reference to baptism. This gift is given to a person because he is a disciple and belongs to Jesus. The messenger who is sent is recognized as embodying the person who sent him. An act of kindness to a disciple is thus actually an expression of faith and obedience to Jesus. Therefore, Jesus recognizes the cup of water extended to a disciple as given to himself.

Jesus admonishes his followers in every age that "whoever is not against us is for us." In our interactions with non-Christians or non-Catholics, we need to regard them as pilgrims on their way to the fullness of faith and obedience to Jesus. When they use his name with reverence and belief in his power, they are, in fact, approaching Jesus with an initial faith. When they welcome the disciples of Jesus with kindness and acts of hospitality, they are welcoming Jesus himself in them. The Christian response should be a recognition that this person is welcoming Christ in their person; we are to engage them in a dialogue, sharing faith and inviting them to greater knowledge and communion with him.

Just and holy Father, lead us to celebrate our union with you, initiated in baptism. Show us how to approach others while anticipating the working of your Holy Spirit in their hearts prior to our encounter with them.

Scandal

Sister Mary Timothea Elliott, R.S.M.

"Whoever causes one of these little ones who believe [in me] to sin, it would be better for him if a great millstone were put around his neck and he were thrown into the sea." (Mk 9: 42)

In our present times, the term "scandal" is not generally used with its exact meaning. Today a scandal usually refers to a shocking or sensational piece of news involving criminal behavior on the part of a public figure, such as sports stars using strength-enhancing drugs, financiers executing scams that create tremendous losses to investors, or political figures engaged in unethical behavior. The public response may be curiosity or condemnation, harsh judgment or disillusionment. However, aside from the emotional shock, the acts themselves do not encourage similar behavior by those who hear about them.

Scandal in the strict sense is defined here by Jesus as "causing one of these little ones who believe in me to sin." The *Catechism of the Catholic Church* expands the definition somewhat. "Scandal is a grave offense when by deed or omission it deliberately leads others to sin gravely" (2326). "Little ones" does not necessarily refer to small children. The little ones may be those who are young and vulnerable in their faith. One who deliberately shakes the faith of a simple Christian or leads others astray is guilty of grave sin. Jesus underscores the seriousness of scandal by a dramatic image. He says it would be better "that a great millstone were put around his neck and he were thrown into the sea." Execution by binding a person to a heavy object, like a huge stone or iron anchor, and casting him in the sea to drown was commonly practiced by the Romans, and especially feared by the Jews.

A few moments of simple reflection can make us aware of how many occasions of scandal we are subjected to daily, and of instances where we might personally give others scandal. These may occur within our immediate families, our work situations, or our places of recreation. Far more important is the consideration of ways that we might counter the effects of scandal in our society by the habit of giving a good example and reinforcing habits of virtue in the lives of the little ones among the faithful.

Good and gracious Father, in your Son you have given us the model of One totally pleasing to you. Strengthen us as we seek to imitate Jesus in our lives and to refrain from any act or omission that might lead another into sin.

Eternal Life, the Ultimate Goal

Sister Mary Timothea Elliott, R.S.M.

"If your hand causes you to sin, cut it off. It is better for you to enter into life maimed than with two hands to go into Gehenna, into the unquenchable fire. And if your foot causes you to sin, cut it off. It is better for you to enter into life crippled than with two feet to be thrown into Gehenna." (Mk 9: 43-45)

Whereas the preceding verse dealt with a person who causes a little one to sin, these three verses deal with scandal that comes from within oneself. The hand and the foot are important members of the body through which a person may carry out a sinful act. In this sense, the hand or the foot may cause one to stumble, to fall into sin. Jesus urges us, his disciples, to take the most extreme and decisive measures to avoid sin and enter into life. "Life" refers to everlasting life, that life promised to those who believe in him, that life which is the goal of our earthly existence. To lose this life is the greatest imaginable tragedy.

This is the second time that Jesus focuses upon the importance of always keeping the goal of our existence in mind. After the first prediction of his Passion (Mk 8: 31) and the disciples' resistance to his teaching regarding the cross and suffering, Jesus says to them: "What profit is there for one to gain the whole world and forfeit his life? What could one give in exchange for his life?" (Mk 8: 36-37). The stark language of the imperative "cut it off!" urges us to look deeply within ourselves and ask the question, "What are those things within myself that lead to sin?" "What are the habits, desires, passions, or human goals that make me forget my ultimate goal of everlasting life with God?" Jesus counsels us to become aware, and be ruthless in removing them.

The alternative is Gehenna. Gehenna refers to the Valley of the son of Hinnon. At an early stage of Israel's history, infants were offered as human sacrifices to the god Moloch in this ravine south of Jerusalem. Later it was used as a dump for every sort of refuse, a place of constantly smoldering fires. Gehenna and hell are used synonymously here and in the writings of the prophets. To land in Gehenna means to miss the transcendent goal of one's life and to die in a state of eternal meaninglessness.

Merciful Father, strengthen my will in the pursuit of good and the decisive conquest of those things within me that cause me to separate myself from the only Person who offers true happiness.

Choices Have Consequences

Sister Mary Timothea Elliott, R.S.M.

"And if your eye causes you to sin, pluck it out. Better for you to enter into the kingdom of God with one eye than with two eyes to be thrown into Gehenna, where 'their worm does not die, and the fire is not quenched.'" (Mk 9: 47-48)

It is noteworthy that in these sayings Jesus refers to members of the body that come in pairs – hands, feet, and eyes. At the same time he speaks of only one of the members: if your hand or your foot causes you to sin, cut it off… if your eye causes you to sin, pluck it out… Focusing upon only one of two members suggests a choice. The hand, the foot, or the eye may be directed toward good or evil. The choice may be toward virtue or sin. The decision is important and it is ours to make.

The teaching of Jesus here appears harsh, and even startling. He seems to exaggerate in order to make the point that nothing is too great a sacrifice to avoid sin. Nothing – not even loss of the most important members of our bodies – not even our human life itself is worth sin.

The choices we make have eternal consequences. Choices for good lead to the acquiring of virtue and the end for which God has created us. This end is eternal life with him and joy in the kingdom of heaven. Choices that tend toward sin also have consequences. They lead to separation from God and everlasting, gnawing regret. Jesus urges us to take responsibility for our actions, to realize what is at stake, to be aware that scandal is given and received both from exterior sources and from within our very selves.

Failure to strive actively for holiness of life, resting content with mediocrity, or simply drifting through life without keeping our eyes fixed attentively on our eternal goal, often means placing ourselves in the near occasions of sin. The author of the Letter to the Hebrews encourages us: "Let us rid ourselves of every burden and sin that clings to us and persevere in running the race that lies before us while keeping our eyes fixed on Jesus, the leader and perfecter of faith" (Heb 12: 1b-2a).

Eternal Father, often it is too easy to neglect the daily reflection necessary to examine the effects our choices, acts, and omissions have upon the lives of others. We can slide easily into habits that weaken our resolution to strive for holiness. Give us the graces we need to hope confidently in you as we make the radical choices leading to eternal life.

Salt and Fire

Sister Mary Timothea Elliott, R.S.M.

"Everyone will be salted with fire. Salt is good, but if salt becomes insipid, with what will you restore its flavor? Keep salt in yourselves and you will have peace with one another."
(Mk 9: 49-50)

Jesus concludes his teaching on discipleship using puzzling references to fire and salt. What does it mean? It seems out of context with the verses that come before it. The fire of Gehenna in the previous verse signified a means of punishment, while salt suddenly appears for the first time.

The significance of "fire" changes here. Now it pertains to "sacrifice" rather than punishment. To avoid sin one must be ready to sacrifice anything, even a hand, a foot, or an eye. The disciple of Jesus must come to terms with the possibility of becoming a sacrifice for God through suffering, persecution, and even death. "I urge you therefore, brothers, by the mercies of God, to offer your bodies as a living sacrifice, holy and pleasing to God, your spiritual worship" (Rom 12: 1). In biblical times, holocaust offerings were first salted and then totally consumed by fire. In this context, "fire" stands for purification through renunciation and suffering. A disciple must be ready to become a holocaust, offering his very life.

In the ancient world, salt was a necessity of life. It was used for seasoning and for the preservation of food. Much of the available salt was not usable, however, due to its combining with impurities or becoming tasteless. Salt is used here as a metaphor for true discipleship. The disciple who loses his devotion to Christ, who does not willingly take up his cross, loses his saltiness. He is no longer effective for the life and salvation of the world.

The disciples are cautioned to "keep salt in yourselves." This salt is a sacrificial love, a willingness to carry the cross, and to lose one's life for Jesus' sake. If the disciples have this salt there will be peace with one another. Thus, Jesus' teaching corrective on discipleship has come full circle. It began with the disciples quarreling about who was the greatest. Jesus instructs them that if they have the "salt" of true discipleship in themselves, there will be peace with one another.

Forgiving Father, we give ourselves over to your purifying love. Restore us so that we may be the salt that preserves and flavors the spirit of true discipleship in your kingdom.

Transitions Are Significant

Sister Mary Timothea Elliott, R.S.M.

[Jesus] set out from there and went into the district of Judea [and] across the Jordan. Again crowds gathered around him and, as was his custom, he again taught them. (Mk 10: 1)

Until this point in Mark's narrative, Jesus' mission is centered in Galilee. Following his baptism by John in the Jordan, he appears first of all in the northern region and there begins his proclamation of the Gospel. The early period of his mission is marked by teaching and healing, giving evidence that he has been sent by God and that his power comes from God. Crowds follow him everywhere. However, even from the beginning he faces opposition and confrontation with religious leaders. At a certain point, he withdraws from the crowds and only travels with his chosen disciples. It is a time of intimacy with them, and also a time in which he endeavors to prepare them for what lies ahead.

At this significant moment, Jesus leaves Galilee and travels to Judea, across the Jordan where he was anointed by the Spirit for his mission. Judea and Jerusalem are the places where his mission is to be completed. It is a time of transition. "Again crowds gathered around him." He receives them and teaches them *again*. Mark's repetition of "again" along with the expression "as was his custom" could give the impression that Jesus is returning to a former mode of operation. But this is not the case. Jesus' movement into Judea marks his commitment to accomplish his Father's will by means of his suffering and death. Jesus is in a new place both geographically and interiorly. Everything takes on heightened meaning.

Transitions are significant for us twenty-first century disciples also. Transitions are vulnerable moments. They are especially significant when they are the result of new understandings of God's will for us. At times they require radical expressions of our baptismal commitment. Transitions often entail a journey, initiated by God, into a new land shown to us by God, and filled with promise and challenges to faith, hope, and love.

Gracious Father, even small transitions present challenges to faith, hope, and love. Show us how to follow your will with alacrity trusting that you have prepared the Way before us.

Testing God

Sister Mary Timothea Elliott, R.S.M.

"The Pharisees approached and asked, "Is it lawful for a husband to divorce his wife?" They were testing [Jesus].
(Mk 10: 2)

The manner in which the Pharisees were "testing" Jesus reminds us of the way that children or teens test their parents or teachers. The young desire to know where their boundaries are. The child will ask, "May I stay up and watch a TV show after my usual bedtime?" Or, "May I ride my bike to visit a friend who lives in a neighborhood across a busy highway?" The teen asks a teacher, "What is the minimum amount of work that I must do to pass this course?" Or pushes his parents, "Do you *really* mean I have to be home by 10:00 PM?" They will test the limits by stretching them, even a little, to see what happens.

In this episode, the Pharisees approach Jesus with a question about the law of God regarding divorce. Their question has little to do with the spirit of the law and more to do with how much one can push the limits of the law. It is like the teen wondering how much he or she can get away with without incurring a penalty for actually breaking the law.

The question, as it is presented, approaches the topic of divorce from only one point of view. "Is it lawful for a husband to divorce his wife?" Phrased in this way, the question focuses only upon the husband and omits any consideration of his wife and family. The Pharisees, teachers and interpreters of the law, ask Jesus to answer a question to which they believe they know the answer, and they seek only his confirmation of the manner in which they interpret the law.

How often do we go to Jesus in prayer with questions that deal with living our faith, and ask, "How little can I do and still get to heaven?" Or approach a moral question from only one point of view – our own? Are we not "testing God"?

Heavenly Father, we are your children and we know that you love us. Help us to grow and mature in "wisdom, age, and grace" until we are one with the mind and heart of your Son, Jesus.

Hardness of Heart or Stability of Purpose?

Sister Mary Timothea Elliott, R.S.M.

[Jesus] said to [the Pharisees] in reply, "What did Moses command you?" They replied, "Moses permitted him to write a bill of divorce and dismiss her." But Jesus told them, "Because of the hardness of your hearts he wrote you this commandment." (Mk 10: 3-5)

Jesus responds to the question of the Pharisees with another question: "What did Moses command you?" Knowing their hearts, he knows they are testing him, and testing the limits of God's law. The Pharisees reply, "Moses permitted him to write a bill of divorce and dismiss her" (see Dt 24: 1-4). Jesus underscores the fact that Moses made a concession here, for there is no commandment of God behind this "permission." In fact, the original purpose of writing a bill of divorce was to protect the wife. The Pharisees had interpreted it as giving permission for the male to divorce. Jesus told them the reason for Moses' relaxing the law: it was the hardness of their hearts. Given man's sinfulness, situations arise where man and wife are separated. However, Jesus' reference to the Pharisees' "hardness of heart" removes any ethical basis for the practice of divorce.

In his Message for the 2011 World Youth Day in Madrid, Spain, entitled "Planted and built up in Jesus Christ, firm in the faith," Pope Benedict XVI highlighted how these words from Saint Paul's Letter to the Colossians run decisively against the tide. "Who nowadays suggests that young people should be 'planted' and 'firm'? On the contrary, uncertainty, mobility and volubility are exalted; all aspects which reflect a culture hesitant over its fundamental values... I wished to offer a message which, following the style of the Bible, evokes the image of the tree and the house. Young people indeed are like growing trees: in order to develop correctly they need deep roots which, when storms blow, keep them firmly rooted to the ground. In the same way, the image of a building in construction recalls the need for proper foundations, in order for the house to be solid and secure."

The Pharisees and the world look for concessions. Jesus answers with clarity in terms of God's law. Pope Benedict XVI in his message to youth addresses the higher nature of the person, what he is capable of with grace, and calls for sinking deep roots in the law of God as interpreted by his Son.

Merciful Father, through our encounters with Jesus in prayer and the sacraments, help us to appreciate the heights of sanctity to which we have been called in your commandments.

From the Beginning of Creation

Sister Mary Timothea Elliott, R.S.M.

"But from the beginning of creation, 'God made them male and female. For this reason a man shall leave his father and mother [and be joined to his wife], and the two shall become one flesh.' So they are no longer two but one flesh. Therefore what God has joined together, no human being must separate." (Mk 10: 6-9)

Jesus anchors his position on divorce, not in law, but in God's will "from the beginning." The existence of two sexes was ordained by God in his act of creation (see Gn 1: 27; 2: 21-24). His true will must be discerned from the order of creation itself. This law of nature existed before any other law or covenant existed. Prior to Moses or the commandments, it was so. There has never been any other way.

Jesus teaches that the union of man and woman in marriage is indissoluble. He renews the first plan that the Creator inscribed in the hearts of man and woman. Further, in the celebration of the sacrament of matrimony he offers a "new heart": thus the couples are not only able to overcome "hardness of heart," but to remain faithful to each other for ever, beyond every difficulty and trial. Above all, by their baptism they are placed within the new and eternal covenant, in the spousal covenant of Christ with the Church. Because of this indestructible insertion, the intimate community of conjugal life and love, founded by the Creator, is elevated and assumed into the spousal charity of Christ, sustained and enriched by his redeeming power (see *Familiaris Consortio* by Pope John Paul II, articles 13 and 20).

The Pharisees' question presumes a very narrow view of marriage. It is one in which the will of the husband can terminate the relationship with his wife by a writ of divorce on the basis of something in his wife that displeases him. This is not unlike the situation of our current society where a divorce rate of fifty percent prevails. Any reason appears sufficient. Jesus calls spouses to a high degree of discipleship. Their union is to be an icon of his own love "to the end."

Good and gracious Father, pour out your Holy Spirit into our hearts and give us a truly supernatural love that participates in the union and communion of your own Trinitarian life.

Sacrificial Love

Sister Mary Timothea Elliott, R.S.M.

In the house the disciples again questioned [Jesus] about this. He said to them, "Whoever divorces his wife and marries another commits adultery against her; and if she divorces her husband and marries another, she commits adultery." (Mk 10: 10-12)

The context of this saying begins in Mark, chapter 10. Jesus has set out from Galilee and traveled into Judea, on his way up to Jerusalem. After his exchange with the Pharisees on the question of a husband divorcing his wife, Jesus enters the house where his disciples question him "again."

Although the essential things have already been said, the ethical implications of divorce are taken up here. In this encounter between Jesus and the Twelve, the focus is no longer on the separation of the spouses but on remarriage after divorce. Jewish practice allowed only the man to dissolve the marriage, and he could marry again. Women could neither initiate a divorce nor remarry after divorce unless the husband consented. Jesus makes the application more universal in order to take into account the practice in the Greek-speaking world, and attributes the sin of adultery to any man or woman who remarries after divorce. This is because the first marriage bond is indissoluble and has never been broken.

This passage from Mark along with Saint Paul's teaching established the Church's practice of forbidding remarriage to divorced couples. "To the married, however, I give this instruction (not I, but the Lord): a wife should not separate from her husband – and if she does separate she must either remain single or become reconciled to her husband – and a husband should not divorce his wife" (1 Cor 7: 10-11).

The teaching of Jesus on "discipleship for the married" is clear and demanding. Each Christian vocation, without exception, must deal with the cross. Due to our wounded human nature, relationships inevitably involve suffering and require forgiveness over and over. Because of the call to union and communion at every level – physical, spiritual, and psychological – marriage demands a continuous growth in unselfish love as a way of holiness.

Loving Father, bless spouses and give them the courage continuously to nurture sacrificial love for one another that they may be striking images of Christ's love for his Bride, the Church.

Let the Children Come to Jesus

Douglas Bushman

And people were bringing children to [Jesus] that he might touch them, but the disciples rebuked them. When Jesus saw this he became indignant and said to them, "Let the children come to me; do not prevent them, for the kingdom of God belongs to such as these." (Mk 10: 13-14)

After his son's First Confession, a father said: "When I think that my son opens the mysteries of his heart to Christ's representative, I realize he is more God's than mine. Only Jesus can give him what I want most for him." That realization could have come with baptism. It applies for every reception of Holy Communion. Only God can forgive sins, reconcile us to himself, love us to our full capacity to be loved, and grace us to share in his own life. These are what really matter.

Parents with Catholic faith know where Jesus is. They have access to God's love for their children through the Church's ministry. And even if clergy sometimes fail to carry out their mission, it does not negate Christ's promises to his Church. He is there to give new life in baptism, strengthen that life in confirmation, nourish it with his redeeming love in the Eucharist, and heal it with merciful forgiveness in confession.

The love of Jesus appeals to the love of parents: "Let your children come to me." It means: "These children are entrusted to your love. Together let us love them. Bring them to me for the love that only God can give." This requires parents to prioritize. How many miles are logged bringing children to doctors, dentists, coaches, instructors? How many phone calls and searches on the web – all motivated by love? All of these are important, yet all of them together cannot meet the most fundamental need, namely, to know that the one who created us did so out of love, and that he does not give up on us even when we sin. What doctors, dentists, coaches, and teachers impart contributes to a full and meaningful life, but without God's love revealed in Jesus Christ and made available in the Church, there is no lasting meaning. Only God's eternal love meets the deepest needs of the human heart.

Father of all, through the intercession of Saint Mark and Saint John the Baptist, turn the hearts of fathers and mothers to their children.

The Kingdom Belongs to Children

Douglas Bushman

"Amen, I say to you, whoever does not accept the kingdom of God like a child will not enter it." Then [Jesus] embraced [the children] and blessed them, placing his hands on them.
(Mk 10: 15-16)

The quality of children that Jesus commends is trust. Little children are pure receptivity. They do not question whether what is given to them is good; they do not verify that the gift is rooted in love. These are assumed. This is why children are so vulnerable. Their natural openness has no defenses. Jesus links this quality of children to the kingdom because with God there is no need for questioning, verifying, or defenses. Trust in him can be unconditional because his love has no limits.

Children learn to love by being loved. Once, a little girl wanted to get her dad a birthday present. He always gave her presents, and that made her feel loved. So it was natural that, at an age when she could conceive of making someone else happy, she would do for her father what he had done for her. Thinking only of her father's joy, she ran to him and said, "Daddy, can I please have some money to buy you a birthday present?"

It never entered her mind – she was so much a child – that if she could not purchase the present with her own money it would not be meaningful. Nothing was more obvious to her than that she had no means to obtain the present. If she wanted to make her father happy, she needed his help. She thought nothing of her dependence. And neither did her father! What father would not be filled with delight upon seeing his daughter's heart so full of love and humility?

The kingdom of God is his gift of love, and it can only be received with childlike trust. God's love unleashes love in us and the desire to bring joy to our heavenly Father, yet for this we need his grace. Our asking for this grace is already his joy, for he desires nothing more than our fullest happiness, and there is no greater happiness than love.

Heavenly Father, grant me the grace to trust in you and to desire your joy above all other things.

The Wisdom of Loving the Poor

Douglas Bushman

As [Jesus] was setting out on a journey, a man ran up, knelt down before him, and asked him, "Good teacher, what must I do to inherit eternal life?" (Mk 10: 17)

It is wisdom to seek God: "God looks down from heaven/ upon the human race,/ To see if even one is wise,/ if even one seeks God" (Ps 53: 3). By his teaching and miracles, Jesus makes God present. Aware of this, a man, looking for the answer to the most fundamental question that can be asked, runs up to him. He does not ask for a healing or any temporal benefit, as so many others do. His question shows that even someone enjoying good health and a comfortable life still finds himself in need. Without the truth about eternal life he lacks definitive direction for his life. Man's greatest need is to discover the essential meaning of his life.

It is a grace to live on the level of this man's question. It is a greater grace to discover the answer in the teaching of Jesus. How easy it is to become preoccupied with concerns about the body, income, possessions, career, and retirement. Jesus' warning is for all times: "Do not worry about your life and what you will eat, or about your body and what you will wear. For life is more than food and the body more than clothing… Instead, seek his kingdom" (Lk 12: 22-23, 31). He warns of the fool who "who stores up treasure for himself but is not rich in what matters to God" (Lk 12: 21), and what matters to God is to make use of one's treasure to help the poor (Lk 16: 19-31). This is precisely how Jesus will answer this man's question: "Go, sell what you have, and give to [the] poor, and you will have treasure in heaven; then come, follow me" (Mk 10: 21).

Eternal life with God begins here on earth. It is participation in God's own love, and his love is directed in a special way to the poor. The wisdom that begins in seeking God ends in discovering him in serving the poor.

Father of infinite mercy, forgive me for shutting out the poor in my pursuit of a comfortable life. Help me to find eternal life in loving those poor whom you love.

The Greatest Inheritance
Douglas Bushman

Jesus answered [the man], "Why do you call me good? No one is good but God alone. You know the commandments: 'You shall not kill; you shall not commit adultery; you shall not steal; you shall not bear false witness; you shall not defraud; honor your father and your mother.'" (Mk 10: 18-19)

Jesus' answer to the question about inheriting eternal life could not be more basic. The word "inherit" is key. To inherit something, a person must be in another's will. Typically, this is the prerogative of children. So, the man's question really means: "What must I do to be an heir to what only God can give, eternal life?" Only Jesus knows what it means to be Son of the Father. He knows it means to do his will in all things: "a son cannot do anything on his own, but only what he sees his father doing" (Jn 5: 19). "I do just as the Father has commanded me" (Jn 14: 31).

Every loving parent knows the wound caused by a child's disobedience. The use of parental authority is an act of love. Commanding a child is for the child's own good, giving direction according to a parent's superior wisdom, truth that keeps a child free from all sorts of harm. If the command is disregarded or disobeyed, it is in fact a rejection of the love that motivated it. A perfect child is one who is obedient in all things, and this is not because this makes life easier (which it certainly does!) but above all because this is what is best for the child! A perfect child, then, is one who always receives his parents' love concretely by obeying all of his parents' commands.

This, then, is where Jesus' answer leads, right to the heart of what it means for God to be the loving Father of all, who desires nothing less than eternal life for all his children, and what it means to fulfill the fourth commandment – the one Jesus lists out of order in order to end with it – in relation to God our Father. Those who keep his commands are truly his beloved children, and they will receive the inheritance of eternal life.

Father of all patience and kindness, help me to receive Jesus' answer to my questions about eternal life by receiving your love and by keeping your commandments.

The Loving Look of Jesus

Douglas Bushman

[The man] replied and said to [Jesus], "Teacher, all of these I have observed from my youth." Jesus, looking at him, loved him.
(Mk 10: 20-21a)

The moral integrity of this man who has kept all the commandments evokes a loving look from Jesus. Jesus knows what it means to be the object of God's loving look, for at his baptism he heard the Father's voice: "You are my beloved Son; with you I am well pleased" (Mk 1: 11). This loving look of the Father is extended to all in whom the Father sees his Son, and he sees his Son in all who obey him as Jesus does.

Is it really possible that a creature has the power to elicit a look of love from the Creator? Well, after each of the first five days of creation God stepped back as if to admire his work, and "saw that it was good." That is a look of love. And after the sixth day, having created man in his own image, God "found it very good." That too, was a look of love. God takes delight in the goodness of creation, and most of all in man. Because he loves, God delights in seeing and hearing the one he loves: "O my dove…/ Let me see you,/ let me hear your voice,/ For your voice is sweet,/ and you are lovely" (Song 2: 14).

His look of love affirms the moral goodness of this man who keeps the commandments. By dying to send the Holy Spirit who renews us and makes us able to keep the commandments, Jesus establishes the condition for his Father to look upon us all with such love. In him we observe what the Father commands. "If you keep my commandments, you will remain in my love, just as I have kept my Father's commandments and remain in his love" (Jn 15: 10). Thus, as a beautiful Preface prayer puts it, the Father can love in us what he loves in his Son. Through, with, and in Christ, God affirms us with his look of love.

Father of our Lord, Jesus Christ, give me the grace of an upright conscience, that I might know how to please you and to merit receiving your look of love.

God Has More to Give

Douglas Bushman

And [Jesus] said to [the man], "You are lacking in one thing. Go, sell what you have, and give to [the] poor and you will have treasure in heaven; then come, follow me." At that statement his face fell, and he went away sad, for he had many possessions.
(Mk 10: 21b-22)

Reading this text, Saint Anthony was overwhelmed by a grace to live it and gave away all he had to follow the poor and humble Christ in a life of poverty and penance. Not everyone is called to do as Saint Anthony did, but everyone is called to divest himself of anything that is an obstacle to receiving God's love.

Even good things can be an obstacle to God's love if we love them too much. This is why the saints call for detachment, which does not mean not to love; it means to love appropriately. To be detached from health, possessions, even spousal and family relationships means to love these in God and for God, and never in a way that would lead to a compromise in loving God with one's whole mind, heart, soul, and strength.

God invites everyone to be one with his Son who "became poor although he was rich" (2 Cor 8: 9). We can only become rich in God's love if we are poor in our own eyes. Then we receive another kind of wealth and become "rich in what matters to God" (Lk 12: 21). What is that heavenly currency? It is love, justice, friendship, and solidarity, especially with the poor. It is valuing relationships based on the fundamental dignity of human beings, not on great possessions or accomplishments.

Jesus' mission is to bring that heavenly wealth to earth, where sin has produced a profound poverty in relationships. In him God's will is done on earth as it is in heaven. In calling the rich man to forsake his wealth, Jesus invites him to become his friend, his associate, and collaborator, to participate in Jesus' own forsaking of comfort as the one who "became poor although he was rich, so that by his poverty you might become rich" (2 Cor 8: 9). This is the condition of true joy. The alternative is to walk away from Jesus in sadness.

Most generous Father, give me a heart to trust you for my true happiness, to count my wealth in terms of love, and never to walk away from the call of Jesus, your Son.

The True Wealth of Heaven

Douglas Bushman

Jesus looked around and said to his disciples, "How hard it is for those who have wealth to enter the kingdom of God!" The disciples were amazed at his words. (Mk 10: 23-24a)

Jesus sets forth the truth in unambiguous terms, knowing how sinful attachments can resist the truth. He knows that a death-event is required for truth to take root in our hearts, that we must be transformed by a renewal of our minds in order not to conform to the world's way of thinking (Rom 12: 2) and to have the mind of Christ (1 Cor 2: 16).

Jesus knows truth is a matter of life and death. He knows that his death must precede our own death to sin. He utters every word that challenges the rich man, and us, fully aware that his mission will lead to the cross. "But now you are trying to kill me, a man who has told you the truth" (Jn 8: 40). Jesus speaks every word under the sign of the cross. In him the text is definitively fulfilled: "I have set before you life and death, the blessing and the curse. Choose life" (Dt 30: 19).

Wealth is an obstacle to entering God's kingdom when it inhibits the perfection of love. Wealth can create a division of classes. It can cause a person to see others as competitors. It can cause others to be envious. It can be a source of security in this world, and numb the need for God. It can command so much attention that a person becomes poor in relationships, destitute in love.

Perfect love requires the evangelical counsel of poverty. Every Christian is called to live this counsel because everyone is called to the perfection of charity. Poverty sets the heart free for love, assuring that there will never be a reversal of the priority of persons over things. It is lived by generosity, especially to the poor, and by denying ourselves certain goods of this world so that we remain mindful that "the world in its present form is passing away" (1 Cor 7: 31). Poverty makes us depend on God, our surest hope.

Father of eternal wisdom, grant me the grace to see that all things are vanity if they do not bring me closer to you and to my neighbor in perfect charity.

Prioritizing Money

Jack Sacco

So Jesus again said to [the disciples] in reply, "Children, how hard it is to enter the kingdom of God! It is easier for a camel to pass through [the] eye of [a] needle than for one who is rich to enter the kingdom of God." (Mk 10: 24b-25)

It has long been a common worldview that money is the ultimate solution to all problems. And it is certainly easy to make the case that the more wealth one has, the easier life becomes. Providing for necessities such as food, clothing, housing, and even health care, become non-issues when sufficient resources are available. On a grander scale, the luxurious trappings of wealth – things such as mansions, jewelry, cars, international travel, first-class amenities, and the like – all seem to indicate that money does, indeed, elevate life to a much higher form.

Many people idolize the wealthy, often looking enviously at their fortunes and lifestyles. Some even refer to the rich as being "blessed" by God, and they fantasize about how vastly different their lives would be if they only had immense wealth.

But Jesus offers us a very different view when he points out how difficult it is for one who is rich to enter the kingdom of God. For Jesus, the accumulation of riches has nothing to do with our ability to love and serve God and our neighbor, the requisite acts of goodness that open the gates of heaven for us. In fact, an unquenchable desire for riches and a preoccupation with worldly possessions can often lead us in the opposite direction of holiness, making it difficult for one who worships the glitter of gold to enter the eternal kingdom of heaven.

Having lived for years among the Hollywood elite in Beverly Hills, it has become apparent to me that money does not make us happy or unhappy or good or bad; it only magnifies the type of person we already are. And while wealth may solve a variety of worldly issues, it does not have the ability to make us holy. It is therefore imperative that we place money in its proper perspective, realizing that holiness, not riches, will ultimately save us.

God the Father, give us the wisdom and strength to master money while never allowing it to master us. Help us to provide financially for our families, but never to jeopardize our eternal happiness for the sake of wealth.

What Are the Rules?

Jack Sacco

[The disciples] were exceedingly astonished and said among themselves, "Then who can be saved?" Jesus looked at them and said, "For human beings it is impossible, but not for God. All things are possible for God." (Mk 10: 26-27)

People love rules. Sure, we may complain incessantly about whatever rules we are asked to follow, but we still feel a certain comfort in knowing what they are. What should I do? When should I do it? What are the limits? What is permitted? What's considered out of bounds? What is required of me in order to be rewarded? What exactly does it take to be saved?

Jesus' answer likely surprises his disciples. In fact, the notion that "for human beings it is impossible" may have even made them feel a bit helpless. But his point is that we must rely on God for salvation, not on our possessions or on a set of rules and regulations.

I briefly did business with a man who followed every religious rule one can imagine. He was fond of bragging that he said three complete rosaries each day, and that he fasted on bread and water twice per week. However, he'd often boast that he had blazed through the prayers, "getting in" all three rosaries while having his morning coffee and muffin. And his fasting would end abruptly at midnight, when he would pig out on everything in sight.

Worst of all, while strictly adhering to all the rules, he seemed to have no problem with unethical business practices and even racist rhetoric. Needless to say, despite his professed religiosity, I took my business elsewhere.

There are always people who are capable of following the letter of the law while having no regard for its spirit.

But Jesus clearly lets us know that all the rules in the world will not save us, and that no matter how hard we try, we will never be able to save ourselves. Our salvation is not a matter of our ability to follow a rule or manipulate a system. It is infinitely simpler than that, for it is God alone who can save us.

Heavenly Father, plant deep in our souls the truth that salvation comes not from earthly power or possessions, but from you. May we live a life of service to you and to our fellow man, knowing that all things – including our salvation – are possible for you.

Giving Up

Jack Sacco

Peter began to say to [Jesus], "We have given up everything and followed you." (Mk 10: 28)

It feels good to be generous, to give of oneself, to make a sacrifice on behalf of another. And, quite honestly, it feels kind of nice to receive a little recognition for your altruistic deeds.

But for some people, their "generosity" is only palatable as long as it doesn't actually cost them anything, especially the lifestyle to which they have grown accustomed. They don't mind giving a little something from their surplus, but would never take it beyond that.

Peter reminds Jesus that the disciples had given up their livelihoods, their belongings, and quite possibly their personal dreams in order to follow him. In doing so, he wasn't regretting his decision, nor was he hoping to receive a pat on the back. He was simply making a declaration of the faith that he and his fellow disciples had in Jesus, thus renewing his pledge to give not only of his surplus, but also of those things the world may deem essential – jobs, houses, financial security, and prestige.

A close friend of mine was an Academy Award-winning actress whose estimated wealth was in excess of forty million dollars. She once told me that she wanted to give away every cent by the time she died. And that's exactly what she did. But what was most impressive about her generosity was that the vast majority of her fortune was given anonymously to those most in need. She donated to hospitals, churches, and schools, but always without fanfare of any kind. Mostly, she gave to individuals who needed help, whether it was to lift a financial burden or to have life-saving surgery.

By the time she died, she had quietly given away all of her earthly possessions, and had changed countless lives along the way.

It feels good to be generous, especially when the cost is low and the recognition is high. But what are you really willing to give up in order to follow Christ?

God the Father, your Son willingly gave up everything, including his own life, for our sake. May we readily give up the things of the world for the sake of your kingdom.

Letting Go

Jack Sacco

Jesus said, "Amen, I say to you, there is no one who has given up house or brothers or sisters or mother or father or children or lands for my sake and for the sake of the gospel who will not receive a hundred times more now in this present age: houses and brothers and sisters and mothers and children and lands, with persecutions, and eternal life in the age to come." (Mk 10: 29-30)

Letting go is never easy, whether it's of a possession, a relationship, a long-held idea, or even an emotion. We naturally like the notion of holding onto what we have, and even adding to our stockpile. To do so gives us a sense of security, whereas to give up too much in the way of worldly goods may seem somewhat irresponsible.

I've often been told that if I were to make a financial sacrifice on behalf of this or that organization, I will be rewarded greatly in heaven. According to their scenario, they imply that they – the nonprofit employees – have the power to bestow the eternal blessing of heaven upon me, all for the price of a hefty donation.

However, that logic often leads us down a slippery slope, wherein one group can take advantage of another, claiming that they are doing the impoverished group a favor by guaranteeing them lavish rewards in heaven.

But Jesus tells us something quite different. Unlike those who may wish to manipulate others, he directly states that those who have sacrificed greatly for his sake and for the sake of the Gospel will receive "a hundred times more now in this present age," along with "eternal life in the age to come."

By doing so, he not only delivers wonderful news to those who have given of their time, talent, and treasure for his sake, but he also exposes those who would take advantage of others in his name, those who would deny others earthly payment while promising them the eternal rewards that only Jesus himself can bestow.

We therefore can let go of earthly possessions for Jesus' sake, certain that he understands the pressures and demands of the world, and that he has no desire to shortchange us. And unlike those who may wish to take advantage of us, Jesus will reward our faithfulness and sacrifices in this life as well as the next.

Loving Father, your generosity can never be outdone by man. May we always remember that our sacrifices on your behalf will be rewarded both here on earth and in heaven.

Jockeying for Position

Jack Sacco

"But many that are first will be last,
and [the] last will be first."
(Mk 10: 31)

It's natural to want to be at the front of the line. People often camp out on sidewalks in order to be the first to purchase a hot new product or tickets for a blockbuster movie. How do you suppose those in line would react if someone came along and instructed them to reverse their order so that the ones at the back of the line would now be at the front, and the ones at the front would now be at the back?

My guess is that the instructions would be met with something of a backlash, specifically among those who were originally at the front. After all, what's fair about moving someone from the front of a line to the back or vice versa? Nothing.

But when Jesus poses this exact scenario to us, is he talking about people patiently waiting to purchase movie tickets or the latest gizmo at an electronics store? Hardly.

Just as we like to be first in line at the ticket window, we also like to be first in line for rewards of any kind, be they earthly or heavenly. Jesus has already given us the good news that our sacrifices on his behalf will be rewarded here in this life. However, it is important to remember that when it comes to entering the kingdom of God, those things that make us important on earth – things such as fame and fortune – will not move us ahead of those with fewer worldly possessions.

At the same time, he also warns those who openly parade their holiness and sacrifices – those who walk around with the pious self-importance of the Pharisees of old – that they too may find themselves at the back of the line, while those who have truly lived with charity and humility will have been moved to the front.

Eternal Father, we know that we are reliant on you – not on our own power or reputation – in order to attain eternal salvation. May we therefore live in accord with your commandments to love you and to love our neighbor as ourselves.

Are You Afraid?

Jack Sacco

[Jesus and the disciples] were on the way, going up to Jerusalem, and Jesus went ahead of them. They were amazed, and those who followed were afraid. (Mk 10: 32a)

Would you be afraid to follow Jesus? It's easy to answer no, but what if you were convinced that following him would necessarily entail some form of physical, emotional, or financial suffering?

There are many people – some well-meaning – who would have you believe that to follow Jesus is to commit yourself to a life of misery, poverty, and injustice, a life devoid of any enjoyment and laughter. His way, they would tell you, is always accompanied by suffering and pain. The way of the world, on the other hand, is portrayed as being filled with glamour and excitement, with wealth and freedom.

We've all heard phrases like, "You should thank God for the suffering," or "God never gives you more than you can handle," or even "God is just testing you." While such pseudo-theological sayings may sound nice, they can also have the unintended consequence of instilling fear, and even alienating us from the very God who seeks to help us.

Following Jesus requires that we trust him, and that we know with certainty that despite the many tribulations of life, he desires for us to be joyful. But unlike those who advertise that our lives can be transformed into unending bliss simply by buying their products, Jesus is honest about the fact that certain sufferings of life can never be totally avoided. He then goes a step further, promising us that though pain is inevitable in this life, when we walk with him, we will ultimately share in his resurrection.

The truth is that Jesus only wants what is best for us, and he takes no pleasure in our pain. Despite our fears, he will never lead us into difficulties. Following him is not a call to misery, but a call to victory. Suffering will always be part of the human condition, but we can overcome that very suffering, no matter how intense it may be, when we follow Jesus.

Heavenly Father, grant us the wisdom and the courage to follow Jesus, knowing that he will always lead us to safety. We trust your plan for us, and we know that with Jesus as our guide, we can live unafraid.

I've Got Good News and Bad News

Jack Sacco

Taking the Twelve aside again, [Jesus] began to tell them what was going to happen to him. "Behold, we are going up to Jerusalem, and the Son of Man will be handed over to the chief priests and the scribes, and they will condemn him to death and hand him over to the Gentiles who will mock him, spit upon him, scourge him, and put him to death, but after three days he will rise." (Mk 10: 32b-34)

Everybody likes good news. Unfortunately, it often comes packaged together with some form of bad news. We can generally accept the bad, as long as it is clearly outweighed by the good. But here, the sheer volume of bad news in Jesus' prediction seems to overwhelm the astounding revelation contained in his final seven words.

If someone were to predict that you would be arrested, mocked, spit upon, scourged, and put to death, you would likely assume that there could be no amount of accompanying good news that could possibly balance out the scales. And it is very likely that the Twelve had the very same reaction.

In fact, even if they closely listened to his final prediction – that after three days he would rise – it may have been unlikely that they really understood what it meant. Mocking, spitting, scourging, killing... these are easy concepts to understand. Rising after three days... not so much.

But Jesus' message is deeper than a mere prediction of what was about to happen to him. In addition to providing his disciples with a sense of reassurance in the midst of the distressing events they were about to witness, he also presented a clear and powerful message that would echo throughout the ages.

No amount of tribulation – up to and including death itself – can keep us from the victory that Jesus has promised us. Just as he was unafraid of the verbal and physical assaults of the world, so should we be.

We may not know the details of our future, but we can always be assured that if we follow Jesus, we will share in his victory – no matter what the cost, no matter what the odds. And that good news will far outshine any amount of bad news the world has in store for us.

Eternal Father, you've blessed us with the Good News of salvation as revealed through Jesus Christ. Help us to live life unafraid, so that we may share in your Son's resurrection.

225

What's in It for Me?

Jack Sacco

Then James and John, the sons of Zebedee, came to [Jesus] and said to him, "Teacher, we want you to do for us whatever we ask of you." He replied, "What do you wish [me] to do for you?" They answered him, "Grant that in your glory we may sit one at your right and the other at your left." (Mk 10: 35-37)

No one likes the idea of sharing in someone else's misfortune, but we all relish the notion of benefiting from their successes. It's human nature. For example, if your best friend happened to win a multi-million-dollar lottery, wouldn't you love to receive a nice gift? Would you expect to receive one? Would you be disappointed if you didn't? Would you be so bold as actually to ask your friend for a gift or favor?

What if you were the one who won the lottery? To whom would you hand out benefits? Would you be afraid of disappointing friends and family members who may have legitimate needs?

It's natural to wonder how events will affect us and those around us. So it's not completely surprising when James and John approach Jesus and ask him for a favor. At least they had been paying attention when he said he would rise again.

What is surprising is what they actually request: "We want you to do for us whatever we ask of you." That's pretty bold. And when pressed to explain exactly what they mean, they once again prove themselves not to be shy, asking to be seated beside him in glory.

Do they see Jesus as Messiah and Savior, or do they, at least at that moment, see him as an opportunity for their own glorification, as someone who can help them attain their own place in history? After all, they have believed in and followed him for nearly three years, even when others have left him. If, indeed, he is now destined for glory, then wouldn't he surely be willing to share a portion of that glory with them?

From a distance, it's easy to indict James and John for their boldness. However, in what ways do we make similar requests of God and our neighbors? How will you answer when Jesus asks, "What do you wish me to do for you?"

God the Father, thank you for inviting us to share in your Son's glory. Please help us live humbly and selflessly so that we might inherit eternal life in heaven.

Be Careful What You Wish For

Jack Sacco

Jesus said to [James and John], "You do not know what you are asking. Can you drink the cup that I drink or be baptized with the baptism with which I am baptized?" They said to him, "We can." (Mk 10: 38-39a)

For ages, people have been inspired by their dreams and goals. But sometimes one can allow his or her aspirations to take center stage, often to the exclusion of everything else. History has provided us countless examples of brutal kings and dictators whose ambitions have had deadly consequences for the people under their control. Fortunately, most people don't go as far as killing or even harming another in pursuit of their quests. However, our ambitions can still compel us to do things that might not be in our best interest, or in the best interest of those around us.

It is interesting to note that Jesus does not respond to the request of James and John by simply answering yes or no. Instead, he states that they do not know what they are asking, almost as if to say that their enthusiasm for glory has blinded them to the sufferings that would await them if that very request were to be fulfilled.

Through his follow-up question, he gives them the opportunity to identify their own motivations and to understand better what it truly means to be his disciples. At the same time, Jesus challenges each of us to assess our own devotion to him so that we can honestly decide whether we are willing to follow him through the valley of death or if we are only interested in the glory of resurrection. As he clearly states, it's impossible to have the latter without the former.

How often do we allow our own ambitions to blind us to the truth behind our motivations? How often do we not really understand what we are asking or even why we are asking it? Are we seeking full union with Christ, sufferings and all, or are we only interested in the part about sitting with him in glory? Do we understand that by asking to rise with Christ, we are also asking to die with him?

Heavenly Father, grant us purity of heart, that we may always follow Jesus with humility and love, and that we may do so without an agenda for our own glory.

227

Status

Jack Sacco

Jesus said to [James and John], "The cup that I drink, you will drink, and with the baptism with which I am baptized, you will be baptized; but to sit at my right or at my left is not mine to give but is for those for whom it has been prepared."
(Mk 10: 39b-40)

It can be easy to become obsessed with status. We tend to be interested in questions such as who has the biggest house, who has the nicest car, and who has the most expensive watch or the finest wine. Here on earth, we like to think that our status says something about our value as people.

But Jesus offers a different take on the subject. When James and John acknowledged that they'd be willing to make any sacrifice in order to be granted what would amount to the ultimate status in heaven – that of sitting at Jesus' right and left – he responds that they will, in fact, be called to make that sacrifice, but that he cannot grant them the favor that they are seeking.

At face value, his response seems a bit unfair. After all, they had openly proclaimed that they were willing to pay the price for their upgraded status. Jesus seems to tell them, "Okay, you will indeed suffer, but you won't be rewarded for your suffering."

After hearing Jesus' answer, I wonder if they considered retracting their request. Perhaps. But then again, perhaps they understood Jesus' words to be more profound than a simple case of deal-making gone bad.

The kingdom of heaven is not about status. Our rank, our titles, our possessions, our popularity will all mean less than nothing in the next life. Only our openness to love, coupled with our capacity to forgive, will determine our experience of heaven. In a place of perfect happiness and joy, how can one person be happier or more important than the next?

Suffering will come to us all, but once we have cleansed ourselves of our sins and petty jealousies, we will be able to finally sit with Christ at the heavenly banquet. And none of us will be concerned about the status of the seating arrangement.

God the Father, grant us the ability to see beyond earthly status, that we might treat our fellow man with equality in preparation for the joy of eternal life with you.

Power
Jack Sacco

When the ten heard this, they became indignant at James and John. Jesus summoned them and said to them, "You know that those who are recognized as rulers over the Gentiles lord it over them, and their great ones make their authority over them felt. But it shall not be so among you." (Mk 10: 41-43a)

Numerous studies have found that when people are placed in positions of power over others, they sometimes abuse their newfound authority by mistreating those placed in their charge. This has even been known to happen when the subjects were relatively well-adjusted.

One study at Stanford University in 1971 placed twenty-four psychology students – each deemed to be physically and emotionally stable – in the random roles of prisoners and guards. Once the roles were assigned, a mock prison was set up in the basement of the psychology building. Within thirty-six hours, those chosen to act as guards were showing signs of abuse toward those playing prisoners. By day six, the experiment was abruptly halted due to increasingly excessive abuse of the "prisoners" by the "guards."

The truth is that there's something about power that tends to corrupt. Sadly, we're all familiar with politicians who beg for our votes, and then, once in office, seem to carry out their own agendas with little or no regard for the will of the people who elected them. While authority is obviously necessary, unchecked power can lead us to believe that the recognized rules of civility don't necessarily apply to us.

A measure of this tendency may be human nature (as reflected in the studies mentioned above), but another, more distressing factor may be that it is often a behavior learned from those who have preceded us. Politicians often learn it from other politicians. Employees often learn it from their bosses. Children often learn it from their parents. Examples of how to lord one's authority over another are in abundance in our world.

But Jesus offers us a different mode of operation, making it a point to inform us that even though we may find such behavior all around us, it shall not be this way with us.

Eternal Father, grant that we might turn away from the temptations to abuse whatever authority is given us, so that instead of following the examples of those who lord their power over others, we might truly understand and follow the teachings of Christ.

Greatness

Jack Sacco

"Rather, whoever wishes to be great among you will be your servant; whoever wishes to be first among you will be the slave of all. For the Son of Man did not come to be served but to serve and to give his life as a ransom for many." (Mk 10: 43b-45)

We sometimes encounter things in life that are, at first glance, counterintuitive: retreating as a method of advancing, speaking less as a method of saying more, and even giving one's life as a method of saving it. Each seems to defy the common rules of logic, creating instead a paradox that might not be readily apparent.

Hundreds of books on leadership skills populate library shelves, each putting forth a blueprint on how to attain greatness, wealth, and power in the world of business. And almost all of them use the same basic formula – be shrewd, be able to market yourself properly, and be prepared to play whatever political games may come your way, even if you have to manipulate those around you in the process.

Jesus offers a dramatically opposing view, informing us that those who wish to be great must, instead, humble themselves by becoming servants, and that those who desire power must first become the slaves of all. To call that line of reasoning counterintuitive would be an understatement of the first magnitude.

Unlike any number of politicians and self-help gurus out there, Jesus is not interested in manipulating others for his own gain. Instead, he is allowing us to glimpse into the mind of his Father by understanding truths that are certainly not apparent to those caught up in the power and glory of the world around us.

He thus provides us with the benefit of both his wisdom and example. He humbles himself as our servant, as a lamb to be sacrificed for our sins. And in the process, he rises to a higher level of greatness than any of us can ever achieve.

Ours is not to grasp for the greatness that is Christ, but to absorb the truth of his words, to follow the example of his actions, and to share in the glory that he has promised us as his children.

Heavenly Father, grant that we may seek to follow the example of Jesus by serving our fellow man. May we seek to attain greatness as defined by Christ, not as defined by the world.

Getting His Attention

Jack Sacco

[Jesus and his disciples] came to Jericho. And as [Jesus] was leaving Jericho with his disciples and a sizable crowd, Bartimaeus, a blind man, the son of Timaeus, sat by the roadside begging. On hearing that it was Jesus of Nazareth, he began to cry out and say, "Jesus, son of David, have pity on me." (Mk 10: 46-47)

There seems to be an almost unending series of disasters and emergencies – earthquakes, fires, floods, famines, epidemics, political turmoil, and all manner of catastrophes, natural and manmade – taking place in the world on a daily basis. Each profoundly affects the lives of those in their path, and each has the power to render its victims helpless and alone.

Millions of innocent people thus find themselves in dire situations every day. And most of them turn to God and ask for his help. That adds up to a lot of prayers and a lot of high-priority emergencies.

At the same time, it seems logical (to me, at least) that if I were kneeling beside both a pope and a cardinal, God would probably listen to their prayers before he'd listen to mine. After all, they outrank me by a long shot.

Considering all of this, it sounds reasonable to assume that God might be a little too busy fixing big things in our world or answering the prayers of the powerful to help us with whatever minor issues might arise in our lives.

But Bartimæus, a beggar and a blind man (and therefore not a member of the elite), is sitting by the side of the road when he realizes that Jesus of Nazareth is passing nearby. Jesus is leaving town with his disciples and a large crowd, meaning that he probably doesn't have time to stop and chat. But the blind man cries out anyway, and asks that the son of David have pity on him.

When we consider the many vital matters and important people demanding God's time each day, how is it possible that we might even get his attention? And if we feel ourselves to be so insignificant, then why even bother to call out for him?

In a world filled with emergencies, it's important to remember that despite the crowds and the circumstances around us, Jesus always has time for us.

God the Father, please give us the courage to call out to Jesus, no matter how insignificant we may consider ourselves or our requests to be. May we have faith that your Son will always be willing to hear our plea.

Persistence

Jack Sacco

And many rebuked [the blind man], telling him to be silent. But he kept calling out all the more, "Son of David, have pity on me." Jesus stopped and said, "Call him." So they called the blind man, saying to him, "Take courage; get up, he is calling you." He threw aside his cloak, sprang up, and came to Jesus. (Mk 10: 48-50)

There's an old axiom that says, "If at first you don't succeed, try, try again." The lesson is as clear as it is timeless: never give up. However, we're often led to believe that there are certain things which we should not ask of God, and that even if we are so bold as to do so, we should go quietly on our way if there seems to be no response.

I've personally had experiences in which presumably well-meaning people advised me not to pray for this or that situation in my life, almost as if doing so would pester God. "If he had wanted to answer your prayer," they say, "he would've done so by now."

These same people sometimes take it a step further, intimating that one should reconsider persevering along any difficult pathway. Their logic, once again, is that if a course of action were God's will for you, then he would have instantly cleared the way.

However, I've heard it said that God's delays are not God's denials. My own opinion – and I believe that Jesus would agree with me – is that God is never "pestered" by his children and that he is pleased by our perseverance. In fact, there are a number of instances throughout Scripture, including this one, in which he rewards those who are persistent both in their prayers and their efforts.

Instead of heeding the advice of those who rebuke him, the blind man continues to call out for Jesus, knowing that the Lord would have pity on him. By being persistent, the blind man may prove that he has a deeper faith in Christ than do those who demand his silence.

How often do we silence ourselves when we feel the need to call out to Jesus? How quickly do we give up in our prayers? How persistent are we willing to be?

Eternal Father, please give us the grace of persistence, so that we may ask repeatedly for your mercy, even when we feel that we are not worthy.

What Do You Want?

Jack Sacco

Jesus said to [the blind man] in reply, "What do you want me to do for you?" The blind man replied to him, "Master, I want to see." (Mk 10: 51)

If you could ask Jesus for anything, what would it be? It's easy to answer, "I'd ask for world peace," or "For all the children to be fed," or "That all diseases be cured." But honestly, how much courage does that take?

Do you have the faith actually to ask for something tangible, for something specific that really affects your life? If you were blind, would you have the audacity to ask for the restoration of your sight?

It's very likely that Jesus knows what the blind man wants. Even so, he asks him anyway. The man, to his credit, doesn't beat around the bush, nor does he attempt to manipulate Jesus by requesting world peace or something nebulous that might sound selfless and altruistic.

He simply comes out with it. He wants to see. And by answering so directly, he demonstrates that he has great faith in Jesus' ability to heal him of his malady.

Often, when given the opportunity to ask for something in prayer, we try to act as if we have no actual personal needs. Some may even view the consistent making of generic requests to be a form of humility. Their reasoning is that God knows what is best for us, and that if he desires something for us, then he will grant it without our asking. To ask for our own will to be done or for our own needs to be met, the logic goes, is prideful and, therefore, wrong.

But Jesus has said, "Ask and you shall receive, seek and you shall find, knock and it shall be opened to you." And, as in the case of the blind man, he wants your requests to be specific.

So, tomorrow morning, when Christ asks you what you would like him to do for you, will you have the courage to ask for what you really want, or will you disappoint him by asking for nothing?

Heavenly Father, your Son has instructed us to ask anything of you in his name. I therefore humbly ask you to grant the personal requests that I hold close to my heart, and that I now share with you.

The Way

Jack Sacco

*Jesus told [the blind man], "Go your way; your faith
has saved you." Immediately he received his sight
and followed him on the way. (Mk 10: 52)*

E veryone is interested in knowing "the way": the way to get rich, the way to be happy, the way to find true love, the way to get a promotion, or even the way out of an uncomfortable situation. It is natural for us to want to find our way and to secure our way of life. The way, no matter how it is defined, is very important to us.

The preponderance of self-help books on the market attests to our insatiable appetite to know how to achieve and attain, how to perform our tasks, and how to solve our problems. However, it's possible – and even probable – that many of the ways proposed to us by the self-proclaimed experts might be at odds with the way of the Gospel.

Jesus informs us that our lives can be transformed by our faith, not through some secret or complex methodology. "Your faith has saved you," he says to the blind man. Simple. Succinct. Profound.

It's interesting to note that he doesn't say, "Your faith has healed you." Instead, he uses the words, "Your faith has saved you." But he takes it a step further. He doesn't put conditions on the salvation he had just bestowed upon the man. He doesn't say, "You will be saved as long as you follow me." In fact, he starts by giving the man permission to go on his own way.

The blind man, now saved, is then healed. He then makes a personal decision to follow Jesus "on the way." One can assume that Jesus wishes for the man to follow him, just as he wishes for all mankind to follow. But his desire isn't that anyone follow him out of duty, but that we do so out of gratitude and love.

Our free will, which is always respected by God, allows us to give the Father the ultimate gift – that of our decision to follow his Son.

*God the Father, deep within our souls is the desire to know the
way home to you. Grant that despite the distractions of the world,
we may listen carefully to the words of Jesus, and that we may
follow him on the way.*

Drafted Donkey

Father John Dominic Corbett, O.P.

*When [Jesus and his disciples] drew near to Jerusalem,
to Bethphage and Bethany at the Mount of Olives, [Jesus]
sent two of his disciples and said to them, "Go into the village
opposite you, and immediately on entering it, you will find
a colt tethered on which no one has ever sat. Untie it
and bring it here." (Mk 11: 1-2)*

There are two points to consider here that are difficult for us to get used to.

The first is that Jesus seems to know the future. Jesus tells the disciples what will happen, and it does. Jesus intends not to manifest knowledge as a clairvoyant might but intends to show his control over the future. What will be is not outside of God's control. While we remain free in our actions God remains God and in charge.

The second point is that the colt is so far unused. It seems to have been reserved for Jesus.

Jesus acts as if he owns the colt. Of course, he does. As the Son of God, "all things come to be through him" (including, we may presume, colts); he has claims on all creation.

Do we acknowledge this? I think that this is harder for us to take than for more ancient peoples. We are egalitarian to our bones, and we sometimes feel that the universe ought to be a community of peers. This sometimes shows up in decrying "specism," the supposedly pernicious belief that our species – *homo sapiens* – is especially beloved of God and has purposes and proper uses by God. The donkey knows nothing of the Master's use of him. Yet the Master does make use of him as he sees fit. Do we object if the Lord uses something we think of as ours – our talents, our sorrows, our loves, indeed our life – for purposes of his own at which we can only guess? Then we do not fully understand the one with whom we must reckon. He has called us friends, but on another level we are servants of the good and hidden providential purposes of him and his Father. Blessed are we if we are not scandalized by this and trust that his use of us is always ennobling and ordered to a share in his glory.

Father, we are sometimes overly conscious of our "rights" and are insufficiently aware of your providence. Give us lively trust in your rule.

The Courtesy of Kings

Father John Dominic Corbett, O.P.

*"If anyone should say to you, 'Why are you doing this?' reply,
'The Master has need of it and will send it back here at once.'"*
(Mk 11: 3)

The Master has need of it. It's a strange thing to say. Being the master ordinarily means that one does not need things. Yet here he is claiming need of a donkey.

There is something fitting and humbling about the Lord needing something like a donkey. After all, his every act of redemption is a gracious choice to use and to need human things. He needs Mary and her consent in order to become human. The Lord of the cosmos becomes a baby at Bethlehem and a boy at Nazareth, and therefore chooses to need parents.

Once here, he could have relied on his miraculous powers as a shortcut to achieve his ends. Although he gives signs of who he is, he never uses his powers as cheap conveniences. He chooses to use and to need ordinary things.

He needs ordinary people too. He chooses fishermen, not professional scholars. He spends most of his time talking with the cabdrivers and cashiers of his day. His connections are with the people who pay exorbitant taxes and, once, with someone who collects them. None of them are certified geniuses. But he chooses to need them.

He needs a ride into town. He needs a special ride sending a special message of authority and smallness. Only a colt will do. He needs it. He asks for it. He promises to return it with the courtesy of a King.

There are days when we feel small and mulish. We feel insignificant and stubborn. There are days when we seem untried (especially in virtue). So we might feel as though the Lord will never ask us for a favor or need us for anything. But this is our blindness. The one who is not above needing a donkey will not hesitate to make use of us if we will let him ask.

Father, help us to be alert to the many ways you request our cooperation in your loving plans. Give us the responsiveness that comes from the Holy Spirit.

A Royal People

Father John Dominic Corbett, O.P.

So [the two disciples] went off and found a colt tethered at a gate outside on the street, and they untied it. Some of the bystanders said to them, "What are you doing, untying the colt?" They answered them just as Jesus had told them to, and they permitted them to do it. (Mk 11: 4-6)

What does he need the colt for? He needs it to manifest his royal authority. He intends to ride into town, not walk, and such a ride signifies that he is coming as a conqueror. But he does not come with a military parade with the chariots and the pride and the pageantry such as Caesar might command. Nor is the colt such a beast as David or Solomon or as another mighty king would ride. He chooses a colt to fulfill the prophecy of Zechariah: "See, your king shall come to you;/ a just savior is he,/ Meek, and riding on an ass,/ on a colt, the foal of an ass" (Zec 9: 9).

Why was a colt appropriate? This is a donkey which would be the ride of the less powerful members of the community. It would be the mode of transportation of the poor, the meek. The colt would be the symbol of the humble nature of the Lord's Kingship. The colt would also serve as a symbol of the character of the Lord's people as they are conformed to his image.

The Lord would be Lord of a people who would fulfill the words of the prophet Zephaniah: "I will leave as a remnant in your midst/ a people humble and lowly…/ They shall do no wrong/ and speak no lies" (Zep 3: 12-13). These poor in spirit would know their need for God and would thus be receptive to his instruction. But this very receptivity to God would make them powerful, especially against the force of the lie that would undo the ties that bind the people to their Lord and the people to one another in steadfast love.

The Lord's people are meek but not spineless. They are receptive to God's rule, and being so receptive they are able to cooperate with God as he makes his will done "on earth as it is in heaven."

Father, may your will be done on earth as it is in heaven. May we your people receive your gracious rule and welcome your triumphal procession into our hearts.

Warhorse

Father John Dominic Corbett, O.P.

*So [the two disciples] brought the colt to Jesus and
put their cloaks over it. And he sat on it. (Mk 11: 7)*

What color are the cloaks? I think the cloaks are of four colors. One is white. One is red. One is black. One is green. Why do I say this?

A text from Zechariah (1: 8) suggests it, as does a text from the Book of Revelation (6: 1-8). I am referring, of course, to the figures of the Four Horsemen of the Apocalypse. These are the horsemen who inaugurate God's judgment on the world. The white cloak is given to the rider who is "the Word of God, conquering and going forth to conquer." Jesus will speak God's merciful judgment and it will be victorious. He goes forth to conquer and he does not go forth in vain.

One is red. "He went forth to make war on the earth to take away peace." Jesus himself says he does not come to bring peace but a sword. His word will divide and cut his people in two. Those who will be slain by the word of God will be joined to him and removed from the world. His coming brings peace, but not before it brings war.

One is black. This symbolizes black hunger and famine. The judgment of God brings a renewed need for the food of the word of God. People are starving for the truth, are starving in lies, and the coming King will feed his people.

One is green. This is the color of sickness unto death. The meek Messiah will face this as his final trial. He will face and endure the terrible process of life ebbing away, and he will face and endure death itself.

Jesus' coming to Jerusalem is also the approach of the Four Horsemen executing God's judgment by speaking God's own truth, exposing false peace, manifesting the famine in the land, and enduring death. But he, in this act, establishes true peace, fills the hungry with every good thing, and brings the dead to life.

Father, before you enter into judgment with a man, you give him the gift of truth. Send your Spirit to our hearts so that we may receive your judgment in love.

Knowing Your Audience

Father John Dominic Corbett, O.P.

Many people spread their cloaks on the road,
and others spread leafy branches that they had cut
from the fields. (Mk 11: 8)

The word is out. The King is beginning to make his way into the city. The crowds are beginning to form and there is jostling for a good seat, shoving and pulling and pushing to get in on the action and to be part of what is that culture's equivalent of the six o'clock news. Everyone is worked up and everyone who is anyone wants to be there.

What goes through Jesus' mind as he sees the crowds form? Does he get caught up in this moment too? It is only human to savor a crowd's enthusiasm and faith. Does he, even if only for a moment, succumb to the spell and listen to the cheers and believe that they have finally believed him? Is he joyful in their joy?

No, he cannot have been. He is God and not simply man. He knows very well how this drama will play out. He knows Peter and Judas and the other apostles will desert him. He knows very well that this crowd which is now singing his praises will soon be baying for his blood. If he were man, and only man, this knowledge would surely embitter him and turn the cries of jubilation into a mockery of his hopes for the redemption of man.

I believe that he is neither intoxicated with illusions of approaching grandeur nor embittered by the soon to be confirmed and endlessly reconfirmed fickleness of his followers. I believe he sees the crowds not as they are on that day but as they will be on another far-distant day when he will return to earth in glory – when the mass of men will acclaim him this time with love purified and unshakable, made so only by the death he chooses to die on their behalf.

Father, the day your Son entered the city of Jerusalem he saw the vanity of all purely human hopes and yet was filled with joy. May our hope in him be purified.

Now, Please!

Father John Dominic Corbett, O.P.

Those preceding [Jesus] as well as those following kept crying out:/ "Hosanna!/ Blessed is he who comes in the name of the Lord!/ Blessed is the kingdom of our father David that is to come!/ Hosanna in the highest!" (Mk 11: 9-10)

What is in the minds of the crowd that surround Jesus as he makes his entrance into the holy city? They must know that something great is in the offing.

They are crying out "Hosanna," which means "save now." It is both a prayer for salvation and a declaration of praise. They are looking for God to act and are already praising him for his act of deliverance. The word "blessed" in the Bible often means being the recipient of a divine favor. They want this favor of God's acting now. These people have been waiting for millennia and the longings of a thousand years since King David come together that day as the people cry their praise to God for finally showing the world that he is in charge of the world and that these people, these ragtag Jews, are his favored children.

They are also saying, "Let faithfulness have its reward. It often seems that no good deed goes unpunished. We are told that the good is its own reward and that wickedness sooner or later punishes itself. But so often this doesn't happen. In the nature of things, those who love God should prosper. Let goodness, let faithfulness, have its reward. Once and for all show us that goodness does pay."

They are also saying, "Please, God, turn things around. We have seen how the wicked triumph. We see that the Romans rule our land. We saw the Greeks before them. We saw the Persians before them. We saw the Babylonians before them. Everywhere we look we see the enemies of God's people in triumph. Stop it. Please, please stop it. Please, God, reverse things, turn the world upside down, establish your Kingdom."

They are ecstatic because they are sure that their prayer is heard and that in Jesus all this will happen. And they are right. But it will not happen in any way they can possibly dream.

Father, our prayers for what is good often seem to go unanswered. Help us to have confidence that our deep desire for your salvation will have its reward.

Late in the Day

Father John Dominic Corbett, O.P.

*[Jesus] entered Jerusalem and went into the temple area.
He looked around at everything and, since it was already late,
went out to Bethany with the Twelve. (Mk 11: 11)*

I t is late. The sun is setting, the shadows are getting longer, the crowds are already drifting home. Jesus looks at the temple, his Father's house, and remembers being here so many years before as a child, listening to the doctors but already knowing by heart the Scriptures they expounded. He is uniquely at home here. Here is the place. Everyplace is the place where he can hear his Father, but this place, this representation of Mount Sinai, is the place where his people should be able to hear his Father speak as well.

This place recalls those pristine days when his people wandered in the desert freshly escaped from Egypt but still untutored in the ways of the One who had rescued them. On Mount Sinai his Father spoke the ten words which served as his preliminary self-portrait. No idols could be carved, because he who had fashioned man in his image could not be captured in any human image. No stealing men into slavery, because he had called this people to liberty. No murder, because he was the Lord of Life. No adultery, because he was deathlessly faithful. No perjury, because he was all truth. On Mount Sinai the ten words rang out as one word: "You shall be holy as I am holy."

That was early in the story. That day, at least, they had understood. Later it all becomes cloudy for them. They fail in love of God and love of neighbor and strain out gnats and swallow camels. The temple is the privileged place to hear his Father, but they turn his very temple into a place to be safe in sin. A purification of this place will be necessary. A new temple, a new place to hear God will be needed and will be given. But not now. It is very late in the day.

Father, the crucified and risen body of your Son is the privileged place from which we can hear you speak. Through this Word, make us your sons and daughters.

The Passover Harvest

Father Stephen Dominic Hayes, O.P.

The next day as [Jesus and his disciples] were leaving Bethany [Jesus] was hungry. Seeing from a distance a fig tree in leaf, he went over to see if he could find anything on it. When he reached it he found nothing but leaves; it was not the time for figs. And he said to it in reply, "May no one ever eat of your fruit again!" And his disciples heard it. (Mk 11: 12-14)

The fig tree of Jerusalem stands green as Jesus, in classic prophetic style, comes looking for fruit as he goes up to cleanse the temple. Figs in the Holy Land are harvested at their earliest in June; the Lord seems to expect this tree to have fruit in Passover's early spring. There is, of course, no fruit, and by this prophetic sign, the Messiah passes judgment on his fruitless creation, of which the fig tree itself is a traditional sign – the city of Jerusalem and the people of God themselves. The warnings of ancient prophets are renewed: "gather them all in…/ No figs on the fig trees,/ foliage withered" (Jer 8: 13); "Like the first fruits of the fig tree in its prime/… Ephraim is stricken,/ their root is dried up;/ they shall bear no fruit" (Hos 9: 10, 16). The Lord's visit to Jerusalem and its temple is the beginning of its doom. Within a generation, Jerusalem will lie in ruins and its inhabitants will be dead or scattered by Rome, not having recognized that Jesus' advent offered what could have been rescue.

Sometimes when the Lord comes to us – as he often does in our sins or in the midst of our just being busy without him – we find him in like manner reproving us for our sins and our spiritual fruitlessness, for our greed, our disordered desires, and especially our laziness in pursuing an authentic relationship with him and his Father. It's easy to start making excuses for ourselves, or perhaps even to question the fairness of his criticism of us – "It is not the season for figs." Yet his loving reproach always promises a richer sweetness. He comes to Jerusalem and to us to reap a Passover harvest of his own planting: the fruit of his cross – eternal life together – coaxed into ripeness by his own blood watering that dry, unfruitful wood.

Merciful Father, may we never fail to see your Son's reproach of our sins as anything other than medicinal; grant that we may enjoy the rich spiritual fruit which he has obtained for us by the sacrifice of the cross.

God's Holy House

Father Stephen Dominic Hayes, O.P.

[Jesus and his disciples] came to Jerusalem, and on entering the temple area [Jesus] began to drive out those selling and buying there. He overturned the tables of the money changers and the seats of those who were selling doves. He did not permit anyone to carry anything through the temple area. (Mk 11: 15-16)

One Advent weekend in a certain parish, the pastor let a parish organization sell Christmas decorations and the like in the back of the church after the Sunday Masses. This was not usual practice, and only happened because two organizations had been assigned to the same room. Nevertheless, it caused a certain amount of scandal – for example, one teen was heard muttering, "Buying and selling in the church! Haven't they read the Gospel?" The pastor, overhearing this, heard in the boy's voice the reproach of Jesus himself, and made a mental note to see his confessor. He had let the day-to-day needs of the parish impinge inappropriately upon the holiness of his church.

The house of God, whether we speak of the temple in Jerusalem, or the parish church, is a house dedicated to prayer – to "the lifting of the mind and heart to God," in the words of Saint Augustine – and is for that reason not to be used for any lesser purpose. The temple merchants are not there to pray, but to make money, even though their services assist worship. Similarly Jesus permits no one to "carry anything through" the temple area, no matter that the temple courts make an efficient passage to the Jerusalem markets. The temple is for prayer; it is holy because of the God who dwells there. To use it for anything else, however innocent, is a sacrilege, because such use fails to acknowledge the holiness of the One who dwells there. How easy it is for us to forget the presence of God, even in church! To miss a genuflection before the sacrament, to have a social conversation while others are praying – these are not far from actual buying and selling in the temple. A heart pure for prayer will always keep God's presence carefully in mind and keep his holy house holy.

Ever present and holy God, your Son Jesus taught us to treat the times and places dedicated to you to be holy in mind as well as in fact; may I never compromise the holiness of prayer.

The Place Where God Dwells

Father Stephen Dominic Hayes, O.P.

Then [Jesus] taught them saying, "Is it not written:/ 'My house shall be called a house of prayer for all peoples'?/ But you have made it a den of thieves." (Mk 11: 17)

My father died in December when I was preparing for my final term examinations as a seminarian in Washington, DC. At 2:30 in the morning my brother called to tell me that Dad was very near death. There was no way I could possibly travel to Boston. I told my brother to give Dad my best, and to tell him that I would be in the chapel for him. I went to our small Eucharistic chapel, and prayed the rosary as best I could. I was a mass of emotions, and not well recollected at all. But I was not alone. Almost palpably, Jesus was there in the midst of my pain and need, to be with me in that moment which comes to every man who must learn how to bury his father and go on without him. My father died, but the Friend of my heart stayed with me.

There is a kind of prayer that asks and asks of God without making any personal commitment to him, that sees him as blessing and benefit without being interested in the divine offer of personal presence and communion. The first purpose of the Jerusalem temple was to be a meeting point between God and his people; not merely a place for petitions to be offered, but to be a place where God would dwell with those souls he had called to himself. Jesus is the foundation stone of the better, spiritual temple which is his Church, built to the same end: he desires to dwell with us as friends. If we treat him only as a dispenser of gifts to be wheedled out of him by contract and bargain, how do our hearts differ from those of thieves? The new Way is better; God has become man precisely to be our friend and companion for ever – the Friend of our hearts present now among us.

Blessed holy Father, your Son pitched his tent among us so that through his communion as a man we might come to know the Trinity's inner life; never let me take this precious gift for granted.

Power and Lordship

Father Stephen Dominic Hayes, O.P.

The chief priests and the scribes came to hear of it and were seeking a way to put [Jesus] to death, yet they feared him because the whole crowd was astonished at his teaching.
(Mk 11: 18)

Jerusalem's leaders understand power games well; in Jesus they meet someone plainly claiming to be the Messiah, fulfilling the words of the prophets, in particular, those of Malachi: "He will purify the sons of Levi…/ that they may offer due sacrifice to the Lord" (Mal 3: 3). Thus they will test the Messiah and be tested by him. Hypocrites themselves, the one idea they seem unwilling to entertain is that Jesus is actually the Christ. When Jesus comes "refining and purifying" them, they hand him over to the Romans; then, as prophesied, Jesus offers the pure sacrifice of the cross for healing the sins of the world.

Power gaming is something of which we are all too familiar. Children find ways to manipulate their parents, spouses find ways to manipulate each other, and so on, from the home, to the workplace, to the government, to the Church herself, and even with God. All of us share this in common with the high priests and the scribes: we are trained from our early years to get our own way; life becomes an exercise of egoism and pride. For us and them something else is true: Jesus' coming into our lives means that we have to choose between him, his Lordship, and his Way, or the life of power games that we know so well. It is a life and death choice: if Jesus lives in us, then the kind of life we have without him must die. The high priests and scribes understand this and make their choice: if Jesus is in charge they cannot be. But the saints know that the life of mutual manipulation and trading in power is better dead. Jesus promises to refine and purify us for a life of love, so that we may participate with him in his perfect sacrifice of praise to the glory of his Father.

Beloved Father, grant me to love your Son's Lordship rather than my own will, especially in those moments when being refined and purified by him are difficult; let me choose him rather than my own ego to rule me.

Faith Is the Door to Life

Father Stephen Dominic Hayes, O.P.

*When evening came, [Jesus and the disciples] went out of the city.
Early in the morning, as they were walking along, they saw
the fig tree withered to its roots. Peter remembered and said to
[Jesus], "Rabbi, look! The fig tree that you cursed has withered."
Jesus said to them in reply, "Have faith in God." (Mk 11: 19-22)*

When Peter remarks to Jesus that the fig tree he cursed has withered, Jesus points immediately to faith, the theological virtue that first unites the soul to God. The withering of the fig tree is both the expression of truth manifesting prophetically the mind of God, and a divine warning to those who can read the sign. Both the prophetic sign itself and the understanding of it require a union of the mind with God in a personal way in order to be rightly understood.

The Jerusalem of the chief priests and the scribes is doomed by its faithlessness; it does not understand the mind of God and does not wish to do so. It has cut itself off from the God who is life, and the withering of the fig tree from its root prophesies Jerusalem's end. Peter, speaking for all Jesus' disciples, recognizes the divine and prophetic power at work in the Master. Jesus shepherds them toward his own Father and a relationship with that Father after the shape of the Son's own. The union with the Father brought about by faith leads to true union, however imperfect in stages, with the mind of the Almighty. In the perfect union of the Father and the Son, we see the will of the Father perfectly and powerfully expressed in Jesus' prophetic deeds. The disciples' less perfect union with the Father through Christ nevertheless is the seed of their rescue and salvation as well as the basis for their understanding of Jesus' signs. This faith is the beginning of salvation for us, too, and our escape from the path of death and doom exemplified by Jerusalem's stubborn unbelief; it is the beginning of eternal life itself: "Now this is eternal life, that they should know you, the only true God, and the one whom you sent, Jesus Christ" (Jn 17: 3).

*Father of Truth, grant that I may always seek to know you more
perfectly; increase my faith, that I may possess life with you and
your Son, and better understand the path through life you have
marked out for me.*

To Move Mountains

Father Stephen Dominic Hayes, O.P.

"Amen, I say to you, whoever says to this mountain, 'Be lifted up and thrown into the sea,' and does not doubt in his heart but believes that what he says will happen, it shall be done for him."
(Mk 11: 23)

This verse from Mark needs to be understood in the context of the verses before and after it, which situate it in the life of prayer. Moving the mountain into the midst of the sea would seem to be a sheer exercise of the power of a superhero or demigod. In fact, Jesus' use of this example in the middle of a discussion of prayer points out that the work of moving the mountain is in fact divine, and the words addressed to it a deed of prophecy. The man who can move the mountain does so as an agent of God, for such things happen only in accordance with the divine will. The man who says these words to the mountain can say them with certainty only if his belief is in fact in accordance with the divine will.

Saint Augustine's definition of prayer as "the lifting of the mind and heart to God" implies a union of the human heart and mind with the mind of God; imperfect in the beginner in prayer, powerful in the saint and the prophet. Through the Holy Spirit's gift of understanding, which aids the act of faith, the one who prays finds a home in the mind and will of God as a fish does in the ocean, perfectly at home in it without encompassing it. If the mountain moves, it is because the two wills act as one. As in the case of Jesus himself and the fig tree's withering, the believer who moves the mountain into the midst of the sea does so because God has willed it first. If we truly know the heart of God through prayer, intimacy with the divine will removes all doubt and produces a holy boldness that trusts utterly that what has been revealed by God in prayer shall be accomplished, no matter how impossible it seems.

God almighty, you instructed prophets and saints bold in prayer and deeds of power. Fill me with a thirst for prayer, that I may share their zeal for a holy life in union with your will.

Petitions That Never Fail

Father Stephen Dominic Hayes, O.P.

"Therefore I tell you, all that you ask for in prayer, believe that you will receive it and it shall be yours." (Mk 11: 24)

In a department store, I once heard a five-year-old boy arguing with his dad about a birthday present: "Dad, can I have a BB gun? I promise to be careful." "You're too little for a BB gun right now," said the father. "Bobby has a BB gun; you're not being fair!" said the boy. "Bobby is fourteen years old, you aren't there yet," said the father. The boy kept pressing his case nonetheless.

No sensible father gives his child gifts that are dangerous or hurtful or counterproductive to the child's growth and development. Our Father in heaven is no less careful about the gifts he gives us. This is why so many prayers for merely worldly goods and benefits go unanswered – they aren't good for us, in fact, from God's long and accurate point of view. Far more important than money, goods, security, or even good health – all of which are of passing utility for this life – are the things that we can actually take with us from life, in particular the virtues: charity, generosity, self-control, temperance, honesty, patience – those qualities that give us a spiritual resemblance to Jesus himself and which are the seed of the glory of our resurrection.

In our text, Jesus asks us to ask "in prayer," that is, having consulted our Father in heaven as to his own will for us. Does the petition we wish to make reflect that which is certainly his will for us? Getting a pay raise or a second car may or may not improve my life as God sees it; growth in the virtue of patience certainly will. Anything, therefore, that increases my spiritual resemblance to Jesus will be a petition that the Father will never refuse. Above all, he will never refuse a request for the Holy Spirit's gifts. Prayers like these will be granted without fail.

Loving Father of Jesus Christ, make me grow daily in a desire to imitate your Son in all his virtues and his holiness of life; in particular, in his desire to do your will perfectly at every moment.

Mercy Received, Mercy Bestowed

Father Stephen Dominic Hayes, O.P.

"When you stand to pray, forgive anyone against whom you have a grievance, so that your heavenly Father may in turn forgive you your transgressions." (Mk 11: 25-26)

To be a Christian is to be a member of God's household. With that intimacy with God comes the need to reflect his love in what we say and do. As the deeds and misdeeds of children reflect upon their parents, so do those of Christians reflect upon the God they profess to worship and by whose law they claim to live. If God is love, and Jesus Christ is love made flesh, then Christians must act in a way that authentically reflects the Father and the Son as they are. For a Christian to hold a grudge, or to refuse to forgive, makes a lie and a mockery of the Son of God who asked his Father to pardon his persecutors as they drove the nails into his hands and feet.

It is necessary, therefore, at the beginning of our prayer, says Jesus, that we should examine our relationships and forgive from the heart anyone with whom we have a grievance. That this principle is at the root of basic Christianity is exemplified by its inclusion in that basic pattern for all prayer, the Our Father. This prayer is given at baptism, prepares us for the reception of our Lord in Holy Communion, and is used to sum up and purify all the other petitions we place before God in prayer. Saint Augustine writes that, in his day, some people at Mass used to drop out of the Our Father at the words "and forgive us our trespasses," as we forgive those who trespass against us – as if they thought they would not be held responsible for them if they did not say them! They were at least thinking carefully about what that prayer meant. Likewise, you and I need to understand these holy words, pray them, and do them from the heart. In this we show ourselves to be true children of the Father of mercy.

Merciful Father, never allow anger or hurt to prevent me from forgiving others from my heart. You have forgiven me my many sins, and have been patient with my wandering ways; make me merciful to others as you have been to me.

The Blessing of Authority

Father Michael Nolan

[Jesus and his disciples] returned once more to Jerusalem. As [Jesus] was walking in the temple area, the chief priests, the scribes, and the elders approached him and said to him, "By what authority are you doing these things? Or who gave you this authority to do them?" (Mk 11: 27-28)

On his final trip to Jerusalem, Jesus acts in a way that opens him up to questioning. He is welcomed as king as he enters the holy city. He cleanses the temple area of the merchants. One can argue that it is perfectly reasonable for those entrusted with religious power in Jerusalem to question the authority of this outsider.

Questioning and determining the authority of another is often an act of fidelity and responsibility. It is only natural to check if someone has the right credentials. A priest only serves in a parish if his bishop grants him that privilege and puts it in writing. Doctors hang their big diplomas on their office walls to encourage their patients to trust their diagnoses. The Lord doesn't spend time convincing people that he has the authority to make divine claims, even though belief always requires an authority. His works, by themselves, are signs of his authority. The words he speaks reveal the heavenly source of his authority. Those who see his deeds and hear his words with an open heart receive the certainty, that one hundred percent certainty, which can turn any person into a believer and disciple.

Jesus' authority is questioned, yet he is not always the target of such an investigation. Sometimes it's directed at those who follow him. Those who question God frequently aim their doubts at those who follow God. Remembering this can help us preserve our faith which is always fragile. For faith is real when it withstands the challenges posed by living in the world. Remembering this helps us trust more in the authority of the Church whenever she is questioned the way Jesus was questioned. Affirming this reminds us that the Church exercises her authority to feed and nourish, to heal and cure her sons and daughters "as a hen gathers her young under her wings" (Mt 23: 37).

God our Father, your Son gave himself over to evil men to reconcile us to you. May I imitate his example by turning hatred into love and conflict to peace.

Faith Is Life

Father Michael Nolan

Jesus said to [the chief priests, the scribes, and the elders], "I shall ask you one question. Answer me, and I will tell you by what authority I do these things. Was John's baptism of heavenly or of human origin? Answer me." (Mk 11: 29-30)

One of the greatest reforms of the Second Vatican Council is the restoration of the catechumenate. Today those who wish to enter the Church are accompanied by the prayers and the witness of the Church's faithful. These adults pass through this process before they are baptized so they can live out their faith the rest of their lives. At the same time, the majority of Catholics are still baptized as infants at the request of their parents. Most of us discover we were baptized long after it happens. When I begin preparing parents for the baptism of their children I usually inquire whether they have questions about the sacrament before I make my presentation. Sometimes a parent is concerned about the garment or the candle or the time of the ceremony. No parent has ever expressed the desire to know what baptism means for their child's immediate or future life. Yet if parents are unaware that baptism affects the very meaning of life, this great gift from God is reduced to a mere ritual.

Jesus asks his interrogators a question about the baptism of John. When John was baptizing across the Jordan, the authorities in Jerusalem went out to investigate him just as they are investigating Jesus now. He asks if John was sent by God when he called the people of Jerusalem to repentance. The Lord's question isn't designed to learn what they thought of John. Nor is he trying to argue with them over theology. He asks this question to begin the process of educating their hearts.

To determine which authority to submit to depends on what dwells in your heart. If we believe our baptism truly washes us clean, then we can trust from that moment on that God is willing to guide us. Then heaven becomes not only our future or our origin. It becomes our dwelling place in our passing world.

Merciful Father, your Son died and rose to give us happiness of life. May I devote this day to sharing that joy with those who still do not know you.

No Reason to Fear

Father Michael Nolan

[The chief priests, the scribes, and the elders] discussed this among themselves and said, "If we say, 'Of heavenly origin,' he will say, '[Then] why did you not believe him?' But shall we say, 'Of human origin'?" – they feared the crowd, for they all thought John really was a prophet. So they said to Jesus in reply, "We do not know." (Mk 11: 31-33a)

The Lord's question not only starts a conversation. It provokes an identity crisis. Accepting that John the Baptist was sent by God opens the priests, scribes, and elders up to the devastating charge that undermines the foundation that all authority rests upon. That charge is hypocrisy. At the same time, this group of leaders possesses all the outward signs of power, yet they are afraid to say what they believe for fear of the crowd. So they choose the option that will preserve their position even though it must have made them wince. They admit ignorance. They say to Jesus, "We do not know." Leaders who are afraid and choose publicly to profess ignorance, rather than say what they believe, trigger an identity crisis for themselves.

Everyone in authority faces the threat of such a crisis. So does every Christian. We want to live by faith, but hesitate when the consequences might penalize us. We want to build up our treasure in heaven, yet the concerns of the world dominate our attention. We wish we could pray better, but neglect to make time for prayer. We want to be faithful to the tradition, yet worry about not being relevant.

Christianity, however, isn't about relevance. It is concerned with fidelity to the Lord. The Christian can never fear the opinion of the crowd. Anyone who has ever stood in a crowd knows how it unexpectedly shifts direction from one moment to the next. Yet all Christians need to ask ourselves what fears we have that inhibit us from professing and practicing the faith. Discovering those fears can help us overcome them either immediately or over time; refusal to admit our weaknesses or fears can reduce us to mere practitioners of religious rituals – to hypocrites – instead of disciples who want to be saints. We never have to fear this identity crisis as long as we respond faithfully to the Lord.

Gentle Father, your Son made disciples to show us the way to seek you. Help me to recognize the hidden suffering of those near me so I may lift up their needs in prayer.

The Love That Isn't Easy

Father Michael Nolan

Then Jesus said to [the chief priests, the scribes, and the elders],
"Neither shall I tell you by what authority I do these things."
(Mk 11: 33b)

Jesus' enemies find it difficult to answer his questions. Their fears overrule them. They are afraid of the crowd and even more afraid of the truth. So they plead ignorance, which leads the Lord to ignore their question. But he doesn't walk away from them. He takes them down the path of repentance with the parable of the wicked tenants. This is the mercy of God.

To defend his authority before those chief priests, elders, and scribes won't bring them any closer to salvation. Their hearts are so hardened that the only reason they converse with him is to find a reason to convict him. He tells a parable to those who wish to kill him. The parable is the mercy of God. It is an acknowledgment that he is aware of their intentions. It is a warning that by pursuing their wicked ways they will forfeit all that has been entrusted to them. It is told so they won't be surprised how they will be judged when they don't change their behavior. It is the mercy of God not to agree to everything while never abandoning anyone.

Every Christian encounters people who have departed or drifted away from the Church. They are our co-workers. We live in the same homes. We are friends with them in all areas of life, except when it comes to the Church. Jesus is our guide in how to love them. He doesn't force his enemies to cooperate with him. Nor does he agree to submit to their demands. Yet he continues to speak with them. There is only one Jesus, and Jesus is our teacher. We can learn from him how not to force God on those we love while still remaining faithful ourselves. We can share in his wisdom and learn his methods in the hope that those whom we love will one day learn again how to love the Lord.

Eternal Father, your Son persevered in love and sincerity. May I be humbled this day and be ready to help others with the loving power you give us.

He Warns Because He Loves

Michael Nolan

[Jesus] began to speak to [the chief priests, the scribes, and the elders] in parables. "A man planted a vineyard, put a hedge around it, dug a wine press, and built a tower. Then he leased it to tenant farmers and left on a journey." (Mk 12: 1)

The parable of the wicked tenants was told to benefit us today just as it was to help those who questioned his authority. The wisdom in a parable is always a benefit to anyone who can uncover its hidden meaning. Yet each parable targets a specific audience. Certain parables are told to certain people. In this case, the parable of the wicked tenants is told to the authorities of Jerusalem – the chief priests, the scribes, and the elders. They question him in public to turn the people against him. He knows it. Jesus responds with a parable to highlight their misuse of authority. He wants to warn them that it is they who should be worried about being convicted. They should worry a great deal. They think they are protecting the integrity of Israel but in reality they are rejecting the gifts of God. The Lord's description of the vineyard makes this clear.

The householder made a vineyard, put a hedge around it, dug a wine press, and built a tower. After leasing the land to farmers, he departs on a journey. The vineyard is God's kingdom entrusted to Israel. The hedge represents the law built to promote justice and keep out evil. The wine press signifies the prophets who were crushed for preaching repentance. The tower is the temple entrusted to those chief priests, scribes, and elders to make sacrifices to the Lord. The lease and the journey symbolize the trust and patience of God.

We have no need to question Jesus' authority today. That was proven when he laid down his life and took it up again. Yet the parable can still help us to grow in trusting God. This same parable reminds us that God has given us everything we need to gain eternal life. The Church, the virtues, the sacraments, and the Creed have been entrusted to the apostles and make it possible for us today to be faithful tenants until he comes again.

Father of creation, your Son's life reminds us that without you we are nothing. May I treasure the blessings you bestow on me more than any material things in my possession.

Permanent Conversion

Father Michael Nolan

"At the proper time [the owner of the vineyard] sent a servant to the tenants to obtain from them some of the produce of the vineyard. But they seized him, beat him, and sent him away empty-handed." (Mk 12: 2-3)

The landowner designs the vineyard to insure an abundant harvest. The tenants rent it with the hedge, wine press, and tower already built. The landowner gives them time before demanding payment. The success of the tenant farmers depends on maintaining the owner's vineyard.

God makes the vineyard. Structurally it is perfect. Yet in that perfect place the tenants produce nothing. The perfect conditions of the vineyard cannot overcome the neglect of the tenants. Their response to the owner's request points to a problem in their hearts. They are violent instead of hospitable. They are greedy instead of generous. Once again, wickedness plants itself in the good soil. The structures can't insure fidelity to God.

Only a change of the heart can do this. The heart of every Christian needs to be changed. The heart of the twelve apostles had to change even though they attended the best seminary in the world. The heart of Saint Paul had to change before he could change the world. The heart of every saint has to change before he can rejoice in heaven. The Church is always changing, *semper reformanda*, as long as her children are being converted back to God. We don't just need conversion. We need conversion back to God.

This coming back to God has mostly been forgotten. We call this confession. Confession is coming back to God. Confession doesn't result in erasing the memory of our sins, but makes it possible, once again, to think of God. In the confessional, we are able to welcome Jesus again even though we sent him away the last time he came. In the confessional, we can acknowledge that we failed to give God what we owe, knowing he will let us remain in the vineyard. In the confessional, we let Jesus know that we won't deny him again.

Father of mercies, your Son came to enlighten all in the world. May my thoughts please you this day so my love toward others will be sincere.

God Always Reaches Out

Father Michael Nolan

"Again [the owner of the vineyard] sent [the tenants] another servant. And that one they beat over the head and treated shamefully. He sent yet another whom they killed. So, too, many others; some they beat, others they killed."
(Mk 12: 4-5)

The rejection of the first servant leads the landowner to send more of them. Instead of giving up on the wicked tenants, the owner keeps open the possibility that they will change. This continues until many more servants suffer shame, beatings, and death. The slaughter of the servants refers back in history to how Israel received the prophets sent by God.

Yet Jesus isn't a history teacher. He educates the heart. He speaks to the hearts of those who refuse to see that they are repeating history. The killing of the servants is mentioned in the parable because those who question Jesus are committing the same sins. He knows they are in denial. At another time he says to them, "Woe to you, you hypocrites… you say, 'If we had lived in the days of our ancestors, we would not have joined them in shedding the prophets' blood'" (Mt 23: 29-30). They deny that they reject God. And so can we who live today.

The Lord sends his servants to us whenever the holy Scriptures are proclaimed in the Mass. Yet how attentive are we while they are being read? The Lord wants to come to us through the Bibles that sit on the shelves of our bookcases. My life was saved the first time I sat down and read the Gospel of Matthew from start to finish. Knowing that I had read the writings of so many other authors before reading the Evangelist filled me with regret. "What took me so long to read this?" I asked myself. I had access to a Bible for many years, but I hadn't bothered to open it. He was reaching out to me through his words. My neglect wasn't the same as Israel's violent rejection of the prophets. Yet I suffered because of it. I had lived longer than I had needed to without really knowing the Lord.

Eternal Father, your Son spoke to reveal our redemption. May I listen to your voice and learn how to cast off my old ways of life.

The Full Truth about God

Father Michael Nolan

*"[The owner of the vineyard] had one other to send,
a beloved son. He sent him to [the tenants] last of all,
thinking, 'They will respect my son.'" (Mk 12: 6)*

We can never know the mind of God. There is a limit to what we can know. Yet the parable gives us a glimpse into his thought process. "They will respect my son." The wicked tenants have rejected the numerous servants sent in the past. This leads the owner to send his beloved son. Does the owner misjudge the depth of their wickedness? Could God in his ultimate goodness be naïve when it comes to facing evil? Of course not! Jesus comes to reveal the full truth about God that can't be shown at a distance. God's full truth is revealed when we experience his forgiveness. God enters the world to forgive the sins of men. God remains in the world by the power of the Holy Spirit to forgive us whenever we are in need of it. Even in this fallen world, by forgiving us, God continues to be God.

God's goodness is revealed whenever the Church is close to those in need. Most see this wherever the Church educates children, feeds the hungry, and cares for the sick and dying. Often people see this witness through the Church's courageous presence in places afflicted by war, poverty, and natural disaster.

Yet none of this charity can fully reveal the ultimate goodness of God. This comes to light when a priest sits in the confessional. There doesn't have to be a long line. The church may even be empty. The priest in the confessional affirms what God thinks: "They will respect my son."

The presence of evil still grips our world. Mercy gets misunderstood as weakness. Man still has not learned how to live among other men. It can appear that maintaining hope is a waste of time, but it isn't as long as somewhere in the world a priest is sitting and waiting in the confessional.

Father of truth, your Son came to take away our guilt. May I not fear to express sorrow for my transgressions and seek to be reconciled with others.

What Makes Peace Possible

Father Michael Nolan

"But those tenants said to one another, 'This is the heir. Come, let us kill him, and the inheritance will be ours.' So they seized [the son] and killed him, and threw him out of the vineyard."
(Mk 12: 7-8)

Every one of us walks through the valley of death. We attend to the dying in nursing homes and hospitals. We read the obituaries and attend funerals. We make out our wills. Yet Jesus lived daily with a much worse threat. He faced the danger of being killed often.

Herod's soldiers are sent to Bethlehem to kill the Christ child. In Nazareth, people try to seize him and throw him over a cliff. In Jerusalem, the leadership whips the crowd into a frenzy until it demands his death. The motives behind killing are often anger and rage. Yet the tenants in the parable kill the son because they think they will gain from it. "Come let us kill him, and the inheritance will be ours." How does killing him gain them his inheritance?

This mentality is one of the pillars of the culture of death. It promotes the lie that fewer children benefit everybody. Yet even those who are open to life and have never entertained the thought of taking a person's life can adopt a similar mentality toward those we find difficult. We think that life will be better by ending contact with those who challenge or betray us. Of course, certain situations demand formal separation when a person's safety is threatened. Yet marriages and families, neighborhoods and parishes weaken when friendships are dissolved, covenants are ended, and people decide to ignore one another.

The most powerful weapon against this twisted mentality is the practice of going to confession. In this sacrament we can discover a joy that comes from honestly admitting our sins and hearing the words of forgiveness. An attitude of patience toward others deepens the more we experience God's patience. The more we go to confession, an awareness can start to grow within us helping us see that we are to be peacemakers and reconcilers, for we know that God hasn't disowned us.

Father of love, your Son set us free from the enslavement of sin. May I face my trials with the awareness that you will never abandon me.

To Pardon the Unpardonable

Father Michael Nolan

"What [then] will the owner of the vineyard do? He will come, put the tenants to death, and give the vineyard to others."
(Mk 12: 9)

One of the most appealing aspects of Jesus' parables is the twist or surprise in them. So many aspects of the parable of the wicked tenants must have confirmed what the chief priests, scribes, and elders already knew about Israel. The actions of the landowner reflect the generosity and patience of God. The murders by the tenants recall Israel's rejection of the prophets. Then the owner puts the tenants to death. He demands justice.

Yet that audience in Jerusalem must have thought they heard Jesus incorrectly when he said the owner gave the vineyard to others. They must have marveled at the generosity of the landowner who lost his beloved son. He gives the vineyard to others. He gives even after losing what was most precious to him. This is a God unlike all others. This God is different. This God is the true God because he can pardon the unpardonable. The worst evil does not have power over him.

A few years ago, I knew someone involved in a bad traffic accident. The driver who was cited for causing the accident was badly injured and without insurance. He sued the other driver who had insurance. The trial brought great stress to the defendant, especially after the jury sided with the driver who had the injuries and hospital bills. A year later, the defendant in that trial was asked to help with food donations in the local parish. The parish was committed to serving those facing hardship. Each week parishioners were sent out to deliver food at the homes of people in need. Unknown to all those involved in organizing the charity, the driver who lost the court case was sent with food to the one who had sued him. That wasn't another accident. That was God letting us know we can be different.

Father of mercies, your Son never hated his enemies. Help me to love those I struggle with, in gratitude for the love you always show me.

Spiritual Reconstruction

Father Michael Nolan

"Have you not read this scripture passage:/ 'The stone that the builders rejected/ has become the cornerstone;/ by the Lord has this been done,/ and it is wonderful in our eyes'?"
(Mk 12: 10)

There is a famous quote: "Jesus promised us the kingdom – all we got was the Church." This is the truth because the Church is what we need. Many doubt that a kingdom is within their reach. While those who just assume they are all prepared to be welcomed are probably the least ready among us. We need the Church on earth to enter God's kingdom.

One of the greatest blessings a parish provides Catholics is the opportunity to prepare adults for baptism. One evening, at the end of one of our final preparations near Easter, a woman wanted to share her joy with us. She had been born and grew up in a rural part of an Asian country that the Gospel has not reached yet. One day she did something wrong, and everyone in her town was made aware of it. The town elders let her know that her sin would remain with her always. There was no way to remove that sin from her. There was no way people could forgive her. That day she lost her reason to live. They denied her hope. Yet on this night, years later, she told us in that church basement hall that for the first time since that day in her town she had a reason to live again. She had hope. She said there is Jesus. She believed that he could forgive her.

All we got was the Church, but the Church rests on a foundation – the risen Jesus. Rejected and put to death, Jesus returns to save even those who had abandoned and rejected him. Rejected by his people in front of Pontius Pilate, he becomes the cornerstone of the place where lives can be rebuilt. He becomes the cornerstone of the Church where he reconstructs our spiritual and personal lives into living stones attached to him and one another.

Father of all blessings, your Son conquered death and sin. May I work with the help of your grace to reject sin and follow him more faithfully.

Learning to Do It Right

Father Michael Nolan

[The chief priests, the scribes, and the elders] were seeking to arrest [Jesus], but they feared the crowd, for they realized that he had addressed the parable to them. So they left him and went away. (Mk 12: 12)

John Cardinal O'Connor often recounted a surprise that took place when he became Archbishop of New York. At the Mass in the cathedral, he spotted Mother Teresa standing near a column. She summoned him. He left his chair to speak to her. Her first words to the most powerful prelate in the United States were, "Don't get in God's way." None of us wants to stand in the way of people seeking God. All of us know we can make it difficult for God to reach people. It is always painful when a Christian leaves the faith. Often we bend over backwards to keep everyone in the flock so we aren't the reason they choose to leave. Yet people walk away.

They walked away from Jesus – the rich young man, those who heard him speak on the Bread of Life, and these chief priests, scribes, and elders who heard a parable about themselves. The parable let them know that their wickedness sets them far apart from God, but it didn't change their hearts. Only by walking away was it possible for them to learn. Knowledge without devotion makes conversion almost impossible. Blessed John Henry Newman says, "People learn to do right by having done wrong." Sometimes we have to let people walk away.

After a few years in a parish, a pastor begins to remember where people sit at Mass. He starts to notice when they disappear. I try to contact these missing parishioners to make sure they are okay. Once I called a parishioner whom I had not seen in months. After telling me that he had left the parish, I invited him to meet and talk about it some more. He said he would think about it and also mentioned that he was "old-fashioned and probably a little bigoted." As the pastor of a parish that ministers in three languages, I decided it was best to offer my prayers for him and wished him good-by.

God our Father, your Son always shows us the way to you. May I look at all those around me and see them as your gift to me.

Whom We Belong To

Father Michael Nolan

[The chief priests, the scribes, and the elders] sent some Pharisees and Herodians to [Jesus] to ensnare him in his speech. They came and said to him, "Teacher, we know that you are a truthful man and that you are not concerned with anyone's opinion. You do not regard a person's status but teach the way of God in accordance with the truth. Is it lawful to pay the census tax to Caesar or not? Should we pay or should we not pay?" (Mk 12: 13-14)

The parable of the wicked tenants falls on deaf ears. Being warned that they will forfeit their authority doesn't change their hearts. It just leads them to switch tactics. Saint Ambrose says, "It does not please God to save his people in dialogue." Only the Lord's death and resurrection has power over the hardest of hearts.

The priests, elders, and scribes seek other ways to trap him. Their desire to pursue him shows that it is they who are ensnared in sin. For sins that do not spark contrition usually lead to more sinning. This time they sin by sending others to question him. The Pharisees monitor the adherence to Mosaic law. They will complain if his answer favors the foreign power. The Herodians enforce respect and obedience to the emperor. They will arrest him if he undermines Roman authority.

They ask Jesus his opinion about paying taxes to Caesar. The question is designed to threaten his status with either the Jews or the Romans. He can favor the world or God. Yet Jesus does not belong to the world. He comes from God. His answer is a truthful one that disappoints his enemies. Jesus knows who he is and that he is sent by God. We forget we belong to God. It is easy to forget that we don't belong to this world.

It gets even easier when we neglect the sacrament of confession. In the sacrament, the Lord consecrates us in the truth so that eventually our attraction to the world may be overcome. Confession allows us to face the truth about ourselves and our past affiliations. We are not God and don't always withstand the attacks of our enemies. Yet confession helps us to face the truth about ourselves so that we can answer every question and make future decisions without worrying what others may think.

Father of all, your Son came to call the righteous and the sinner alike. May I trust that following you at every moment will bring me a lasting joy and happiness.

Where God Listens

Father Michael Nolan

Knowing their hypocrisy [Jesus] said to [the Pharisees and Herodians], "Why are you testing me? Bring me a denarius to look at." They brought one to him and he said to them, "Whose image and inscription is this?" They replied to him, "Caesar's."
(Mk 12: 15-16)

Jesus answers their question by looking at reality. He asks to see one of the coins used to pay taxes to the emperor. That piece of metal has an image and inscription of Caesar chiseled on it. Today we often think of an image as something we craft for ourselves to control how others view us. We observe the fashion and behavior of others to discern what they are like on the inside. Yet no clothing or behavior or association with others can reflect the true image of a human being. For a human person is fashioned in God's image. You are God's image. Every person is made in the image and likeness of God.

Yet how can we be God's image when God is holy and perfect? Anyone with the slightest self-awareness knows his faults and his dark side. Our memories are never cleansed of the times we showed indifference to those around us. We carry with us the results of our mediocre efforts. How can the glory of God possibly be reflected through my being? It can't be true unless we are honest and admit that we need God's mercy and forgiveness.

Admitting our faults to ourselves does not cut it. We need someone who can listen. The confessor's primary role is to listen in a way that allows us to say everything. The confessor is also saved by taking on this sacred role. At times, the parish priest has to speak all day. He gets called upon to counsel. He must preach. Yet in the confessional, the priest can listen in a way that shows that God is listening. It is a privilege, even though it is never easy, to hear another person tell God that he is sorry. Here, the priest listens, making it possible for the person to tell God that he wants to be restored and reflect his holy image.

Almighty Father, you always heard your Son when he prayed to you. May I pray more this day knowing that you always hear me.

Method of Payment

Father Michael Nolan

So Jesus said to [the Pharisees and the Herodians], "Repay to Caesar what belongs to Caesar and to God what belongs to God." They were utterly amazed at him. (Mk 12: 17)

Regular Sunday attendance at the Eucharist is in decline. Commentators offer many explanations for this phenomenon. People work on Sundays. Sundays are a day for football and soccer and hockey. Many don't know it is a sin to miss Mass on Sunday. Yet Catholics who have stopped worshiping God on Sundays often say it is because the Mass "doesn't do it for them." Many have said to me, "I don't get anything out of the Mass." As a priest, I wish I could help them in their frustration. I sympathize with them. But I don't bother to do anything about it except respond by saying, "You are not supposed to get anything out of the Mass. You go to Mass to give – not to receive."

This is one of the tensions of Christian life. We practice it to fulfill our need, but it is only fully practiced when we give to God. We have to give to God when it isn't easy. We give to God when things are good and when they are bad. We give to God when we are weak. We give to God when it is inconvenient. We give to God when we heal and when we bury someone.

How does the Lord wish to receive his payment? The Lord wants something much more precious than any coin made by Caesar. He wants what he gave us – our lives. God wants to receive back what was given to us – his Son. He wants us to live our lives refashioned in the image of his only begotten Son, Jesus Christ. He wants our good deeds. He wants to hear from us in prayer. God wants to celebrate. For a great feast is held and there is never more joy in heaven than when just one sinner returns to the Lord.

Father in heaven, your Son is our gift for our life today. May I see that in giving to you I receive everything back one hundredfold.

Asking for an Answer

Father George William Rutler

Some Sadducees, who say there is no resurrection, came to [Jesus] and put this question to him, saying, "Teacher, Moses wrote for us, 'If someone's brother dies, leaving a wife but no child, his brother must take the wife and raise up descendants for his brother.' Now there were seven brothers. The first married a woman and died, leaving no descendants. So the second married her and died, leaving no descendants, and the third likewise. And the seven left no descendants. Last of all the woman also died. At the resurrection [when they arise] whose wife will she be? For all seven had been married to her." (Mk 12: 18-23)

There are two ways to ask a question: to get an answer or to prove a point. The latter is insincere because it does not want to learn. The Sadducees, being materialists, thought that matter is all that matters. They ask Jesus an intentionally absurd question – about an imaginary widow of seven brothers – in order to make themselves look right and Jesus wrong. While they would have been reasonable in saying that they saw no evidence of life after death, they were unreasonable in denying resurrection simply because they had no evidence. They exalted their opinion to the rank of a truth. By so doing, they assumed that truth is only opinion. Faith roots us in something more, not less, substantial than opinion: "Faith is the realization of what is hoped for and evidence of things not seen" (Heb 11: 1).

The Sadducees thought they "knew it all" because they did not know how small what they "knew" was, and how vast "all" is. That was simply because they had a limited definition of "it." All these years after 1735, when Carl Linnaeus published his system for classifying plants and animals as well as minerals, it is estimated that scientists have discovered as few as ten percent of the species living on our planet. Linnaeus would have been amazed, for he thought thirteen pages of his book had pretty much exhausted the subject. Recently, physicists have learned that their measure of the universe is also perhaps about ten percent of its true size, since they had based their calculations on light emitted by hydrogen which was trapped within the galaxies emitting it. So "it" is much more than "it" was said to be. If the Sadducees had been more reasonable, they could have learned from Jesus that life after death is part of a reality far grander than their closed minds.

Heavenly Father, open my mind and strengthen my will that I might seek and find eternal life.

The Language of Heaven

Father George William Rutler

Jesus said to [the Sadducees], "Are you not misled because you do not know the scriptures or the power of God? When they rise from the dead, they neither marry nor are given in marriage, but they are like the angels in heaven." (Mk 12: 24-25)

Those who have had an intimate contact with heavenly beings could feel frustrated when trying to describe the experience. Saint Bernadette was saddened by the sculptor's rendition of the Lady of Lourdes. Moses pleaded, "Do let me see your glory!" (Ex 33: 18), but God would only give him hints. Jesus says patiently, "I have much more to tell you, but you cannot bear it now" (Jn 16: 12).

We must keep that in mind when interpreting descriptions of heaven. The prospect of heaven without marriage may not seem heavenly at all for those whose vocation is to wed. But everyone has a vocation to union with the divine Love that made the world: this is true of those who consecrate their celibate state as well as of husbands and wives. To be "like" the angels is not to be angels, for humans have a different glory, but that splendor comes from being "wed" to the love of God. In heaven, that union is inexpressibly more joyful than the greatest happiness on earth. Grace does not destroy nature, but perfects it, so when "all is grace" in heaven, our human nature is more vivid than now, but in a way that human language stumbles over itself to express, like Saint Bernadette's sculptor. Various heretics have imagined paradises according to materialist delights which, if they actually existed for ever, would be hellish. As marriage in time and space is meant to be open to procreation, that aspect is no longer needed in eternity, and yet the joy of resurrected life surpasses the bliss of the lover and the beloved. The risen body will be incorrupt, beautiful, strong, and unconfined by space. Aquinas spoke of these as impassibility, clarity, agility, and subtility. This cannot be completely clear now, but "then I shall know fully, as I am fully known" (1 Cor 13: 12).

Blessed Lord, I thank you for the promise of joy with you for ever, and ask for the simplicity to trust that happiness now is only a taste of the happiness yet to be.

God of the Living

Father George William Rutler

"As for the dead being raised, have you not read in the Book of Moses, in the passage about the bush, how God told him, 'I am the God of Abraham, [the] God of Isaac, and [the] God of Jacob'? He is not God of the dead but of the living. You are greatly misled." (Mk 12: 26-27)

I f we practice patience, the same people who would exasperate us can also sanctify us. Christ needed no sanctification, but he had plenty of opportunity to have his patience taxed in his human nature. When unimaginative and cynical people ask him about life after death, he certainly is ironical in asking these supposed experts in the Book of Moses if they had ever read it. Then the patient Master uses masterly understatement: "You are greatly misled." Saint Paul would say from his own experience what applies to all of us, and not just those who tried to bait Jesus: "Avoid foolish and ignorant debates, for you know that they breed quarrels. A slave of the Lord should not quarrel, but should be gentle with everyone, able to teach, tolerant, correcting opponents with kindness" (2 Tm 2: 23-25). No amount of arguing will persuade the doubter that the dead can be raised. Death alone can convince the doubter. We do know that Jesus quotes the Book of Moses, specifically Exodus 3: 6, on the Wednesday before he died and rose again. Instead of trying to win an argument, he wants to win souls. That is why he immediately gave the apostles power to forgive sins on the day he rose. Mortal sins are called that because they are little deaths, blocking his gift of life. In saying that God is not God of the dead but of the living, he is saying that nothing can die in his presence. His voice, that raised the daughter of Jairus from her deathbed and summoned Lazarus from his tomb, draws us back to life after sin has blocked his grace. He even sustains us when we spend a third of our lives in that little death we call slumber. Instead of arguing, it is better to pray before going to sleep, and to confess our sins instead of trying to be clever.

Dear Master, forgive our foolish questions and give us the faith to trust you, so that when we die and face you as our judge, we will rejoice and not be ashamed that we doubted your power and glory.

Fully Alive

Father George William Rutler

One of the scribes, when he came forward and heard [Jesus and the Sadducees] disputing and saw how well [Jesus] had answered them, asked him, "Which is the first of all the commandments?" (Mk 12: 28)

If Jesus held a press conference today, it is unlikely that any reporter would rush up to ask which commandment is the most important. More likely, he would be asked about why there are commandments at all, and if it might be possible to drop a few. The scribe loves the commandments but he sees in Jesus someone who loves them even more than he does. Surely the scribe knows the ritual formula about what law ranked first, but he wants to hear it from someone who might give life to what had become stale. This is the attraction of saints in our day: they have a lively fascination greater than pundits or professors, which is why they can be threatening. The saints are the most extraordinary people who ever lived, and yet they are conspicuously absent from university curricula, because to acknowledge their existence is to acknowledge the power of God to change lives.

This is why our Lord wants us to ask him for help. "Ask and you will receive…" (Lk 11: 9). If we lack the humility to propose a question, we will be like the driver who hates to ask for directions when he is lost. At least the scribe is willing to admit that someone great might be passing by with a great answer. The scribe is not like those people who pretend to be asking a question when in fact they are making a speech. His question is heartfelt: like the rich young man and the Ethiopian eunuch and Saint Paul's prison guard. All of them wanted an answer to the meaning of life. When they asked what they must do to be saved, they may have not even have known what that means, but they wanted contact with something bigger than themselves. In Christ, the something is someone, whose first law is to become fully alive by living like him.

Father of Life, on whom all law and teaching depend, I humbly praise you for giving me a mind to ask worthy questions and a heart to receive the answers that you alone can give.

The Greatest Commandment
Father George William Rutler

Jesus replied, "The first is this: 'Hear, O Israel! The Lord our God is Lord alone! You shall love the Lord your God with all your heart, with all your soul, with all your mind, and with all your strength.'" (Mk 12: 29-30)

The first sound ever heard was that from God: "Let there be light." Only God himself could have heard it. When he made us "in his image," he entrusted to us the ability to speak of him and to him. "Much will be required of the person entrusted with much, and still more will be demanded of the person entrusted with more" (Lk 12: 48). The greatest commandment begins with a commandment within itself: to "hear" what God requires of his people. Twice a day the Jew would, and still does, recite the *Keriath Shema* ("Hear, O Israel"), making holy the rising and setting of the day (Dt 6: 1-9). Jesus knew how to write this commandment to love God and to wrap it on his wrist and forehead and to place it on the doorpost of his humble house in Nazareth. Our human dignity is nurtured by loving God in our actions and thoughts and in our homes.

There may be in this *Shema*, and indeed there must be since this commandment is from God, a prophecy of the love that is within the Holy Trinity. The very rhythm of the greatest commandment is threefold: The Lord, our God, is One. The Lord is Father and our God is the Son and the Holy Spirit makes them One. So our Creator gave the human race a clue to the Three in One and One in Three in the age of Moses, and his people were praising the Triune God unaware of what they were doing, rather like the man in Molière's play who was speaking prose without knowing it. As to love God is life, so to curse God is death to our dignity (Jb 2: 9). If we do not wrap the commandment on our wrists and foreheads, surely we can show our love by praising the Lord whenever we hear someone curse.

Blessed are you, O Lord God of Israel. And ever blessed are we by your revelation to us as Father, Son, and Holy Spirit, whom we love by the gift of love which comes from you.

We Are Wonderfully Made

Father George William Rutler

"The second is this: 'You shall love your neighbor as yourself.'
There is no other commandment greater than these."
(Mk 12: 31)

Jesus knows us better than we know ourselves. That is the bad news for the selfish, but it is also Gospel good news if we are selfless. He knows the depths of human depravity, which is why he weeps for Jerusalem, but he also knows our potential, which is why he actually says on the night before his death that we are his Father's "gift" to him (Jn 17: 24). So an aging actress insisted, "I am not a has-been. I am a will-be." In Old Adam shows the "has-been," but the New Adam, who is Christ himself, shows the "will-be." He commands us to love others as ourselves. If I do not love myself, I cannot love anything outside myself. The Renaissance writer Montaigne said, "Of all our infirmities, the most savage is to despise our being." But if I am tied up in myself, I shall never get untied by myself. When God made the first man, he did not stop. He made from his side another being, for it was not good for the man to be alone. A priest will often hear a hesitant penitent say, "I want to feel good about myself." That wallows in the narcissistic cult of "self-esteem" until it matures by loving others. A baby after only a few months is able to distinguish a smile from a frown. The infant cannot see its own smile, and learns what happiness is from seeing other faces. Happiness with ourselves grows by smiling with other selves and, ultimately, with God. The Psalmist sings of himself, but makes that a hymn to his Creator: "I praise you, so wonderfully you made me; wonderful are your works!" (Ps 139: 14). Saint John Mary Vianney said, "I would rather die loving you, than live without loving you." By loving Christ in others, the self we loved first never dies.

Eternal Father, I praise you for having made me a gift to your Son, who then gave his own Mother as a gift to me from the cross, to teach me to love others as I am loved.

Love and Sacrifice

Father George William Rutler

The scribe said to [Jesus], "Well said, teacher. You are right in saying, 'He is One and there is no other than he.' And 'to love him with all your heart, with all your understanding, with all your strength, and to love your neighbor as yourself' is worth more than all burnt offerings and sacrifices." (Mk 12: 32-33)

This amiable conversation takes place a few days before Passover, when lambs are being prepared for sacrifice. Jesus and the Torah teacher can smell the smoking altars. The scribe may even be pointing to the curling smoke in the sky as he commends Jesus for affirming the prophecy of Hosea: "For it is love that I desire, not sacrifice." He does not realize that Jesus is the "I" made visible.

It would be the worst kind of literalness to take this to mean that altars should go and that there be no temple. It is easy, but spiritually myopic, to reduce all the commandments to philanthropy: "I love my neighbor, so I don't have to go to church." Christ skewers that kind of rationalization with true reason: "Do not think that I have come to abolish the law or the prophets. I have come not to abolish but to fulfill" (Mt 5: 17). Human priests begin each day kissing countless altars throughout the world because, in the words of the Preface for the Fifth Sunday of Easter, Christ "showed himself to be the priest, the altar, and the lamb of sacrifice." Not to worship him is to evaporate divine love into a kind of benign largesse which is not large enough to embrace God and man together. Egoism quickly turns a humanitarian into a sociopath who says, "I love humanity. It's people I can't stand." Blessed Teresa of Calcutta once told me to remember her every time I put the drop of water into the wine in preparing the chalice at Mass. Love for neighbor becomes a holy sacrifice when mingled with love for God. Through no fault of his own, the scribe treats Christ as his equal. "Well said, teacher" is meant as a compliment, but to agree with God only because he agrees with us makes us look foolish.

Heavenly Father, may the gifts we present at your holy altar became a living sacrifice through the perfect love of your only begotten Son who offered himself for us on the altar of the cross.

The Kingdom among Us

Father George William Rutler

And when Jesus saw that [the scribe] answered with understanding, he said to him, "You are not far from the kingdom of God." And no one dared to ask him any more questions. (Mk 12: 34)

The school of philosophy founded by Aristotle was called "Peripatetic" because of its walkways or colonnades. Aristotle liked to think while walking, and he knew that this also helped to keep his students awake because they had to walk with him. Jesus walked while talking about the kingdom of God because that kingdom is active: not a visible thing, but his own presence, so it might just as well be called the kingship of God. He once told the Pharisees, "No one will announce, 'Look, here it is,' or, 'There it is.' For behold, the kingdom of God is among you" (Lk 17: 21). The kingdom is himself in their midst. Now he says that the scribe is "not far" from it. The scribe was one voice away, but he had to let the sound move into his very soul.

Those who mourn for human kings are solaced by the fact that there is a successor: "The king is dead. Long live the king." When King Edward VII noticed the royal standard at half-mast on the boat carrying the body of his mother, he ordered it raised back up the pole because the moment she breathed her last he took his first breath as the new monarch. As Alpha and Omega, Jesus has neither predecessor nor successor. He himself is the procession to heaven. In his case, "The king is dead. Long live the king" is the shout of his own resurrection. The scribe was one heartbeat away from that kingship, but one heartbeat can mark the difference between life and death. King Agrippa will tell Saint Paul that he was "almost" becoming a Christian (Acts 26: 28). But there is no halfway to heaven because there is no half of heaven. No one dared to ask Christ any more questions. Nor did they have to. Christ wants from us only the answer that is the Church's most ancient creed: "Jesus is Lord!"

Heavenly Father, may the kingdom promised by your Son be opened to me by the grace of your Holy Spirit, who lives and reigns with you and the same Lord who is among us now and for ever.

Lord and God

Father Stephen Dominic Hayes, O.P.

As Jesus was teaching in the temple area he said, "How do the scribes claim that the Messiah is the son of David? David himself, inspired by the holy Spirit, said:/ 'The Lord said to my lord,/ "Sit at my right hand/ until I place your enemies under your feet.'/ David himself calls him 'lord'; so how is he his son?" [The] great crowd heard this with delight. (Mk 12: 35-37)

Jesus is not disagreeing completely with the scribes; the Scriptures are clear that the Messiah, the Anointed One of God, when he comes, will be of the house of David. When David the king wished to build a temple to God, the Lord forbade him to do so because he had spilled so much blood in war. God promised that his son would build a temple (which, of course, Solomon did) and that David's royal house would last for ever. The problem with the scribes' teaching is that it can be taken to suggest that the Messiah will be an earthly ruler only, with human imperfections and failings. Such a Messiah might be a very great king in his own time but, in the end, like David, Solomon, Cyrus the Persian, and other historical rulers, would be only one more weak and sinful child of Adam in a long lineage of inevitable human failure.

Jesus' words open up another possibility to our imagination: that the Messiah will be more than an earthly man. Jesus points out that God in the psalm speaks to someone who is "lord" of David the king: who can this be but God himself? And yet it is God who places this mysterious figure on his own divine throne in honor and power.

We the Church have been given the full truth of what Jesus is suggesting: that the Messiah of God is both truly human and fully divine – one divine Person who simultaneously brings to the earth a salvation and healing by the hand of God which is also truly and fully the work of him who is one of us, the son of Mary, and of David, of Abraham, and Adam. In Jesus, the human race cooperates in its own rescue, and receives a king who teaches us a perfect self-mastery by his own example.

King of the Universe, Jesus your Son gave divinity a human face, and showed us what you hope each of us your children should become; help me subject myself to your Christ that I may share in his reign.

Clothed in Justice

Father Stephen Dominic Hayes, O.P.

In the course of his teaching [Jesus] said, "Beware of the scribes, who like to go around in long robes and accept greetings in the marketplaces, seats of honor in synagogues, and places of honor at banquets." (Mk 12: 38-39)

In a culture where cloth is made by hand, inch by inch, long robes are a sign of prosperity and respectability – only the settled and wealthy can afford them. The scribes, who in Jesus' time were the scholars and masters of the texts of the sacred law of Moses, tended to follow the Pharisees in their casuistry, legalism, and emphasis on externals. In the honor paid to them by the common people on the street, and at synagogues and banquets, they found great benefit in being outwardly pious. They seemed to be clothed in righteousness as well as in the fine linen and wool which indicated their high status in society. Many of them belonged to the Sanhedrin, and would eventually hand Jesus over to the Romans to be stripped and crucified. Jesus warns his hearers in this passage against mistaking external trappings for true righteousness.

The scribes made sure that they were always seen more than merely decently clad; Jesus will show himself authentically righteous in the sight of God, stripped of his clothes and his dignity. He will be condemned to death by the well clad and self-righteous so that he can clothe poor sinners in authentic justice. In Genesis, God sheds the blood of animals to clothe Adam and Eve with leather garments and dignity after their sin; this prophesies Christ's work on the cross, which clothes us sinners in grace, and is signified by the white robe we receive at our baptism. This is righteousness that reaches to the core of our soul, a healing (*salvatio*) visible to the world as we imitate Christ in living alive to God and dead to sin, sharing in Jesus' victory: "I will satisfy her poor with bread. Her priests I will clothe with salvation and her saints will shout for joy" (see Ps 132: 15-16).

Almighty Father, never let me forget what Jesus suffered on the cross in nakedness and indignity for the sake of my salvation. Strip me of earthly attachments so that I may always serve you with an undivided heart.

Gleaning God's Grace

Father Stephen Dominic Hayes, O.P.

"[The scribes] devour the houses of widows and, as a pretext, recite lengthy prayers. They will receive a very severe condemnation." (Mk 12: 40)

In a traditional culture, widows, especially elderly widows, suffer much. Often without strength or health because of advanced age, unable to give a new husband or family more children, suffering debility, weakness, and illness, they frequently have difficulty finding the means to live, or even eat. The law of Moses permits them to glean grain from fields already harvested, and landowners are told not to go back over a harvested field precisely to leave something for these poor souls. Their neediness and vulnerability are not merely economic but social, and their want of food, clothing, and shelter is accompanied by loneliness and doubt. It is, therefore, an especially evil thing when widows are preyed upon by the unscrupulous. This is precisely what Jesus accuses the scribes of doing – making a racket of cultivating such widows, promising them special access to God in exchange for donations in support of their "ministry." Like ravens circling a sick animal, they come not to aid God's poor, but to feed themselves on them. Jesus implies that there will be a very serious comeuppance for them when God finally works his justice toward them.

By contrast, the poor widows thus preyed upon are vulnerable religiously precisely because they are seeking God. In their poverty and loneliness they stretch out their hands to God because he is the only infallible source of assistance they truly have. In her later life, our Lady manifests this widow's deep thirst for God in a preeminent way. The Lord's mother lived as maiden and mother, but after the death of Saint Joseph, she too seems to have lived as a widow. She is a perfect image of the prayerful heart, and, in a widow's profound faith and spiritual poverty, embraces the promises given by God to her in her Son fully and completely.

God of Wisdom, keep before me at all times the example of the Blessed Virgin Mary, who lived her whole life unmindful of worldly things, intent upon her Son and his grace. Holy Mary, Seat of Wisdom, pray for us!

God Is Watching

Father Stephen Dominic Hayes, O.P.

[Jesus] sat down opposite the treasury and observed how the crowd put money into the treasury. Many rich people put in large sums. A poor widow also came and put in two small coins worth a few cents. (Mk 12: 41-42)

The temple of God, from its early institution as Moses' tent of meeting, has functioned as a kind of stage where the great drama of salvation has played itself out in one form or another. It was here that the Holy Spirit fell upon the elders of Israel (Nm 11: 24-30), where Samuel received his call (1 Sm 3: 1-21), that was the scene of so many incidents from the Old Testament, and which becomes so again when the Messiah of God unexpectedly appears at the temple, as prophesied from of old. Like the angel of judgment in the time of Abraham, Christ visits his people to "see whether or not their actions fully correspond to the cry against them that comes to me" (Gn 18: 21). He comes to the temple to purify them so that "the sacrifice of Judea and Jerusalem/ will please the Lord" (Mal 3: 4): a prophecy which comes true in the sacrifice of the cross.

When Jesus sits down to observe the people contributing to the treasury, therefore, it is not a casual act, but a prophetic one. His Father is also watching: "The Father and I are one" (Jn 10: 30). On this ancient and holy stage, God looks into his people's actions and sees their hearts. He has, in the past few verses, looked into the hearts of the prideful, greedy scribes; now he shows the holiness in the heart of a poor widow. The two judgments are related, if we look carefully: the remedy for the pride and avarice which afflicts the scribes has a cure in the practice of the widow's humility and generosity. The Lord heals as he wounds. In this moment he is acting as both savior and judge of those who frequent the temple of God, making visible, as he will when enthroned on the cross, the Last Judgment before its time.

King of the Universe, through the grace of your Son's cross you have manifested the thoughts of many hearts; grant that this same grace bring perfect healing to my mind and body in this world unto eternal life.

Love and Risk

Father Stephen Dominic Hayes, O.P.

*Calling his disciples to himself, [Jesus] said to them, "Amen,
I say to you, this poor widow put in more than all the other
contributors to the treasury. For they have all contributed from
their surplus wealth, but she, from her poverty, has contributed
all she had, her whole livelihood." (Mk 12: 43-44)*

When my brothers and I as children used to argue with one another, you would often hear the challenge, "Put your money where your mouth is!" "Talk is cheap," we say; "actions speak louder than words." Whatever your favorite way to put it, the principle which Jesus is pointing out to us is clear: the truth of a person's heart is seen not so much in what they say, as in what they do. He who is the all-seeing God as well as the Christ invites us to look into the heart of the widow by observing carefully what she does. And what God sees there delights him.

Jesus is not directly castigating the wealthy donors to the temple treasury. Rather, he is showing us the purity and holiness of this poor widow's heart. The two small coins she gives are everything she has to live on. How will she eat? Where will she sleep tonight? She has so little to call her own, and yet she boldly gives it all back – to the God from whom she has received it, and whom she challenges by her gift to continue to give her life and support. Her gift, small as it is, shows how much she trusts God. The rich contributions made by others are "out of their surplus," and do not cut to the bone this way. The widow, on the other hand, makes a spiritual holocaust of herself in pure and utter faith. Greed in a rich man finishes in complacency and coldness of heart toward others, but the poor can be greedy, too. In them, avarice finishes differently, in envy, fearfulness, and bitterness. By her gift of two small coins, however, this poor widow shows her heart to be free from the grasp of avarice and worldly fear because she has first reached out boldly to her Creator by faith.

Father of the poor, cleanse my heart from greed, and from fearfulness about my daily needs; keep me faithful to you whose plans for me are for good, both in this world and in the world to come.

Becoming Living Stones

Father Stephen Dominic Hayes, O.P.

As [Jesus] was making his way out of the temple area one of his disciples said to him, "Look, teacher, what stones and what buildings!" Jesus said to him, "Do you see these great buildings? There will not be one stone left upon another that will not be thrown down." (Mk 13: 1-2)

Herod the Great, the same Herod who sought to destroy the child of Bethlehem (Mt 2: 16-19), was responsible for beginning the rebuilding of the Jerusalem temple in the breathtaking magnificence noted by the disciples. He began his work for reasons of policy: he was not a Jew, but an Idumean, a descendant of Esau, not of Jacob, and therefore built with a view to binding himself more closely to the hearts of a people who saw him as a usurper to the throne of David. Long after Herod was dead, and during the whole period of Jesus' life, the temple continued to be rebuilt. It was not completely finished until a few years before its total destruction in AD 70 during the First Jewish War. Built for worldly purposes, its glory was fleeting and its existence short. "Unless the Lord build the house,/ they labor in vain who build" (Ps 127: 1).

The advent of God's Messiah to the temple is in fact the prophecy of its doom and its fulfillment. In Jesus Christ, God works the construction of a new, spiritual temple – Holy Church – "built upon the foundation of the apostles and prophets, with Christ Jesus himself as the capstone" (Eph 2: 20). The same Christ who proclaims the imminent death of the old temple will institute the new one by his death, and erect this edifice of souls mortared together in the power of the Holy Spirit. This will be the new temple where God preeminently dwells with his people. Every Christian heart is a spiritual stone within it, and needs to be shaped by the hand and desire of Christ the builder. Let us open our hearts to him and surrender our petty lordship over ourselves to the immortal son of David who is also the divine Son of God.

Maker of heaven and earth, smooth my roughness, grind out my imperfections, and polish my virtue so that your Son may see in me a spiritual reflection of his holy humanity, and set me firmly in the indestructible fabric of Holy Church.

The Sign of the Cross

Father Stephen Dominic Hayes, O.P.

As [Jesus] was sitting on the Mount of Olives opposite the temple area, Peter, James, John, and Andrew asked him privately, "Tell us, when will this happen, and what sign will there be when all these things are about to come to an end?" (Mk 13: 3-4)

Jesus' revelation of the imminent doom of God's temple has shocked the devout imagination of the disciples, and so the four who have been longest with Jesus approach him privately to inquire further. They ask the Master how long it will be before the end, and how to recognize its coming. Their question occasions Jesus' discussion of the end times, the whole subject of Mark, chapter 13.

The sign of the "end," however, is Jesus himself, who is about to ascend the cross. There's a double significance here with regard to the destruction of the Jerusalem temple: the end of the temple and the form of worship that goes on there is definitely an end of an age, as well as of the form of life which goes with it. This simultaneously marks the beginning of the visible life of the Catholic Church and the beginning of a new age of grace. The temple's doom furthermore points to the final destruction of the world which God made and which the ancient sin of men and angels ruined. The temple, built for the service of God, has become a stage for avarice, pride, and even unbelief, and is a portrait of God's fallen universe in miniature. Jerusalem, the city where God dwells, is also the city that kills prophets, and it stands for the larger universe which rebels against its Creator in every age. The sign of the temple's destruction begins with Jesus' arrival there as Messiah, and culminates in Christ's crucifixion and resurrection. The sign that "all these things are about to come to an end" which the apostles seek is already here – for the drama of Jesus' coming to the temple moves inexorably to the sacrifice of the cross. The new age of grace which begins there contains the seeds of the end of all ages, and the final destiny of each one of us.

Loving Father, you sent your Son Jesus among us to give divinity a human face, and humanity a vision of its final destiny. His cross kills our sins and brings us to life with you; keep us always in its grace.

False Messiahs

Father George William Rutler

Jesus began to say to [Peter, James, John, and Andrew], "See that no one deceives you. Many will come in my name saying, 'I am he,' and they will deceive many." (Mk 13: 5-6)

Our Lord gives practical advice. He told his apostles, "I am sending you like sheep in the midst of wolves; so be shrewd as serpents and simples as doves" (Mt 10: 16). Now, in the Garden of Olives before his crucifixion, he warns four of them that they will have to deal with heretics: false messiahs who confuse their egos with the truth. In his own earthly time, there was Theudas who led four hundred people to their deaths with his claim that he could part the River Jordan. One disciple, Simon the Zealot, had been a client of Judas the Galilean who made extravagant claims for himself. Soon Simon bar Kochba would lead a three-year messianic revolution ending in the destruction of Jerusalem, as the true Messiah forecast. In the fifth century, Moses of Crete convinced hundreds of people that he could part the Mediterranean. Many leapt to their deaths off cliffs, though some were rescued by Christian fishermen. Their number was less than the nearly thousand souls who drank poison in Jonestown at the behest of a modern equivalent. Another colorful imposter, Moses al-Dar'i, left credulous followers destitute after persuading them to sell all their possessions in preparation for the advent of the Messiah in 1127. One would-be messiah in 1666, Sabbathai Zevi, led a band of devotees to Constantinople, but he converted to Islam to save his own life.

These imposters are no more extravagant than self-appointed messiahs whose reforms deform the Church in every century, who deny God in universities, and who offer social change as the only salvation. The loving Christ who warned the apostles also warns us. His followers will have their own share of his cross. He does not dissuade us from spiritual combat. He only cautions us against following liars, for all who follow the true Messiah will inherit a fullness of life which the world cannot give.

God and Father of all, we bless you for the inestimable gift of your Son the Messiah, who is the way and the truth and the life. Give us strength and wisdom to follow him, to obey him, and to live with him now and for ever.

War and Peace

Father George William Rutler

"When you hear of wars and reports of wars do not be alarmed;
such things must happen, but it will not yet be the end."
(Mk 13: 7)

Fighting is the result of the fall of Man. Once our first ancestors succumbed to the fatal lie that they could replace God as though they were gods themselves, their sons battled, and Cain slew Abel. Since then, wars have brought out the worst and best in people. Fighting exercises the lowest passions, but it also occasions high valor. Only the armchair soldier is amused by war. So Erasmus said, "War is sweet to those who do not know it." My own father was silent about World War II, and only after he died did I find all his decorations in a drawer. A friend of mine who survived one of the worst single naval casualties in the same war said, "I was no hero. It's just that I could swim." To have fought real battles is to want to forget them, but not to forget their cost.

Theologians have worked hard to explain the difference between ignoble wars and "just" wars. But there will always be combat so long as there is unresolved warfare in each human soul. It takes as great an effort to establish peace as to fight a war, and so Pascal held that, "Peace is war in masquerade." But any peace established by human concordat is frail and likely not long lived.

Jesus speaks of wars for he lived in an age of war. Few were the times in human experience that were any different. In 1097, Pope Urban II banned the use between Christians of what was considered the ultimate weapon, the crossbow, and this was repeated in a "disarmament" clause of the Second Lateran Council in 1139. Although the details of that are obscure, it is clear that Pope Innocent II tried to bring peace. Every age may think it is on the verge of destruction, but all that really matters is the destruction of souls, and that can only be resolved by peace of soul.

Almighty Father, arm me with the weapons of faith, hope, and love, that I may withstand the onslaughts of the enemy and share the victory of your blessed Son, the Prince of Peace.

Earthquakes and Famines
Father George William Rutler

"Nation will rise against nation and kingdom against kingdom. There will be earthquakes from place to place and there will be famines. These are the beginnings of the labor pains."
(Mk 13: 8)

Wars in one way or another are the result of human weakness. As the clouds of World War II were looming, Pope Pius XII said, "The profound and ultimate roots of the present evils is the refusal to accept a standard of universal morality… in social life and in international relations; that is disregard and forgetfulness of the natural law whose foundation is God."

Natural violence is another matter. Human sin does not account for earthquakes and famines. "Why do bad things happen to good people?" Even keeping in mind Christ's reminder that only God is good, often the most innocent suffer the most from calamities they did not cause. Armchair theologians, who say that natural disasters are God's way of punishing others, call them inexplicable tragedies when they happen to themselves. Evil is a mystery, and Saint Bernard said that mysteries are to be worshiped, not analyzed. But intelligent analysis can be a form of worship. The best analysis is in scrutinizing the body of Christ suffering on the cross. He says that all human calamities are the beginning of the labor pains. They give birth to a triumph over suffering in the resurrection, after which all suffering becomes a means of strength, when united with Christ's suffering. On seeing the first detonation of an atomic bomb, Robert Oppenheimer quoted ancient lines from the *Bhagavad Gita*: "Now I am become Death, the destroyer of worlds." The risen Christ is Life, the Savior of all who believe in him. Pope Gregory the Great, suffering from gout and gastritis in a time of plagues and earthquakes and floods, wrote, "It is a great consolation to us if, when we suffer afflictions, we recall to remembrance our Maker's gifts to us. Painful things will not depress us if we quickly remember also the gifts that we have been given."

Almighty God, save me from the dangers of this earthly life and give me the grace to serve your Son who fasted for my sake, and whose death for my salvation made the earth quake.

Watch out for Yourselves

Father George William Rutler

"Watch out for yourselves. They will hand you over to the courts. You will be beaten in synagogues. You will be arraigned before governors and kings because of me, as a witness before them. But the gospel must first be preached to all nations."
(Mk 13: 9-10)

Christ had no faith. It was the one virtue he did not need, because, as Aquinas says, "The object of faith is a divine thing not seen. From the first moment of his conception Christ saw God's essence fully." But Christ does endow us with faith, and for a reason. Those who tell the truth in a world of lies will be put on trial. Sometimes that will actually involve a courtroom, but all Christians are on trial each day, being called by a skeptical world to show evidence that Christ is real. This is the chance to "preach the Gospel." That preaching has priority, and even the risk of individual lives is of secondary importance to it. It takes faith to take up this challenge, and that is why the old baptismal rite begins by asking what the one about to be baptized seeks, and the answer bluntly and boldly is "Faith." This enlists the Christian at the baptismal font in a spiritual battle that lasts as long as life itself. Faith is the necessary weapon, for while Christ has secured eternal victory, even soldiers in a victorious army can be killed. Faith sustains us when the enemy looms large. In 1944, army journalist Ernie Pyle described a scene on the Normandy beach the day after D-Day: "I walked around what seemed to be a couple of pieces of driftwood sticking out of the sand, but they weren't driftwood. They were a soldier's two feet. He was completely covered by the shifting sands except for his feet. The toes of his GI shoes pointed toward the land he had come so far to see, and which he saw so briefly." Christ points his followers toward a land that can be lived in for ever, and by faith we know that when he says, "Watch out for yourselves," he is watching out for us too.

Lord, increase my faith so that I may never retreat from the struggle that leads to the vision of your glory and the dwelling place of peace.

God on Trial

Father George William Rutler

"When they lead you away and hand you over, do not worry beforehand about what you are to say. But say whatever will be given to you at that hour. For it will not be you who are speaking but the holy Spirit." (Mk 13: 11)

Courtroom dramas, in fiction or fact, have never surpassed the magnificence of Christians on trial. Saint Paul defended himself with such eloquence in Caesarea that the minor King Herod Agrippa II said, "You will soon persuade me to play the Christian" (Acts 26: 28). The same inspiration moved the teen-aged saint of Arc, Joan, to say at her trial: "You say that you are my judge; I do not know if you are: but take good heed not to judge me ill, because you would put yourself in great peril. And I warn you so that if God punish you for it, I shall have done my duty in telling you." Twenty-four years later, in 1455, Pope Calixtus declared her death sentence wicked and unjust. By the same Holy Spirit, Saint Thomas More said in his trial: "My lord, for one bishop of your opinion I have a hundred saints of mine, and for one parliament of yours, and God knows of what kind, I have all the General Council for one thousand years, and for one kingdom I have France and all the kingdoms of Christendom." In 2010, Pope Benedict XVI honored that witness by speaking to the people of England in the same Westminster Hall where More had testified. Having been arrested in 1975 by the Communist government of Vietnam, Cardinal Nguyen Van Thuan spent thirteen years in prison, nine of them in solitary confinement. In 1976, he said, "I am happy here, in this cell, where white mushrooms are growing on my sleeping mat, because you are here with me, because you want me to live here with you. I have spoken much in my lifetime: now I speak no more. It's your turn to speak to me, Jesus; I am listening to you." It was not these holy ones, and countless others through the ages, who spoke, "but the Holy Spirit."

Almighty God, whose justice makes right what is wrong in the world, give me the strength to love the truth and to live according to your laws.

Rome or Babylon

Father George William Rutler

"Brother will hand over brother to death, and the father his child; children will rise up against parents and have them put to death." (Mk 13: 12)

Cecil B. De Mille's explanation for why he made so many biblical films was simple: "Why let two thousand years of publicity go to waste?" Wild animals attacking Christians in the arenas of the Roman Empire have been a staple of lurid fascination, partly because it is hard to imagine such cruelty being real. Yet the modern age showed sadism on a vaster scale. Sadistic entertainment and the callous indifference to the most innocent lives today are part of the continuum of sin which goes back to the killing of Abel. Anyone who is a "Christ-bearer" will be treated as Christ was. Christians will be dragged before councils, as he was before the Sanhedrin; beaten in synagogues as he was lashed within an inch of his death; taken before governors as obtuse as Pilate; brought to trial and "handed over" as he was given to the mob; their own brothers will betray them as Judas sold him; and they will be hated in Jesus' name as the crowds on Calvary hated the name inscribed above the cross.

The suffering of Christians now lasts longer than a brief encounter with a lion. There is the mockery of the media, and the scorn of the social establishment. A young man seeking the priesthood may be shunned by his own family as in the first century. Yet the merit gained from such struggle is the fuel of great holiness.

Saint Mark was an interpreter for Saint Peter in the city they called "Babylon" (1 Pt 5: 13). That most likely was a code for Rome. After Rome embraced Christ, the two cities came to be opposites. So the poet novelist Thackeray, frustrated by the logic of a lecture given by John Henry Newman on the truth of Catholicism, stood up and declared: "It is either Rome or Babylon, and for me it is Babylon." That has always been the choice.

Father of mercy, strengthen what is weak in me, so that when I face the foe I may use all the grace that you have given me through your Son.

The Grace of Perseverance
Father George William Rutler

"You will be hated by all because of my name. But the one who perseveres to the end will be saved." (Mk 13: 13)

When Saint Peter once tried to block Jesus from going to Jerusalem, the Lord knew that the real obstacle was not Peter but Satan (Mt 16: 23). The Deceiver's ultimate strategy is to discourage us from walking with Jesus who is the Way. The conductor Arturo Toscanini was not without an artist's temper, and he let it flare when he shouted at a trumpet player during a rehearsal: "God tells me how the music should sound, but you stand in the way." Amidst all this world's noise, God has let us know "how the music should sound." The music is the voice of Christ. Saint Augustine called it the "grace of final perseverance." By this power, says Newman, God arranges "the course of our life so that we may die at a time when he sees that we are in the state of grace." The Greek Stoics tried to develop self-control to such a degree that they might persevere through any trial. But that was human perseverance with a human goal. Christ promises that those who hate his disciples "because of my name" will not ruin the way to eternal life. Saint Thomas Aquinas was clear about this: "We cannot command our final perseverance, but must ask it from God." Saint Francis de Sales said, "Though perseverance does not come from our power, yet it comes within our power." Newman, in a time of deep affliction, prayed that this grace, as a "kindly light," would guide him "O'er moor and fen, o'er crag and torrent, till/ The night is gone." If I were able to write the Stations of the Cross, for each time Jesus falls, I'd add: "And then he got up." Jesus gets up a first time, and a second time, and a third time. Now we know that by getting up he went on to change the world, and each one of us.

Almighty Lord, make firm my steps, that I may walk the paths of this world until I reach you as my goal and glory.

The Abomination of Desolation

Father Joseph T. Lienhard, s.j.

"When you see the desolating abomination standing where he should not (let the reader understand), then those in Judea must flee to the mountains, [and] a person on a housetop must not go down or enter to get anything out of his house, and a person in a field must not return to get his cloak." (Mk 13: 14-16)

The translation provided here reads "desolating abomination." Older versions had it as "the abomination of desolation," an intriguing phrase – mostly, perhaps, because we don't know what it means, although it has an ominous ring to it. To be desolate is more than to be alone; it is to be deserted, to be unwanted, to be rejected. Perhaps the phrase meant that an abomination, a horror, made a place desolate. That is what the phrase means in the Book of Daniel, where it first occurs (Dn 11: 31).

The central place of Jewish worship was the temple in Jerusalem, which Solomon had built. At the heart of the temple was the Holy of Holies, a room that held the ark of the covenant, the throne of the unseen God. The temple was destroyed in the sixth century before Christ, and the ark was lost. When the temple was rebuilt, the Holy of Holies was left empty, for God does not need a throne on earth. In the year 168 BC, the temple underwent a horrible desecration: the statue of a pagan god was erected in the courtyard of the temple, and swine were sacrificed to it. It was this act that was called the abomination of desolation. Ironically, the presence of the true God was marked by one empty room; when a false god, an abomination, was set up in the temple, its presence was called "desolation." In the course of many centuries, God had taught the Jews that he is invisible and incomprehensible; he cannot be confined in any space. The Jews learned that lesson well, and so they were horrified by the idol in their temple.

God has continued to teach us. We worship the one invisible, incomprehensible, eternal God. In Christ, however, God has revealed something else about himself: he is indeed incomprehensible, but he is also wholly present in Jesus the Christ, reconciling the world to himself.

Almighty, ever-living God, hid from our eyes by the splendor of light, help our hearts to see you as you are: one God in three Persons, revealed to us in Christ, who lives and reigns for ever and ever.

September 11

Father Joseph T. Lienhard, S.J.

"Woe to pregnant women and nursing mothers in those days. Pray that this does not happen in winter. For those times will have tribulation such as has not been since the beginning of God's creation until now, nor ever will be." (Mk 13: 17-19)

One needs only to say, "September 11," and all sorts of images flood into our minds. The picture of those two planes crashing into the World Trade Center; the horror of the two buildings collapsing, one and then the other; the nearly three thousand dead; the many more who escaped; the courageous rescue workers; the hideous pile of rubble. Jesus speaks of "tribulation such as has not been since the beginning of God's creation until now." Since September 11, many of us have a sharper idea of what "tribulation" really means. Of course, September 11 was only one of many horrors in the history of civilization, but to many of us it is the most vivid, because it was so close to us.

Such a horror can lead us to ask: Why does God allow this? Can a good God permit such horrors? When Saint Thomas Aquinas asks, in his great work the *Summa Theologiae*, whether God exists, he first – as he always does – brings forth arguments against the position he wants to hold. In this case, he offers two arguments against God's existence: first, God is unnecessary; we can explain the world without him. And second, the fact of evil: the existence of a good God is incompatible with the existence of evil. Of course, Saint Thomas goes on to affirm God's existence. But we should not pass over his objections too easily, or try to explain away suffering. Pregnant women, nursing mothers… and our Lord does not mention abortion or infanticide. Tribulations will come.

What our Lord speaks of is mysterious, and we should not rush to say we know what he means. But we know for sure that he acknowledges the existence of evil in the world, what is called the mystery of iniquity. And we also know for sure that he experiences it on the cross, and that he answers it on Easter morning.

Eternal God and Father, you are all good and the source of all goodness; deliver us, we pray, from the bondage of sin and evil, and bring us into the fullness of grace, through Christ our Lord.

The Meaning of Providence

Father Joseph T. Lienhard, s.j.

"If the Lord had not shortened those days, no one would be saved; but for the sake of the elect whom he chose, he did shorten the days." (Mk 13: 20)

We are invited to reflect on a mysterious verse: what does our Lord mean when he speaks of shortening the days? Does he mean that the times of tribulation, mentioned in the preceding verse, will not be as long as they might have been? Does the phrase "no one would be saved" apply to those times, or to something else? Perhaps it is the second half of the verse that should draw our attention, for it contains words of deep consolation. The Lord has acted for the sake of those he had chosen, for the sake of the elect, we read. Such actions of God are summed up under the phrase "divine providence."

Our faith tells us that God did not simply create the world and then leave it to run its course. That was the view of the deists, who saw God as the great watchmaker, one who made the watch and wound it up, but then walked away and left it to run on its own. Our faith teaches us that God is provident – that God knows all things, even how we will use our freedom; and that God, in his power and wisdom, sustains and governs all things. Divine providence extends even to the flowers of the field and the birds of the air; how much more to us and to our eternal destiny! God, in his eternity and utterly outside of time, guides the course of history to its goal. And that is the source of the word "elect" in the verse we are reflecting on. In the infinite mystery of God's will, he guides the world through its history and, at its consummation, he will bring it to its goal. Our prayer will be one of absolute surrender to God's will, the very opposite of the stubborn pride that is the root of sin.

All-powerful God and Father, in your loving providence you guide and guard all you have made; bring us, we pray, to the life and the joy you have prepared for us, through Christ our Lord.

Messiahs and Prophets

Father Joseph T. Lienhard, s.j.

"If anyone says to you then, 'Look, here is the Messiah! Look, there he is!' do not believe it. False messiahs and false prophets will arise and will perform signs and wonders in order to mislead, if that were possible, the elect." (Mk 13: 21-22)

Jesus warns us against false messiahs and false prophets. Perhaps, we might think, such a warning was needed in his day, but surely not in ours. But then we might reflect for a few moments longer on his warning. "Messiah" means "the Anointed One"; it is equivalent to "Christ." What is a false messiah? Someone who is not Christ, but who tells us, "I am the way to salvation." Of course, most of us have seen street-corner preachers, with long beards and signs saying "The End Is Near" – mostly in cartoons. In our age, the message of a false messiah is different: it might be trivial, like "eat all you want and lose weight" or "this exercise machine requires no effort." Or it might be painfully deceptive, like "we can cure your cancer when no one else can." And, what is a false prophet? One who says, "I can bring you the final truth." Maybe that truth is religious; or maybe it is political, or economic, or social.

And what is our Christian, Catholic answer to such claims? There is one true Messiah, we confess, one final Prophet: Jesus the Christ, true God and true man, eternal Son of the Father, in the last days, for us and for our salvation, born of Mary the Virgin. He is the anointed One of God. In Jesus Christ, we not only find the final, unchanging truth; we discover what no philosopher could ever have dreamed: that truth is a person. In Christ we encounter the center point of the universe, from which all other reality is measured. In Christ we encounter God's final Word to the human race. He is the Messiah because he was anointed by God, as priest, prophet, and king; and, as the anointed prophet, he speaks God's definitive word to humanity. It is the Church who says truly, "Here is the Messiah!" And the Church speaks the truth.

God, our eternal Father, you anointed Jesus Christ the Messiah and Savior; by his cross and resurrection, confirm us in the truth you revealed and bring us to the life you promised, through the same Christ our Lord.

How the Story Ends

Father Joseph T. Lienhard, S.J.

"Be watchful! I have told it all to you beforehand."
(Mk 13: 23)

Each year, on the last Sunday of the Church's cycle of time, we celebrate the Solemnity of Christ the King. On that beautiful day, in the Preface of the Mass, we hear a description of Christ's kingdom: "a kingdom of truth and life, a kingdom of holiness and grace, a kingdom of justice, love, and peace." These are more than melodious words. They are what Christ has promised: they are what we look forward to and hope for; they are our future. For on that Solemnity of Christ the King, we celebrate, by anticipation, how the Great Story is going to end.

There is a crucial difference between optimism and hope. Optimism does not see the future; it blindly asserts that the future will be better than the past, and optimists reinforce their conviction by reassuring each other that things must be getting better. The one who has received the Christian virtue of hope does not need optimism, because he knows how the story is going to end: and it is going to end with Christ as the King of the universe. As our Lord says, "I have told it all to you beforehand." We do not know what God has prepared for us between now and the triumph of Christ the King. But we do know the direction we are being carried in.

Jesus himself knew, too. As he hung dying on the cross, the sign over his head read "Jesus of Nazareth, the King of the Jews." With those words, Pontius Pilate, that most trivial of all men, had written, for once in his life, a profound truth. Jesus is indeed the king of the Jews, and more than that – he is the king of all creation. And that is how the Great Story is going to end, as our hope is fulfilled: Jesus is the King of the universe! He has told it all to us beforehand.

Almighty, ever-living God, you have made Christ your Son the King of the universe; by your grace, we pray you, let him reign in our hearts, now and always and for ever and ever.

Light from Light

Father Joseph T. Lienhard, s.j.

"But in those days after that tribulation/ the sun will be darkened,/ and the moon will not give its light,/ and the stars will be falling from the sky,/ and the powers in the heavens will be shaken./ And then they will see 'the Son of Man coming in the clouds' with great power and glory, and then he will send out the angels and gather [his] elect from the four winds, from the end of the earth to the end of the sky." (Mk 13: 24-27)

In modern times, and especially since electric power became widespread, we can have good light whenever we want it. For most of the history of the human race, however, that was not the case. Our distant ancestors had to make the best use of daylight that they could. Often enough, they rose at dawn, at first light, before sunrise. They worked by daylight, and they retired soon after dark, for there was little reliable light after sunset. If you've ever tried to read by candlelight, you understand this well. Hence, Jesus' threat was acute to his hearers: "the sun will be darkened, and the moon will not give its light."

Think, by contrast, of the liturgy of the Easter vigil. The vigil begins in darkness; then the new fire is struck. But that new fire is just that, a fire that gives some irregular light. From that new fire the paschal candle is lit, and now fire and light take on meaning, profound meaning. The deacon carries the candle up the central aisle of the church. Three times he stops and sings, "Christ our Light!" and the people answer, "Thanks be to God!" Gradually the light spreads from the one candle to the whole congregation, and Christ the Light illumines the entire church.

We can extend our reflection on light even further. Perhaps the phrase in the Creed that receives the least attention is "light from light." It stands in the middle of three phrases: "God from God, Light from Light, true God from true God." All three phrases are meant to affirm the same truth: God the Son is begotten by God the Father, but the Son is equal to the Father in every way. "God is light," Saint John writes, "in him there is no darkness" (1 Jn 1: 5). The sun may be darkened, but God is pure light.

God our Father, you are eternal light and splendor; bring your light, we beseech you, to the darkness of our hearts, and make us shine with the splendor of Christ, who lives and reigns for ever and ever.

He Is Near

Father Joseph T. Lienhard, S.J.

"Learn a lesson from the fig tree. When its branch becomes tender and sprouts leaves, you know that summer is near. In the same way, when you see these things happening, know that he is near, at the gates." (Mk 13: 28-29)

The world of the Bible is a world of nature, agriculture, and animal husbandry, a world that is far different from the cities that many of us live in. The world of the Bible was a world without electric power. Transportation was by mule or donkey. The people were close to the rhythms of nature: day light and night darkness, the seasons, planting and harvest, fishing on the lake, herds of sheep and goats, the cycles of the stars. The Gospels reverberate with this rhythm: lilies of the field, sowing seed, wheat and tares, sheep without a shepherd, the lost sheep, the Lamb of God. Without CNN or the Weather Channel, much less central heating or air conditioning, people lived by the rhythm of the natural world. Perhaps the closest we come to that rhythm is the fact that the date of Easter is fixed by the first full moon of spring, although many of us probably never notice it.

Jesus encourages us to learn from the signs of the times, the signs of nature. He uses a rather obvious example: the fig tree sprouts leaves, and we know that summer is near. But what this lesson teaches us is deeply mysterious: when certain events happen, the Son of Man is near, even at the gates. From its earliest days, the Church has puzzled over these words of Jesus. Do they apply to some future general cataclysm? Do they concern the destruction of the city of Jerusalem, which happened in AD 70? Or do they apply to our own lives and deaths? We have no answer, except perhaps the one proposed by Saint Luke, "The kingdom of God is within you." But we need to distinguish. The signs of Christ's coming are ambiguous, but the fact that Christ will come is certain. Year by year, century by century, the body of the whole Christ is being built up. "Learn a lesson," he says.

Almighty God and Father, fill our hearts, we beg you, with longing for Christ your Son; free us from love of this passing world and fill us with love for yourself, through the same Christ our Lord.

My Words Will Abide for Ever

Father Joseph T. Lienhard, s.j.

"Amen, I say to you, this generation will not pass away until all these things have taken place. Heaven and earth will pass away, but my words will not pass away." (Mk 13: 30-31)

Jesus makes a remarkable claim: "Heaven and earth will pass away, but my words will not pass away." Spoken words are fragile things; the air vibrates for a moment, and the words are gone. A few words are written down and remembered; President Lincoln's address at the Gettysburg battlefield is one example. Most printed words fare no better; each day we discard piles of newspapers, and most of what is delivered to our mailboxes goes into the trash unread. Shakespeare's plays are remembered; how many more plays are forgotten! We can even go back much longer in time, centuries before Christ: G.K. Chesterton wrote that the last man alive would do well to quote the *Iliad* and die. What Jesus says, however, goes far beyond any of these examples. His words, he says, will last beyond the existence of heaven and earth; they will last into eternity. Who can make this claim? No mere human being, surely, but only God. That is our faith, and we affirm it gladly.

But what are those words? Are they the texts of the Gospels? Perhaps. But will Bibles exist when the earth passes away? The early Christian writer Origen speaks of something mysterious, something he calls an "eternal Gospel." Is there a key message, a heart of the Gospels, that stands behind the four Gospels of our New Testament? Surely there is. I could hazard a guess at what that Gospel might be, some key phrase from the New Testament, perhaps. But to do so would surely be to risk error. It is better to remain silent, and to point to the crucifix. One who fully understands the cross of Christ understands the eternal Gospel, perfectly. His words will never pass away, because his cross is the central point of all time and all history. "We adore thee, O Christ, and we bless thee, because by thy holy cross thou hast redeemed the world."

God our Father, you have spoken to us in Christ the Word, and in the Holy Scriptures; make us, we pray, attentive hearers and faithful followers, through the same Christ our Lord.

Only the Father Knows

Father Joseph T. Lienhard, s.j.

"But of that day or hour, no one knows, neither the angels in heaven, nor the Son, but only the Father." (Mk 13: 32)

Jesus asked Saint Peter, "And who do you say that I am?" In a sense, all of Christian theology is an attempt to answer that question. The starting point is the apostles' and the earliest Church's experience of Jesus the Christ. Among the first answers were some that were wholly inadequate. Some, for example, basing themselves on reason alone, said that God could not become man; Jesus must have been simply an excellent human being. Others – and there were more of them – thought that becoming man was utterly beneath God; Jesus' humanity must have been an illusion or a deception.

Once these extreme errors had been put to rest, another one arose, at the beginning of the fourth century. Its name was Arianism. These Christians – and there were many of them – readily confessed that Jesus the Christ was the very pinnacle of the created order, the first and greatest of all that God had brought to be. Out of a sense of reverence and awe, one might even call him "God." But he was not God in the same way that the High God, the Father, is. And the biblical text that the Arians appealed to, more than any other, is the one we are meditating on. If, indeed, there is something that the Father knows but the Son does not, then does it not follow that the Son is less than the Father? The question should not be dismissed lightly. The Fathers of the Church, who battled Arianism for a century and more, taught that, in these words, Jesus was speaking in his human nature. They often quoted Jesus' other words: "The Father and I are one" (Jn 10: 30).

Arianism has never wholly died out, and it is among us today in different guise. Our best answer to Arianism is the Creed we affirm every Sunday: the Son and the Father are related as "God from God, Light from Light, true God from true God."

Almighty, ever-living God, in your eternity you have begotten the Son, true God from true God; confirm our faith, we pray you, and fill our hearts with joy in your name, through the same Christ our Lord.

Trust

Father Joseph T. Lienhard, S.J.

"Be watchful! Be alert! You do not know when the time will come. It is like a man traveling abroad. He leaves home and places his servants in charge, each with his work, and orders the gatekeeper to be on the watch." (Mk 13: 33-34)

Our Lord describes an intriguing situation. A man is about to set off on a long journey. He leaves his home – and his home probably includes a large farm and herds of animals – in the hands of his servants. In fact, he puts them in charge. And further, the gatekeeper is put in charge of keeping the owner's property safe. In other words, the owner puts profound trust in his servants.

What is trust? To trust someone means much more than giving him a job to do. With trust, we hand ourselves over, as it were, to another person. We say, I will live and act on the assumption that you have my best interests at heart, that you will do what is best for me, that you will even put me before yourself. The one we trust has the opportunity to damage or steal our property, to harm a member of our family, or even to injure us. Yet when we make an act of trust in another person, we say to him, "I am confident that you will respect and protect my property, my family, me." Of course, we could not live without trust. We trust a babysitter, who watches children when we are away, to keep them safe. We trust a doctor, who injects something into our arm, to do what will heal us, not harm us.

What is distinctive about trust? Trust relates to the future; hence, it is not knowledge. Some of the synonyms for trust are confidence, reliance, and dependence; but the best one is faith. When we make the act of faith, we put ourselves into God's hands, saying: I accept as true and life-giving all that you have revealed in Jesus Christ and recorded in the Holy Scriptures. And is there anyone more trustworthy?

Eternal Father and Lord, we believe all the truths that you have revealed, and we place all our trust in you, who will never deceive us; so we pray, through Christ our Lord.

The Hour of Our Death

Father Joseph T. Lienhard, s.j.

"Watch, therefore; you do not know when the lord of the house is coming, whether in the evening, or at midnight, or at cockcrow, or in the morning. May he not come suddenly and find you sleeping. What I say to you, I say to all: 'Watch!'"
(Mk 13: 35-36)

Most of us probably say the Hail Mary at least once a day. Lovers of the rosary say it at least fifty times a day. The prayer has two parts. In the first part, we quote words addressed to Mary in the Gospel – the words of the archangel Gabriel and the words of Mary's cousin Elizabeth. "Hail, Mary, full of grace. The Lord is with you. Blessed are you among women," Gabriel said. "Blessed are you among women, and blessed is the fruit of your womb" were Elizabeth's words to Mary, echoing in part the words of the archangel Gabriel. The second part of the prayer is the Church's composition: first the archangel had spoken, and then Elizabeth; and now we speak. "Holy Mary, Mother of God." "Mother of God": this phrase represents a victory won at the Council of Ephesus in 431: if Mary were not the Mother of God, then Jesus Christ would be two persons. Then, we make our humble confession: "pray for us, sinners." When? "Now and at the hour of our death." We know with absolute certainty when "now" is; we do not know, we cannot know, when the hour of our death is.

And that is what Jesus warns us about in the passage we are meditating on. "You do not know when the lord of the house is coming... May he not come suddenly... What I say to you, I say to all: 'Watch.'" And "watch" is what we do: we anticipate the hour of our death each day – not out of fear, not out of morbid despondency, but in the calm certainty that, at some moment, the Lord of the house will come to us. Our prayer each day, our prayer to Mary, is the way we heed Christ's warning: each time we say the Hail Mary we are living out his command: "Watch."

Eternal God and Father, by the intercession of the Blessed Virgin Mary, preserve us in your grace all the days of our lives and, at the hour of our death, bring us into everlasting joy, through Christ our Lord.

The Passover Lamb

Father Mark Daniel Kirby, O.S.B.

The Passover and the Feast of Unleavened Bread were to take place in two days' time. So the chief priests and the scribes were seeking a way to arrest [Jesus] by treachery and put him to death. They said, "Not during the festival, for fear that there may be a riot among the people." (Mk 14: 1-2)

From all eternity, the Father foresaw the identification of his beloved Son, the Word made flesh, with the paschal lamb of his chosen people, the Jews. With the approach of the last Passover of Jesus' earthly life, the fulfillment of the Father's eternal plan begins to unfold. For this reason, year after year, the Church enters into the sacred paschal Triduum on Holy Thursday evening by reading the account of the first Passover in the twelfth chapter of the Book of Exodus.

The Passover lamb prefigures Jesus, the lamb provided by God himself for immolation by Abraham on Mount Moriah (Gn 22: 8), the lamb who, silently and meekly, goes obediently to the slaughter. "Though he was harshly treated, he submitted/ and opened not his mouth;/ Like a lamb led to the slaughter/ or a sheep before the shearers,/ he was silent and opened not his mouth" (Is 53: 7).

It is significant that when our Lady, together with Saint Joseph and Saint John the Evangelist, appeared to a group of men, women, and children in the Irish parish of Knock on a rainy evening in 1879, it was in reference to Christ Jesus, the true Passover Lamb, who appeared with them, standing upon an altar, before a large cross. The Passover of the Old Covenant points to the sacrifice of Calvary, made present, again and again, in an unbloody manner in the holy sacrifice of the Mass.

The coincidence of our Lord's bitter Passion and death with the Jewish festival of Passover was willed by the Father. Saint Mark's explicit mention of the timing of our Lord's sufferings allows us to see in Jesus, and in the sacrament of the Most Holy Eucharist, the perfect fulfillment of the promises made to the prophets, and of the Passover sacrifice faithfully carried out by the Jews.

Eternal Father, may the Blood that flows, even now, from the heart of the Lamb protect our homes, purify our hearts, and keep us faithful to the covenant of love revealed in the sign of the cross.

Love Is Lavish

Father Mark Daniel Kirby, o.s.b.

When [Jesus] was in Bethany reclining at table in the house of Simon the leper, a woman came with an alabaster jar of perfumed oil, costly genuine spikenard. She broke the alabaster jar and poured it on his head. (Mk 14: 3)

Jesus is at table in the house of one Simon, identified as a leper. Simon is, in fact, a shortened form of the name Eleazar, which means "God has helped." This suggests that Simon, having suffered from leprosy for a time, was cured of the dread disease that marked him as an outcast unfit for sharing a meal with others. Simon, then, represents all of us who have found a place at table with Jesus, after having experienced the alienation of sin, the leprosy of the soul.

The woman who enters the house of Simon, bearing an alabaster jar of perfumed oil, intuits that Jesus is the merciful Lover of humankind, the divine Physician of souls and bodies. Approaching Jesus, she is confident of being welcomed by him. She knows that she will not be turned away by the one who says, "Everything that the Father gives me will come to me, and I will not reject anyone who comes to me, because I came down from heaven not to do my own will but the will of the one who sent me" (Jn 6: 37-38).

Both Simon and the woman with her jar of perfumed oil experience in Jesus the mystery of the Divine Hospitality. Jesus knows them through and through; their past holds no secrets for him. He welcomes them both, allowing himself to be fed and touched by those whom he has come to feed with his body and blood, and to touch with his healing hands. The lavishness of the Divine Hospitality calls for a lavish response, for love is never stinting or calculating.

Simon provides a banquet and, at that banquet, the woman breaks open the jar of precious perfume, using it to anoint Jesus' head. Each, in his own way, understands that love is lavish, and that God is glorified by the grateful outpouring of a trusting heart.

Most merciful Father, through the sacraments of the Church you pour forth your lavish love and abounding mercy. May we who receive these gifts, time and time again, show ourselves ever grateful and lavish in love.

Learning to Waste

Father Mark Daniel Kirby, O.S.B.

There were some who were indignant. "Why has there been this waste of perfumed oil? It could have been sold for more than three hundred days' wages and the money given to the poor." They were infuriated with [the woman]. (Mk 14: 4-5)

God values what the world judges wasteful. While the world, often unjustly, measures and calculates the investment of its resources, the saints are loathe to measure their response to love, and incapable of calculating the cost of glorifying God.

Those who were infuriated with the woman's waste of costly perfumed oil have successors in every generation. There will always be pragmatic types incapable of grasping the heart's expression of love.

Recently, a talented young man, full of promise, graduated from a prestigious mid-western university. It was assumed that he would make a name for himself in the medical field, in human services, or in some socially useful endeavor. What his family and friends did not know was that he had, during his last year of university, found himself irresistibly drawn to adoration of the Blessed Sacrament. Kneeling in the radiance of our Lord's Eucharistic Face, he discovered the burning love of the Heart of Jesus, and found himself compelled to respond passionately and generously to so great a love. To the consternation of many and the scandal of some, he entered a monastery precisely to waste his life in adoration of the Blessed Sacrament. Today he spends up to six hours a day adoring and praising God.

The Church thrives in proportion to the number of souls compelled by the Holy Spirit to waste time – even the best hours, days, and years of their lives – in adoration of Jesus in the Blessed Sacrament. The Father "so loved the world that he gave his only Son" (Jn 3: 16). Even today, the Holy Spirit raises up souls to make reparation for those who would calculate and shrink their response to the Father's love. What the world judges useless is, in the eyes of God, supremely precious and mysteriously efficacious, bearing "fruit that will remain" (Jn 15: 16).

Father, you so loved the world that you did not spare your own Son. Grant that we may respond to so great a love with hearts that dare to spend themselves in a holy wastefulness, for the measure of loving you is to love you without measure.

A Beautiful Thing

Father Mark Daniel Kirby, O.S.B.

Jesus said, "Let [the woman] alone. Why do you make trouble for her? She has done a good thing for me."
(Mk 14: 6)

Jesus reproaches those who criticize the extravagance of the woman who anoints his head with precious oil. They scrutinize her and pass judgment on her action, discounting it as the wanton waste of a capital resource. Being hard-nosed realists, they are annoyed at what they perceive as folly, the gross mismanagement of more than three hundred days' wages. To justify themselves, they add that the sum netted by the sale of the ointment could be given to the poor.

Jesus tells them, in plain language, to mind their own business. They have no right to impede what Jesus calls "a beautiful thing." Although some translations render the Greek word used here as "good," the same word can also be translated as "beautiful."

Saint John Mary Vianney was tireless in making his parish church a place of beauty. When, in 1818, he arrived in Ars, France, he found the church neglected, dirty, and unadorned. The state of the little church mirrored the spiritual condition of souls in the parish of Ars. Straightaway, he set about caring for the house of God. He cleaned it, set it in order, and succeeded in making it beautiful.

To a soul steeped in the ugliness of sin, outward beauty stands as a reproach. A soul moved by grace, on the other hand, is compelled to pursue harmony with the outward beauty offered to God. Christ is the "fairest of the sons of men" (Ps 45: 3, RSV), and the "light [of] the knowledge of the glory of God" (2 Cor 4: 6) is given to those who fix their gaze upon the beauty of his face.

Christians, having discovered the beauty of Christ, understand that the house of God and the worship offered him by the Church require beauty. The Church, in her wisdom, knows that virtue blossoms in an environment of beauty. Exposure to what is beautiful ennobles the human heart and causes the soul to aspire to the beauty of holiness.

Almighty Father, inspire us with zeal for the beauty of your house and, by your grace, make us temples fit for the indwelling of your presence, together with your Son and the Holy Spirit.

Caring for Christ

Father Mark Daniel Kirby, O.S.B.

"The poor you will always have with you, and whenever you wish you can do good to them, but you will not always have me." (Mk 14: 7)

These words of Jesus have a mysterious ring. He is obliged to measure them to the capacity of his hearers to receive them. Saint Mark records that Jesus says, "You will not always have me," while Saint Matthew records him saying, "And behold, I am with you always, until the end of the age" (Mt 28: 20). From the day of his Ascension into heaven until his return in glory, the bodily presence of Christ on earth remains veiled by the humble appearances of bread and wine.

The poor will be Christ–in–the–world until the end of time. "Whatever you did for one of these least brothers of mine, you did for me" (Mt 25: 40). Great figures of charity such as Saint Vincent de Paul, Saint Martin de Porres, Blessed Mother Teresa, and Dorothy Day spent themselves utterly in the service of Christ in the poor.

Other holy men and women, such as Saint Margaret Mary Alacoque, Saint Peter Julian Eymard, and Saint Sharbel of Lebanon illustrate a different grace: that of the direct service of Christ for his own sake, especially in the sacrament of his love. Just as there are men and women called by God to lay down their lives in service of the poor, there are others whom he calls to lay down their lives in adoration before his Eucharistic Face.

Jesus is not indifferent to the love that we lavish upon him in our adoration of the Blessed Sacrament. The service of Christ's members cannot be used as a pretext for neglecting adoration of the Christ the Head, any more than adoration of Christ the Head can be used as a pretext for neglecting the service of his members. Recognize Jesus in the breaking of the bread and you will recognize him even more keenly in the least of his brothers. Care for the least of his brothers, and you will be compelled to approach his Eucharistic Heart.

Holy Father, open our eyes to recognize the living Bread dwelling in the tabernacles of the world where, even now, he awaits the fragrant offering of hearts poured out in his presence.

Love's Gestures Not Forgotten

Father Mark Daniel Kirby, O.S.B.

"[The woman] has done what she could. She has anticipated anointing my body for burial. Amen, I say to you, wherever the gospel is proclaimed to the whole world, what she has done will be told in memory of her." (Mk 14: 8-9)

Sacred Scripture tells us of two women whose names are recalled wherever the Gospel is proclaimed. The first is the Blessed Virgin Mary who, in her canticle of praise, prophesies, "from now on will all ages call me blessed" (Lk 1: 48). The second is the woman, often identified as Mary of Bethany, who anoints Jesus' head with a costly perfume in the house of Simon the leper.

Jesus is fully conscious of going toward his death and burial. "I came from the Father and have come into the world. Now I am leaving the world and going back to the Father" (Jn 16: 28). He receives the oil poured over his head as a portent of the spices with which Mary Magdalene, Mary the mother of James, and Salome will anoint him after the sabbath rest.

Wholly engaged in carrying out his Father's will until the end, Jesus integrates every detail of his final days into the unfolding of his mission. "I am troubled now. Yet what should I say? 'Father, save me from this hour'? But it was for this purpose that I came to this hour" (Jn 12: 27). Jesus' ascent to the altar of the cross gains momentum; the anointing of his head prepares it to receive the crown of thorns and, after that, the linen bands, until, rising all-glorious from the tomb, he is crowned with a splendor surpassing that of all the stars in the firmament.

The triumphal cortege of the risen and ascended Jesus includes, first of all, his most holy mother, and with her the other holy women who ministered to him in Galilee, and who, in the final hour, accompanied him even to the cross. Jesus forgets nothing of what is done for him or for his sake. Every gesture of love is assumed into his sacrifice and borne with him into the sanctuary of heaven where he lives for ever to intercede for us.

Father of infinite majesty, we praise you that our humble gestures of love on earth are not forgotten in the sanctuary of heaven, for they are offered to you there in the hands of Christ Jesus, our perfect sacrifice and eternal priest.

Never to Despair of the Mercy of God

Father Mark Daniel Kirby, O.S.B.

Then Judas Iscariot, one of the Twelve, went off
to the chief priests to hand [Jesus] over to them.
(Mk 14: 10)

Our Lord loved Judas even after he had gone off to the chief priests to betray him. Saint John completes Saint Mark's account by adding this significant detail: "And it was night" (Jn 13: 30). The all-seeing eyes of Jesus followed Judas into his night and, while the Heart of Jesus grieved over his friend turned betrayer, his love for him remained unchanged.

There is no one who, at one time or another, is not tempted to go alone into the night, forsaking the companionship of Jesus and of his friends. The door of the Upper Room – the place of Eucharistic communion with Jesus – remains unlocked, even after the tempted disciple has closed it behind him and taken the first steps in his betrayal. One has only to turn around – the very meaning of conversion – to reject the darkness and choose the light.

There is one pithy phrase in the age-old Rule of Saint Benedict's seventy-three chapters that never fails to fill me with hope. It is, I think, the most important phrase of all, and even if one falls short in carrying out all that one seeking God ought to do, this one last injunction remains: "And never to despair of the mercy of God" (Rule of Saint Benedict, Chapter IV).

At any point in the drama of his betrayal, Judas could have reversed his steps, turned back to Jesus, forsaken the blackness of the night, and re–entered the Eucharistic light of the Upper Room. Judas' tragic decision to betray his Divine Master served, in the end, the Father's mysterious plan for the triumph of light over darkness, and of mercy over judgment on the tree of the cross. While, in the end, Judas went to the tree of despair to take his own life there, Jesus went to the tree that is our only hope, the cross, there to offer himself for the life of the world.

Father, rich in mercy, give us the grace never to despair of your mercy, because the darkness is passing away and the true light is already shining on the face of your beloved Son.

Betrayal

Father Mark Daniel Kirby, O.S.B.

When [the chief priests] heard [Judas] they were pleased and promised to pay him money. Then he looked for an opportunity to hand him over. (Mk 14: 11)

So many sins are made possible because people see others as a means to an end. Fallen human nature is inclined to use others by appealing to the desire for power, pleasure, and possessions. In this way, Satan weaves a web of iniquity, and makes use of human instruments to attain his hateful ends.

The chief priests see in Judas, the disciple of Jesus, someone useful to them. Judas, for his part, sees in the chief priests men of power and influence capable of furthering his own dark designs. Satan, by appealing to greed, envy, and the lust for power, drives the operation in both parties. Thus is Jesus betrayed into the hands of those who hate him.

Jesus' betrayal is played out again and again in the history of the Church. How many martyrs for the faith are handed over to their torturers in exchange for favors, promises of protection, or money?

Just a few days before his own betrayal, our Lord speaks to his witnesses in every age: "Say whatever will be given to you at that hour. For it will not be you who are speaking but the holy Spirit. Brother will hand over brother to death, and the father his child; children will rise up against parents and have them put to death. You will be hated by all because of my name. But the one who perseveres to the end will be saved" (Mk 13: 11-13).

No one is immune to the allurements of power, pleasure, and possessions. Already in Genesis we read, "Sin is a demon lurking at the door: his urge is toward you, yet you can be his master" (Gn 4: 7). The saints through the ages attest to the power of the name of Jesus, by whose grace tempted souls are changed into triumphant souls, and betrayers into witnesses.

Most merciful Father, touch the hearts of those who are tempted to betray the friends of your Son, and strengthen those who, for his sake, are delivered up to their enemies, that in all these things we may conquer overwhelmingly through him who loves us.

Bread for the Journey

Anthony Esolen

On the first day of the Feast of Unleavened Bread, when they sacrificed the Passover lamb, [Jesus'] disciples said to him, "Where do you want us to go and prepare for you to eat the Passover?" (Mk 14: 12)

Jesus and his disciples wish to celebrate the Feast of Unleavened Bread, commemorating that night when the Hebrews ate the Passover meal as people taking flight, with their loins girt, and walking-staff in hand. Then too those Hebrews would slay the Passover lamb, sacrificing it to God, not knowing that in the fullness of time God himself would become the sacrifice, both on the cross and in the holy sacrament of the altar.

Imagine the moment. The disciples, having no idea what is about to happen, think they are about to partake of a tradition many centuries old. It is what all the Jews would be doing. For all they know, what they need is but a place for the supper, and the bread, and the lamb. So they ask Jesus the obvious question, "Where do you want us to go?" What they cannot have conceived is that this would be in more than one way a Last Supper. That is, Jesus would fulfill and transcend the tradition. God now provides the lamb, who is Jesus, led to the slaughter; and Jesus willingly gives of his broken body and sheds blood to feed his people. He would set them free from a bondage more terrible than that of Egypt: the chains of sin and death.

And we too partake of his body as sojourners on the way – since our home is not here. When we approach the altar to receive the body of Christ, we confess that without the food that God provides, we must grow faint and weary. We need not ask, "Where do you want us to go?" We know already. We need Christ's holy rations, not once a year, to commemorate some event long ago, but now, here, continually, that Christ's death and resurrection might nourish us, ushering us into his life in glory.

Father, never abandon us on our journey, but give us the Son; let his life make us live, that he whom we receive in the Eucharist may make us like himself, through the same Jesus, our Lord.

Moments of Grace

Anthony Esolen

[Jesus] sent two of his disciples and said to them, "Go into the city and a man will meet you, carrying a jar of water. Follow him." (Mk 14: 13)

Did Jesus have the Passover meal planned? Sought out by men who wished to take his life, had he arranged for a secret meeting between his disciples and a man carrying a jar of water? Or was this but another miracle wrought by the Son of God, who knew that there would be such a man, and that he would lead the disciples to a room fit for the celebration?

I like to believe that the meeting was as much a surprise to the man with the jar as it was to the disciples. Such is life, such are the subtle workings of divine Providence. When Simon traveled all the way from Cyrene in Africa to Jerusalem to celebrate the holy days, he had no idea that he would be taking part in a crucifixion – and that his life would be changed for ever. The man with the jar was no doubt only going about his business, serving his master. We are not told whether he then also served in the upper room when Jesus instituted the Eucharist, though it seems well within the bounds of possibility. If so, did he understand what was going on? When, a few weeks later, those same disciples preached the risen Lord, was he one of the thousands who came to believe?

Rather, how often are we like the man with the jar of water? We too have our daily habits and our business. But in the midst of it all someone approaches us with a request. We may not perceive it so, but the question is the same. The Teacher needs a room to celebrate the feast. Where shall he go? To which our answer must be, "Come here, Lord, come to me, or let me serve at the table where you give yourself to others. Let there be an Upper Room in my heart."

Father, come to me in the humblest tasks of everyday life, touching me upon the shoulder, and in the heart, that I may be granted the inestimable grace to be of service to you, through Jesus, the suffering servant, and our Lord.

Jesus, Our Teacher

Anthony Esolen

"Wherever he enters, say to the master of the house,
'The Teacher says, "Where is my guest room where I may eat
the Passover with my disciples?"' Then he will show you a large
upper room furnished and ready. Make the preparations
for us there." (Mk 14: 14-15)

We don't know who owned the upper room where Jesus and his disciples ate the Last Supper. He must have known who Jesus was, since the disciples were instructed to say to his servant, "The Teacher says, 'Where is my guest room where I may eat the Passover with my disciples?'"

He knew Jesus as "the Teacher." In some ways, we know him far better. We know him as our Lord and Savior, the eternal Word of the Father, begotten before all ages. He is the redeemer of mankind, who alone reveals to man what it means to be fully human. He is the way, the truth, and the life; he is the door to the kingdom; he is the vine, and we are the branches. Yet for three years he went about working signs and wonders, to give the seal of authority to his teaching. He was the Teacher first of all – as is shown by the fact that the Gospels call his followers his "disciples," meaning those who learned from him.

What do we learn from Jesus? No less than our humanity. The world, wise in its crooked ways, teaches us how to lord it over others, grasping after a flashy and shallow greatness. Jesus teaches us that he who would be greatest must be great by giving, by serving his brethren, by being the least of all. The world teaches that freedom is the license to do as you please. Jesus teaches us that the truth about ourselves and God will set us free; we must commend ourselves in grateful obedience to God. The world teaches us to look out for ourselves, and to punish our enemies. Jesus died for his enemies, and teaches us that God has pardoned us even when we were estranged from him. Compared with Jesus' preaching, and his very life and person, the greatest moral philosopher in the world is but a trader in platitudes.

Father, show us in your Son the Teacher of all good things, that we may be numbered among his faithful disciples, partaking of the blessed supper with him, now and forevermore.

It Is As He Says

Anthony Esolen

The disciples then went off, entered the city, and found it just as [Jesus] had told them; and they prepared the Passover.
(Mk 14: 16)

When the disciples entered Jerusalem to prepare for the Passover, they found the man with the water jar "just as [Jesus] had told them."

We shouldn't be surprised. Yet how many are the things Jesus tells us which, if we troubled to look into them, we would find exactly so! The world says, "Seek after greatness." Jesus says, "If anyone among you wishes to be great, let him be the least, and serve the others." And is it not so? The communist dictators of the last century strutted in their pride, murdering and oppressing their own people to harden their grasp upon power. Yet they were defeated by a humble patriot who had not one armed soldier to command, a man who considered himself the servant of the servants of the Lord. In a hundred years, no one will remember the Polish general he confronted in 1978; but as long as there are people in the world, the name of John Paul will be honored. The world says, "Gratify your appetites," but Jesus says, "A new commandment I give you: love one another, as I have loved you." So the mass of people pursue what is not bread, spending their wages for what fails to satisfy. But one diminutive nun from Albania gave her heart to the destitute, the orphaned, the homeless, the hungry, the abandoned, and the dying of Calcutta; and her love has brought forth a hundredfold, and far more.

If Jesus said to us, "Go into town and you will meet a certain man," would we not believe him? But he says more. He says he and the Father are one. He says he has living water to give us. He says that if we eat his flesh, we shall live for ever. He says that he goes before us, to prepare a place. Then let us trust him.

Father, help us to heed the words of your Son, placing our firm trust in him, because in him alone do we find the truth that sets us free, through the same Jesus Christ, our Lord.

The Meal with Jesus

Anthony Esolen

When it was evening, [Jesus] came with the Twelve. And as they reclined at table and were eating, Jesus said, "Amen, I say to you, one of you will betray me, one who is eating with me."
(Mk 14: 17-18)

All animals eat – our family dog certainly does. But only human beings enjoy a meal, because only for us is the food an occasion for love – for conversation about the trifles of the day, or about what most stirs our hearts. There is no telling where the talk at a meal will go.

Here Jesus is reclining at table with his closest friends. They have trodden many a weary mile at his side. They have slept in one another's company, under the open sky. They have known sunshine and rain, fair winds and storms. They have heard together the grateful and joyous shouts of some of the people, and the malevolent whisperings of the others. Together they have besought the Father, the God of Israel, and Maker of heaven and earth. They have done so on this very evening, when Jesus blessed the bread and the wine, and transformed them into his body and blood. And now, at a meal, and at this of all meals, Jesus announces that one of the men reclining with him will betray him.

How can this be? Judas, who broke bread with Jesus, who was one of the blessed few to share his most intimate conversation, is even now, as he shares the meal with his fellows, revolving in his mind how he might hand Jesus over to his enemies. Can he have been with Jesus so long, and never known him? Or is it rather because he did understand – something, no doubt, distorted and misconstrued – that he betrayed him?

We who partake of the Eucharist have also been invited to this supper. We have come to know Jesus through the Scriptures, through the Church, and through the Spirit he has sent to strengthen us. But the nearer Jesus draws to us, the more urgent is his call. Judas heard it – and rose from the table.

Father, send forth your Spirit upon us, that we may ever seek the love of Jesus in the holy sacrament of his body and blood, nor let us ever be parted from him.

Surely Not I!

Anthony Esolen

*[The Twelve] began to be distressed and to say to [Jesus],
one by one, "Surely it is not I?" (Mk 14: 19)*

When the disciples hear Jesus say that one of them will betray him, their response, deeply human as it is, shows their faith in him. For they do not say, "You are wrong! None of us will betray you." Stranger still, they do not look at one another, wondering if the man next to them is the one. Instead they react in fear. Each of them worries that he might be the betrayer, and cries out, "Surely it is not I!" Evidently they assume that Jesus knows them better than they know themselves – that Jesus may see the treason that harbors in their hearts, of which they themselves are unaware.

The disciples are quite right. What do we really know of ourselves? The Pharisees looked upon themselves as righteous, and made sure others saw them so too, taking the seats of honor at banquets, making a show of their gifts to the synagogue, and taking pride in their not being like the great mass of sinners around them. They judge as man judges, and that means they get things wrong. When the important Simon invited Jesus to dine with him, and that harlot, weeping, came to Jesus to anoint his feet and dry them with her hair, Simon judged Jesus in his heart. He did not know that he himself would fall under judgment, for the lukewarmness of his love.

It is not just that Jesus can read the thoughts we would hide from others. He reads the thoughts we hide from ourselves. That should instruct us to be humble. There is a certain kind of sin that is so close to us, so intimately woven into all our habits, that we cannot see it. And then the Spirit may be working quietly in the heart of our sinful neighbor, making him like Jesus, though he himself would not be so bold to say so.

Father, you who know our coming and our going, grant us the graces we do not know enough to request, and the benefits we need, rather than those alone for which we pray, through Jesus Christ, our Lord.

Was Judas Not Listening?

Anthony Esolen

[Jesus] said to [the Twelve], "One of the Twelve, the one who dips with me into the dish. For the Son of Man indeed goes, as it is written of him, but woe to that man by whom the Son of Man is betrayed. It would be better for that man if he had never been born." (Mk 14: 20-21)

"The one who dips with me into the dish," says Jesus, will be his betrayer. At which point one wonders what must be going through the minds of his disciples. Have they already dipped their bread into the oil with Jesus, and is that what he means? Or will it be the next man to do so? Then the disciples must have stayed their hands, in tense expectation. But why would Judas have gone on to dip his bread into the dish? Did he not hear what Jesus said? Was he not listening?

Think of it. At this, the most terrible moment of their lives so far with Jesus, one of the twelve, Judas, may be stunningly unaware of what is going on. How is that possible? We should recall, though, how often the prophets say that blindness and deafness are fit punishments of sin. And Jesus too has said to the Pharisees, after he had cured the blind man, that because they say in their pride, "We see," their sin remains. It is not simply that we sin because we are deaf to God's call. We grow deaf to God's call because we sin. And not only to God's call, but to all the goodness and holiness in the world. We begin by loving the darkness because our deeds are evil; we end by no longer being able to tell the light from the darkness. We begin by being worldly, and we end in utter incomprehension of that very world around us. We are, to invert Saint Paul's saying, of the world, but not in it.

So Judas sits at the table, and does not hear, or does not care. The Lord of life speaks to him in sadness, yet he, Judas, simply mulls over the plot he will soon execute, with a kiss.

Father, give us ears to hear the words of your Son, and the grace to open our hearts to them, that we may then proclaim them to a world grown blind and deaf. We beg this through Jesus our friend and redeemer.

Sacred Moment, Sacred Persons

Father Romanus Cessario, o.p.

While [the Twelve] were eating, [Jesus] took bread, said the blessing, broke it, and gave it to them, and said, "Take it; this is my body." (Mk 14: 22)

When Saint Mark recounts the establishment of the Eucharist, he places us in company with Jesus on the night before he died. During the sacred banquet that the Lord shares with his disciples, these chosen men receive Christ himself. The gift of the Eucharist lasts throughout the ages. In order for its continuance until the end of time, this mystery of Christ's abiding presence in the Church requires the ministry of priests. The priesthood of Jesus Christ also begins on the night when Jesus was eating with the Twelve. Like the original Twelve, priests come from diverse backgrounds. They display the various traits of personality and character that distinguish one man from another. Christ's priests are taken from among men who themselves require the same Eucharist that Jesus confides to their care.

What remains unique about the ordained priest lies in the nature of the consecration that he receives. Since our eternal salvation depends on their preaching the word and enacting the seven sacraments, God has made priestly consecration a permanent reality in those men who receive it. Given the stakes, we should not wonder that priests can always effectively celebrate the sacraments. Once ordained, the priest carries out his sacramental and other ministries in the person and name of Jesus Christ. Whatever virtues a priest may develop, the effectiveness of his sacramental action depends not on his personal dispositions but on the power of Christ working through him. This consoling provision proves the importance that Christ attaches to the Eucharist. We need the sacrament of Christ's body and blood. For the words that Saint Mark records are addressed to each of us: "Take it; this is my body." The Eucharist however only comes to us from the hands of those men whom God has made priests of Jesus Christ.

Heavenly Father, you provide the Church with the Eucharist. Confirm my belief in the Real Presence of your Son Jesus Christ. Bless your Church with holy priests so that all may receive this sacrament of salvation.

Costly Love

Father Romanus Cessario, O.P.

Then [Jesus] took a cup, gave thanks, and gave it to
[the Twelve], and they all drank from it. He said to them,
"This is my blood of the covenant, which will be shed for many."
(Mk 14: 23-24)

When Saint Mark records the words that Christ speaks over the cup of wine, we realize that the Eucharistic meal comes at a costly price. For as one ancient authority has observed, no man makes the offerings to be the body and blood of Christ, but Christ who was crucified for us. Shedding of blood signifies the ultimate kind of sacrifice. The Christian religion finds its highest expression of worship in the shedding of Christ's innocent blood on the altar of the cross. It ordinarily requires a period of spiritual training to appreciate that the Eucharist is both meal and sacrifice. While the Eucharistic meal brings a holy communion with the Lord, the Eucharistic sacrifice makes us participants in the death of Christ. Sacrifice and communion together make up this sacrament of Christ's love.

By renewing our participation in Christ's sacrifice, we unite ourselves to the source of forgiveness for all sins. The Church in fact holds that the Eucharist cleanses us of venial sin. While only penance and reconciliation absolves grave sins, fervent participation in the Eucharist can wipe away our everyday sins. Once united with "the blood of the covenant," the communicant discovers a new source of charity. Still there exists the perennial temptation to embrace Christ without his cross. Similarly, we can find ourselves thinking about the Eucharist and forgetting Christ's "blood of the covenant, which will be shed for many." The words of institution that the priest repeats each time he celebrates the Eucharist should forestall such forgetfulness. When Christ speaks of his "blood of the covenant," he announces the fulfillment of all legitimate sacrifices offered to God. Now the blood flows from the pierced side of God's own Son. Unlike any other religious action, Christ's precious blood makes of us perfect offerings to God's glory.

Almighty Father, the death of your Son inaugurates a new covenant. Make me a fervent participant in the Eucharistic sacrifice. Then I can expect the kingdom where the new wine of Christ's blood creates saints.

A Eucharist for Ever

Father Romanus Cessario, O.P.

"Amen, I say to you, I shall not drink again the fruit of the vine until the day when I drink it new in the kingdom of God." Then, after singing a hymn, they went out to the Mount of Olives.

(Mk 14: 25-26)

While the Eucharist itself lasts only as long as the world does, the saints recognize in this sacrament a pledge of future glory. Those who regularly frequent the Eucharist – faithful communicants – develop the conviction that their communion with Christ under the appearances of bread and wine gives way to another kind of communion on high. When Christ refers to drinking the fruit of the vine anew in the kingdom of God, he himself points to this future dimension of the Eucharist. We should not pass over lightly this aspect of the Eucharistic mystery. The promise of eternal life provides a fixed point of reference for our everyday lives. Poets like Flannery O'Connor encouraged their readers to regard everything under the aspect of eternity – *sub specie aeternitatis*. In other words, they urge Christians to make moral choices in light of the particular judgment that comes at the moment of death. As the Church announces, this judgment determines how we spend our eternity – whether in love or despair. Even those who do not believe in Christ's resurrection can suspect that human persons must render an account of their free actions. For those who remain faithful to the Eucharist, the prospect of judgment should gladden them.

Observe that Jesus sings as he leaves the room where he celebrates the First Eucharist. When we encounter difficulties in undertaking Christian life and witness, we too can remain joyful. Christ's ascent to the Mount of Olives also signals that once the Eucharist has refreshed us, we find ourselves ready to embrace a high spiritual calling manifested in both the observance of the virtues and a willing surrender to the Holy Spirit. On the stage of life, the Holy Spirit acts like a prompter. The more we follow his lead, the more we will welcome confidently the bright dawn of immortality.

Most merciful Lord, the Eucharist of your Son rejoices my heart. Make me ready to sing a constant hymn to your glory. Then I shall find a home among your saints for all eternity.

Why We Need Shepherds

Father Romanus Cessario, O.P.

Then Jesus said to [the Twelve], "All of you will have your faith shaken, for it is written:/ 'I will strike the shepherd,/ and the sheep will be dispersed.'/ But after I have been raised up, I shall go before you to Galilee." (Mk 14: 27-28)

While the concrete expressions of opposition to the Gospel change with the passage of time, the challenges remain substantially the same. Jesus acknowledges the difficulties that face even the devout. So he tells his apostles, "All of you will have your faith shaken." One may inquire why a message of love and salvation should meet challenges and opposition. The answer lies in the fact that people do not welcome truth, especially when accepting the truth entails woeful suffering. Jesus of course predicts his disciples' troubles as he enters the final moments before his Passion and death. Even the prediction of the resurrection does not suffice to keep these disciples, save one, from fleeing the sight of Calvary. Significantly, Christ indicates that an attack on the Shepherd will scatter the sheep. And still, the very men who abandon him must take up the office of Shepherd in the Church. Ancient Christian writers agree that Christ allows his disciples to confront their timidity and weakness so they will learn not to trust their own resources. As future Shepherds of the flock, these apostles are learning to repose their confidence completely in the power of the risen Lord.

The apostles' experience instructs us. Each of us needs to learn to avoid undue self-reliance and to discover in Christ the source of our spiritual strength. No other recipe for a happy life conforms to what the Church holds about Christian practice. What is more, the practice of turning to Jesus for moral energy and spiritual motivation relies heavily on the encouragement we receive from the preaching and sacramental ministrations of our pastors. Their unique participation in the Headship of Christ ensures that they can steady us in living by faith. On the night before Christ died, his chosen band learned this lesson for all.

Loving Father, the power of your risen Son sustains Christian loving. Grant me the grace to turn frequently to Jesus. Then I shall find what I need to overcome my fears and failures.

The Pope and the World

Father Romanus Cessario, O.P.

Peter said to [Jesus], "Even though all should have their faith shaken, mine will not be." (Mk 14: 29)

Betrayal strikes at the heart of friendship. One rule that distinguishes friends from acquaintances stipulates that friends share intimate thoughts with each other. Everyone needs a friend. No man is an island. We are not made for isolation. When a friend betrays intimate sharing, the suffering increases in proportion to the excellence of what the friends have shared between them. So we can understand why Christ's apostles reacted sadly to his foretelling of their betrayal. Their friendship with Christ entails a most excellent sharing between friends. The Eucharist. No wonder that the apostle Peter spoke up to protest his loyalty. He declares that he will remain faithful to Jesus. Notwithstanding these avowals, the Prince of the Apostles undergoes a powerful purification that readies him for his office in the Church.

In the overall plan of divine providence, Peter's faith does not fail. Even now, Peter's grace enjoys a central place in the Church. The Bishop of Rome and Peter's Successor occupies the Church's still center point from where God strengthens Christian believers worldwide. Throughout the course of two millennia one worldly force and another have tried to limit the universal scope of the pope's authority. While the best of political geniuses have made the mistake of trying to destroy Peter's confession of faith, to undermine the Rock, these efforts have failed and always will fail. The apostle Peter for ever remains at the head of the apostolic band. Peter's impetuousness that pressed him forward to remonstrate with Jesus does not win him a privileged place among the other apostles. Personal bravado does not sustain a worldwide communion of faith. Bravura creates sects, not communion. What makes Peter's confession of faith a permanent feature of the Church's life lies in the grace that comes to this apostle after his repentance for failure.

Father, you give the Church apostle Peter as her Rock. Grant me the strength to remain loyal to the Successor of Peter. Then I shall rejoice in the friendship that binds those who abide in your truth.

What Peter Forgot

Father Romanus Cessario, O.P.

Then Jesus said to [Peter], "Amen, I say to you, this very night before the cock crows twice you will deny me three times."
(Mk 14: 30)

Peter's threefold denial occurs as the religious authorities seek a way to destroy the Lord. Christ predicts precisely the manner in which Peter's cowardice will express itself: "before the cock crows twice..." Commentators observe that Saint Mark describes the particulars of Peter's denial in greater detail than the other evangelists record. We can infer that a special bond of friendship bound the evangelist Mark to the apostle Peter. Later in Mark's Gospel we learn that the recollection of the words that Jesus spoke to him moved Peter to sorrow: "And immediately a cock crowed a second time. Then Peter remembered the words that Jesus had said to him, 'Before the cock crows twice you will deny me three times.' He broke down and wept" (Mk 14: 72).

Sadly, Peter forgot the lessons that Jesus had taught throughout the course of his public ministry. In a word, he forgot that Jesus came to save sinners. Peter forgot about the cleansing of the leper, the healing of the paralytic, and the man with a withered hand. Peter forgot about the healing of the Gerasene demoniac, the raising of Jairus' daughter, and the cure of the woman with a hemorrhage. Peter forgot about the healing of a deaf man in the Decapolis and of the blind man in Bethsaida, the healing of a boy with a demon, and the blind Bartimaeus. Peter even forgot about the cure of his own mother-in-law! Peter forgot all the miracles that Jesus worked to reveal that the incarnate Son of God came among sinners so that they might find healing and salvation. Instead of remembering his own penchant for weakness, Peter thought that he must demonstrate his personal excellence. As often happens in this life, Peter's own strength failed him. Therein lies an important lesson for us.

Merciful Father, hear my petition. Grant me the grace to remain united with your Son. Then I can learn from my past sins, and remain confident in your love for me.

What Peter Remembered

Father Romanus Cessario, O.P.

But [Peter] vehemently replied, "Even though I should have to die with you, I will not deny you." And they all spoke similarly.
(Mk 14: 31)

To appreciate the full significance of Peter's repentance, we must go beyond making him a model of humility and penitence. While Peter's repentance displays certain traits proper to Christian life, his sorrow after sinning primarily exemplifies the paradigm for Christian conversion. Peter's confident attachment to Jesus explains his return to God's grace. Peter remembered that Jesus preaches God's unconditional love for the human person. This recollection helps explain why Peter did not follow the example of the other apostle who betrayed Jesus. This Judas, one may suppose, shared the same sense of regret as Peter showed. What then explains why poor Judas takes his own life in despair, whereas Peter finds himself at the head of the apostolic college? We discover the answer in what Peter remembered about Jesus' teaching.

While the ultimate explanation remains hidden in God, we can distinguish the psychological dispositions that explain Peter's trust and Judas' despair. Judas obviously had failed to grasp the message of love that Jesus taught throughout his public ministry. So when he realized that he had committed a most wicked deed, handing Christ over to his enemies for a paltry financial consideration, Judas concluded that he had excluded himself definitively from the friendship of Jesus. Since he finds himself alone, isolated from all that he once loved, this judgment precipitates his self-destruction. Poor Judas offers nothing to instruct us. Peter, on the other hand, recognizes that he too denied Christ before those who were complacent with his arrest. While Peter spills the bitter tears of regret, he however does not exclude himself from the company of the Savior.

What did Peter remember? He remembered that Christ remains faithful when we fail him. Whatever we may have forgotten from our Catechism lessons, we should never forget this great truth of God's love.

Loving Father, keep me in your love. When temptations threaten, draw me close to the mercy of the Lord Jesus Christ. Then, secure in the pierced recess of his heart, I shall fear no evil.

When I Survey

Father Lawrence Donohoo

Then they came to a place named Gethsemane, and [Jesus]
said to his disciples, "Sit here while I pray."
(Mk 14: 32)

With his retreat into the Garden of Gethsemane, Jesus' Passion now formally begins. You'll not find a more ardent proponent of the power of the word than Saint Paul. Yet even he faces the problem of talking about the stupidity of the cross whereby evil men gain the upper hand and Goodness himself is crucified. Even if Christ rises from the dead, evil still has its day in the sun. What a complex world we will hear described! Romans and Jews, pagans and believers, friends and enemies, Barabbas, the convicted centurion, the unwilling cross-bearer, Pilate's wife, high priests, and low thieves. And with the complexity comes the might-have-been. What if Pilate had obeyed his spouse? What if Simon had broken free? What if Barabbas had lost the wager? Jesus is the victim of spousal insubordination, of help that hurts. He is the loser who dies so Barabbas can go free. If our crucified Lord went through so much work and pain for our redemption, then we can make a first step by reflecting on what he has done for us. If our salvation proved so complex in reality to achieve, we should be willing to grapple with it in our minds and hearts.

But the first task is not trying to figure it out with analysis, but taking it in with humility. The opening posture is not sitting behind the desk, but kneeling before the cross. That's where Paul begins, and so must I. How does eloquence even dare to speak of the cross when the mocked Word was pinned shamelessly on it? If we sing, "Let all mortal flesh keep silence" before the mystery of the incarnation, how much more silent must we stand before this most awesome of wonders. Saint Paul teaches us that the difficulty in grasping the cross arises not simply because we're slow, but because we're sinful. Jesus on the cross will address both issues.

Loving Father, your intricate artistry in wresting redemption from this chaos of sin and web of intrigue is beyond amazing. Give me a heart of wonder and gratitude.

Waiting for the Dawn

Father Lawrence Donohoo

[Jesus] took with him Peter, James, and John, and began to be troubled and distressed. Then he said to them, "My soul is sorrowful even to death. Remain here and keep watch."
(Mk 14: 33-34)

When Jesus took with him Peter, James, and John up the Mount of the Transfiguration, they didn't seem to have any problem staying awake. Keeping watch when shimmering glory unfolds before your very eyes and the terrifying awe of the supernatural floods your spirit is no great feat. And frankly, it shouldn't be tonight either because then was a preparation for now. Something more was granted to the three on the Mount of Glory, and now something more is expected on the Mount of Olives. If the other eight disciples are simply to "sit," these three are to "keep watch." Elementary though it sounds, sitting certainly implies staying awake. But it also means being there, knowing what's up, supporting through presence. Watching is a good deal more. The sentinel sees it coming because forewarned is forearmed. He also sees him coming: "My soul looks for the Lord/ more than sentinels for daybreak" (Ps 130: 6). Watching means watching *with* Jesus, watching *over* Jesus, and above all, watching *for* Jesus.

We have a lot to be on the lookout for because there is "terror on every side" (Jer 20: 10). But above all, we need to be on the lookout for the Lord, since we not only don't know *when* he's coming, we don't know *where* he's coming from. I expect him in the chapel, but he's there knocking at the front door in the person desperate for help. I expect him to console me, but he appears in a disquieting word that requires yet another conversion on my part. The Lord of the Dance can appear anywhere anytime under any form. If he shows up under the appearances of bread and wine, I should be prepared for him anywhere anytime in any manner. Preparation for this, thankfully, is not difficult because he is also the Good Shepherd already at my side. The Lord helps me get ready for himself.

Merciful Father, it's so easy for me to overlook the presence of your Son. Since he's closer to me than I am to myself, help me be closer to him than to myself.

Willing in Slow Motion

Father Lawrence Donohoo

[Jesus] advanced a little and fell to the ground and prayed that if it were possible the hour might pass by him; he said, "Abba, Father, all things are possible to you. Take this cup away from me, but not what I will but what you will." (Mk 14: 35-36)

Recently someone in search of a spiritual director visited me to ascertain my suitability. After our meeting, he thanked me for my remarks and time and said that he would let me know what God's will had determined for him. I was not surprised that I was not chosen since I had concluded that anyone with direct access to the divine will was clearly at a stage of spiritual maturity far beyond my capacity to direct him.

In the famous and wrenching scene of the agony in the garden, it's so easy for us to read the end of the story into its beginning. We assume that Jesus knows at the outset of this personal struggle not only his own will (escaping from his enemies and their cross-purposes once again) but also the Father's will (this time, facing them down). But perhaps Christ's agony here is a double one: not only struggling to accept the Father's will, but learning beyond a reasonable doubt what it truly is. In that case, his prayer to the Father is not primarily to convince him to abandon his will, but above all to clarify it.

So it is with us. How often don't we complain: "If only the Lord would tell me in plain English what I'm supposed to do!" For the Father's will is occasionally what we least expect. It's not necessarily the most difficult course of action or the most pleasant, what most fulfills us or least fulfills us, what first occurs to us or what last comes to mind. Rarely do we have certain knowledge of this will, and we often lack the personal resources to embrace what we think it is without his immediate help. This means we need divine grace to know the divine will as well as to execute it. And all this ambiguity suggests that it is the Father's will that we struggle with knowing in the first place.

Heavenly Father, your will is often a process. Help me to calm down and accept it as you offer it, sometimes in struggle, often in morsels, usually in twilight.

Seeing Is Loving

Father Lawrence Donohoo

*When [Jesus] returned he found [Peter, James, and John] asleep.
He said to Peter, "Simon, are you asleep? Could you not keep
watch for one hour? Watch and pray that you may not undergo
the test. The spirit is willing but the flesh is weak."*
(Mk 14: 37-38)

The three apostles sleep because they simply don't understand that the hour is at hand. Their inability to stay awake shows that they do not read the situation. They do not see the deep sadness and anxiety in Jesus' demeanor. They don't feel the danger in the air. Even before they nodded off they missed his crescendo of references to suffering and death, his poignant actions at the Last Supper, the troubling departure of Judas, his unusual request that they pray with him. Or is the problem rather that the apostles *do* read the situation aright, at least in part, and that their depression becomes an exercise in avoidance? But even in that case they would have failed to see because they would have failed to love.

Those who are awake obviously see more. Charles Dickens had an incredible capacity not only to observe the details of nine-teenth-century English life but to preserve it in revealing prose. His careful eye missed nothing because it was as much sharpened by empathy as intelligence. Reading the situation aright also requires the capacity to care. When her son was pinned under his Chevrolet after the jacks gave out, Angela Cavallo lifted up the car high enough and long enough for two neighbors in the small Georgia town to pull her son from beneath the car. Before it came to this, she saw the solution in the problem. The lesson for weight-lifters here is that love will supply the adrenaline. To read the situation aright is only possible for those who love – who see not only what's there, but what can be done about it. In the apostles' case, it simply meant watching in prayer. In Dickens' case, it meant painting social injustice in prose. For Angela Cavallo, it meant lifting high the car. If I do not see, I cannot respond. But if I do not respond, it cannot be said that I have really seen.

Almighty Father, there is so much going on that I miss, particularly your divine work hidden behind the veil. Help me wake up to life, get focused, and see you.

Sleeping on the Job

Father Lawrence Donohoo

Withdrawing again, [Jesus] prayed, saying the same thing. Then he returned once more and found [Peter, James, and John] asleep, for they could not keep their eyes open and did not know what to answer him. (Mk 14: 39-40)

This threefold pattern of sleeping and awakening is a hint for the pre-warned Peter: three times he manifests this sleepy betrayal of love before his far graver betrayal of Christ when wide awake. Jesus issues a command and three remonstrations, but none of this works because Peter, James, and John are intent on their sleep. What's so troubling about this unconscious stubbornness is that it's so predictable, so inexorable, so tedious. Such bad habits possess their own stubborn logic that resides on the other side of critical speech. They don't speak back to us; they just don't know how to answer us. They nod in agreement that they're wicked and lazy, and then continue to do their thing. Unsurprisingly, the text gives us no response on the part of the apostles other than to tell us that they can't provide a response – and then fall asleep again. The same troubling habit that refuses to face itself honestly lives off this crafty mix of a reputation for helplessness and a penchant for resistance.

Perhaps the most dangerous feature of our bad habits, especially those that put us to sleep, is that they numbingly attack our knowing and loving. In some sense, I *am* my habits, good and bad, so that my capacity to engage God, others, and myself is in large part assisted or resisted by them. Because I rest in my bad habits and they are mine, I need divine help in naming them, analyzing them, and provoking them in order to vanquish them and discover the larger world that they prevent me from entering. Otherwise I face the embarrassment of not staying awake for my Lord, but manifesting impressive vim and vigor when my life or fortune is on the line. Which means that Peter, James, John, and I need to address our problem in prayer and ask the Lord for help. The vigil in the garden is an ideal time to begin.

Eternal Father, without you I can do nothing. With you I can do something. Help me to do what I can for me, and do for me what I can't.

Timing Is Everything

Father Lawrence Donohoo

[Jesus] returned a third time and said to [Peter, James, and John], "Are you still sleeping and taking your rest? It is enough. The hour has come. Behold, the Son of Man is to be handed over to sinners. Get up, let us go. See, my betrayer is at hand."
(Mk 14: 41-42)

The Gospel of John owns the image of the hour, from Jesus' insistence at Cana that his hour has not yet come, to that hour when the beloved disciple takes our Lady into his own home. In Mark, only five references to the hour appear, but three of them are compressed into these verses in all of their foreboding intensity and relentless advance. The hour has now arrived. This means that in the life of Jesus, as in our own, all moments are not equal. Some stand out, define the others, and build a story. For no matter which Gospel we read, we find Jesus aware of his mission that leads him from active ministry to Passion, death, and resurrection. This mission is not a career, but a vocation: Jesus is sent by the Father on a path marked by lesser moments and greater hours.

Each of us as well has been sent by the Father into the world with a work to do and with hour and minute hands with which to do it. Like that of Christ, every human life is a story to be told with a beginning, a long middle, and an ending that does not end. Some of its major hours we know in advance or at least can expect in all probability. They may ring in joyous events or toll for deep sorrows. But it is in the remaining minutes that most of our lives are played out. Here we prepare either well or poorly for the great hours that mark our days, interpret our past, infuse our present, and inflect our future. In imitation of Jesus, we too from time to time can take time out to get a sense of our story, to look for the major plot, plan the best moves, and judge the characters – always looking, of course, for the invisible hand of our divine ghostwriter.

Loving Father, you are author not only of my life, but of my lifespan. Yet you assign me an indispensable role in its unfolding. Help me help myself.

They Can All Be Wrong

Father Lawrence Donohoo

Then, while [Jesus] was still speaking, Judas, one of the Twelve, arrived, accompanied by a crowd with swords and clubs who had come from the chief priests, the scribes, and the elders. His betrayer had arranged a signal with them, saying, "The man I shall kiss is the one; arrest him and lead him away securely."
(Mk 14: 43-44)

Sociology, or psychology writ large, has its hands full with crowd control. We might want to avoid crowds altogether except that the Book of Revelation sees one in our future: "a vision of a great multitude… from every nation, race, people, and tongue" (Rv 7: 9). The desire to belong, to be part of something larger than ourselves, finds its glorified expression in the communion of saints. This is the creaturely image of the perfect community of divine Persons. But that's not what Jesus encounters tonight. Belonging, to be sure, is in the air: the heavy march of the many, the unwavering sense of purpose, the swords and clubs that give this the feel of the official, the paramount, the divinely ordained. These folks are out on a mission to do God's will, even if it hurts, and nothing is going to get in their way. They're cousins to the crowd that brought Stephen down, who "cried out in a loud voice, covered their ears, and rushed upon him together" (Acts 7: 57).

One need not be Christian to be alarmed by all this. Socrates, way back when, consigned the crowd mentality to the lowest form of political life. And contemporary studies show the frightening willingness of people to do ghastly things when even mildly coerced by the "group." The unanimity that Saint Paul is aiming for not only forbids this false religion, but requires that individuals be respected with their God-given and individual intellects, wills, freedom, and rights. A hint that these goods may be lost from sight is the crowd armed with clubs but void of speech. For it is *logos* – the capacity to slow down and reason about problems – that provides the genuine link from the one to the many. The frenzied crowd should jolt us all into assessing our own partiality for their false righteousness. The Father at least was ready for it, and bent it into a useful tool for our salvation.

Heavenly Father, only when I come to self-possession and other-possession in you can I take a rightful place in your communion of saints. Make me worthy of it.

Appointment at Golgotha

Father Lawrence Donohoo

[Judas] came and immediately went over to [Jesus] and said, "Rabbi." And he kissed him. At this they laid hands on him and arrested him. (Mk 14: 45-46)

With the arrest of Jesus, we reach an entirely new place in the Gospel. From a human perspective, any newcomer would conclude that Jesus' salvific work of teaching, preaching, healing, exorcising, and forgiving has now ended. No one could see this arrest as the beginning of his most decisive work of salvation. Not only does God take a salvific path different from human expectations, he chooses a way that even runs counter to some scriptural texts. One psalm, for example, offers a job description of the Messianic king that we can accept: to "defend the oppressed among the people,/ save the poor and crush the oppressor" (Ps 72: 4). But with Jesus' arrest, the Savior himself must now be saved. This will come to a climax on Golgotha when the Rescuer is challenged to rescue himself: "save yourself by coming down from the cross" (Mk 15: 30). Just when we needed him most, he has fallen prey to the enemy.

The problem with Psalm 72's prescription is that it presumes the wall between good and evil separates the virtuous from the vicious. But the enemy is not only at my gate, but inside my city walls. The salvation I need is one that not only frees me from "them," but from myself – a salvation with the precision of surgical instruments "sharper than any two-edged sword, penetrating even between soul and spirit" (Heb 4: 12). The first thing to do here is to cast aside my list of needs that I keep shoving in God's face and learn from him what is really necessary. By watching Christ in his moment of extreme vulnerability – by seeing how he is saved – I learn what kind of salvation I need most deeply. The first task for all would-be recipients of salvation, then, is to "look on him whom they have thrust through" (Zec 12: 10). We need that two-edged sword that on Golgotha will lay bare the heart of God.

Most merciful Father, while it is true that my enemies without are numerous, the truth is that too often I'm on their side. Overcome me with your saving love.

An Alarming New Twist

Father Lawrence Donohoo

One of the bystanders drew his sword, struck
the high priest's servant, and cut off his ear.
(Mk 14: 47)

Now we're talking! As with a good Hollywood thriller, we expected the good guys here to take a few hits early to whet our appetite for revenge. Then you turn the tables and the bad guys get pinned under them. But no... it just keeps getting worse. What is wrong with this picture? To appreciate the divine strategy here, we should observe that God remains faithful to his game plan. The salvific sufferings of Christ didn't come from nowhere: his life was a study in suffering. At the dawn of his ministry he underwent active suffering in his desert struggles against the world, flesh, and devil. The sufferings of his ministry arose from the demands on his time, the process of triage always placing him last, night prayer because of day schedules – the sheer exhaustion of it all. Add the suffering occasioned by enemies: defending victims of oppressors, withstanding attacks against himself and his Father, remaining steady under fire while proclaiming the Gospel of love. Most recently, we have betrayal and abandonment: Judas escaping into the night, and now the disciples starting to follow suit with the limelight trained on Christ.

What's new with this policy of non-resistance is that in all his previous sufferings, Jesus was both actor and acted upon. He was a player on the human scene, and a mighty one. But he so played the game that everyone else had a chance to show what they could do. Christ's Passion we call it: to be acted upon, to let it be done unto him. Having acted his entire life – as shepherd and savior, physician and consoler, leader and teacher, wonder-worker and friend – Jesus today lets everyone else take center stage. Let's see them in action. As with Pilate, he is now in their hands and they can do with him what they will. In this way, he shows us how to act when our capacity for action is gone.

Almighty Father, our lives are a mix of action and passion, giving and receiving. Help us know and then adopt the correct posture for each passing moment.

Really Tough Guys

Father Lawrence Donohoo

*Jesus said to [the crowd] in reply, "Have you come out as against
a robber, with swords and clubs, to seize me? Day after day I
was with you teaching in the temple area, yet you did not
arrest me; but that the scriptures may be fulfilled."*
(Mk 14: 48-49)

When the Passion account is analyzed, it's always the disciples who are blamed for cowardice, but what about all these little foot soldiers armed with swords and clubs? The reason they're working after hours is because they fear a backlash among the people – the simple folks, God's people, the beneficiaries of Jesus' ministry, who just might make a fuss if a daytime arrest were attempted. With these people sound asleep, it's easy to form a mob and seize Christ when he's basically defenseless. What we witness here is a common tactic of cowardice: hitting the opposition where it's weakest and attacking in numbers. Which brings us back to the monolithic crowd, that specialist in cowardly deeds.

Courage was so critical for the ancient Greeks that their word for virtue originally meant bravery in the face of adversity. In a soft culture such as our own with an elite intelligentsia that encourages socialization for everyone else, courage can be a pain in the neck. It is likelier to appear when it is seen not as a luxury for the few, but as a necessity for all. But it will only be valued by those who do not take their intellectual and moral bearings from the approved teachings of the culture. This includes Christians. Courage, then, will only come into view for those who struggle to know the Truth that alone can make them free. Since the truth can only be known by struggling against the *Zeitgeist*, the cross will always be a neighbor of freedom. But the cross of opposition can only be borne if truth is loved more than the package of rewards promised to the conforming. It is for this reason that John gets down to brass tacks when he teaches that "perfect love drives out fear" (1 Jn 4: 18). Which explains why the disciples are about to hightail it out of there – and the armed thugs are there to stay.

Eternal Father, I recognize that every Christian is called to follow Christ with courage, not simply the saintly few. Make me strong in seeking the truth and living it.

329

Last Man Running

Father Lawrence Donohoo

And [the disciples] all left [Jesus] and fled. Now a young man followed him wearing nothing but a linen cloth about his body. They seized him, but he left the cloth behind and ran off naked.
(Mk 14: 50-52)

There are those who come early and leave late, those who come late and leave early, those who come early and leave early, and those who come late and leave late. Our midnight streaker belongs in the last category, and for this he's to be commended. Who is he? The received wisdom, and it's probably right, is that the author of the Gospel of Mark is here leaving eyewitness evidence that he was there. Since it was under less than flattering conditions, you can believe him. Contemporary scholarship calls this the criterion of embarrassment. Now why is he lightly clad? Probably because he was awakened in the middle of the night when news of trouble brewing began to spread. Instead of taking time with inessentials, like finding clothes, he ran out in his pajamas. He had his priorities right. Also to be commended is his lasting a round longer than any of the other disciples – and then, once again, to have the shamelessness to leave naked rather than remain caught and clothed. Or perhaps he should have remained.

No matter how you view it, there is something impressively authentic here that no reporter would want to miss. The young man's clothing is actually the perfect metaphor for his actions. Just as he stays longer than the other disciples, so he goes much further, risking everything – or almost everything – until he loses his shirt. This is good news for me. Whenever I go one step further in tracking down Jesus or staying with him, even if it's not far enough, I can build on the step taken instead of critically measuring the distance yet to be traversed. Commendation is far better than censure for making spiritual progress, not only for everyone else, but even for myself. With past results acknowledged, even if imperfect, I can plan the next step in following unreservedly my Lord for whose vesture they cast lots.

Heavenly Father, your Holy Spirit is a lamp for my steps and a light for my path. Help me make even incremental steps in the direction of your love.

Practice Makes Perfect

Father Lawrence Donohoo

[The crowd] led Jesus away to the high priest, and all the chief priests and the elders and the scribes came together. Peter followed him at a distance into the high priest's courtyard and was seated with the guards, warming himself at the fire.
(Mk 14: 53-54)

Again, we're quick to point out Saint Peter's threefold denial, but at least he's attempting a comeback. Where are the other ten? Does no one else return to give witness? We saw Peter disappear earlier into the waves, but forget that he alone dares to learn to tread water. Peter, of course, is a combination of temerity and caution. In this sequence, it's caution that makes him run, and it's temerity that brings him back. But now it's cautious temerity as planner whose first task is to gather information. To this end, he gets as close to the action as possible without compromising his identity. Unfortunately, his cover is blown, just like the naked young man. But at least I can give him credit for trying, just as I remember the times I fled pell-mell and never turned back at all.

To be sure, Peter will be absent from Golgotha, but on Easter Sunday he will run back in quest of the risen Lord and on Pentecost boldly proclaim him. He will successfully open the doors of the young Church to the Gentiles without legal or ritual preconditions, but then will stand corrected by Saint Paul for not practicing what he preached. Over and over again this pattern returns in Peter's life: fall and rise, rise and fall. Like a wrestler who can't see that he can't win, Peter keeps picking himself up and proving they're wrong and he's still in there. In the end he will return to Golgotha where the rock who once fell into the water will stand his ground, which is that of his Lord. In this he serves as an inspiration to us when our sins and bad habits keep shouting that it's a losing battle. We can win, and we need to be reminded that divine grace does not measure future success by past failures. It's there before, during, and after our next attempt, whether on sea or land.

Almighty Father, I too have sunk beneath the waves and fled in the darkness. With your Son ready to steady and secure me, give me always another chance.

Keeping Up Appearances

Father Lawrence Donohoo

The chief priests and the entire Sanhedrin kept trying to obtain testimony against Jesus in order to put him to death, but they found none. Many gave false witness against him, but their testimony did not agree. (Mk 14: 55-56)

These poor stooges are doing their best, but they obviously need help in bringing Jesus down. They have been primed by the leaders, but in their big moment when all that hard practice and all those payoffs should pay off, they collapse. It further looks as if they're trying to embarrass Jesus the preacher since he earlier taught that a kingdom divided against itself cannot stand. Fortunately, their kingdom does crumble, so no harm done to the Lord's words. But this bungling is instructive since it shows that evil is often intertwined with good. What we see here is an awkward attempt by unjust men to play by the rules and abide by the law even as justice is skewed in order to obtain a wicked result. So why all this meticulous attention to judicial procedure? Why not simply get to the evil result by the most direct means possible? Because evil often needs the good to provide cover for its nefarious deeds. Because evil occasionally needs to be convinced that it is righteous. Because evil is more dangerous when it cloaks itself in the garments of justice.

What we can take home from this is that the ways of evil demand careful study. Its advocates are occasionally fooled by their own duplicity since consorting with goodness may convince evil that the false appearances it hides behind are the real thing. In this way, the maxim that hypocrisy is the homage that vice pays to virtue eventually can deceive even the deceiver – that seasoned practitioner of wickedness. The sober warning to those who attempt to avoid evil both in its substance and its appearances is that the greatest evil is often perpetrated by those most convinced of their own righteousness. And the positive photograph of this negative is that justice is most attractive when it also appears to be so. We can rest our case with the Accused standing before them.

Loving Father, so tortured is the human heart that it can be consistent neither in good nor evil. May your Spirit probe my depths and throw his light.

Warm Logic

Father Lawrence Donohoo

Some took the stand and testified falsely against [Jesus], alleging, "We heard him say, 'I will destroy this temple made with hands and within three days I will build another not made with hands.'" Even so their testimony did not agree.
(Mk 14: 57-59)

Their testimony doesn't agree because they twist the good of truth for their evil intentions. Aristotle taught centuries earlier that truth is the good of the intellect. Since knowing is our first access to the real world, our ability to know the good and then to do it requires an ability to access this world. Anyone who has ever been wrong about anything knows that truth is not always gained with ease. The mysteries of faith, insofar as they make sense to us, are no exception – even if they are revealed. What the Lord expects is not simply that we listen, but that we absorb what he is saying and doing. So we find the Scriptures replete with logic, arguments, and all kinds of reasoning. Most of the Wisdom books, beginning with Proverbs, appeal to common sense and experience. In the Gospels, Jesus is constantly inviting us to think by teaching in parables, asking questions, and dismantling received opinions that are simply – or complicatedly – wrong. In large part, the Letter to the Romans and the Letter to the Hebrews are extended arguments for the primacy of faith and the superiority of the new covenant, respectively. Saint Paul uses a logical argument in First Corinthians to prove our resurrection on the basis of Christ's resurrection. While we accept on faith what the Lord has revealed, much of his revelation and even the way he reveals it requires a God-given and grace-infused reason to receive it.

Christian holiness, then, depends in part on critical thinking, and today more than ever. In order to navigate our faith through the troubled waters of secularism, appraise competing claims and testimonies of believers, negotiate our vocation in the world, and join the Holy Spirit in probing the depths of our spirit as well as the deep things of God, we need to appreciate the role of reason in our Catholic belief. This is something to think about.

Most merciful Father, to know your truth is already to possess salvation. Help me to develop my understanding of your wonderful ways and your saving truth.

Your Turn

Father Lawrence Donohoo

The high priest rose before the assembly and questioned Jesus, saying, "Have you no answer? What are these men testifying against you?" But he was silent and answered nothing.
(Mk 14: 60-61a)

What is the Father's strategy here? That Christ suffer and die against his better judgment? Saint Anselm argues that the Father cannot directly will to condemn his Son to free the guilty. Jesus must freely consent to his Father's will, even if his excruciating suffering and death is the consequence. But what exactly is the Father's will? Not precisely that his Son die, but that he live life to the full – that for the first time in history a human being place no conditions on representing God's justice and love to the very end. That his Son not back down, that he stand firm in the face of immovable opposition and defend the work he has done on behalf of the Father's kingdom. Jesus thus accepts the full consequences of his life and his actions by going all the way for the Father, representing him in this eerie silence of near-total passivity. This Word stands silent in court, giving the human race the podium for its day in the sun (as long as it would last).

Now is the time for all those with grievances against Goodness to show up and file their complaints. Now will God, in the person of his Son, set his face like flint and reveal by listening. Job, whose face was covered with boils, received an answer to his long complaint in terms of divine power. But now a more adequate answer is given by One whose face will be covered with blood. If the divine answer to Job's suffering is power out of the whirlwind, the new answer to our accumulated complaints is one of powerlessness in Jesus Christ on the cross. What a consolation to know that God takes on not only our sin, but our criticism. We are assured that we can file any complaint we have against him, recognizing that our relationship with him needs this issue resolved, whatever it may be.

Eternal Father, allow me to present the offering of my heart, even when it is troubled, broken, or angry. Please give me your answers to my questions.

Identity Crisis

Father Lawrence Donohoo

Again the high priest asked [Jesus] and said to him, "Are you the Messiah, the son of the Blessed One?" Then Jesus answered, "I am;/ and 'you will see the Son of Man/ seated at the right hand of the Power/ and coming with the clouds of heaven.'"
(Mk 14: 61b-62)

Jesus breaks out of his passive mode because he is required to do so. He didn't have to respond to the incompetent witnesses, but he must answer the high priest. And he does so by saying that he will return from on high, claiming as his own the brief image in Daniel of the mysterious Son of Man. In this way Jesus helps everyone: the ineffective perjurers, the determined elders, the frustrated high priest – all who need convincing and convicting evidence against Jesus. And he provides it – by not providing it. For what is blasphemous about Jesus admitting that he is the Messiah if in fact he is? This is precisely the question before the court. But with their predetermined conclusion that Jesus cannot be, the leaders accuse him of blasphemy who would only be guilty if he denied his identity. Jesus further employs an image packed with power, glory, clouds, and action to help them find a Messiah whom they don't recognize in Isaiah's Servant – the one charged to "bring glad tidings to the lowly,/ to heal the brokenhearted,/ To proclaim liberty to the captives/ and release to the prisoners" (Is 61: 1). By speaking the truth, then, Jesus cannot provide them what they are looking for – a blasphemer. And by not providing it, he is convicted of blasphemy and so continues his inexorable march to death. The Servant then becomes the Suffering Servant, who "was pierced for our offenses,/ crushed for our sins,/ Upon him was the chastisement that makes us whole,/ by his stripes we were healed" (Is 53: 5).

Can I accept all the various portraits that Scripture offers me – the prophetic images of the old covenant, the textual images of the Gospels, the interpretative images of the other New Testament writings? Can Jesus be for me Son of Man and Son of God, Anointed King and Suffering Servant, Wonderful Counselor and Mighty God, Good Shepherd and Slaughtered Lamb?

Loving Father, your Son has truly become all things to all people. Help me to study his various portraits etched in your sacred Word and his saving deeds.

Redeeming the Incarnation
Father Lawrence Donohoo

At that the high priest tore his garments and said, "What further need have we of witnesses? You have heard the blasphemy. What do you think?" They all condemned [Jesus] as deserving to die. (Mk 14: 63-64)

Note all the reasons that Jesus is *not* condemned to die: threatening to destroy the temple, cleansing it of money-changers, forgiving sinners, sabbath healings. No, he is convicted for identifying with the heavenly Son of Man who consorts with the Ancient One. This is sheer fabrication to his judges because a man of flesh and blood cannot be the Son of Man in glory. One who is divine cannot be human, all too human. By claiming his incarnate status, Jesus becomes the cause of our redemption. His death is a complex case of mistaken identity.

Thus do the Passion and death of Jesus complete his incarnation. All of his life he lives this simple principle of being here now: first assuming human nature in his Mother, then taking on a full human life in our world. We know him as the Man of Sorrows, but he is first the Man of Joys. The life of the party, he comes eating and drinking, and his parables are full of both. It runs in the family: Mary is concerned that wine might give out. No one lived life nor ranged the spectrum of human experience as does Jesus. Not despite, but because he is acquainted with joy, he becomes a study in sorrow. Only one who knows joy can weep, and laughter comes most easily to those who learn to cry. Jesus does not avoid the edges of human existence, nor does he claim the middle of the road as the straight and narrow way. The one who comes to give life abundantly meant to possess it first.

Because he so lives and so dies, Jesus expects no less of us. Only those who have truly lived deserve to die – in order to live more fully. To join Christ in his sufferings, I can embrace his life here and now abundantly, stop taking life's temperature before I jump in, start following his will wherever it leads me.

Almighty Father, since life is short I need each moment to seek the wonders it conceals. Thank you for the drama of your Son's life, by which I am redeemed.

Helplessness

Father Joseph T. Lienhard, S.J.

Some began to spit on [Jesus]. They blindfolded him and struck him and said to him, "Prophesy!" And the guards greeted him with blows. (Mk 14: 65)

We are asked to ponder a verse from Saint Mark's Gospel that describes Jesus in a moment of absolute helplessness. Elsewhere in the Gospels, Jesus is always in command of the situation he is in. At the age of twelve, he explains to Mary and Joseph why he was right to stay in Jerusalem. Throughout his public life, he dominates each situation – by his wisdom, by his power, by his strength. Even on the cross, his lordship is manifest: he asks for forgiveness for his executioners, and he even chooses the moment of his death.

But in the verse we are meditating on, Jesus allows himself to be utterly helpless. He was made physically helpless: he was blindfolded; his sight was taken away. Think for a moment what it is like to be blindfolded – not to know where you are, or where you are being taken; not to know what danger is near you, or where you may step next. His tormentors also begin to spit on him, a unique kind of insult. And they strike him, hit him, punch him. All these acts are aimed at Jesus' body.

The final insult is different: it is aimed at his person. "Prophesy!" "Be Jeremiah!" "Be Isaiah!" "Be Ezekiel!" In the Old Testament, the words that introduced a prophecy were often, "The word of the Lord came to [the prophet], and he said." Those who are mocking Jesus are saying to him, "Make the Scriptures alive again in our day." They would never know that the one standing before them – blindfolded, bleeding, silent, covered with spit – had far more to give than the passing word of a prophet. This man was the Father's eternal Word; and all that he suffered, he suffered "for us and for our salvation," as the Creed tells us.

God our Father, we ponder the Passion and death of Christ your Son, and all that he suffered because of our sins; fill our hearts, we pray, with sorrow for sin, and guide us on the way to life, through the same Christ our Lord.

Peter's Three Denials

Father Joseph T. Lienhard, S.J.

While Peter was below in the courtyard, one of the high priest's maids came along. Seeing Peter warming himself, she looked intently at him and said, "You too were with the Nazarene, Jesus." But he denied it saying, "I neither know nor understand what you are talking about." So he went out into the outer court. [Then the cock crowed.] (Mk 14: 66-68)

As Saint Mark presents Saint Peter's three denials of Jesus, we see clear progressions, in several ways. The first is in the one who makes the accusation against Peter. The first two times, it is one of the high priest's maids. The third time, the number of accusers increases: it is now the bystanders, several if not many. Then, too, the charges become more pointed. First the maid says to Peter, "You too were with the Nazarene, Jesus." Judas had been with Jesus, too. The maid is not accusing Peter of any wrongdoing; she is simply associating him with Jesus. The maid's second charge is more ominous: "This man is one of them." Somehow, the very vagueness of this statement makes it more unsettling. To be one of them – we do not yet know who they are, or what their purpose is. But we do know that this group exists, and we are suspicious of them. And finally, the bystanders adduce a vague sort of proof, but a proof that is enough for them. They add "surely" to their charge. And what is their proof? "For you too are a Galilean."

Peter, for his part, ups the ante in the same way. He makes his first denial an assertion of ignorance: I don't know what you are talking about. The second denial is more specific: You say that I belong to that group, whatever it is. I say I don't. Peter's third and last denial is the most explicit, and the most painful: "I do not know this man." But you do, Peter, you do! And you know him better than anyone else, for once you said, "You are the Messiah, the Son of the living God" (Mt 16: 16). We see what fear can do to a man. Do we see something of Peter in ourselves?

Almighty God and Lord, you have given us the gift of faith in Jesus Christ your Son; keep us true to your word all the days of our lives, through Christ our Lord.

To Be "One of Them"

Father Joseph T. Lienhard, S.J.

The maid saw [Peter] and began again to say to the bystanders,
"This man is one of them." Once again he denied it.
(Mk 14: 69-70a)

To write off another person as one more member of a group can be a mean and nasty thing to do. It denies the person's individuality, his freedom. It says, "I already know how you think, what you will say, how you will act, because you are 'one of them.'" Each of us can easily think of groups that are dismissed in that way; there is no need to create a list. Often enough, the members of such a group do not join it voluntarily; they are born into it. Then there is another sort of group, one that a person joins voluntarily. Such groups may also be despised and rejected, but such treatment does not deter the members.

We can think, of course, of the resounding sentence in the Acts of the Apostles, about the city of Antioch in Syria: "It was in Antioch that the disciples were first called Christians" (Acts 11: 26). This designation, "Christian," was meant as an insult; but soon it became the name that its adherents were most proud of. Saint Gregory Nazianzen writes that, when he and Saint Basil the Great were students in Athens, they had one great goal: to be and to be called Christians. Thousands of martyrs had stood before judges for interrogation and said, *"Christianus sum,"* "I am a Christian," knowing the sentence that that statement would entail. Tertullian, the sharp-witted Christian apologist, summed up the situation well: If the Tiber floods, if the Nile does not, if the sky does not move, or the earth does, if there is famine, if there is plague, there is one cry: "The Christians to the lion!" What – he adds sarcastically – all of them to one lion? At one moment in his life, Saint Peter did not want to be "one of them." Later he was proud to be, and he died on a cross, like his Lord and Master.

God our Father, you have given us the name of Christian; make us worthy, we pray, to bear the name of your only Son, Jesus Christ the Lord.

Friendship

Father Joseph T. Lienhard, s.j.

A little later the bystanders said to Peter once more, "Surely you are one of them; for you too are a Galilean." He began to curse and to swear, "I do not know this man about whom you are talking." And immediately a cock crowed a second time.
(Mk 14: 70b-72a)

We have just been reflecting on Peter's denial of Jesus. We might reflect here on Peter's friendship with Jesus, a friendship he betrayed so meanly in his denial. A friend is someone we want to be with, someone we trust, someone we know will help us when we are in need. Saint Augustine of Hippo was the first to elaborate a vision of Christian friendship. The Roman philosopher Cicero had defined friendship as agreement on all things divine and human, with good will and affection. Augustine rethought what Cicero had written and conceived of friendship as the bond between souls that cleave to each other by the love that the Holy Spirit pours into their hearts. We owe Christian charity to all; friendship adds an attraction or liking that we feel for certain people.

We probably do not often think of the friendship between Jesus and Peter; but surely there was one. Jesus liked Peter – boisterous, compulsive, a little hotheaded, deeply loving as he was. And then, after his arrest, Jesus knew what Peter was doing. As one of the Gospels records, Jesus turned and looked at his friend. What Peter had done may have hurt Jesus more than all the slaps and whips: his friend had denied him. But that look, that meeting of their eyes, may also have been Peter's salvation, for even at that moment, Jesus looked at his friend, and his eyes asked, will you come back? Those same eyes can look at us, as we approach the sacrament of reconciliation. Peter was to experience repentance and sorrow. Was he tempted to think, God can never forgive this sin? That is what Judas thought, and Judas hanged himself. Peter had hope. Still, what did he expect when the risen Christ appeared to him on Easter? That beautiful moment is a secret between Jesus and Peter. But one look into Jesus' eyes must have said everything to Peter.

God our Father, by the intercession of Saint Peter, prince of the apostles, stir up a spirit of true repentance in our hearts and help us to cling to you in trust, through Christ our Lord.

Peter's Repentance

Father Joseph T. Lienhard, S.J.

Then Peter remembered the word that Jesus had said to him,
"Before the cock crows twice you will deny me three times."
He broke down and wept. (Mk 14: 72b)

Simon Peter is one of the best known and most appealing of the apostles. He was the brother of Andrew; their father was Jona. Peter and Andrew were the first disciples whom Jesus called; Saint Luke records that Jesus showed Simon Peter his power by commanding him to cast out his nets after Simon had spent the whole night fishing and caught nothing (Lk 5: 1-11). It was Simon Peter, too, who confessed that Jesus was the Messiah, the Son of the living God. According to Saint Matthew's Gospel, Jesus changed Simon's name to Peter and said, "You are Peter, and on this rock I will build my church, and the gates of the netherworld shall not prevail against it" (Mt 16: 18). Whenever the twelve apostles' names are mentioned, Peter's is always first. With James and John, he was with Christ on Mount Tabor and witnessed the Transfiguration.

In light of his rank and privilege, Peter's denial was a dreadful act. But it was also a lesson for the Church, and for all future Christians. Peter shows us that there is no sin that is unforgivable, unless we decide and choose not to seek forgiveness. In the days between Jesus' arrest and his appearance to Peter on Easter morning, Peter must have suffered greatly. What had he done? How could he have done it? What will become of him now? But his suffering is the suffering of any sinner between the sin and reconciliation; the difference is only one of degree. If one were to imagine an ideal father confessor, who would be better than Saint Peter? Who could know, better than Saint Peter, what it is like to experience God's loving mercy? Is it not consoling to approach the sacrament of reconciliation with the thought that Saint Peter might be hearing my confession?

God our Father, fill us with a true spirit of repentance and a firm purpose of amendment; help us to celebrate the sacrament of reconciliation often and worthily, through Christ our Lord.

The Hands of Jesus

Father Mark Daniel Kirby, O.S.B

*As soon as morning came, the chief priests with the elders
and the scribes, that is, the whole Sanhedrin, held a council.
They bound Jesus, led him away, and handed him over to Pilate.*
(Mk 15: 1)

The sight of Jesus being led away with his hands bound causes me to stop, and look, and wonder. His are the hands that molded the earth. His are the hands that set the stars in the firmament. His are the hands that fashioned man from dust of the earth. The Psalmist sings: "When I see your heavens, the work of your fingers,/ the moon and stars that you set in place –/ What are humans that you are mindful of them,/ mere mortals that you care for them?" (Ps 8: 4-5).

The hand signifies power, action, and creativity. The palm of the hand represents a place of tenderness, and of protection. "Can a mother forget her infant,/ be without tenderness for the child of her womb?/ Even should she forget,/ I will never forget you./ See, upon the palms of my hands I have written your name" (Is 49: 15-16).

Cruelly bound by his captors, the hands of Jesus remain the human hands of God, just as his face is the human face of God, and his heart the human heart of God. These are the hands that touched the leper and made him clean, raised the daughter of Jairus from the sleep of death, took up the five loaves and two fish, and blessed the little children. These are the hands that held the bread changed into his body, and the chalice of wine changed into his blood. These are the hands that, after having been bound with cords, were stretched from east to west on the wood of the cross.

The mystery of this one sentence in Saint Mark's account of the Passion is that God allowed his hands to be bound. He allowed his power to suffer limitations. He allowed the wicked to foreshorten his reach. "He was crucified out of weakness," says Saint Paul, "but he lives by the power of God" (2 Cor 13: 4).

Father, we adore the hands of your Son, bound by his captors and nailed to the wood of the cross. We adore the hands of our Eternal Priest, raised before you in the sanctuary of heaven, bestowing grace upon the weak, and setting captives free.

Christ the King

Father Mark Daniel Kirby, O.S.B.

Pilate questioned [Jesus], "Are you the king of the Jews?"
He said to him in reply, "You say so." (Mk 15: 2)

Every three years the Church uses this very passage in her liturgy for the feast of Christ the King. Our Lord does not deny his kingship, for he is king from before all ages, nor does he affirm it, lest Pilate represent it in limited earthly terms. In Saint John's Passion, Jesus says, "My kingdom does not belong to this world" (Jn 18: 36).

The kingship of Jesus is one of love, not of coercion. He establishes his reign in the hearts of those who enter into his own prayer to the Father, saying, "Thy kingdom come." To accept the love of Jesus is to submit to his kingship, and to submit to his kingship is to accept his love.

Some years ago, a certain monk who had tried for many years to practice the ceaseless prayer of the heart learned of the prayer indulgenced by Blessed John XXIII, "O Jesus, King of Love, I put my trust in your merciful goodness." One day, kneeling before the Blessed Sacrament, he realized that the prayer was repeating itself ceaselessly and effortlessly in his heart. He found himself praying the little invocation at every waking moment and even during the night, in a way similar to the "Jesus Prayer" of monks of the Eastern Church.

Individuals from all walks of life have called upon Jesus, the King of Love, in this way. Having accepted the love of Jesus and submitted to his kingship, they attest to the graces received: inner healing, victory over persistent and deeply rooted habits of sin, trust in the mercy of Christ, and ceaseless prayer.

The kingship of Jesus liberates; it is never oppressive. It ennobles; it never humiliates. It heals; it never crushes. Surrender to Jesus, the King of Love, is the beginning of true freedom, of dignity, and of wholeness.

All-powerful Father, send your Holy Spirit upon us, that with confidence and boldness we may invoke your beloved Son, saying, "O Jesus, King of Love, I put my trust in your merciful goodness."

The Silence of Jesus

Father Mark Daniel Kirby, O.S.B.

The chief priests accused [Jesus] of many things. Again Pilate questioned him, "Have you no answer? See how many things they accuse you of." Jesus gave him no further answer, so that Pilate was amazed. (Mk 15: 3-5)

"See how the wicked string their bows,/ fit their arrows to the string/ to shoot from the shadows at the upright" (Ps 11: 2). To the amazement of Pilate, Jesus responds to the accusations of the chief priests with silence. The silence of Jesus sends the lies of his accusers, like so many barbed arrows, back into their own hearts. Their accusations cannot touch him, for lies have no hold upon Truth. In his silence, Jesus is in dialogue with his Father.

Nothing is less fruitful than dialogue with the Accuser, who is the devil, and with those who are in league with him. "He was a murderer from the beginning and does not stand in truth, because there is no truth in him. When he tells a lie, he speaks in character, because he is a liar and the father of lies" (Jn 8: 44).

Nothing is more fruitful than dialogue with God, the Father of lights, and with the angels who surround his throne, ready at every moment to execute his commands. "Whoever belongs to God," says Jesus, "hears the words of God" (Jn 8: 47).

All the martyrs, from Saint Polycarp († 155) to Blessed Jerzy Popieluszko († 1984), have found strength and grace in silence, not in the silence that signifies a breakdown of communication, but in the silence that opens onto communion with the Father, through the Son, in the Holy Spirit. Even when the martyrs speak, their words, like those of Jesus in his Passion, emerge from silence and return to it.

I have learned by experience that much speaking in times of suffering dissipates precious energy, and weakens the soul's ability to recollect herself in prayer. Silence, on the other hand, allows the soul to exercise more freely the gifts of fortitude and of counsel; silence is the language of the love that yearns for union.

Set a guard, O Father, before my mouth, and a gatekeeper at my lips, that I may keep my soul in silence, and become all attention to your Word.

In Imitation of the Lamb

Father Mark Daniel Kirby, O.S.B.

Now on the occasion of the feast [Pilate] used to release to them one prisoner whom they requested. A man called Barabbas was then in prison along with the rebels who had committed murder in a rebellion. The crowd came forward and began to ask him to do for them as he was accustomed. (Mk 15: 6-8)

"On the occasion of the feast": Saint Mark alludes again to the liturgical setting of our Lord's betrayal, condemnation, and sufferings. Jesus is the Passover Lamb, spotless and unblemished. The innocence of the Lamb of God shines out in contrast to the guilt of the man called Barabbas.

The crowd asks that the pardon customarily granted at Passover be given not to Jesus, but to Barabbas. Jesus thus takes upon himself the crushing weight of the crimes of Barabbas, of the murderous rebels in prison with him, and of the whole world. Jesus suffers: the Author of Life for murderers, the Just One for the unjust.

"Whenever," says Saint Peter, "anyone bears the pain of unjust suffering because of consciousness of God, that is a grace. But what credit is there if you are patient when beaten for doing wrong? But if you are patient when you suffer for doing what is good, this is a grace before God. For to this you have been called, because Christ also suffered for you, leaving you an example that you should follow in his footsteps" (1 Pt 2: 19-21).

The lives of the saints are a living commentary on every word of the Gospel. The saints are, in fact, those who, by suffering for doing what is good, follow in the footsteps of Christ. When, for example, in 1941, Saint Maximilian Maria Kolbe offered his life in exchange for that of a fellow prisoner in Auschwitz, he was following in the footsteps of Christ, the Lamb of God. In every age there are victim souls: men and women who, in imitation of Jesus, accept the chalice of suffering, so that others may be set free.

In the mysterious designs of God, such incomprehensible exchanges work justice where there is injustice, obtain pardon where there is but guilt, and, by turning back the wrath of God, open the floodgates of mercy.

Holy Father, your wisdom surpasses all that we can think or imagine, and your mercy is inexhaustible. Give us the grace to imitate Christ, the immolated Lamb, so that our sufferings may be united to his for the deliverance of souls from darkness, and the pardon of sinners.

345

Guarding My Thoughts

Father Mark Daniel Kirby, O.S.B.

Pilate answered, "Do you want me to release to you the king of the Jews?" For he knew that it was out of envy that the chief priests had handed him over. (Mk 15: 9-10)

D riven by envy, the chief priests deliver Jesus over to Pilate. Our Lord's own words are fulfilled: "He began to teach them that the Son of Man must suffer greatly and be rejected by the elders, the chief priests, and the scribes, and be killed, and rise after three days. He spoke this openly" (Mk 8: 31-32a).

Pilate himself sees that envy is the hidden motive of Jesus' arraignment. The goodness that radiates from Jesus, the compassion that shines from his face, and the healing power that goes forth from him to heal the sick, act as an irritant on the pride of the chief priests and scribes. Whereas the humble rejoice in the signs wrought by Jesus, to the proud the same signs are a cause of sadness. Sadness in the face of an incontrovertible good is the vice of envy. Envy unchecked becomes bitter hostility. Bitter hostility quickly escalates into a murderous hatred. "It was out of envy that the chief priests had handed him over" (Mk 15: 10).

A long ascetical tradition, beginning with the Fathers of the Desert, teaches me to be attentive to my thoughts. When I feel an irritant being rubbed into my pride, when another's good makes me sad, when another's misfortune makes me glad, I need to lay hold of my thoughts and dash them quickly against the rock who is Christ.

Thoughts intensify feelings. Feelings express themselves in words and in actions. By keeping guard over my thoughts, and by dashing every envious thought against the rock who is Christ, I am making room for "whatever is true, whatever is honorable, whatever is just, whatever is pure, whatever is lovely, whatever is gracious" (Phil 4: 8).

In this way, almost imperceptibly, but surely, do the fruits of the Holy Spirit germinate day after day, and blossom, and begin to mature.

Merciful Father, make us watchful over the thoughts of our hearts, that we may dash against the rock who is Christ all that is evil, and preserved from envy, rejoice in all that is good.

Compunction

Father Mark Daniel Kirby, O.S.B.

But the chief priests stirred up the crowd to have him release
Barabbas for them instead. Pilate again said to them in reply,
"Then what [do you want] me to do with [the man you call]
the king of the Jews?" They shouted again, "Crucify him."
(Mk 15: 11-13)

The shout of the crowd, "Crucify him!" resonates, year after
year, in the Holy Week liturgy of the Church. One cannot
sing it or hear it sung, read it or hear it read, without being
inwardly pierced. Again, making the Way of the Cross, the same
shout strikes the ear of the heart at the First Station, "Jesus is condemned to death."

God so speaks his word in Sacred Scripture, in the liturgy of
the Church, and in personal meditation, that often it cuts into the
heart, opening there a wound of repentance and of love. This grace
of compunction – an inward piercing of the heart – can, at times,
cause tears to flow. Tears of compunction are a grace; they disin-
fect the heart, heal the effects of sin, and strengthen one's resolve
to walk in newness of life.

It happened (in thirteenth-century Saxony) that Saint Gertrude
the Great was acutely distressed at being unable to satisfy her
desire for a relic of the wood of the cross. Bringing her want to
Jesus in prayer, she heard him say, "Friend of my heart, there are
no relics more precious than the words of Sacred Scripture that
recount my sufferings. If you would have a relic of my cross, fix
your mind upon my Passion, learn the words of the Gospels and
cling to them, for you can possess no relics more wonderful than
the words that came forth from my heart."

An intimate familiarity with the Passion of Jesus as recounted in
the Gospels will dispose you to the grace of compunction. Compunction, in turn, opens a wellspring of tears in the depths of the
soul. Even when these tears do not moisten your cheeks, they are
softening your heart and allowing you to receive the impression of
the word. Seek this grace, and draw near to the Crucified.

Eternal Father, let the shout of the crowd, "Crucify him!" so pierce
my heart, that I may recognize in it all the malice of my sins, and
sorrow over them with tears of repentant love.

What Evil Has He Done?

Father Mark Daniel Kirby, O.S.B.

Pilate said to [the crowd], "Why? What evil has he done?"
They only shouted the louder, "Crucify him."
(Mk 15: 14)

Pilate asks the raging crowd to justify their cries for Jesus' crucifixion. Caught up in a hellish frenzy, the crowd roars in reply again and again, "Crucify him."

Focus for a moment on the Face of Jesus: the shining icon of innocence and of love in the midst of the encroaching darkness. The gaze of Jesus is disarming. Those who dare to meet it are, in fact, obliged to disarm themselves. Those who expose themselves to the Face of Jesus risk being judged by his innocence, stilled by his silence, humbled by his meekness. The crowd, being incapable of meeting the gaze of the Lamb, chooses blindness over seeing. And Pilate acquiesces to their unseeing hatred.

Contemplation of the Face of Christ opens the soul to the light of truth. He who stands before Pilate, he whom the raging crowd would soon see hanging from a cross, says, "Whoever believes in me believes not only in me but also in the one who sent me, and whoever sees me sees the one who sent me" (Jn 12: 44-45). By refusing to put their faith in Jesus, those who demand his crucifixion choose darkness over light. By rejecting Jesus, they reject the Father. By spurning the Father, they choose death over life.

Contemplation of the Face of Christ illuminates the soul with the light of hope. "I came into the world as light," says Jesus, "so that everyone who believes in me might not remain in darkness. And if anyone hears my words and does not observe them, I do not condemn him, for I did not come to condemn the world but to save the world" (Jn 12: 46-47). Even in the hour of his own condemnation, Jesus remains the Savior of the world. A single glance of faith and hope, directed toward his Face, is enough to unite the soul to him in a living bond of love.

Father of lights with whom there is no variation or shadow due to change, open the eyes of my soul to the Face of your beloved Son, that in gazing upon him, I may believe in him; and that believing in him, I may rejoice in hope, and abide in love.

Jesus Handed Over

Father Mark Daniel Kirby, O.S.B.

So Pilate, wishing to satisfy the crowd, released Barabbas to them and, after he had Jesus scourged, handed him over to be crucified. (Mk 15: 15)

By order of Pilate, Jesus is scourged; then, robed in the priestly vesture of his own blood, he is handed over to be crucified. Had Jesus not handed himself over to the will of the Father, Judas could not have handed him over to the chief priests and scribes, and Pilate could not have handed him over to be crucified.

The Passion of our Lord is a sacrifice that he embraces freely from within. "This," says Jesus, "is why the Father loves me, because I lay down my life in order to take it up again. No one takes it from me, but I lay it down on my own. I have power to lay it down, and power to take it up again" (Jn 10: 17-18).

Jesus enters his Passion willingly, as a priest, prepared to offer sacrifice, approaches the altar. The liturgy of our Lord's priestly sacrifice begins, in effect, at the very moment of his incarnation in the womb of the Blessed Virgin Mary. Thus do we read in the Letter to the Hebrews: "When he came into the world, he said: 'Sacrifice and offering you did not desire,/ but a body you prepared for me;/ holocausts and sin offerings you took no delight in./ Then I said, "As is written of me in the scroll,/ Behold, I come to do your will, O God"'" (Heb 10: 5-7).

"The Son of Man indeed goes," says Jesus, "as it is written of him" (Mk 14: 21). Already, in the Upper Room, the ancient paschal sacrifices give way to the one sacrifice of the true and everlasting victim without blemish, "the Lamb of God who takes away the sin of the world" (Jn 1: 29). The temple priesthood, too, passes away, giving place to the one High Priest who, after offering himself at table in the Upper Room, will offer himself on Calvary from the altar of the cross and, then, eternally in the sanctuary of heaven.

Most merciful Father, by the grace of the Holy Spirit, unite me to the sacrifice of your only-begotten Son, our eternal high priest, that with him and cleansed in his blood, I may be lifted up to you as one single oblation perfect and pleasing in your sight.

Divine Satire

Father Anthony Giambrone, O.P.

*The soldiers led [Jesus] away inside the palace, that is,
the praetorium, and assembled the whole cohort.
They clothed him in purple and, weaving a crown
of thorns, placed it on him. (Mk 15: 16-17)*

The Roman poet Juvenal declared: "*Difficile est saturam non scribere*," "It's hard not to write satire." The world is maddeningly upside-down and even relishes standing on its head. The absurd offense plainly beckons some shot of moral irony.

If there is any moment in the Gospels worthy of a Juvenal's art, it is here in the praetorium. The Third Sorrowful Mystery is compact with untold irony, as the world blindly celebrates its own insane inversion. The King, anointed by the unction of the Father at the Jordan, is at last crowned by humankind in an act of unimaginable insubordination. The scene is monstrous – far more grotesque than the discrete, pious images we've so often seen: two or three soldiers simply having their cruel fun. In fact, a whole Roman cohort is assembled against the Lord in the grand staging of a mock acclamation.

To be sure, the wild disproportion of this military display is not purposeless amplification. It means quite clearly to cast Christ as a Caesar; for we must recall that the army made the emperors. The title, it is true, will be "King of the Jews" – but the mode of mocking is a Roman conceit. Whereas the Jewish kings were heirs by descent and the high priests' taunt will target Jesus' "blasphemous" claims, the Romans reverenced commanding power as their principle of rule and they thus parody the Lord's inglorious weakness. He is "an unarmed prophet," to borrow a line from Machiavelli.

The truth, of course, is that Jesus, bound and insulted, has tied his own hands. "Do you think that I cannot call upon my Father and he will not provide me at this moment with more than twelve legions of angels?" (Mt 26: 53). This misguided world is upside-down, and the Lord couldn't resist *his own parody*: treading underfoot the golden crowns of human glory to wreathe his head in a diadem of thorns.

Father, you alone are the Lord. All things are in your power and you have dominion over all. Give me the grace to see through this world's perverse pretenses and to reverence your inversion of our twisted values.

Hail to the King

Father Anthony Giambrone, O.P.

[The soldiers] began to salute [Jesus] with, "Hail, King of the Jews!" and kept striking his head with a reed and spitting upon him. They knelt before him in homage. And when they had mocked him, they stripped him of the purple cloak, dressed him in his own clothes, and led him out to crucify him. (Mk 15: 18-20)

The soldiers' mockery of Christ is strangely contained. It is almost a theatrical interlude. The men let loose a violent rush of derision, then suddenly pack up their props and get back to their bloody business.

If (as seems quite certain) the abuse of a prisoner was a kind of informal ritual – the sort of overlooked illegality that kept the grunts happy – this only highlights the indiscriminate malice hurled at the Lord. Clearly the soldiers know the royal charge against him, and this greatly piques their genius for taunting. Still, there is a strong suggestion of sweeping racism in their fun, and one cannot resist the impression that these men would have been quite as happy to beat the head of poor Barabbas, had the fatal lot that day fallen the other way. In a very real sense, Jesus was simply filling a role, taking in the face the full-forced mockery of the Jewish people. It is the horrible shame heaped on God's elect that the Christ bears here in silence. Like the miserable kings of old, cruelly abused and deported from Jerusalem, the Son of David now takes his seat on the fallen throne of his nation to endure ridicule from the pagans, be led outside of the city, and die as a pretender in exile.

The solidarity of Jesus with the humiliated kings of his line is his solidarity with the fate of all his chosen people. Though by nature we are sinners from the Gentiles, by grace we are numbered among God's elect. It is thus also our shame that Christ here sanctifies; for against the new Israel, the *world* harbors, not a racism according to the flesh, but a hatred on the order of the spirit. As Christians we are mocked as a matter of course. If we have never tasted the sting of this ridicule, perhaps our allegiance to the King is unclear.

Father in heaven, your Son was obedient unto death, heedless of the shame. Give me the strength to be a bold Christian. Help me endure the world's mockery and hatred, and learn obedience through what I suffer.

Coming in from the Country

Father Anthony Giambrone, O.P.

*[The soldiers] pressed into service a passer-by, Simon,
a Cyrenian, who was coming in from the country, the father
of Alexander and Rufus, to carry [Jesus'] cross. (Mk 15: 21)*

I n the best chapter of his best novel, Charles Williams (the Ringo Starr of the Inklings) develops what he calls "The Doctrine of Substituted Love." The idea, simply, is that Paul was deadly serious when he told us to "bear one another's burdens" (Gal 6: 2). The communion of saints, he avers, somehow allows the power of Christian love to penetrate even the spiritual burdens of others. We can thus come to the direct relief of those around us through a mere act of the will, the decision to enter charitably in and *experience* the weight we see pressing down upon them.

This doctrine of substitution has a clear patron in Simon of Cyrene. What is so puzzlingly paradoxical, however, is that *Jesus* is the true vicarious victim at the Fifth Station. Simon shoulders the cross, and bears the Lord's burden; yet it is Christ who bears the iniquity of us all – including the sins of Simon.

In one way, Simon's righteous deed exposes the mystery of Christ's failing human nature. Through no sin and no fallen imperfection, the Lord's sacred manhood is debased to the point of need. The cross is too heavy. At another level, though, Jesus' encounter with Simon reveals that the doctrine of substituted love derives its viability from the insertion of Simon's action into the larger substitution enacted by the Lord. In the mechanics of redemption, Christ leaves a space open for others to play his vicarious role.

The impressing of Simon makes his service uncertain, yet the experience evidently transformed him. His sons became Christians, known to Mark's readers. If we choose to bear one another's burdens, we too will be transformed; for we will become participants in the mystery of redemption. We need only selflessly substitute the misfortunes of others for our well-earned trip home from the fields.

Heavenly Father, strengthen me when I am tired and self-centered. Open my heart to the troubles of others, and transform me by the power of compassion and love.

The Smile of Satan

Father Anthony Giambrone, O.P.

[The soldiers] brought [Jesus] to the place of Golgotha (which is translated Place of the Skull). They gave him wine drugged with myrrh, but he did not take it. (Mk 15: 22-23)

I once had a professor who advertised his exams by hanging the Jolly Roger. While I do suspect he felt some regret at not following the career of a pirate, the ostensible point was simply to shiver our timbers in fright at what was before us.

The skull, of course, is the face of death. It is a banner flown to conjure fear, to confront us head-on with our human mortality. Golgotha is thus the fitting sign for this chosen ground, this mountain where the cross is staked like a claim; for here, on the field of the Skull, Christ combats Death: *mors et vita duello conflixere mirando*. The marvelous conflict is no metaphor, nor is the ghoulish grin of this place a mere geological quirk. Pure malice and perverse delight haunt this hill, and an evil Agent greedily lurks here, ready to rob the human species of Life.

"God did not make death,/ nor does he rejoice in the destruction of the living... By the envy of the devil, death entered the world" (Wis 1: 13; 2: 24). Satan is the predator, the primal pirate and murderer from the beginning; and it is his wicked smile which creeps across Calvary. It is he who stripped humankind of original justice and he who would hijack God's incarnation and run it into death and oblivion.

Death smiles at us all. It silently mocks with a calm air of assurance. "No one escapes me." Whenever the fever of fear grips us, it is this induced terror of final defeat; for all fear is fear of death. Yet we know that Satan's smile will rot in the end, and every threat that he makes is a lie. Jesus enters the jaws of the beast, swallowed by the earth in a hungry fit of destruction. But as in the medieval pictures, Christ will swing open the monstrous maw of hell, leading out Adam and Eve by the hand.

Father, help me to unmask the lies of the Evil One. Overcome my fear of failure, lead me to the place of your cross, and help me trust that death has no sting for the Christian.

Gaming for Heaven

Father Anthony Giambrone, O.P.

*Then [the soldiers] crucified [Jesus] and divided his garments
by casting lots for them to see what each should take.*
(Mk 15: 24)

I t is a startling narrative stroke that Christ's crucifixion gets less
than half a sentence. All the detail and description goes to the
garments, as if to underscore by imbalance the rank inhuman-
ity of giving more attention to a man's clothes than his life.

We might dwell on this judgment of *worthlessness* passed on the
death of our Lord. To the eyes of those who killed him, Jesus of
Nazareth was a penniless pretender who left to this world only the
clothes on his back. Dice played executor of his estate. If indeed
Christ was expendable, innocent but expedient, a peasant born
to die at the whim of some or another misfortune – if indeed the
kingdom of God had nothing to do with the life of this "King," it
is right that *chance* should thus have had the last word. The envy
of the high priests, the greed of Judas, the fear of Pilate, and the
shouts of the crowd – a thousand sub-rational reasons put this
poor man on the cross.

Chance, though, is a creature and subject to God's direction:
an elemental power marshalling under its influence a vast coun-
ter-history, the fallen mastermind and author of all irrational action, yet destined in the end to bow to God's own wisdom. For
providence works its way and orders all things sweetly; and with
due respect to Dr. Einstein, God does play dice in the Acts of the
Apostles.

Christ hangs on the cross for a reason. The very value of his
divesture, of his abject material poverty reveals the deep mystery
of his death. "For your sake he became poor although he was rich,
so that by his poverty you might become rich" (2 Cor 8: 9). We are
the ones who inherit the true treasure bequeathed from the cross.
He gave his divine life that we'd be clothed in immortality. May we
be greedy as the soldiers to win and wear that wedding garment.

*God our Father, you order all things sweetly by your Word. When
confusion and disorder seem to reign in my life, give me the grace
to find peace in the wisdom of the cross.*

An Unalterable Inscription
Father Anthony Giambrone, O.P.

It was nine o'clock in the morning when [the soldiers] crucified [Jesus]. The inscription of the charge against him read, "The King of the Jews." (Mk 15: 25-26)

There is a magnificent scene in Bernanos' *Diary of a Country Priest* where the young curé perceives that the seditious whispering against him has not been driven by lying rumors. He is slandered with no false charge, but simply hated for being who he is and misunderstood for doing what he did. For Bernanos this sketches a key mystery of the priestly identity: Christ was rejected for who he truly was, and so must all be who act *in persona Christi*.

The charge "King of the Jews" is no crime. It is a chosen role, prosecuted (or persecuted) only by those who stand outside of the kingdom. In John's Gospel, the chief priests understand this well and scramble to rewrite themselves back into the center. "Do not write 'King of the Jews,' but that he said, 'I am the King of the Jews.' Pilate answered, 'What I have written, I have written'" (Jn 19: 21-22). In handing to the nations the Davidic Messiah, they hand over their right to his kingdom.

The irreversible inscription of this *titulus* thus promulgates a sentence on Christ's executioners. This irony need not rally a hue and cry of deicide. It shows, however, that rejecting the Lord is not without consequence for the covenant. If Israel thus fails and forgoes its inheritance, this deed redrafts the testament. The kingdom of the Jews as a Jewish conceit has been handed to the nations to destroy. Jesus dies despised, King of the Jews, but rises to reign, King of kings.

Christ is thus our King. But do we reject him? Do we indict the Lord's meekness and charge him with not acting in power? If we do, we oppose not what he should be but what he is; and we write for ourselves our own sentence. Let us then love our Lord for his meekness, for what he has written, he has meekly written: our name with nails on the palms of his hands (Is 49: 16).

Father, your Son Jesus is truly King of kings and Lord of lords. Help me never resent suffering, but reverence and worship his humble reign and follow him on the path to his cross.

The Balance of Salvation

Father Anthony Giambrone, O.P.

With [Jesus] [the soldiers] crucified two revolutionaries,
one on his right and one on his left. (Mk 15: 27)

Early Christians enjoyed the untold tales of cameo characters. Thus we have some unlikely accounts starring Jesus'
two associates: Saint Dismas, the Good Thief, and Gestas,
his rotten friend.

The desire to know more about these men in particular is quite
understandable. After all, it is hardly an incidental thing to be
there on Calvary sharing the exact same fate as the Savior of the
world. What should one make of it? From one perspective, the
idea that Jesus' redeeming death must share the stage and even ac-
commodate itself to a routine round of political executions gives
the whole scene a peculiar insignificance and contingency. Mary
was not the only mother mourning that day, and there are other
stories one could tell of Good Friday in which *Jesus* would have
the cameo role.

The legends, however, all lead to one place; and the traditional
instinct is theologically sound: the lives of these thieves, whoever
they were, only make sense when they finally meet Jesus. The im-
plication is broad, and Mark is wise to preserve the men's anonym-
ity, for these two represent the whole human race. Every human
life, our lives, finally wind down to this shared fate of death for
our sins, when we will find ourselves pinned up on account of
our guilt. In the end we are all rebels. The decisive question will
be how we address that man in our midst. Why does he share our
fate? Is he just another like us, doomed to die a miserable death?

The slanted footrest on Russian crosses is tilted like a scale, up-
wards to the right, signaling salvation for Dismas, and downwards
to the left, portending Gestas' trip to Gehenna. Jesus' cross is the
fulcrum of the balance of salvation. We are weighed on its beam,
not by merit but a promise. Let us beg for that promise in faith,
hope, and love, with Dismas who knew that Jesus was just.

Father in heaven, help me believe that your crucified Son is truly
the King of heaven, and help me put all my hope in his promise.
Above all, help me in love to comfort Jesus in his sufferings.

The Temple of the Cross

Father Anthony Giambrone, O.P.

*Those passing by reviled [Jesus], shaking their heads and saying,
"Aha! You who would destroy the temple and rebuild it in three
days, save yourself by coming down from the cross."*
(Mk 15: 29-30)

The head shaking of the passers-by is their "No" to the sign of the cross. Whatever they thought of his rumored stunt – destroying and rebuilding the temple – it is now clear that this naked man on a tree was overplayed. The crushing humiliation of Jesus' crucifixion kills any imagination that he holds some wondrous and ultimate power.

The irony, of course, is that the very taunt the crowds hurl is the key which unlocks this stumbling block of a sign. Unlike John, Mark lets the riddle stand; but we know the answer. Jesus' body is the Temple, because it bears the Presence. This thought is heavy with meaning. It makes Christ's Paschal Mystery into a kind of a Ring Cycle, a condensed three-day telling of Israel's great national story, from covenantal trauma to final vindication. As God abandoned Israel to Babylon, so the Father abandons Jesus to the Romans. But as the razed temple was remade, so will the true Dwelling of Christ's body rise again.

Christ lives through the history of his people. To call the Lord down from the cross is thus to ask him to halt his solidarity. We must recall this when we find sanctified suffering unworthy of true divine power. The cross is not the Lord's invention; it was manufactured by man as a prodigy of evil. It is an emblem of what creatures have made of creation, and for Jesus to hang helpless upon it is his tasting our own helplessness before this wreck we have made of the world.

We build crosses, while God makes temples. We may wish that we had never fallen, but suffering cannot be denied, nor will Christ's solidarity be stopped. The sign of God's power is not in forsaking our tragedy and springing down from the tree, but in rebuilding our cross as his temple. May we worship his Presence in our suffering, for truly "something greater than the temple is here" (Mt 12: 6).

Father, help me accept the sign of the cross. Give me the grace to recognize suffering as a holy temple of your presence so that I might enter and endure it with gratitude and awe.

The Simony of Assent

Father Anthony Giambrone, O.P.

Likewise the chief priests, with the scribes, mocked [Jesus] among themselves and said, "He saved others; he cannot save himself. Let the Messiah, the King of Israel, come down now from the cross that we may see and believe." Those who were crucified with him also kept abusing him. (Mk 15: 31-32)

The chief priests and scribes imagine that they can set their own conditions for faith. "Come down now from the cross that we may see and believe." These men seem to suppose that some certain measure of evidence will simply bring its own convicting power. With a sign sufficiently potent, faith will freely flow.

This idea is no private conceit. It is an almost irresistible human inclination. We make our belief a bargaining chip, to curb God's behavior to our own expectations. So long as God acts as we imagine a God to be, we are ready to acknowledge his lordship. The problem, of course, is that to agree to such terms limits God's wisdom to the weak imagination of our own miniscule minds. It makes *us* the craftsmen who mold the divine image, which means it is simply idolatry: the worship of a god in our power.

Faith is not for leverage, nor does God gain from our consent to his claims. The gift of believing is a treasure for us, a grace that opens our tiny, weak minds to the massive horizon of divine wisdom. To be stingy in believing is, then, not to be shrewd or discerning; it is the bankruptcy of rejecting the Truth, the folly of confounding docility and credulity.

Jesus, in the parable of poor Lazaraus, speaks of those who prostitute faith for a sign. "If someone from the dead goes to them, they will repent," insists the rich man. To which father Abraham responds: "If they will not listen to Moses and the prophets, neither will they be persuaded if someone should rise from the dead" (Lk 16: 30-31). Faith is a gift of God; one word is enough to conceive it. But our Lord must show himself as he truly is, and not as we would buy him. It is for us to pray to be given faith, not pretend it is ours to dispense.

God our Father, give me faith to believe the truth of your Word. Let me never put you to the test, but welcome your revelation with grateful joy.

Amid the Blaze of Noon

Father Anthony Giambrone, O.P.

At noon darkness came over the whole land until three in the afternoon. And at three o'clock Jesus cried out in a loud voice, "Eloi, Eloi, lema sabachthani?" which is translated, "My God, my God, why have you forsaken me?" (Mk 15: 33-34)

There is a famous Della Robbia of the crucifixion in which the sun has become a dramatic mask of mourning. The Great Light which rules the day cannot bear to look, cannot bathe in light this treachery against the Creator. Primordial darkness returns, and there is a halt in the fixed times, the days, and the years.

This is the dream "hour." This is the moment beyond all time, when the Son and eternal radiance of the Father is extinguished, veiled in death. A cosmic blackout drapes the world, and the grim shadow penetrates even Jesus' human heart. "My God, my God, why have you forsaken me?"

"Dark, dark, dark, dark, amid the blaze of noon/ irrecoverably dark, total eclipse/ without all hope of day." Like Milton's blind Samson, the Lord is stripped of his strength, cast out and abused, a plaything for the pagans. God plays the buffoon before men. What devastating confusion! He who was anointed from the womb to judge captive Israel is shrouded in death and failure.

What miscalculation has brought Christ to this fate? Has the Father forgotten his Son? If vision yields no answer, the verdict of love cannot waver. No distance or darkness can break its bond. "Can a mother forget her infant,/ be without tenderness for the child of her womb?/ Even should she forget,/ I will never forget you" (Is 49: 15).

The eyes of Samson (a name which means "sun") were gouged, but a light still burns for the Lord. The Sacred Heart of Jesus – that core mystery of the incarnation which reduces to human proportions all the infinite love of God – this anguished heart still burns with the fire of charity and sees by a daystar stronger than the sun. The cross drenches the world in a light too bright to bear. Unbelieving eyes are dazzled when, like Samson, the hero Christ stretches out his arms in one final deed of valor.

Father, when you feel distant, fire my heart with deeper love. Let me see the proof of your presence in the pledge Christ has made on the cross.

Toasting the Kingdom

Father Anthony Giambrone, O.P.

Some of the bystanders who heard it said, "Look, he is calling Elijah." One of them ran, soaked a sponge with wine, put it on a reed, and gave it to [Jesus] to drink, saying, "Wait, let us see if Elijah comes to take him down." (Mk 15: 35-36)

This is really one of the strangest scenes in the Gospel. What precise logic moves us from Jesus calling on Elijah (a curious idea in itself) to some man taking the peculiar step of hastily offering the Lord wine on a sponge?

Often, the man's beverage service is simply seen as a kind act, a little ray of light in the Passion; but this hardly explains the context. It is more helpful to recognize that at some point (we are not sure exactly when) Jewish Passover meals began to include a cup of wine reserved for Elijah. It was the fifth cup of the Seder meal, a cup never drunk but left waiting for the messianic era.

Just before he was nailed up, Jesus refused the offer of some drugged wine (a kind of cigarette before the firing squad). Mark gives no hint of whether Jesus drinks this wine here or not. If we follow John, though, the Lord does indeed sip it. This is not a capitulation to the wrenching pain of the cross. Jesus drinks the wine now, because "It is finished" (Jn 19: 30). By the immolation of the true paschal Lamb, the messianic era has now been consummated and the exodus begun. Jesus' proclamation at his last Seder has been fulfilled: "I shall not drink again the fruit of the vine until the day when I drink it new in the kingdom of God" (Mk 14: 25).

Every year at Passover, faithful Jews set a place for Elijah, pour him a cup of wine, and open the door to receive him: a beautiful witness to their eager expectation of the messianic kingdom. The urgent "Wait, let us see…" still lingers in their hearts; yet by faith we know that "Elijah has come" (Mk 9: 13). May we be so eager to celebrate the joyful arrival of the kingdom, as these faithful bystanders are ready to welcome and toast it one day.

Heavenly Father, give me a spirit of joy. Support me with a deeper awareness of the power and presence of your reign. Comfort me with the announced arrival of your kingdom.

The Breath of His Mouth

Father Anthony Giambrone, O.P.

*Jesus gave a loud cry and breathed his last. The veil of
the sanctuary was torn in two from top to bottom. When
the centurion who stood facing him saw how he breathed
his last he said, "Truly this man was the Son of God!"*
(Mk 15: 37-39)

M ark's Gospel abruptly began with the baptism of Jesus by
John. That dramatic scene was vividly described as a literal "tearing" of the heavens. The sky was ripped open,
the Spirit released, and the Father's voice was heard: "You are my
beloved Son; with you I am well pleased" (Mk 1: 11).

As at "the beginning of the gospel of Jesus Christ [the Son of
God]" (Mk 1: 1), so now again at the end, we behold a portentous
tear. And again, it is a rending of the heavens; for the temple veil
mentioned was (according to Josephus, the first-century Jewish
historian) a grand tapestry wrought in blue and exquisitely spun
with a depiction of all the starry sky. John's baptism obliterated a
barrier between the realms of heaven and earth, for it had opened
the way for the Son of God to announce the coming of the kingdom. On the cross, the final screen separating the holiness of God's
presence from the unclean world outside is completely destroyed.
The kingdom is let loose from the sanctuary.

The pairing of Jesus' baptism with his cross recalls John's prophecy: "I have baptized you with water; he will baptize you with the
holy Spirit" (Mk 1: 8). Christ's baptism is in his last breath; for it
was no normal death gasp, but the pouring forth of his Spirit. Indeed, it is this momentous breath that stuns the centurion (a man
familiar with death) and elicits his amazing confession.

Where the Lord sends forth his Spirit, uncleanness is driven like
chaff before the wind; and when the breath of Christ baptized this
pagan soldier with faith, the old dividing wall was toppled. There
is much impurity still alive in our hearts. We are still strangers to
the temple of his Presence. May God's Spirit blow through our
outer-courts and make them holy, until our every breath resounds
in that Spirit: "Truly Jesus Christ is the Son of God!"

*Father in heaven, at the dawn of creation you blew your breath
into man and made him a living creature. Blow your Spirit into
me now that I might come to new life in holiness.*

361

Affection and Service

Father Vincent Nagle, F.S.C.B.

There were also women looking on from a distance. Among them were Mary Magdalene, Mary the mother of the younger James and of Joses, and Salome. These women had followed [Jesus] when he was in Galilee and ministered to him. There were also many other women who had come up with him to Jerusalem. (Mk 15: 40-41)

An American with long experience running an educational institution in Palestine asked me a question that took me by surprise: "Well, you have had a lot of experience in the Middle East. Why it is that women seem to be generally so much more, ummm, 'efficient' than men in this culture? Why is it that, if you really need a practical job to get done well, it is often better to hire a woman?"

In a tribal culture, the status of a family is a more important factor to the welfare of all its members than we in the West can easily understand, and that status is represented by the man. While what a man can do matters, it does so relatively less than for the woman. The position the man holds in the family or in society is what tends to give status to the man and through him to his whole family. Women, on the other hand, tend to be raised with a view to their practical abilities and the ability to respond to the real needs around them.

So when Saint Mark talks to us about these women from Galilee who ministered to Jesus, we can well imagine how grateful our Lord was to them. While the men, urged on by the women of their families, vied for status in his company (Mk 10: 37; Mt 20: 21), these women sought to be useful to him in the here and now and were not preoccupied with how Jesus could be useful to their status. And, as we see in these holy women, this is where our affection for him has the opportunity to grow, in serving him practically in the needs of those around us. May God grant that our status be born of the affection between the Lord and ourselves that comes through service.

Father of all, I desire to grow more rooted in your kingdom. Help me to choose the path of these women, simple service to your Son's suffering body, through the same Jesus Christ our Lord.

Courage Born of Expectation

Father Vincent Nagle, F.S.C.B.

When it was already evening, since it was the day of preparation, the day before the sabbath, Joseph of Arimathea, a distinguished member of the council, who was himself awaiting the kingdom of God, came and courageously went to Pilate and asked for the body of Jesus. (Mk 15: 42-43)

One of the stories that made a particular impression on my younger brothers and me as we grew up was about a brother and sister who, in a dreamlike world, twice have to negotiate a maze of choices. The first time around, frightened and bewildered by this unexpected situation, they choose in an instinctual and reactive manner, grabbing at anything that attracts their attention and running from what seems painful. They end up facing only options that are repulsive. The second time around, later in the story, they help each other always to keep in mind the deepest desires of their hearts, and so take courage to choose carefully even the things that seem difficult in light of what they hope for. In this way they end up in front of options that are mysteriously beautiful far beyond their childlike imaginings.

This connection between a deep expectation of something that we are hoping for, and finding our courage in the face of fearful circumstances is what we see in Joseph of Arimathea. Saint Mark makes a point of telling us that Joseph was "awaiting the kingdom of God," and that he was "courageous." The two are linked. Without the expectation that comes from believing in something greater that has been promised, we are afraid of losing what is in front of us, and we grasp and squeeze. Similarly, we cannot see beyond the pain of difficulties, and we run the other way, not having the patience to understand what goodness these painful things may lead to. Joseph is described as having "fear" of the circumstances he found himself in (Jn 19: 38), yet it is his "awaiting," his choosing in light of the promise he believes in, that allows him to see past the darkness and danger and choose the road to salvation. May our expectation grow, and so too our courage to live without enslavement to our circumstances.

Father, free me from my cowardice by filling me with the expectation of meeting Jesus here and now, ready to welcome his kingdom, for he lives and reigns for ever and ever.

True Strength

Father Vincent Nagle, F.S.C.B.

Pilate was amazed that [Jesus] was already dead. He summoned
the centurion and asked him if Jesus had already died.
And when he learned of it from the centurion, he gave
the body to Joseph. (Mk 15: 44-45)

I remember a little elderly woman whom I met as I was doing sick rounds in the hospital. I can still see that special sparkle in her eyes, that tired but welcoming smile, and still feel the warmth of her fragile hands. She was one of those people you do not easily forget. She was physically frail and had no particular air of command. But what she did have was a remarkable sense of peace in her sickness, a grateful acceptance. She had been ill for a long time and lived a kind of contemplative life of prayer with her Nigerian housekeeper of many years. They were more than sisters. When she finally died and her body was taken away, instead of people feeling tired from all the energy they had expended in caring for this person, they felt that this strange patient had somehow given them strength. Her death was much less of a battle lost than a joyful offering completed. It is a kind of strength that the world is not used to seeing.

While the struggle to survive can very much impress us, and human endeavor can overcome many obstacles, this was a different kind of strength.

But what is strength? Pilate, a man of power, considers himself very well qualified to answer that question. He knows that quality when he sees it. He saw it in the strange man from Nazareth, but he interpreted Jesus' strength as he usually finds it – a will to survive and conquer. However, the infinite strength of Jesus is of a different sort. It is, like the grace that he granted to that woman in the hospital, the strength of belonging, of a serene consigning himself to the Father.

Pilate is shocked because he expected a long struggle against death. Instead, our Lord's victory is a free act of laying his life down for his sheep, placing himself into the hands of the Father.

Father, you see how I am obsessed with "winning." Let me instead
imitate the true strength that I meet in your Son, who consigned
himself to your loving will.

A Hidden Gesture

Father Vincent Nagle, F.S.C.B.

Having bought a linen cloth, [Joseph] took [Jesus] down, wrapped him in the linen cloth and laid him in a tomb that had been hewn out of the rock. Then he rolled a stone against the entrance to the tomb. (Mk 15: 46)

Today, one of the objections to the claim that the Shroud of Turin is the very burial cloth of Jesus of Nazareth is that it is made of a weave that is far finer and more costly than the usual cloths used for burial during the period. Should it be otherwise?

The gesture of Joseph of Arimathea is extravagant, and, apparently, hidden, even as his discipleship has been (Jn 19: 38). Though rich (Mt 27: 57) and a member of the council who nonetheless disapproved of the council's treatment of Jesus (Lk 23: 51), yet he did not manage, nor perhaps even attempt, because of his fear, to save his secret master. With what deep sentiments of sorrow, shame, and desire for reparation does he choose the cloth for the burial? Even as his discipleship has been kept secret, so too, perhaps, does he believe that this last, seemingly late, and useless gesture will be covered by the earth, never to see the light of day. Would he not choose the best kind of cloth, not just the usual, for such a gesture?

But such gestures of compassion have a way of coming to light. Unseen acts of mercy in the name of Christ can, through God's providence, live on in ways that those who perform them in love can hardly expect.

It fills us with sympathy for Joseph, this man who came forward – after what seemed to be the end – to embrace his Lord. Now this gesture, giving a wildly expensive cloth as a burial shroud, which must have seemed undiscoverable and gratuitous, is on display for all the world to see in Italy. Is there any act of ours, no matter how buried, carried out in the name of our Lord, out of compassion for his suffering humanity, that our Father in heaven does not make use of for the building up of his kingdom?

Father, let me always be conscious of living under your compassionate gaze, so that even far from the gaze of others, I might act as a servant of your mercy, which we meet in your Son.

The Power of Silent Witness

Father Vincent Nagle, F.S.C.B.

*Mary Magdalene and Mary the mother of Joses
watched where [Jesus] was laid. (Mk 15: 47)*

A distant cousin, with whom I had only a passing familiarity, and I were just starting as students at a university institute for Great Books – in fact classes had not yet begun – when her father suddenly died. I was a little shocked to see the staff of this institute, where we had only just enrolled, show up at the funeral which was at least an hour's drive from the university. The institute staff knew no one there. Yet, because it was a student's father, they had come.

One might think that being at the funeral of someone you had never met, and whose relatives you only barely knew, would be a little senseless. It was not. I was surprised to see how much it meant to everyone there, including me.

How could their presence mean so much? To place oneself as a witness to the burial of the dead, even when there is nothing to be done and little or nothing that can be said, is a powerful gesture. The eyes of those who stand in prayerful solidarity are visible signs of the eye of our God in heaven who has not forgotten, who is not absent, and who is even now guiding the journey of the deceased to judgment and eternity.

These women, Mary Magdalene and the others, still fully under the shock of the day's events, standing there in the evening's unnatural obscurity, were just such witnesses. Their stance was neither passive nor helpless. It was an active gesture stating that even now, when all seemed to be at an end, God's judgment was in play. Men of violence might have tortured and crucified their adored master, but the story was still being written in the judgment of the Father. This was their silent certainty. May it be ours as well.

Father, you have sent your Son so that your children might be with you for ever. May we rejoice in being able to stand as witnesses to him through whom you save the world.

Small Tasks, Great Mystery

Father Vincent Nagle, F.S.C.B.

When the sabbath was over, Mary Magdalene, Mary,
the mother of James, and Salome bought spices so that they
might go and anoint [Jesus]. Very early when the sun had risen,
on the first day of the week, they came to the tomb.
(Mk 16: 1-2)

Though I've never been very talented at manual work, in my youth I put in thousands of hours trying to get good at it. So, it took me by surprise to discover an unexpected dimension to a straightforward task, beyond the satisfactions of skill and accomplishment (something I rarely experienced in any case due to my awkwardness). I was working with a friend wrestling wrenches in order to dismantle a structure on a river bed, closing down for the summer a camp where we had been working. Sweating together over this task at the end of a long hot day of physical labor, I was struck by the powerful sense of intimacy that this practically wordless alliance forged. It was as if undertaking this simple yet arduous job was our opportunity to engage the mystery that unites us. I have never forgotten since then that obedience to the mundane tasks of life is a way to open myself to the mystery that is creating our existence.

Mary Magdalene rises from her troubled rest with the other women and sets out to go to the tomb to anoint the Lord, bringing the spices that will keep off the stench of death for the first days of his entombment. They are the ones that have cared for his practical needs all along. It is what is expected, and indeed required of them. It is their duty. Nothing is very remarkable in this action. But their simple obedience to that duty with trust in God opens them up, and through them opens the world up to the mystery communicating itself. What do we need to be doing in order to collaborate in the revelation of God to the world? Nothing more than engage in the task at hand, mindful of our Lord.

All-seeing God, let me not disdain the daily duties that are mine,
but grant that I undertake them in communion with your Son,
in expectation of the revelation of your glory, through the same
Christ the Lord.

Hope Sets Us in Motion

Father Vincent Nagle, F.S.C.B.

[The women] were saying to one another, "Who will roll back the stone for us from the entrance to the tomb?" When they looked up, they saw that the stone had been rolled back; it was very large. (Mk 16: 3-4)

I once went to visit some relatives of mine, most of whom I had never met before. They were very nice people, but my being a priest clearly disturbed them. As I calmly answered their increasingly aggravated questions regarding the faith, one of them came right up to me and challenged me: "And just what do you think that you are going to be able to do there for those people [in the Holy Land]?" In other words: "What good can you do, powerless as you are? Do you think that you are just going to show up there and solve problems that decades of involvement by some of the world's most powerful and persuasive people have failed to resolve? Who do you think that you are?"

Keeping calm, I answered, "I intend to go and suffer all things with them in order to share with them my hope."

The question that the women ask themselves, "Who will roll the stone for us from the entrance to the tomb?" reminds me of this. We do not set off on our tasks only if we think we have the answers, or if we are certain that we have the resources to see the job through, nor even because we have confidence in ourselves to come up with the solution eventually. We set off on our tasks because we are certain of the One who is asking us to perform them. Without trust in providence, without the awareness that we are cooperating with a plan infinitely deeper than our own, then it is only within the horizon of our measured capacities that we are able to act. But a human being's true movement forward comes from something else – hope.

The women know their duty, and with entreaties in their heart to the God of providence, they get going. The end is not in their hands. Their obedience, born of hope, is.

Continue to open up my life to your kingdom, Father, by not letting me be trapped within my measured limits, but by helping me keep my eyes on your Son, who has made me one with you.

Seeing Is Not Believing

Father Vincent Nagle, F.S.C.B.

On entering the tomb [the women] saw a young man sitting on the right side, clothed in a white robe, and they were utterly amazed. (Mk 16: 5)

My father was a World War II veteran, and one of the stories I heard from him has stayed with me. An airborne soldier he knew came across a home that had been bombed as they made their way across Normandy in the first days of the western offensive. He looked inside through a collapsed wall and saw there an entire family, parents and children, seated at a set table – motionless. They were all dead. Apparently the concussion of the bomb that had blown out the wall had instantly taken their lives without disturbing the scene. This soldier went away never speaking of this to anyone, not able to process what he had seen. It was not until many years later at a veterans' reunion, when by chance he spoke to another soldier who had also seen the same sight, that he believed his eyes. For him, as is sometimes true for us, seeing was not enough for believing.

Often we do not know how to make sense of our experience. It only becomes real for us when there is a witness, someone looking with us and who is able to guarantee for us that we have seen aright, helping us to judge and articulate its meaning. Without witnesses we hardly know what to make of the events of our lives.

The women arriving at the empty tomb of Christ cannot know how to judge the scene presented to their eyes. Like the soldier in Normandy, it is beyond their experience and imagining. It is the presence there of this man "clothed in white" and sent by God that gives them any hope of arriving at the significance of what is happening. May God send to us witnesses who can patiently point us in the right direction when, in wonder, we grapple helplessly with making sense of the work of the mystery in our lives.

Father in heaven, I know not how to see your plan in the events of my life. Send me witnesses who help me recognize the victory of your Son, who lives with you and the Holy Spirit for ever.

Daring to Be Human

Father Vincent Nagle, F.S.C.B.

[The young man] said to [the women], "Do not be amazed! You seek Jesus of Nazareth, the crucified. He has been raised; he is not here. Behold, the place where they laid him. But go and tell his disciples and Peter, 'He is going before you to Galilee; there you will see him, as he told you.'" (Mk 16: 6-7)

"He has been raised," says the mysterious young man in the tomb, "as he told you." In these last words we can hear something of a rebuke to the women standing there in amazement, almost an impatience. After all, had not the Lord spoken more than a few times of these things, of how he must suffer, die, and be raised? So why are they so amazed?

Contrary to what is often asserted, we are sometimes very loathe to hope for the best, or to let our imaginations be carried forward by signs and indications of something desired in the deep caverns of our fearful hearts. We dare not. It takes a great deal of courage even to let ourselves articulate certain hopes or yearnings.

I recall the first full-time professional job that I ever got, a very well-paying job as it turned out. I knew things looked good for getting it, yet I could not even let myself articulate my hope that I would be offered the job. The high remuneration meant that much of what I hoped for and envisaged for my life was riding on whether or not this came through. It promised too much. I could not let myself expect it too. After all, if I did let myself hope, and it did not come about, then the disappointment would be crushing indeed.

In the heart of every human being there is an almost unbearable hope that all the gifts that we receive of beauty, love, and life will not be lost, but rather they might fulfill the oath that they speak to us, hinting at "for ever." It is almost too foolish to think about. But as Mary and her companions are discovering, in the company of that unique man, Jesus, we can actually dare to be human. Let us share the joy of redemption that we see dawning in the lives of the women at the tomb.

Lacking the courage to be human and to hope for what the heart desires, I turn to you, my Father, creator of my heart, and beg you to show me your Son, the redeemer of my humanity.

The Mystery Is No Joke

Father Vincent Nagle, F.S.C.B.

Then [the women] went out and fled from the tomb, seized with trembling and bewilderment. They said nothing to anyone, for they were afraid. (Mk 16: 8)

I once spoke with a family about an extraordinary experience they had endured a few short years previously. They had been living in central Washington State not far from Mount Saint Helens when it exploded in May of 1980. They had had an up close view of that huge eruption. I was excited to be speaking with eye-witnesses of that exceptional natural event and hoped that they would give me many details and descriptions of what they had experienced. They did not. Though years had passed, they were still in shock over what they had witnessed. It had completely upset their underlying fundamental assumptions and understandings about nature, life, and reality itself. The sight had been magnificent, yet after all this time they remained shaken and mute, unable and perhaps unwilling to put into words what had appeared before them.

When we encounter a glimpse of the infinite power underlying creation, it is an insight into the bottomless mystery that brought it forth. It is so vastly disproportionate in might and scope to all the categories that we normally use to understand the world around us that we end up as those women did when they "fled from the tomb, seized with trembling and bewilderment."

The mystery is no joke and not fun. And when we encounter it in our lives, we tremble and want to flee. What makes it possible for us, then, to stay in front of the unsettling mystery, where we feel reduced to nothing? It is the certainty that this in-breaking of the divine is a communication of mercy, itself a word that outstrips our human parameters. Let us take recourse often to the mercy of the mystery available to us in the sacraments and prayer, so that in the moment when we are faced with his overwhelming presence, we may yet be able to cry out, "My Lord and my God!"

Saving Father, as the mystery of existence fills us with the terror of annihilation, let us reach out to take the saving hand you extend to us in your Son, who suffered and died for us.

Liberation from Evil Is Not the End

Father Vincent Nagle, F.S.C.B.

*When [Jesus] had risen, early on the first day of the week,
he appeared first to Mary Magdalene, out of whom
he had driven seven demons. (Mk 16: 9)*

Jesus' potent work in Mary, his driving out the seven demons, was hardly the end point of his work in her. It never is. Jesus' redemptive power never has as its end a mere healing or liberation from evil. Jesus has much, much more in mind than that.

It reminds me of a writer who suffered from alcoholism and who, in her recovery from this affliction through Alcoholics Anonymous, ended up a Catholic. In the beginning of her recovery she was keenly averse to the spiritual dimension of the program, having grown up with a disdain for any talk about the supernatural. One day she was voicing her repugnance to a fellow recovering alcoholic, asking caustically why there had to be any talk of God at all in their path. The writer's friend challenged her to think of anyone who had made it to sobriety without turning to the mystery. So the writer did name one woman. Then her friend asked her what kind of person that was. The writer admitted that the person she was thinking of was a bitter person. "Right," answered the friend. She explained that if you somehow manage to do it on your own, you end up ungrateful and empty. It takes everything out of you. What you need is not just to stop drinking, but to be filled with that something that your spirit is missing.

Jesus appears to Mary, from whom he cast out the demons, to fill her with what her spirit is seeking, communion with the Father through the Son's victory over sin and death, not simply to leave her empty of demons. We can be so focused on liberation from our afflictions that it becomes our ultimate goal. But that is not why Jesus has come. As with Mary, he frees us in order to receive him in an eternal and victorious pledge of divine love.

Dear Father, I am so burdened by my weaknesses that I imagine freedom from them is my salvation. Show me that it is you alone who are my salvation and destiny, through your Son Jesus Christ.

Clinging to Death or Receiving Life

Father Vincent Nagle, F.S.C.B.

[Mary Magdalene] went and told [Jesus'] companions who were mourning and weeping. When they heard that he was alive and had been seen by her, they did not believe.
(Mk 16: 10-11)

The inability of the apostles to receive Mary's good news is a reminder that we are divided in ourselves between an attachment to death and an attachment to life. Though we are created for life, yet darkness and death can somehow feel more familiar and thus safer than risking a belief in what we hardly dare believe in, namely, that the promise of life might be true.

It puts me in mind of an attachment I once had to a girl. We had broken up, but she might have come back into my life romantically. I remember the moment when I was most tempted to let that happen. We were talking over our break-up, and began to speak about a moment that had been particularly humiliating for me. Reliving that moment with her right there, I was overcome with black, spirit-crushing misery. That was when I considered getting back together with her. I had rarely had an experience as intense. At the moment, the wretchedness seemed more real and a firmer basis for me than the hard-to-believe promise of life in Christ I was beginning to follow.

The fact is that there are times when we do not give up our wretchedness easily. It can reach deep into our souls, and we can find ourselves very attached to it. It can so color our experience that we do not know who we would be without it.

And we, like the apostles, are left with this fundamental choice: what are we more attached to, death or life? What word is our spirit prepared to receive? They "were mourning and weeping," and not ready to let go of that. Are we ready to risk believing that creation's promise of full life can be fulfilled? Let us pray for the intercession of Mary of Magdala, that she help us make a daily habit of asking to receive the word of life, instead of attaching ourselves to death.

Father, we, your mortal creatures, stand between life and death. Help us always turn to and look for the eternal life that has been won for us by your Son, who is conqueror over sin and death.

Recognizing the Risen One

Father Vincent Nagle, F.S.C.B.

After this [Jesus] appeared in another form to two of them walking along on their way to the country. They returned and told the others; but they did not believe them either.
(Mk 16: 12-13)

I have to know a person well, or there has to be something striking about the features for me to be able to identify him or her by the face. I tend to know who people are by their hair, body shape, or clothes rather than what's between their ears. When I was small, my mother changed the color of her hair, and any time we went out, even to a small grocery store with only a few aisles, I would lose track of her, not being able to pick her out due to the change in her hair. I've learned that there are other ways than just recognizing facial features to identify a person.

After the resurrection, Jesus' disciples recognized him in ways other than by matching up his physical features with the figure in front of them and exclaiming, "Whoa! It's Jesus!" Mark writes that the two disciples who met Jesus "walking along on their way to the country" saw him in "another form." How is it then that we can tell it is him, pointing and saying, "There he is!"?

There is a way. The disciples walking in the country lived an experience with this person whom they casually met that was unmistakably the same experience they lived with Jesus. The irreproducible content of redeeming truth, compassion, and mercy could only be him. Their utterly exceptional experience meeting Jesus before his Passion meant that, even if the form was different, they could unerringly identify their Lord through an encounter that communicates the same experience.

This is our condition even today. What generates the Church is this "exceptional" experience that we see in the Gospels and in the lives of the saints. And it is happening now. Let us pray to meet up with a human presence born of the grace of the Church that constrains us to say, "We have seen the Lord!"

Father, to see your Son is to know your mercy. Give us that unmistakable experience that allows us to recognize him in our lives always, through the same Jesus our Lord.

He Comes to Where We Are

Father Vincent Nagle, F.S.C.B.

[But] later, as the eleven were at table, [Jesus] appeared to them and rebuked them for their unbelief and hardness of heart because they had not believed those who saw him after he had been raised. (Mk 16: 14)

In a period during high school when I was very busy with classes and extra-curricular activities, a brother who had a small business called me at nine in the evening to ask me to come and work with him through the night. He had to get out a job by the next morning. I told him that I could not, and hung up. My father had heard my side of the conversation and asked me what had happened. When I told him, he forcefully corrected me, letting me know in no uncertain terms where my priorities needed to lie. Stung, I picked up the phone, told my brother I was coming in, and left the house.

That lesson has always been with me, and I am grateful. Correction, though painful, is a mercy, in that it comes to meet you when you are in a place you should not be – in my case, self-centered ambition – in order to point the way out to a better place.

Jesus' correction to the disciples is none too gentle either. The angel gave Mary Magdalene, who saw the risen Lord, the message that the disciples were to meet him in Galilee, but they did not believe it. Then the two disciples met Jesus on the road and the eleven did not believe it. So they are not in Galilee where they should be. Not waiting for them to keep the appointment in Galilee, Jesus comes to where the disciples are, where they are not supposed to be, and meets them there. But the meeting is not pleasant. "He rebuked them for their unbelief and hardness of heart."

What mercy our Lord shows his disciples. He does not simply wait around for us to become the people that we should be. He comes to us even as we are, mercifully and painfully pointing to where we need to be, but not leaving us alone. No matter where we are, we can always say, "Come, Lord Jesus!"

Through sin, Father, I often end up other than where you have called me to be. Do not abandon me, but send your Son, by the power of the Holy Spirit, to lead me to eternal communion with you.

A Simple Truth

Father Vincent Nagle, F.S.C.B.

[Jesus] said to [the eleven], "Go into the whole world and proclaim the gospel to every creature. Whoever believes and is baptized will be saved; whoever does not believe will be condemned." (Mk 16: 15-16)

Among the people I love most, some are unbelievers. So I feel a twinge of discomfort at the words of our Lord, "Whoever does not believe will be condemned." They ring harsh. Yet I have come to recognize simple mercy in them as well.

Raised with the various cultural and political strains of the 1960s circulating in full force, including in my own home, I absorbed a worldview that made it hard for me to see the truth and mercy in these words. I saw the world and its people as more or less perfectible but corrupted by the structures of man. I did not see sin and evil coming out of something deep and damaged in the human person, what we call original sin. Everything and everyone in themselves are basically fine; it's just the system that is messing us up.

With this view, a phrase like the one spoken by our Lord seemed arbitrary and despotic. I remember thinking: "Just because someone does not happen to hear, understand, or receive your word, you condemn them? How cruel, when so many non-Christians are better people than many Christians." But in a moment of grace, I came to understand that the world is not basically fine. There is something dark within us. Without seeing our Lord incarnate among us, we cannot recognize the only human path that roots us in hope and allows us to see and say "yes" to the beauty and life that our souls yearn for. We may manage to get many things right and become "basically good people," but ultimately we will not be set free from the darkness.

In other words, without Jesus, at best we are condemned to walk knowing that we can never reach our goal. At worst we never realize that there is any goal at all to reach. Jesus only spoke the simple truth staring us in the face: without him, we are condemned.

Merciful Father, because of sin our minds and hearts are slow to recognize the truth. Let the presence of your Son liberate us from darkness.

The Language of Intimacy

Father Vincent Nagle, F.S.C.B.

"These signs will accompany those who believe: in my name they will drive out demons, they will speak new languages. They will pick up serpents [with their hands], and if they drink any deadly thing, it will not harm them. They will lay hands on the sick, and they will recover." (Mk 16: 17-18)

"There is not too much you can do about it, except try to pay more attention," my friend, a psychologist, was saying to me. We had been discussing the fact that I seem to be continually getting people upset with me without meaning to. "Maybe in your infancy you did not spend enough time close to your mother or something," he opined. "In any case you cannot seem to read people's reactions or understand well what they are signaling. You do not pick up the signs and you end up making a mess."

We are not computers. We do not receive our most important communications or intimate knowledge from mere raw data. Signs are points of reality that speak of something greater than themselves. We fill our lives with signs – banal ones like arrows and letters, and more subtle and moving ones like colors and materials displayed, musical sounds performed, or even fateful ones such as flowers and gemstones offered as tokens. Without signs we do not manage to make ourselves truly understood or truly to understand. The most important and intimate things we need to communicate and receive are not adequately conveyed with mere words.

So Jesus is gently and patiently helping his disciples begin to recognize his presence among them, telling them of some initial and easy-to-read signs, giving them a list, some of which is familiar to us these days and some not. Like infants needing to spend time in intimate contact with their mothers in order to develop the ability to read the signals, so we need to spend time in his company, visible in the life of the Church, in order to learn to recognize the signs by which he makes his presence and himself known. We need to take our first baby steps in becoming familiar with his expressions. He is introducing us to that playful yet dramatic language of intimates and lovers – signs.

Father, you have made us to receive you who are infinitely greater than we are. Make us grow in our ability to recognize the communication of yourself in your Son, our communion with you.

Restoration in Heaven

Father Vincent Nagle, F.S.C.B.

So then the Lord Jesus, after he spoke to [the eleven],
was taken up into heaven and took his seat
at the right hand of God. (Mk 16: 19)

Once when I was a young teenager I mistakenly accused a younger brother of something he had not done. I almost immediately realized my error, but when I saw my father's anger explode, my courage failed me and I did not make a move as my younger brother was hauled off for his punishment, crying out to me, "How could you just lie like that?" As adults, the relationship between my brother and me has been strained, and I have often thought that this incident is at least among the reasons why. Though I have apologized, yet the sometimes hostile distance remains. Now as we grow older, I begin to see that perhaps this rift might remain for our time here on earth.

How can we live with these things, these broken ties that may never find a solution in this life? This state of affairs can lead us either to grow indifferent or to succumb to a fear of loss, becoming unforgiving of errors.

It is precisely Christ's ascension into heaven, his second departure, that gives us hope of the final victory of love, when, as Saint Paul writes, "God [will] be all in all" (1 Cor 15: 28). In our walk with him here on earth we are always in a tension toward our definitive communion with him when we too shall rise from our graves. Saint Paul says, "If for this life only we have hoped in Christ, we are the most pitiable people of all" (1 Cor 15: 19).

The more we can recognize him here through faith, the more certain we grow of his final victory, which allows us to embrace even deep sorrow with peace in our hearts. Let us not fear to embrace what is broken, powerless as we are to repair it. It is precisely this embrace in hope that is the path to the restoration of all things in heaven.

O Father, let the presence of our Redeemer give us the courage to embrace the world's brokenness and bear it to your kingdom, where all things are restored in your Son.

Trusting That He Will Meet Us There

Father Vincent Nagle, F.S.C.B.

But [the eleven] went forth and preached everywhere, while the Lord worked with them and confirmed the word through accompanying signs. (Mk 16: 20)

The truth is that it can be very difficult for me to get on an airplane to start a new mission, or return to a mission that is still struggling and unsettled for me. I have three times managed accidentally to miss my international flights altogether, costing the mission a good bit of money. Ultimately, I missed those flights because in my heart I lacked confidence that the Lord is with me. I remember too how sweaty and nervous I could be before entering the room of a new patient when I was a hospital chaplain. I knew that the questions and issues that I would be placed in front of might well outstrip my intelligence and human empathy, and I would look for excuses not to pass through that door.

In facing what it means to live for the kingdom of God, we are accepting to live for something that is more than we are, and will require more than just what comes from us. Knowing that, how can we even get started? How are the apostles able to step forward into a universe of knowledge and power utterly far above even their wildest estimations of themselves, and to engage the whole world announcing the good news of Christ?

They keep the memory of the one who is sending them, trusting that he will meet them there where they have been sent. In what they have risked and undertaken, they discover that they are not working alone.

Mark says that "they went forth and preached everywhere, while the Lord worked with them." It is only by getting to work that they could discover this, seeing the "signs" that they are accompanied, that more is happening than just what they can do. May God send us aid to keep the memory of his Son, so that we do not fear to depart but rather discover that we are never working alone.

Father, since it is only by getting to work that we can verify that your Son is working with us, help us to be certain of your promise to be with us always, through the same Jesus Christ our Lord.

Brief Biographies of Contributors

- **José Enrique Aguilar Chiu** teaches Sacred Scripture at Saint John Neumann Seminary College and at Fordham University.

- **Douglas Bushman** is director of the Institute for Pastoral Theology at Ave Maria University. He received his S.T.L. degree from the University of Fribourg, Switzerland.

- **Father Peter John Cameron, O.P.**, is editor-in-chief of MAGNIFICAT and author of *Mysteries of the Virgin Mary: Living Our Lady's Graces.*

- **Father Romanus Cessario, O.P.**, serves as senior editor for MAGNIFICAT and teaches theology at Saint John's Seminary in Boston, MA.

- **Father Basil Cole, O.P.**, is professor of moral and spiritual theology at the Pontifical Faculty of the Dominican House of Studies in Washington, DC, and author of *The Hidden Enemies of the Priesthood.*

- **Father John Dominic Corbett, O.P.**, teaches fundamental moral theology at the Dominican House of Studies in Washington, DC. He also preaches retreats and gives spiritual direction.

- **Father Harry Cronin, C.S.C.**, is a priest of the Congregation of Holy Cross. He is professor in residence at the Graduate Theological Union in Berkeley, CA, and a professional playwright, winning two Los Angeles Drama-logue awards.

- **Father Lawrence Donohoo** teaches systematic theology and serves as spiritual director at Mount Saint Mary's Seminary in Emmitsburg, MD.

- **Sister Mary Timothea Elliott, R.S.M.**, is a Sister of Mercy in Alma, MI. She has taught in seminaries since receiving her doctorate in Scripture. At present she is director of Christian formation in the Diocese of Knoxville, TN.

- **Anthony Esolen** is professor of English at Providence College, a senior editor of *Touchstone Magazine*, and a regular contributor to MAGNIFICAT. He is the translator and editor of Dante's *Divine Comedy* and author of *Ironies of Faith.*

- **Father Anthony Giambrone, O.P.**, is a Dominican priest of the Province of Saint Joseph and a doctoral student in Scripture at the University of Notre Dame.

- **Father Donald Haggerty**, a priest of the Archdiocese of New York, teaches moral theology and is a spiritual director at Saint Joseph's Seminary in Yonkers, NY.

■ **Father Stephen Dominic Hayes, O.P.,** ordained in 1988, has served in parochial ministries, currently at Saint Thomas Aquinas Parish, Zanesville, OH.

■ **Mary Healy** teaches Scripture at Sacred Heart Major Seminary in Detroit, MI, and is author of *The Gospel of Mark* (Catholic Commentary on Sacred Scripture).

■ **Father Andrew Hofer, O.P.**, teaches on the Pontifical Faculty of the Immaculate Conception at the Dominican House of Studies in Washington, DC.

■ **Father Mark Daniel Kirby, O.S.B.**, is prior of the Monastery of Our Lady of the Cenacle, in the Diocese of Tulsa, OK. In a traditional monastic life, marked by Eucharistic adoration, he intercedes daily for the sanctification of priests.

■ **Father Joseph T. Lienhard, S.J.**, teaches patristics in the Department of Theology at Fordham University. He is currently translating Saint Augustine's commentaries on the Old Testament.

■ **Monsignor Gregory E. S. Malovetz** is a priest of the Diocese of Metuchen, NJ, and serves as pastor of Saint Charles Borromeo Church in Montgomery Township, NJ.

■ **Andrew Matt** is a member of the MAGNIFICAT editorial team and holds a doctorate in comparative literature. He lives with his wife and two young sons in Chester, CT.

■ **Father Vincent Nagle, F.S.C.B.**, is a missionary priest working with the Latin Patriarch of Jerusalem and assisting in the Latin parish of Ramallah, Palestine.

■ **Father Michael Nolan** is a priest of the Archdiocese of Boston and pastor of Saint Mary's Parish in Waltham, MA.

■ **Father Jacob Restrick, O.P.**, is a Dominican priest of the Province of Saint Joseph. He is presently chaplain to the Hawthorne Dominican Sisters at Rosary Hill in Hawthorne, NY.

■ **Father George William Rutler** is pastor of the Church of Our Saviour in New York City. His latest book is *Cloud of Witnesses* (Scepter Publishers).

■ **Jack Sacco** is an award-winning author. His book *Where the Birds Never Sing* was nominated for the Pulitzer Prize, and his latest novel is *The Resurrection Sequence*.

■ **Father Richard G. Smith** is a priest of the Archdiocese of New York currently completing doctoral studies at Fordham University.

■ **Father Richard Veras** is pastor of the Church of Saint Rita in Staten Island, NY, a member of the lay movement Communion and Liberation, and the author of *Wisdom for Everyday Life from the Book of Revelation*.

Publisher: **Pierre-Marie Dumont**
Editor-in-Chief: **Peter John Cameron, O.P.**
Senior Editor: **Romanus Cessario, O.P.**
Managing Editor: **Catherine Kolpak**
Editorial Assistant: **Andrew Matt**
Administrative Assistants: **Jeanne Shanahan, Nora Macagnone**
Senior Managing Editor: **Frédérique Chatain**
Editorial Coordinator & Permissions: **Diaga Seck-Rauch**
Iconography: **Isabelle Mascaras**
Cover Design: **Solange Bosdevesy**
Translator: **Janet Chevrier**
Proofreaders: **Sr. Mary Paul Thomas Maertz, O.P. et al.**
Production: **Sabine Marioni**

Contributors: **José Enrique Aguilar Chiu, Douglas Bushman,
Father Basil Cole, O.P., Father John Dominic Corbett, O.P.,
Father Harry Cronin, C.S.C., Father Lawrence Donohoo,
Sister Mary Timothea Elliot, R.S.M., Anthony Esolen,
Father Anthony Giambrone, O.P., Father Donald Haggerty,
Father Stephen Dominic Hayes, O.P., Mary Healy,
Father Andrew Hofer, O.P., Father Mark Daniel Kirby, O.S.B.,
Father Joseph T. Lienhard, S.J., Monsignor Gregory E. S. Malovetz,
Father Vincent Nagle, F.S.C.B., Father Michael Nolan,
Father Jacob Restrick, O.P., Father George William Rutler,
Jack Sacco, Father Richard G. Smith, Father Richard Veras**

MAGNIFICAT®